Books should be returned on or before the
last date stamped below

ABERDEENSHIRE LIBRARY
AND INFORMATION SERVICE
MELDRUM MEG WAY, OLDMELDRUM

Bagman to Swagman

Tales of Broome, the North-West and
other Australian Adventures

Alistair McAlpine

ALLEN & UNWIN

First published in 1999 by
Allen & Unwin
9 Atchison Street
St Leonards NSW 1590
Australia
Phone: (61 2) 8425 0100
Fax: (61 2) 9906 2218
E-mail: frontdesk@allen-unwir.
URL: http://www.allen-unwin.com.au

National Library of Australia
Cataloguing-in-Publication entry:

McAlpine, Alistair, Lord.
Bagman to Swagman: tales of Broome, the North-West
and other Australian adventures.
Includes index.
ISBN 1 86508 104 3.
1. McAlpine, Alistair, Lord. 2. Collectors and collecting—
Australia. 3. Australia, Northwestern—Description and travel. 4.
Australia—Politics and government. 5. Australia—Social life and
customs. I. Title

Set in 11.5 on 13.5 Goudy by Midland Typesetters, Maryborough
Printed and bound by Australian Print Group

10 9 8 7 6 5 4 3 2 1

Contents

To Romilly, My Wife

Preface

For forty years I have travelled to and from Australia, sometimes staying only a week or so, sometimes as long as a few months. One year in particular I visited Australia eight times, but since 1964 I have been in the habit of visiting during each quarter of the year.

These are the memories of those visits—events in my social, business and artistic life, recalled as accurately as I am able, given the vagaries of memory and the embellishments of imagination created by the passing of time.

These memoirs are more than a travelogue, or a catalogue of the people, places and objects I have come across during my travels around this fascinating and beautiful country—this is the story of my love affair with Australia.

I

Early Days in Perth

1

If it is wildflowers that you dream of, go to Perth in Western Australia in September. There, in Kings Park, in over eight hundred hectares of natural bush in the middle of the city, are eight thousand species of wildflower. On those cool September mornings, their combined scent has a beauty I have never experienced elsewhere. Kangaroo paw, native iris, the banksia shrub—plants so exotic they have been collected for years and were growing in conservatories in Europe long before the State was settled.

In this peaceful and strange park there are also avenues of ghost gums, each with a plaque to commemorate a Western Australian soldier killed in the First World War. It is a moving experience just to read them: Hall, George F., 10th Australian Light Horse, killed in action, Palestine 19.4.17; Fred Thomas, killed, Pozières, France, 1916. No war memorial can be more poignant than these great white gums, bearing the names of men killed at Gallipoli, the Somme, North Africa, and at Beersheba. These men died on a faraway continent more than thirty years before the centenary of their State.

Under the gums, the wildflowers grow in plumes not unlike the emu feathers that decorated the slouch hats these dead men wore. The flowers are like a great posy at their memorial. The white-tailed black cockatoos circle and shriek in the wind. The blackfellas in the north say that the different varieties of cockatoo call their own names; for me, they are the unquiet spirits of men buried far from the home they loved. Around the trees, children play. On Sunday afternoons, their parents, whose grandparents had never heard of Western Australia, walk in the park. Never is the idea of war more beautiful, never is the futility of war more certain, than when you stand here in one of the most remote cities in the world.

It was to Perth in Western Australia, a State the size of Western Europe—with nothing much but desert lying between it and most of Australia's population in the east—that I came in 1958. The SS *Oriana* was on her maiden voyage, the first of a new generation of ocean liners built to carry both freight and passengers to Australia. This voyage, that I was on with my parents, stopped at many ports before arriving in Australia. The *Oriana* was a fine ship with luxurious first-class accommodation. My parents' cabin had both a balcony and a sitting room attached to it. My accommodation was a comfortable cabin on a lower deck with a porthole bolted closed against the sea. In the event, the sea treated us well as we sailed through still waters in the Mediterranean and the Red Sea and out into the Indian Ocean. At night, the moon reflected on their calm surfaces and the algae disturbed by the liner's wake glowed, a silver slipstream marking our passage. It was a romantic trip, with stops at Port Said, Suez, Aden and Colombo. As each day passed, I became more and more excited. The ship was full: the first-class passengers, mostly elderly, had boarded at Southampton; the steerage passengers, at Nice and Naples. There were few teenagers on the outward voyage. Aged sixteen, I made no shipboard friendships—the balmy nights and romantic silvered seas were wasted as far as I was concerned. However, my excitement on this great journey was such that I did not need the company of contemporaries, seeking instead the companionship of old men and the tales of their youth.

Brigadier Shearer, perhaps the most polite man I have ever met, travelled with his wife, Mary, and my parents. Shearer was a Highland Scot, with all the romance of his people in his soul. As a young man, he had joined the Indian Army. Often engaged in intelligence work, he saw the last acts of what Kipling called 'The Great Game', the battle of wits to keep the Russians from outflanking British India. During the First World War, he was a cavalryman, and fought with Allenby's cavalry in the desert. On the *Oriana*, he was full of stories of the places that we passed. During the Second World War, he had been head of British Military Intelligence for the Middle East based in

Cairo. It had been his duty to tell King Farouk of Egypt that the British no longer required his services. At the time, the British were engaged in the desert war with Germany, and their General Rommel was sweeping across the desert with his forces—Egypt, and particularly Cairo, were threatened. Farouk was a dissolute man whose hobby was collecting pornography. He was also a weak king who could not be relied upon, so the British determined to remove him from the throne and govern the country. Each day, it was John Shearer's habit to breakfast with Farouk's uncle at a café overlooking the palace. At one of these breakfast meetings, Farouk's uncle, not much taken with the idea that his nephew be dethroned, said so. Shearer, now aware that the dethroning was not going to be done quietly, took a white handkerchief from his sleeve—it was the habit of British officers of the regular army to carry a handkerchief concealed in the sleeve of their uniforms—and waved it in the morning air. A nearby British tank fired one shot, demolishing the palace gates. So went the last king of Egypt.

Back in London for a while, Shearer was spotted at a railway station by General Montgomery who realised that Shearer was reporting directly to Churchill. Before long, Shearer had been relieved of his command and left Cairo. He then became the managing director of the French couturier Molyneux. An unlikely post for an ex-general, Molyneux, however, was the cover for British intelligence working in Occupied France. I spent much time with John Shearer, his stories and his adventures inspiring in me a restlessness that has been with me all my life.

Another passenger, Lord Morley, was a singular old man. His family had once owned Dorchester House in London, the mansion that once stood where the Dorchester Hotel now stands. In 1928 my family acquired Lord Morley's London home, pulled it down and built a hotel in its place. The gateway to the old Dorchester House was bought by Rosa Lewis, better known as the Duchess of Jermyn Street, who specialised in finding nice clean girls for gentlemen. She also sold them, when they were in their cups, large pieces of masonry too large to be taken away. One of these pieces of stone was the arch that once had formed the gateway to Dorchester House. In the 1960s, my family rebuilt her hotel in Jermyn Street. The Dorchester arch now stands in the garden of my brother William's house, and very well it looks.

Lord Morley was old and doddery, but he had been a fine young fellow in his time. A Guards Officer at the time of the Boer War, he recalled his departure from Southampton. His regiment was paraded on the dock, as Queen Victoria was to inspect them before they left. Up and down the ranks the Queen progressed, stiff as a ramrod until she came opposite the young Lord Morley. Turning to an aide, she rested her hand on his shoulder and dabbed tears from her eyes. 'My fine young men all going to war', the Queen murmured, 'so few of them will ever come back'. Lord Morley told me that he did not find the Queen's words reassuring as he boarded the liner that was to take him and his regiment to South Africa.

Happily, while the Queen was right as a generality and many of her fine young men did not return, she was wrong in the specific, for Lord Morley survived well into his nineties. Old and doddery he may well have been on that trip out to Australia, but when we reached that great continent and a number of extremely elegant young ladies boarded the *Oriana* for its return voyage to England, he perked up no end.

⚜

As we crossed great oceans, shipboard life fell into a routine until the night came when it was announced that the next morning we would see Australia. My first sight of this most ancient continent in the world was the long, flat coastline of Western Australia. As the *Oriana* closed with that coastline, the Island of Rottnest, which guards the entrance of the Swan River, and the port of Fremantle came into view. When we arrived in Fremantle, the great liner's decks were crowded with migrants—migrants who had left so little and arrived expecting so much, their white skins burned red by the Indian Ocean's sun. The migrants, dragging their children by the arm, walked towards the immigration officers who were seated behind desks; children who looked around, and carried their world in a basket. A lone piper stood and played as the passengers came ashore. This was Australia, the lucky country, the 'Golden West': that is what these people had been told by those paid to persuade them to travel there for ten pounds a head. The Cinderella State: that is what those who lived and worked there called Western Australia. But Cinderella did go to the ball, and what a ball those forty years have been. I had no idea then that I would fall in love with this great continent, let alone with Western Australia, its landscape, its people, and join in its hectic dance.

A ship's officer came towards my father and with him a young man in military uniform, wearing a kilt. We were to take morning tea with the Governor of Western Australia. The young man took us quickly to his waiting car. The government driver saluted; customs officials stood aside. We set out from Fremantle and in a moment were out of the town among the bush that then tracked the Swan River. In those days, the Swan River ran at the edge of the escarpment on which stands Kings Park.

At that time, Perth was barely a city, more a big farming town where you expected to see cattle and drovers in the main street. An elegant street, nonetheless, with buildings of the 1930s seldom more than three or four storeys high, built in soft, yellow Donnybrook stone. Offices were fitted out with dark-brown panelling of jarrah, a tree that grows in Western Australia and can reach several hundred feet in height.

The Governor, Sir Charles Gairdner, was an old friend of my family's travelling companion, John Shearer. We took tea with him and talked about nothing in particular, for Perth was a town where nothing in particular ever happened. There was no talk of an exciting future; indeed, there was no talk about any future. We drove back up St George's Terrace, Perth's comfortable main street. At one end, there was a red brick fortress known as the Barracks, built in the early years of the colony, which blocked the view of Parliament House. The Barracks looked for all the world like a child's toy castle. Back along the road under the escarpment, to our left, a squadron of small yachts sailed on the Swan River.

We did not linger in Perth—just morning tea and then we were away. That night, we rounded the bottom of Western Australia and with the old whaling port of Albany on our port side, we set out across the Great Australian Bight. It was by now the end of January, and the weather in Perth had been hot, extremely hot. You can imagine my surprise when, just twenty-four hours out of Fremantle, I came on deck and found it covered in snow. Wind blew and it was bitterly cold; the sun was nowhere to be seen. The next day we arrived at Melbourne. In my view, it was not as pretty as Perth, but a place of substance; where there had been farming in Perth, there was business in Melbourne. This was no lazy country town, rather a city with a cultural hinterland and prospects. The tide of development was stirring in Melbourne and you could feel it as you walked the streets. The museums, the theatres, the Parliament buildings, even the hotels, had about them a permanence. This was a place where history had been made and, as you listened to the people talk, a place where history would be made again.

Twenty-four hours in Melbourne, lunch at the Windsor Hotel, a drive round the city, each important feature pointed out to us, and then a dinner party at the house of a grand family that had been forewarned of our coming. A fine house, built in the style of a late nineteenth-century manor, set in large gardens where exotic plants grew in profusion. A generous dinner, with Australian wines and excellent food, a dinner conducted with a formality that my mother claimed reminded her of pre-war Britain.

Back on our ship, where all had remained the same, day in, day out, there was a change. The Campbell family had joined the passengers. Mrs Campbell, a pretty woman with blonde hair, and her husband, a good-looking man, tall and strong, but now walking with sticks. It was, however, the Campbell daughters who made the difference: Virginia, a blonde, not tall, pretty with shortish curling hair, very like her mother, and her sister, Susan, a tall, fine-looking girl with long blonde hair. At first, I regarded these girls from afar; in time, we became friends.

A day or so sailing from Melbourne, we arrived at Sydney. Sydney was in 1958 a city caught between the formality of its past—long white gloves and picture hats to be worn on all occasions—and the hurly-burly of its future. Already the foundations of its Opera House were in place, a building which, at that time, was probably the most remarkable undertaking in the world. My father and I were shown over the building site of what was to become the world's most spectacular opera house. The contractor, whose manager was our guide, intended to embark on casting some immensely complicated post-stressed concrete beams. 'Have you ever worked with post-stressed concrete?' my father asked. Post-stressing concrete involves placing wet concrete around piano wires, which are stressed or tightened as the concrete surrounding them sets. Timing in this is everything, and great skill is needed to conduct such an operation successfully. 'No,' replied the site manager, 'there shouldn't be any real problem.' My father, who had seen a great deal of post-stressed concrete used in the nuclear power stations that we were building, was of a different view, but refrained from comment until we were alone.

⌘

After Utzon, its Danish architect, had been dismissed, those charged with the construction of the Opera House had to discover how on earth they were to build the cluster of giant shells that are both roof and building. How could Utzon's vision, that had been sketched in the sand of a beach on the other side of the world, become a reality? The reality of human life, however, is cruel, just as is the reality of nature. In the end, Ove Arup and Partners, a fine partnership of engineers, adapted Utzon's designs to ease the task of construction. Sadly, the architect's light touch was lost; the natural caution of the engineers made the building heavier than was originally intended. What had started with Utzon drawing nautilus shells in the sand became a solid edifice on the edge of Sydney's harbour. Utzon's Opera House would have seemed likely to fly away with the wind. Still a remarkable building, the Opera House is, and always will be, a thing of beauty, but how much more beautiful it could have been if the politics of ambition and greed had not played their dubious role.

For there can be no doubt that, had Utzon's Opera House been built, the building would have been the masterpiece of this millennium and, indeed, most other millennia as well. For years now, the world at large has been content to praise Sydney's great Opera

House. It is only the advent of the museum in Bilbao, built for the Guggenheim Foundation, that makes one wonder whether Utzon and the people of Australia weren't cheated out of the chance to truly make architectural history.

⋄

Later that first day in Sydney, my father and I visited the local chairman of the Caltex Oil Company in his office beside Sydney Harbour Bridge. John Shearer, recently retired as chairman of Caltex in Europe, took us to see this man who was a friend of his. We were shown what seemed to us stunning views of Sydney and its harbour from the windows of this multistorey building. Today, the old Caltex building is but a pygmy among the serried ranks of skyscrapers that make up Sydney's central business district.

The next day, the *Oriana* sailed from the wharf at Woolloomooloo where we were berthed. We sailed, however, not without a slight delay. The ship's doctor had been called from his bed to attend on various members of the crew arrested by the local police force and charged with drunken behaviour. 'Are these seamen drunk?' asked the police sergeant in charge of the station where they were being held. 'Certainly not,' replied the ship's doctor. 'In which case, if you take that view, you must be drunk,' responded the sergeant and, without much ado, locked up the ship's doctor with the crew.

While the *Oriana* might well have sailed without members of her crew, there was no possibility of sailing without the doctor. So we all waited for the matter to be resolved. Fines paid, restitution made for damage done and apologies given all round, the *Oriana* set off from Sydney for New Zealand. As the liner swung away from the wharfs of Woolloomooloo, we passed Mrs Macquarie's Chair, a headland jutting into Sydney's beautiful harbour. Along the side of this headland ran a group of school children accompanied by nuns, their black robes flying in the wind. They waved at the ship, we waved back and the ship's band played 'Anchors Away'. During the voyage across the Pacific, I became friends with Susan and Virginia Campbell, a friendship that lasted while they lived in London. A pair of good-looking girls, they were popular among both the passengers and the officers. Their father had his work cut out keeping an eye on them. As for myself, I was too young to enter into a romantic situation with these beautiful women; I was also short, fat and far from articulate.

New Zealand was, in the words of Marlene Dietrich, 'always closed'. When we reached its shores it seemed as if she was right! Ms Dietrich may never have known how accurate she was when she made that damning observation. In Auckland, we could get neither dinner nor a drink after six o'clock in the evening. Fiji was exotic and wonderful; Hawaii, the most fantastic place that I had ever visited. It was crossing the Pacific that Susan Campbell one day turned up on the upper deck bar wearing the briefest of bikinis. These were, of course, the days before the Swinging Sixties, days when girls dressed with caution and young men behaved with the best of manners. Even the barman, a cockney of considerable experience, was slightly shocked. 'Miss Campbell, how wonderful it is that we are seeing more and more of you in this bar.'

In time, we reached Vancouver. My mother was brought up in Vancouver, so our stay there was an emotional one. She had told us about the town, only to find that the place was not as she remembered it at all. We visited the places of her youth, now changed beyond recognition. My parents and I left the ship at Vancouver to take the train through the Rockies. Fond goodbyes were said all round, addresses exchanged and promises made to meet again, sincere promises as shipboard promises always are. In the event, I did see much of Virginia and Susan in London in the following years, and then our paths drifted apart as the paths of travellers do. My mother had made the trip through the Rockies many times and was much reassured that nothing had changed in this remote but beautiful place. Then across the plains of Canada to Toronto, where we were met by the Canadian manager of my family's business. We were soon looking at building sites, all thoughts of Australia forgotten.

There was, however, one fellow traveller on the *Oriana* who might have changed my life: a woman from Texas who was in the business of building roads across that State. 'Send your son to spend a couple

11

of years with me, it will be great experience for him.' My father agreed but, in the event, I went to work in my family's business and Texas was forgotten as well. This, as I look back, is not surprising, for my family were contractors and they lived for their work. As a child, I had ridden on the foreman's shoulders, seen concrete mixers as big as four-storey buildings and cranes that towered hundreds of feet into the air, and been terrified of the rattle of the giant air compressors. As a young man, I was caught in the excitement of our trade.

My family lived construction and talked construction, and, as a youth, I dreamt construction. Power stations and docks, skyscrapers and hotels were to be built. The construction boom of the late 1950s and early 1960s was well under way. I had neither the time nor the inclination to go to Texas to build roads and neither had my father the inclination to send me, for this woman and her construction business were never mentioned again.

2

It might have been that I would never have returned to Australia and, in particular, to Perth, for on that first visit I came across nothing that would draw me back, met no-one with whom I fell in love, saw nothing so remarkable that I felt compelled to return. My interest in Australia and my association with that continent could have been all over, but for one man and the fact that, by chance one day in the mid-1960s, my father was on holiday when he telephoned. He was Sir Halford Reddish, then the chairman of Rugby Portland Cement. A customer of my family's, Sir Halford Reddish and his reasons for me to undertake the journey to Australia are well-described in my memoir *Once a Jolly Bagman*. Suffice to say here that I knew that if Sir Halford Reddish asked you to go somewhere, you went—and went as quickly as possible.

So it was that I found myself on a long and incredibly tedious journey. The flights took ages and the breaks at various cities along the way were curtailed by the fact that I had miscalculated the time changes, with the result that no sooner had I arrived, for instance, in San Francisco or Sydney, than I had to leave again. Tired beyond belief, I found myself ensconced in Perth's Adelphi Hotel. Built in the 1930s, the Adelphi Hotel was a solid building of local stone, four floors in height. Its doorway was recessed from the street, with a short flight of stone steps leading up to it. These steps were guarded by a pair of knights in armour, knights taken from the romantic fantasies of the Pre-Raphaelites. Each of the knights carried an electric light disguised as a flaming torch. The hallway was brown and dark, and led onto a dining room that owed more to a penal establishment than a first-class hotel, let alone a luxury one. The rooms were small, the service and the bathroom, I felt at the time, defied description.

The highlight of the Adelphi Hotel was a Steak and Oyster Restaurant located in the basement; you could eat a plate of oysters and a steak for less than three dollars. Cheesecake was an optional extra, but as it was served by a voluptuous young Western Australian woman, my friends and I usually ate cheesecake. Swan lager was readily available, also wine, I believe, but I never drank any there. Wine did not then enjoy the popularity it has since achieved. In the bar that adjoined the restaurant was a remarkable cartoon by Rigby. It caricatured many of Perth's notable figures—sportsmen, politicians, lawyers and judges. Later, the cartoon was moved to one of the bars in the new Parmelia Hotel. It is interesting today to look at it and reflect on how the people of Perth have changed in the last 40 years.

⌘

Sir Halford Reddish had promised Charles Court, then the Minister for Industrial Development in Western Australia, that he would build a first-class hotel in Perth. To achieve this, he and my family acquired the Adelphi and the Riviera, a block of flats behind the Adelphi. The Riviera was to be demolished first and the Parmelia Hotel built on the site. After the Parmelia had opened for business, the plan was to demolish the Adelphi and build a multistorey office building, Hamersley House. The whole of this development was carried out in partnership with Sir Halford Reddish's company, Rugby Portland Cement. The architect for the Parmelia Hotel and Hamersley House was Peter Arney, a partner of Oldham Boas Ednie-Brown, a firm working in association with the British firm of architects, T.P. Bennett & Partner. Michael Metcalf and Philip Bennett, the son of Sir Thomas Bennett, the firm's founder, looked after these projects.

One afternoon, Peter Arney took me to meet his retired partner, Harold Boas. We took tea, in the proper sense of the word, at this gentleman's house. Harold Boas poured the tea and Peter Arney offered the sandwiches—delicate things were these sandwiches. The house stood on the edge of the escarpment that edged Kings Park, one of four or so that stood there with a breathtaking view out over the City of Perth and the Swan River. Most of these houses have now been pulled down and replaced with apartments. Harold Boas explained to me that it was only 30 years since he had designed the Adelphi Hotel and now I was going to pull it down. He believed that to pull down this fine old hotel was a shame and, as I reflect on the matter, I am inclined to agree with him in his judgement with, however, one caveat. I believe that to have pulled down that wonderful hotel was, in fact, a crime—among the first of a succession of crimes that systematically destroyed St George's Terrace.

༺༻

Perth in the early 1960s was a large, sprawling country town with a main street of commercial buildings where the lawyers and other professionals worked. St George's Terrace was at that time a noble street. Slowly over the last 40 years, its grand buildings have been knocked down and replaced by pale images of skyscrapers taken from the pages of glossy magazines devoted to the world's architecture. These buildings have neither elegance nor originality. Parliament House, that stands on the hill at the end of St George's Terrace, is a building of solidity, as Parliament buildings should be. It looks out over a motorway beyond which now stands only the brick gateway to the long-demolished toy castle, the Barracks. That gateway stands lonely, lost, irrelevant, a rebuke to the Western Australian parliamentarians who were responsible for an architectural tragedy. I do not refer to the loss of the fine buildings in St George's Terrace—that loss was due only to the natural course of commerce, ignorance and the short-sighted pursuit of greed—but rather to the pulling down of the Barracks, an impediment to the view from Parliament House.

In the days when I first came to Perth, the Barracks housed the civil servants. It was no architectural masterpiece; in fact, it was a nineteenth-century utilitarian building, not unlike the brick armouries that you still find scattered among the buildings of New York. It is true that in this building the civil servants had accommodation of rather a poor quality: they had no views or at least none to compare with those they now have from their office in the block on the hill. Of course, the Barracks had to go and the new motorway that surrounds Perth provided the perfect excuse. With the Barracks gone and its view secured by sinking the vast motorway into a trench, Parliament intended to sit with the bureaucracy in new office towers at its back. Happily, only one of five hard-faced, multi-storeyed office blocks to house civil servants was ever built. On seeing the first of these monoliths, some intelligent politician must have realised that civil servants, a prolific but generally unpopular species in Australia, would not enhance the popularity of politicians with so dominant a presence.

They, the ubiquitous they, caused the peaceful bays of the Swan River to be filled with earth so they could build this motorway. The foreshore of the river's north bank became a spaghetti junction. To ease the pain of the motorway, they planted gardens between its coils, with little bridges and little ponds—small trite gardens that nestle among roads that curl like a tortured snake. Then a grateful Government gave the planner who did all this the Order of Australia. With time, a car park and a bus station have been added, and the trees around the motorway have grown. Even with the motorway, the Barracks could have been saved, though it blocked the views of politicians down the once-grand St George's Terrace. It could have been saved, but it was pulled down. The plan was carried out with precision; the cries of residents in the area went unheard. Only one mistake was made—that fortress's gateway was left standing, a permanent memorial to the folly of planners and their masters in the Parliament behind it.

Now the great motorway, an act of conceit by a Government that saw the future of the State as grand, but not as grand as it became, runs through the city rather than around it, and the politicians' great vision, their desire to be modern, has become, 40 years later, a folly. The true beauty of the city, its peace, is shattered by traffic that another generation will try to eliminate by spending more taxpayers' money. As for the city's foreshore, that is long gone. Try as they may and, indeed, they seem to be trying, there is little option but to start again.

Perth is a great city, its people different from those of other great cities—Perth should have been proud of that difference. Sadly, for some years, it lost its way, seduced by the idea of being modern but ending up being much the same as everywhere else. Where once the architects of Western Australia benefited from their isolation and built small new buildings in scale with their town, in the 1980s they started to read glossy architectural magazines and build glossy buildings. In the depths of the recession of the 1990s, the emptiness of these buildings stared through shiny glass that once reflected the greed of the men who owned them. Their concrete piazzas, emptied of people, had concrete pots and windswept trees—the main street, the once-beautiful St George's Terrace, become a wind-filled canyon. The State Government should take the opportunity that came out of the recession to turn empty city sites into gardens before their value increases with the demand for space. A new road system must be planned and the concrete of the old motorway demolished, its tarmac torn up. Kings Park must be allowed to escape from its escarpment and filter down through the city. The hard core of Perth must be softened before it is too late. As for the gateway to the old Barracks, rebuild the walls that flanked it and use it as an auditorium. In retrospect, one can see that a new centre for the city's business district should have been created away from St George's Terrace. No part of the city centre of Perth is more than 20 minutes' walk from another. It is ridiculous, when you think about it, to pull down buildings just because they are too small. Often I call to mind the image of Harold Boas watching, with a grandstand view, the building that he designed being pulled apart. Now that a building is given a lifespan of thirty years, I wonder when I will see the first of the buildings that were the children of my imagination suffer the blows of the demolition contractor's ball.

꿍

The Riviera flats, despite their grand name, were quite another kettle of fish. If anything deserved to be pulled down, it was that god-forsaken block of jerry-built flats standing in a jungle of bamboo decorated with the waste of successive tenants. The Riviera flats belonged to Alan Bond; they were his first and only property holding within the City of Perth at that time. Bond was known to my lawyer, John Adams, and others, as being a pretty sharp customer. Before he vacated the Riviera, he stripped it of light switches and fittings, water heaters—anything that could be detached. After completion of the contract of sale on the Riviera, Bond offered himself as a partner to Sir Halford Reddish and myself, an offer that Sir Halford turned down quite simply with the words, 'No, thank you, Mr Bond,' and then, before Alan Bond could protest, 'Goodbye, Mr Bond.'

It was many years before I met Alan Bond again, and by this time he was well on his way towards the top of the dung heap created by a small group of corrupt businessmen in Western Australia. Crowing like crazy, flapping his arms, barely a day passed that this consummate publicist did not make out that he was the best thing to happen to Western Australia in years. What is more, many highly intelligent people believed Bond's line. Bankers were falling over themselves to lend him money, the State Government, both Liberal and Labor administrations, treated the man as if he were a king and, in a way, Bond was a king. Tycoons went in fear of him, his holdings in the media were powerful, his holdings in industry and property impressive, his efforts to win the America's Cup admired. His success in winning the America's Cup was applauded by all and sundry, and even sceptics began to soften in their criticism of him. Bob Hawke, the then prime minister, announced that anyone who did not give their work force the day off when 'Bondy' won the Cup was 'a bum'.

For many years, the Swan Brewery had been the greatest industrial force in Western Australia, and the chairman of this institution wore the crown in Perth. Alan Bond needed to own the Swan Brewery, he needed to wear that crown. The Perth business establishment desperately needed to stop him from owning the Swan Brewery and all the prestige that went with it, not to mention the brewery's abundant flow of cash. The Swan Brewery had at this time just completed a brand-new brewing plant some miles outside Perth. This left it with two redundant breweries in the city itself. Both breweries sat on prime sites, and on the site occupied by the Emu Brewery, I had my eye—fourteen acres of land tucked under the escarpment of Kings Park, just across the road from the Bishop's See development, the jewel in my family company's crown. The Bishop's See development was on about four acres of near-derelict land on which sat several old buildings. I had these buildings, which included the particularly fine Bishop's House, restored, and a large area of land became an important West Australian garden. A multistorey office building occupied the balance of the site.

Alan Blanckensee was then the chairman of the Swan Brewery. He was also a partner of John Adams, my chairman, and a good friend of both John and myself. In time, we did a deal: my family company formed a joint company with the Swan Brewery to develop the Emu Brewery site. Plans were under way for a hotel, and Inter-Continental Hotels were keen to be our partners. Enter Alan Bond—suddenly he had a stake of some size in the Swan Brewery, then he had a seat on its board and, before many months passed, he appeared on the board of our joint company. Until this time, the company had been run with a considerable amount of informality, decisions were taken after only a telephone call. John Adams and I ran the company, consulting frequently with our partners. With the presence of Bond on the board, however, formality became the order of the day, as careful note needed to be taken of every word that was spoken and every decision that was made. A board meeting was called and, for convenience, it was arranged to hold that meeting in Europe. For most of my life I have admired the City of Venice, so that was where the meeting was to be held, in the Gritti Palace Hotel. Rooms were booked, all was arranged. I flew into Venice and waited on the arrival of Mr Alan Bond. The weather was perfect, a warm spring, the sun bright, the sky a clear blue, the waters of the lagoon cool.

We met at ten o'clock that morning. The meeting, which should have finished by twelve-thirty in time for lunch with our wives, lasted until two o'clock as Bond argued over every detail. Alan Blanckensee, always an elegant dresser, wore a beige linen suit. We sat down for lunch, a tense affair. Bond was boastful and often rude but, no matter, the strategy was to humour the beast. My wife Romilly asked after his art collection. He told her of it in some detail, rather more detail than her polite enquiry had required. 'But where do you keep all these paintings?' she asked. 'I don't tell people where I keep my pictures, they might steal them,' was the reply. At last, lunch was coming to an end. 'Could you please pass the coffee?' Alan Blanckensee asked Bond. Bond passed the coffee, spilling it all over his chairman's elegant suit.

The end was obviously near for Alan, and within weeks, Bond gained control of the Swan Brewery and became its chairman in his place. As for our joint company, John Adams and I withdrew from the board and appointed Alan Blanckensee and another lawyer as our nominees. Their instructions were to make life as difficult as possible for Bond and they set about this task with relish. In about a year, Bond bought out our interest for a remarkably satisfactory price. After this experience, I began to take a close interest in the affairs of Alan Bond, as indeed did most of Western Australia's population. Bond had become something of a local hero, the local boy who made good; he had become the ambassador of Western Australia's success to the rest of the world. We heard of his triumphs in America and in China; in Britain, his native land, he bought a village and set out to become its squire.

My next encounter with Alan Bond was during the America's Cup in Perth in 1987, a time when he was at the height of his fame and, as it turned out, at his most vulnerable financially. For the Cup, my family's company took over the dock previously used by the Italian team, Italia, which had been knocked out at an early stage. John Adams arranged to have a tent set up the length of the dock. Large television sets were strategically placed so that my guests could eat their lunch and watch the racing at the same time. That dock was a wonderful spot to be in during the week of the Cup; we were at the heart of the action and in great comfort, as well. Unfortunately, the Americans won so convincingly that the racing took a day less than had been expected. Suddenly it was all over and Australia had lost. Frantic negotiations took place to keep the Cup in Australia by offering such advantageous terms to the victors that they would choose Fremantle as the venue for the next challenge. The Government of Western Australia and its supporters from business nearly pulled it off. The reality of life, however, was that had the victorious Americans gone home to Newport and announced that the America's Cup would once again be competed for at Fremantle, instead of a victory parade, there would have been a lynching. Since the tycoons of Perth were at a loose end that day, I invited them all to lunch. It was extraordinary to see the likes of Laurie Connell, Alan Bond and other members of what was to be called 'Western Australia Inc.' sitting all together at the same table. To cheer them up, I told the story of Alan Bond and how he had taken the hot water heaters from the Riviera flats after he had sold the property to me. He really seemed quite proud of what he had done. The others thought it was a great joke, particularly Laurie Connell. For some years after that lunch, I did not meet Alan Bond again; indeed, there was no reason for our paths to cross.

In a few years, however, his name came up at a board meeting of Imre Properties, a public company whose chairman was the charismatic and brilliant financier, David Davis. It was suggested that Alan Bond would buy 50 per cent of the property development that we were undertaking on the site of the old St George's Hospital at London's Hyde Park Corner. Never in my whole business career had I been so definite about anything at a board meeting. Alan Bond was a man with whom I did not wish to be in partnership under any circumstances. There was not a price that Bond could offer that would make me change my mind. On this I was quite clear—Bond should buy the whole scheme or nothing. A few days later, he came back with a highly acceptable offer for the whole development.

While Bond in those days was a man of mercurial moods, one aspect of his character was always constant: he could not resist a gamble, especially in a field that he knew nothing about. At the outset of what turned out to be by any standards a remarkable career, Alan Bond succeeded in cheating me out of the hot water heaters in the Riviera flats. I suppose he felt that he could go on behaving in the same way towards everyone else with whom he did business. Events, however, moved against him—his gambles had been a little too wild and his business practice a little too sharp. His decline was short, his struggle to avoid the consequences of his actions protracted but its result inevitable. While Western Australia was the richer for having Bond as a citizen, it's just a shame that he directed himself towards business rather than politics.

3

My hosts were kind in my first days in Perth. Each evening I was entertained by different people. While the people who entertained me were different, the restaurant that they took me to was always the same one. It was Luis, the city's best restaurant. In those days, it was decorated with printed colour reproductions of the great paintings of Degas, Monet and Renoir—'I am told that these pictures are extremely valuable,' said one of my hosts. The food was awful and the pictures imitation; the proprietor of Luis knew little about French art or cooking. The citizens in those days all seemed to be big men, well over six feet tall, with heads like shopping baskets and faces burned brown by the sun and the wind. They wore grey suits and brown fedora hats, looking at you from under wide brims that made no attempt to hide their eyes.

By chance, I met in Perth in the mid-1960s a man who was to become one of a small group of four or five people whom I consider to be my closest friends. I do not make real friends easily, although I have many acquaintances that others might call friends. I had in London been introduced to the Agent-General for Western Australia, a former Government minister of that State, Gerry Wild. He gave me an introduction to a lawyer friend of his in Perth, called Adams. One morning I went to the office of Mr Adams and asked to see him. Perth was like that then: you just turned up at somebody's office and they would see you; appointments seemed unnecessary. It was the same even with senior politicians. The whole place was extremely casual; there was no noticeable security nor, for that matter, any need for security. The office of premier of Western Australia was about the equivalent of that of mayor of a small European city; the premier's budget for a state the size of Western Europe would at that time have been smaller than that of most large towns in Britain.

Seeing before her a young man, the receptionist assumed that I wanted the young Mr Adams, rather than the older and rather grander Mr Adams to whom I had an introduction. Young Mr Adams, John, appeared and even he did not mention his father. I explained what I wanted done and John explained that he could save my family a lot of tax if we made our land purchases in a particular way. I did not really understand tax then—and I still do not understand it now—so I thought it better if John came to England to talk to experts. 'I am pretty busy,' he told me but, once in the street, as he told me years later, he ran all the way to the travel agent to get a ticket for the next day's flight. When we arrived in England, I took John to my home at Fawley Green, arriving there at about midday on a Sunday. I showed John his room, left him to have a bath and change, and returned with a dry martini. My family prided itself on its dry martinis and I had been taught the art in a hard school: pour a few drops of vermouth into a shaker full of ice, shake it about and throw the liquid away, then add a large quantity of gin, shake it up, pour the liquid into an ice-cold glass, rub a slice of lemon peel around the edge of the glass and serve. John drank the cocktail and said that he would be down for lunch in a few minutes. Time passed and still there was no sign of John. Lunch was delayed and delayed again. After the second delay, I went upstairs to find out what had happened to him. John was fast asleep; he woke only in time for breakfast on Monday morning.

A month after this first visit to London, John Adams joined the board of my family's Australian company and stayed there until 1990, when he left to become a Master of the Supreme Court of Western Australia. In late March 1996, John died of cancer. His death took much of the joy out of my visits to Australia; we had, for thirty years, been extremely close friends. My memories of him are legion but, like so many memories of friendship, they are full of the jokes of fleeting moments, the joinings of two people's sense of humour that, when written down, lose their energy. In print, the events that made us laugh become too laboured to seem humorous at all. Numerous were the travels we made together in those early days, carrying a giant model of the new Parmelia Hotel and the adjacent office block, visiting government office after government office, endlessly answering the question, 'Why would you want to build this hotel in Perth?' The answer was that I had faith in Western Australia—I saw something in the economic climate that attracted me to the place.

∞

In those days in Perth the city did not have much in the way of entertainment, and at a weekend it was a place of peace and particularly quiet. As for vice and crime, they barely existed. In those days, you never saw a policeman; crime was, as a citizen of Perth might say, 'as rare as hens' teeth'. If you saw a girl standing on a street corner late at night, and you often did, she was waiting for a bus. Walking in the streets at any time of day or night was totally without danger. John Adams and I used to set out looking for fun. I was, at the time, a mere twenty-two years old. We liked to drink and, if possible, we liked to drink where women were to be found. Drink was not easy to come by then and the women of Perth were respectable. The morals of the promiscuous society had not reached Perth from London's Kings Road. There was a motel in south Perth, I forget its name, where airline crews stayed on overnight stops. They drank a lot in those days and then the fun and games began. A favourite trick was for two male members of such a crew to hold a woman upside down so she could walk up a wall and across the ceiling, leaving footprints of boot polish on the paintwork, much to the amazement of the room's next occupants. This was considered the height of entertainment.

The airport was popular because the bar was open for longer hours than were the bars in the city hotels. When I first visited the airport, it was packed with people whom I imagined were waiting for their flights but, in fact, were waiting for another drink. Pinocchios, a nightclub in Murray Street was, I believe, dry but full of young women. One night, John and I, tiring of Pinocchios, decided to move on. The car was parked some way off and rain was pelting down; water ran about a foot deep in the gutters. Believing that there was no point in us both getting soaked, John ran to fetch the car while I waited in front of the club's door. Without warning, a customer was ejected from the club. He came out horizontally, hitting me in the small of the back. I was pitchforked into the water rushing down the gutters. That was about as wild as nightlife was likely to become in the Perth of the 1960s.

As a result of the laws restricting drinking, rather than eliminating drunkenness, it became common. On my first stay in the old Adelphi, I was sitting one afternoon in the lounge when a middle-aged woman fell down the stairs from the first floor. I looked on in amazement as she scrambled to her feet, swaying like a galleon in a heavy sea, top-heavy with a large hat not unlike a cream bun, balancing herself with hands hidden in long white gloves. In a flash, the women spotted my amazement. 'What the —— —— are you staring at?' Then, as an afterthought, 'You'd be drunk if it was your son getting married.' Too stunned to apologise, I watched in silence as she felt her way along the wall to the hotel's front door.

On a Sunday, there was no drinking except for a couple of hours in the afternoon. This was called 'the Session'. The beer was served in jugs, each member of the party taking a couple of jugs in each hand, going into the garden of the hotel and drinking long after the place closed. This restriction on a person's right to drink was clearly not designed to attract foreign tourists and it certainly would not help an international hotel earn a living. After much negotiating with the State Government, John Adams and I managed to agree a formula for a liquor licence that would be satisfactory for the new Parmelia Hotel. There was, at that time, no such thing as, for instance, a banqueting licence, and the hours in which a hotel guest was allowed a drink were restricted to the same hours as those allowed the patrons of its bars. The Government had been as helpful as one might expect, bearing in mind that a luxury international hotel in this unlikely city was the idea of Sir Charles Court, then the Minister for Industrial Development, who sold the idea to Sir Halford Reddish, who then sold it to me. I in turn had sold it to my family, none of whom realised quite how bizarre a suggestion this was for the City of Perth in 1965.

John Adams and I were confident that, with the government on-side, we would have little trouble in the matter of this special licence. In due course, John and I set off across the street from the old Adelphi to the Licensing Court. The judge was an old man, or so he seemed to be—in retrospect, he was probably in his mid-fifties. He looked at us with total contempt. 'I have read your submission to the court and I see that you intend to build a five-star hotel. We do not have five stars in this State; we do have four stars but no four-star hotels. You can build a four-star hotel if you have a mind to, although I would not advise it. As, however, we have not got five stars, you cannot build a five-star hotel.' This was an unpromising start, to say the least. He continued, 'I have studied your plans for this hotel and I cannot find any single bedrooms nor can I find a reading room on each floor'.

John explained in a deferential manner that it was the habit these days to build hotels where all the rooms were doubles and there were no reading rooms in modern hotels. 'That may very well be your habit to build hotels in that fashion but it is not my habit and this hotel will have single rooms and reading rooms if it is to have a licence.' John rose to protest. 'Sit down,' the judge snapped. John sank to his seat as if he had been shot. 'What is more, the single rooms will be so small that only one single bed fits in there. The reading rooms will be fitted out with armchairs and all the bedside lights will be screwed to the wall.' I stood up to protest and was firmly shot down. 'You, sir, are clearly unaware of how things are done in Western Australia so I will explain them to you just once. The single bedrooms will be small as I do not want you putting another bed in there after I inspect your premises. I insist on this because you might put two people in the same room who do not know each other and the bedside lights will be screwed to the wall as I don't want you taking them out once I have inspected the place.'

I protested that this was a luxury hotel and there was no possibility of two strangers being forced to share a room. 'That may sound ridiculous to you,' said the judge with some passion, 'but only last week I booked into a hotel in Port Hedland. When I went to sleep, I was alone in my room. When I awoke in the middle of the night, there were two other men sleeping there, and by morning one of them had left taking my wallet. As for the reading rooms, there are a number of people, of whom I might say I am one, who do not want to spend their time in bars. These reading rooms are for us and, what is more, the law provides that we shall have our reading rooms.'

I left the building and had, once again, to seek the help of Sir Charles Court, the dynamo behind the mega-leap to prosperity that Western Australia took during the late 1960s. Sir Charles recognised the problems that I faced with the Licensing Board: Western Australia was to have a five-star hotel and so, in time, work started on the Parmelia Hotel.

⚜

Travelling around with that giant model of the Parmelia became the bane of my life. When I first brought it into Australia, the customs officers made me unpack it, which involved removing almost fifty brass screws that held the lid of its travelling box in place. Then they pronounced: 'This thing is made of wood. You can't bring it into Australia!' Happily, John had met my plane and I was able to say, 'Hold on a moment while I fetch my lawyer.' John persuaded them to allow the model into Australia provided we had it sprayed. Determined, however, to stop something coming into Australia, they picked on the fur coat of my then wife, Sarah. 'How long has that been dead?'

This box travelled with us from Canberra to Sydney, then to Melbourne and then back again to Canberra. Every time we showed the wretched thing, all its screws had to be undone. Every time we changed State, quarantine and health officials would ask, 'What's in that box?' We travelled from banks to borrow money, to the government to ask permission to borrow money, and always we were asked the same question: 'Why would you want to build that hotel in Perth?' Even when our travels around the capitals of the Australian States were over, the problems with the Parmelia Hotel persisted. Even in

Perth itself, officials did not believe that the badly needed hotel of international quality would ever be built.

There can be no doubt that the Parmelia was planned to be as no other hotel in Australia. Sir Halford Reddish wanted the best. 'A small version of London's famous Dorchester Hotel' was how he described his vision of the Parmelia. Sir Halford, apart from being a considerable industrialist, was a man who knew 'the best' when he came across it, and the Parmelia was to be his home in Australia. What is more, he had just the right manager in mind to run the place—Donald Mclean, who ran the Sheraton East in New York, the hotel where Sir Halford always stayed when in that city. The Sheraton East had about this time just been sold and was due to be demolished. Donald Mclean was ready to make a change, although I do not imagine that he ever expected that change to be from New York's Park Avenue to Mill Street in a small Australian city. When Donald Mclean arrived in Perth, he oversaw the outfitting of the building and also hired and trained staff.

A large, florid-faced man in, I suppose, his mid-thirties, he wore the formal clothes of a hotel manager. It seemed, however, that these clothes had been made for another person, as nothing that he wore really seemed to fit him. Mclean was, if nothing else, a great enthusiast. He entered into life in Perth with gusto, gave parties and went to parties. It must, of course, be remembered that by the standards of the world's great capitals, in those days the wild set of Perth was extremely tame. At Donald Mclean's parties, champagne and canapés were served; at everyone else's, beer—and you cooked your own steak or prawns.

Dancing furiously at a beach party on a hot summer's evening, Mclean began to sweat profusely, and damp patches began to appear on the front of his pink shirt. A fellow reveller, a prospector just out of the bush for a week's holiday in the metropolis, took a dislike to Mclean from the moment that he set eyes on him. Walking up to this florid and sweaty hotel manager, he brought Mclean's dancing to an abrupt halt by poking him in the chest. It seemed as if a fight was about to ensue. Mclean, who was winded from the dancing and always had a certain trouble getting the words from his brain into general circulation, stood gasping. The prospector looked him up and down and then remarked, 'It seems to me that that your pink shirt and your pink face were both washed in the same bucket.' Before Mclean could reply or strike a blow, the prospector weaved his way off into the night.

Donald Mclean's efforts at setting up the Parmelia were remarkable: in a city that had never heard of interior decoration and had no tradition of service, he gave Sir Halford the hotel he sought. The Parmelia became a hotel of considerable character, furnished with decorative antiques and a fine collection of Australian paintings all displayed with great style. Most of the paintings were bought from Rose Skinner, who dominated the art market in Western Australia. Mclean's budget was modest but the results he achieved were very grand. While many in Perth bemoaned the loss of the old Adelphi Hotel, the Parmelia was the first sign of the affluence that was to grip Perth in the following decades. Perth was still a long way from everywhere but it now boasted a hotel that people wanted to stay in.

Donald Mclean pleased Sir Halford Reddish in almost every respect except one—Mclean liked a drink. Sir Halford was a teetotaller; no-one who worked around him mentioned drink, let alone took one when he was present. The staff Christmas party at Rugby Portland Cement, the company that Sir Halford chaired and ran as a virtual dictator, was a dry occasion—dry, that is, until some enterprising managing director switched the fruit punch for Pimm's and then convinced Sir Halford that Pimm's was a non-alcoholic drink. Sir Halford was not often in Perth, so the fact that Donald Mclean liked a drink or two went unnoticed for a couple of years. The end came suddenly. Mclean had been to a highly successful party and, although tired, he decided to drive himself home in the early hours of the morning. After a long day's work and a long night's drinking, he fell asleep in his car. But for where it was, I doubt if the police would have noticed him, sleeping quietly in the early hours of the morning. Perth, after all, was in those days a city where the police presence was almost invisible. Mclean was incensed at being woken from a deep sleep by two policemen. 'Drunk, how dare you say that I am drunk?' he said, or words to that effect. The policemen stared at him in total amazement and then asked how he came to be asleep in a car that was parked in the middle of a highway and, what was more, a car that was facing the wrong way? There was no answer. Mclean rang his lawyer who had him released from the police station. At first, it was judged best not to inform Sir Halford of Mclean's indiscretion. It was, after all, a personal matter and did not happen during working hours. Besides, in the nature of their job, hotel managers either drink nothing or rather a lot. However, in every organisation there is someone who delights in passing on bad news. So it was with Donald Mclean—he left his job and left Australia the richer for having known him and the poorer for his going.

⸜⸝

After Mclean's departure, my family sold its interest in the Parmelia to Sir Halford Reddish's company. The hotel was for some years never quite the same; profits were given priority over style. Perth grew and the Parmelia grew with Perth, its customers were no longer farmers uncomfortable amongst the hotel's fashionable decor. Business was booming in Perth. Business people from overseas stayed at the Parmelia, business people used its bars and its restaurants, a nightclub was opened and the place prospered.

In every hotel, stories abound, and the Parmelia was no exception in this respect. It became a step in the career of a number of stars in Perth's hotel and catering industry, among them Gavino Achenza. Gavino is a champion among enthusiasts; for him, every day starts well and can only get better. He is also the sort of man who attracts the unusual as inevitably as dead fish attract flies on a hot day. On his first day as a trainee waiter, he entered the kitchen of the hotel where he was working with his usual enthusiasm, whistling gaily. Seeing the stacked tray of dishes that were ready for serving, he picked them up and, still whistling, moved towards the service door. Almost at the door, he felt a stab of pain in his left buttock and, with his free hand, searched for the cause. Gavino was somewhat surprised when he found a serving fork sticking out of his bottom and blood running down his hand. Putting down the tray, he pulled the fork out and then looked around to find out how it got there. The cause was self-evident—the head chef was standing there with a face of thunder. 'You ignorant young fool,' he shouted at Gavino. 'Don't you know that it's the worst kind of luck to whistle in a kitchen?' Gavino did not know that it was bad luck to whistle in a kitchen but he did now know that the chef was amazingly adept at throwing a two-pronged serving fork a long distance at a small target.

Gavino later took over the management of the Garden Restaurant at the Parmelia. In a restaurant, Gavino moves about the place like a tennis champion. Trained in Britain, he is the sort of head waiter who makes you feel that he has waited all year for you to come to his restaurant, even if you last dined there only the day before. Nothing is too much trouble for him when it comes to his customers. Even if he doesn't have the dishes that they require on his menu and the ingredients are not in the kitchen, he leaves them feeling satisfied, simply by convincing them that they did not really want those dishes in the first place. While Gavino was at the Parmelia, the hotel had an important customer: an elderly gentleman, a local businessman who lunched there every day; his lunch, always just a plate of smoked salmon. He was undemanding and his habits were as regular as clockwork. He would arrive at the same time Monday to Friday, sit at the same table, look at the menu and order smoked salmon. On this particular day, Gavino had greeted the customer and, as usual, asked him how he was. 'Very well, thank you,' the customer replied. He was seated, his smoked salmon ordered and, in the twinkling of an eye, it was served. Gavino, moving around the restaurant attending other customers, noticed that the elderly gentleman only sat and looked at his smoked salmon, making no attempt to eat it. Concerned lest the customer was upset, Gavino wondered how he should approach this problem.

Pulling himself to his full height and selecting his broadest smile, Gavino swung nonchalantly across the room, looking everywhere except at the man and his untouched smoked salmon. 'Well, how is everything today?' he said, as he patted the man on his back. In place of a reply, the man fell forward, his face four-square in the plate of smoked salmon; clearly, he was dead. Gavino quickly pulled him into a seated position and then, sliding his arm around the waist of the corpse, raised it to its feet. Determined not to spoil the lunch of his other customers, Gavino walked with the corpse towards the kitchen. The head waiter and the dead customer appeared to be in animated conversation. It was then that Gavino's problems really began: the chef, Gavino knew, wouldn't have the corpse in the kitchen, and he couldn't leave it in the restaurant.

Chefs, as Gavino well knew, are highly superstitious, and if whistling causes bad luck, heaven alone knows what sort of bad luck a corpse would cause in a kitchen. Gavino was not unresourceful, so he propped the corpse up between the double swing doors of the kitchen's service entrance and went off to ring for an undertaker. Undertaking, however, is not a trade where hurry is of the essence; corpses can usually be counted upon to wait for the undertaker, unlike customers in a restaurant who expect to get fed promptly. When Gavino returned from the telephone, he discovered that the corpse had collapsed and was jammed between the two sets of swing doors. What was worse, the waiters now all knew that the customer who had been lurking in between the swing doors for the last fifteen minutes was dead and not just taking a nap. Gavino was right about the chef—he refused to have the corpse even pass through his kitchen. In addition, the waiters refused to step over the body as they went in and out of the kitchen. Gavino ended up performing a shuttle service between the waiters in the kitchen and those out in the restaurant.

In time, Gavino left the Parmelia to open his own restaurant. With a partner, he ran the Mediterranean in Perth. It soon became the epicentre of Western Australia Inc. His customers planned deals, buying and selling companies as they ate their lunch and drank what in those days appeared to be an endless supply of Dom Perignon champagne.

⸎

At the time of my sojourn in the old Adelphi Hotel, I used to be shaved every morning. The barber was an Italian migrant to Australia, Tony Sgro. In the early days, he was a travelling barber with no shop of his own. Tony shaved me every day that I was in Perth for the best part of 25 years. When the Parmelia was built, he took premises in the shopping arcade and I would remove myself each day from my hotel suite to his barber's chair. As I sat there, behind me, in the centre of the arcade, was a shallow pond that was supposed to stop people bumping their heads on the cantilevered stairway to the ground floor of Hamersley House. Tony Sgro, always helpful, explained to me that far from helping people, this pond was a hindrance—customers coming out of the hotel's bar often as not stepped into the pond which, to be fair, was hard to see. Then, concerned only with their wet feet, these irate customers banged their heads on the stairway. Much as he found this a great entertainment, he believed that we should fill in the pond. Ponds always appear on architects' drawings; in reality they seldom work, becoming either full of litter or people—I took Tony Sgro's advice.

On one visit to his barber's shop, he looked particularly carefully at my chin as the whole surface was badly lacerated. Even his natural politeness could not constrain Tony from asking me what had happened. 'Last night I was waiting in Singapore airport,' I told him. In those days, Singapore airport was a very different place to the all-singing, all-dancing airport it is today. In fact, it was just a large hangar with merchants selling mechanical toys that performed all over the floor. Bored with waiting for the flight and the toys, I noticed a barber's stall. Sitting high in his chair, the barber asked me if I would like a back massage. Foolishly, I accepted the offer. The barber then asked for a small coin, which he slipped into a slot in the side of the chair. The coin deposited, my chair began to vibrate and the barber began to shave me with a cutthroat razor. The result was the chin that Tony Sgro did his best to repair.

༄

In time, the movers and shakers took over from the tall men in grey suits and brown fedora hats who ran Western Australia. The movers and shakers were short and fat, with bald heads and, if they wore a hat, it was a yachting cap. Their suits were blue, too bright a blue, with too much silken thread in the weave—these were shiny men.

The America's Cup came and Perth became a party; the State changed the slogan on its car number plates from 'The wildflower State' to 'The State of Excitement'. Still a small city, the whole world now knew about Perth, the place where the tycoons came from, the place where the deals were done. In time, both the champagne and the luck of Western Australia ran out. Cinderella was about to leave the ball and Western Australia was about to be beset by terrible scandals and the deepest recession that Australia has seen this century. The boom of the 1980s, when anything went, came to an end.

However, Australia is built on bankruptcy, with an endless supply of optimistic Australians waiting to take over where others have failed. Nowhere is this more apparent than in Western Australia, for the West is a hard country and her people hardened by her; as fast as a shop failed, a restaurant or café opened. By the mid-1990s, the whole population of Perth seemed to have given up shopping and taken up eating. There can be nowhere else with so few people and so many restaurants. Not the plush paint and velour of the past, these new places were decorated with whatever came to hand, and all the better for it. The city, for all its changes, again had the feel of the 1960s; the citizens still played bowls dressed in their whites, the peppermint trees still stood in the suburb of Peppermint Grove. The lucky country? The people of Western Australia have learned that the ball is over—Cinderella is back in the kitchen and luck comes only with effort. In truth, both the people and the place are the better for it.

4

The bureaucrats who did not believe the Parmelia Hotel would ever get built were wrong. Not only did it get built but it became the first of a number of buildings that John Adams and I worked on in Perth. Hamersley House, perhaps the least distinguished of them, was the next. In time, everything was in place for the building of Hamersley House; all that remained to be done was the pulling down of the old Adelphi Hotel which occupied the site. As the Adelphi closed, so would the new Parmelia open. On the last night of my visit to make the final arrangements for this demolition to commence, Donald Mclean gave a party, and what a party it was. I drank too much and ate too little. My head would, I believe, be considered hard and the quantity of alcohol that I drank that night was no greater than I had often drunk in an evening before and most certainly no more than I have often drunk in an evening since, without a great effect. Perhaps I had been poisoned by a defective bottle of champagne, or maybe in the general excitement I had eaten a bad oyster. Whatever the cause, its effect was dramatic. When I returned to my hotel room, I was desperately sick. Feeling awful, I decided for some reason to have a bath, so, putting in the bath plug and turning on the taps, I lay on my bed.

Next morning, I awoke to find the room ankle-deep in water. As I believed my room was on the first floor, and the hotel would close the next week, I did not worry too much about the damage. Dressing quickly, I set off for some fresh air. Standing in the street by the hotel entrance, my head aching as never before, I watched guests coming and going. In time, a smart, well-built man in a formal black suit of old-fashioned cut, black tie and a black Homburg hat, descended the steps from the hotel's entrance. He gave me a vicious scowl, and at that moment I remembered that my suite was not on the first floor but on the second. The gentleman scowling at me with such ferocity was the occupier of the first-floor suite, a client who had lived in the hotel for many years. He, poor fellow, must have been soaked during the night. In any event, he had booked out of the hotel that morning. Overcome with an aching head, weak legs and the general lethargy of a terrible hangover, my mind was working too slowly for me to be able to apologise for this terrible accident.

～∘～

This all happened so very long ago and it is only as I write that the events of some of those years become a reality. It was during that week, so long ago, when I was sitting in John Adams's office that John's brother came in to say goodbye as he set off to the Vietnam War. Richard Adams looked a fine figure of a man, wearing the uniform of the Australian Army and carrying a kitbag. It all seemed so natural, this parting of brothers. John did speculate, after Richard had left, whether or not he would ever see his brother again. That war changed Australia—the sense of duty to fight other people's wars, in other people's lands, was for the last time stretched to its very limit. At the same time, prosperity came with the sale of wool, whose price rose to a figure never since repeated, and the influx of American servicemen for rest and recuperation in Australian cities. Sydney changed beyond belief; nightclubs opened as never before and the city was filled with manufactured gaiety. Prostitutes lined the streets around Kings Cross, and traffic accidents were caused by cruising cars which came to a sudden halt to pick up an attractive woman, while the driver of the car behind was also watching the same woman rather than the vehicle in front. The roads in that part of Sydney were like the dodgems at a fair—one car after another bumping into the car in front. Hotels opened and restaurants flourished as, for the first time, tourists really came to Sydney.

Time flies, yet we barely notice that it is happening nor its impact on us. When I was young, I believed people my age were ancient; now, I look at people half my age and believe them older than I was at the same age. A few months ago, I lunched with a childhood friend, a woman a couple of years younger than me. When I mentioned the Vietnam War, she held her hands up in horror. 'Never mention that you remember that war, and on no account ever tell anyone where you were when President Kennedy was assassinated. Young people will think that you are geriatric if you say such things. Just drop into the conversation that you remember the Falklands War; it is socially much safer.'

༄

Hamersley House was built and I tried to decorate it with paintings and sculpture, without much enthusiasm from my colleagues. Glass and brass were the touchstones of modern taste in the Perth of 1968. They hated my modern pictures and detested my contemporary sculpture. Although the plans for Hamersley House included an arcade to join onto one that was to cross the City of Perth, it never happened. Its gardens never really worked: the wind killed the plants and filled its ponds with litter from the street. When a creeper that had been planted in the building's forecourt really took off and had reached the fifth storey—for some unknown reason it liked wind and pollution—despite direct instructions to the contrary, some child in an estate agent's office instructed that this adventurous plant be cut at the roots. With the death of this plant, the last piece of friendliness was stripped from the barren face of the building. No-one that I employed was remotely interested in making this building look better than its neighbours; they could not see the sense in such an idea.

Across the road, a brick building was erected. I was beginning to win the battle to make my buildings people-friendly. Oliver Ford, whom I knew from London, was employed to design the foyer of this building. His job was to give it a dramatic quality—'Make it seem like an old hotel,' I told him, 'forget that it's an office building.' So he did, with a sweeping staircase in the foyer and panelling on its walls. Then we decorated the inside with antique furniture, modern Australian paintings and a variety of strange objects, from farm implements to equipment from Perth's old Mint. It was not a masterpiece but the result was far better than Hamersley House.

Two blocks down was London House, a concrete monster built by others at the time that I was planning the Parmelia. We bought it in partnership with the family store, Boans, then we pulled it down. In its place went New London House, a tall, red-brick building with a grand foyer, again designed by Oliver Ford, with high ceilings, its walls covered by Sidney Nolan's paintings and large Chinese pots placed in the corners. On a carpet in the centre, its design taken from an Aboriginal painting, sat eighteenth-century English furniture. In a smaller foyer off to the side, an entire wall was covered with Aboriginal artefacts and weapons, which made a stark contrast to the elegance of eighteenth-century England. The result was a sensation, the building let at once and in the weeks after opening, thousands of people came just to look at the foyers.

At least three of the foyers that I built in Perth were designed by Oliver Ford. Over many years, he was a great help to my family's business. Not only was he in charge of redecorating the Dorchester Hotel when renovation was needed, but each week he inspected all the suites to check that the furnishings had not been muddled up by careless housekeepers. Through my association with Oliver came the idea to make the foyers of our buildings portable. Instead of designing the foyers of office buildings so that they were all marble and brass, we used paint and plaster, adding expensive paintings and furniture. Oliver was a master at getting just the right colours to make the plaster look expensive, then I would hang often very valuable paintings on his beautifully finished walls. The furniture was always antique; the carpets, often copied from Aboriginal paintings, were woven in Thailand. The total cost of these buildings per square foot was about the same as the ones with the marble and brass foyers, but the scale and the feel of our foyers was domestic. The beauty of the whole scheme was that when we sold our buildings, we could move the pictures, the furniture and the carpets on to the next building that we were developing. No-one so far has discovered a convenient way of shifting marble and brass. Oliver Ford gave me the idea, for he used to make immensely beautiful gardens by acquiring wonderful tubs and planting them with shrubs and flowers. When he moved house, his garden moved with him.

John Roberts, the intuitive contractor who runs and owns the highly efficient Multiplex Construction Company, built many buildings for me in Australia. Over the years, he has become one of my closest friends. A consummate storyteller, John once told me one that involved Ray O'Connor, the man who succeeded Charles Court as premier of Western Australia. They were together in London with Alan Bond. Bond, born in London, claimed that he knew how they should behave. First, they must buy English suits, then English shoes, and then English shirts and ties. Perversely, Bond insisted that they make these purchases at the Scotch House. Equipped to appear as Englishmen, they set out from the Hilton Hotel. On their walk, they passed through Shepherd's Market in London's West End. On a corner about a hundred yards from them was a street musician with an accordion. As they approached, he broke off the tune he was playing and burst into a spirited rendering of 'Waltzing Matilda'.

John Roberts, for all his good humour and funny stories, is one of the smartest contractors that I have ever come across. A man of endless generosity, he has helped many friends when they were in need despite the fact that he is totally focused on his own occupation. Generous with both money and, more importantly, his time, he does not, however, squander either. When you come to choose a builder to work for you, a good question to ask is: 'How long have your key staff been with you?' In the case of John's company, the answer to this question is, in most cases, since he started business. However well-qualified a building business is in a technological respect, a builder is only as good as his or her staff. In the case of John Roberts, they could not be better. In the choice of a builder, another important feature is to decide how you believe that builder would behave if unexpectedly things go wrong. The construction of the buildings on which John worked for me did not always run smoothly; sometimes there were problems but never a crisis, because John always dealt fairly and in good humour with every problem before it even approached the serious stage, let alone a crisis. There is no piece of paper printed with the phrases of lawyers, and signed by all participants in a deal, that I would value above a handshake with John Roberts.

The slogan of Multiplex is 'The Well-Built Builder'. John is just that, like so much about him. His size is deceptive—what at first passes as overweight is in fact strength. I once watched him run down St George's Terrace on his tiptoes, moving with great speed and surprising agility. When I first met him, John was one of Australia's smaller builders; now he is its largest with a successful international business. It wasn't by chance, however, that I met John Roberts—he sought me out. There was no need of his services as I already had a builder, a fine firm named Edwards and Taylor. I had never met Taylor but Vic Edwards was a builder of the old school while John Roberts was a builder of the modern world. When John came to see me in London, I was impressed, for I have always believed that it is a builder's job to seek out customers before they have work to let. In the world of building, persuading a customer to give you a contract is the very essence of your work. So important is this function that I always told my friends that in order to get a contract, I would crawl on my stomach from my family's London offices in Bloomsbury to Tower Bridge in the City of London. Having neither a crawling shape nor the inclination, this would be for me a considerable feat. All my life I was a builder from a family which for generations had been builders. When John Roberts came into my office and we had spent time together, I recognised a builder who was interested in his customers. Soon after John's visit, Vic Edwards died and I had need of a new builder to construct an office block at 90 St George's Terrace so I engaged John Roberts to handle that contract. Later, when my family company was about to build the Intercontinental Hotel in Sydney, I turned again to John Roberts for his help. Even though he had no business in that city, I preferred him to the local builders and how right that decision turned out to be. It would be wrong to say that the contract was completed without a hitch—there were hitches—but, as I have written, John has the ability to resist the temptation of turning a problem into a drama. My man in Australia, at that time, was Laurie Dunn, a highly experienced manager who had completed the construction of several hotels for the American Group Loewes Hotels. Together, Laurie Dunn and John Roberts's staff worked out the problems that arose and with mutual goodwill solved them. By the end of the 1980s, John Roberts had become an extremely rich man and his business, Multiplex, was flourishing.

When the Queen came to Australia, John Roberts was her host during her visit to Western Australia. The Queen and Prince Philip stayed with John and his wife, Angela, at their stud farm in the Swan Valley. Walking with John across his fields one morning, Prince Philip strode ahead of his wife, while John lagged behind with the Queen and a member of the Western Australian police force which was looking after her security. Police were stationed all over the farm and constantly spoke to one another on their mobile radios. Soon the Queen was gaining ground on the Prince, who was striding ahead. Meanwhile, John and the policeman were left far behind. 'There's an old woman following the Prince.' John could hear the words quite clearly as they came over the air from the radio of the officer walking beside him. 'I don't know how she got past us, but she has been following him for some time.' 'Where exactly is she and what does she look like?' went the conversation. 'About a hundred yards behind him dressed in an old mackintosh and a head scarf.' 'Is she any danger?' 'Well, she's gaining on him.' It was only when the police officers began to talk of 'taking her out' that John realised that they were referring to the Queen. At this point, he drew their attention to this fact.

The Queen wasn't the only world figure John Roberts entertained in Perth. When the Pope paid a visit to Australia, John was chosen to greet him. The welcoming ceremony was at the WACA stadium in Perth, and John was selected to lead the procession to the dais in the centre of the stadium. As he walked out, there was no applause; as he came near the dais, there was no applause. Becoming concerned, John quickly looked over his shoulder to find himself alone in the middle of the stadium. For some reason, the Pope had delayed his exit from the reception rooms under the stand, and John had been sent out just before this decision had been made. He was the only member of the procession who was not told what was happening.

It is entirely typical that John Roberts is usually the butt of his own humour. He tells both these stories and many others with

41

considerable relish. He is a man who survived the scandals and the crash in the Western Australia of the early 1990s, coming through the former as fresh and as lily-white as a recently laundered handkerchief, and the latter with both his business and his fortune intact.

The buildings that my family's company owned in Perth let quickly for good rents. My idea of changing the face of foyers in Perth from cold marble halls to human habitations seemed to have worked. By now, I had a team around me who believed, as I did, in conserving the best and rebuilding the rest. There should only be one rule in the matter of conservation—'never knock anything down no matter how badly that building is regarded, unless you can replace it with something that you are convinced is aesthetically superior'. I suppose as a rider to that rule, an open space is far better for a city than a mediocre building. My feelings about conservation and town planning are strong, as the reader of this book will by now be only too aware. Writing about those feelings, I could not help wondering where they have come from. Neither my mother nor my father held these views; possibly theirs would even have been the reverse of mine. Searching, however, through my writings of the past, I came across this piece. It exactly sums up how I feel about the conservation of buildings and the human dimension in planning towns. It goes thus:

A flight to Australia is a long and tedious affair, which I thought could be eased by three days in Singapore to break the boredom. After leaving its mega-airport—a labyrinth of moving staircases, fresh-decked with fluorescent orchids, like some Eastern shrine to the modern world—the traveller encounters, on each side of the road into town, rows of hibiscus, rows of lilies. In fact, serried ranks of tropical plants that seems at first enchanting then monotonous—vast quantities of trees and plants, but of only half-a-dozen varieties.

Singapore is a difficult city to arrive at, for there are so many trees in the city that it seems like the countryside and so many buildings in the countryside that it seems like the city. No smell of exotic perfume here, no smell of oriental spice, just petrol. Its now expensive aroma hangs in the hot and sweaty air, kept captive by banks of cloud, washed almost daily by heavy rain. It is a good rule of thumb that if a country has a large quantity of lush greenery, it always gets a large quantity of rain. There is a monotony about Singapore found, I believe, nowhere else. The shops—Chanel, Cartier, Louis Vuitton, not one, but multiple agencies of these great houses—selling their products half a season behind the rest of the world. Twelve hours by aeroplane from winter to summer, but in Singapore it is hard to tell one from the other. Seasons here become irrelevant and so the fashions in these fashionable shops trail behind, unsold goods lingering on the shelves.

Its buildings, built with all the advantages of blatant commerce, have failed—towers, scaled down from other towns, clippings from architectural magazines pasted into this city then hidden with trailing bougainvillea and filled with potted palms. The high-ceilinged foyers of the early Sixties with their overgrown chandeliers of cascading glass. New buildings that were once Singapore's pride now seem like a reproach. Systematically they have, for nearly twenty-five years, destroyed everything that was old. Hotels everywhere, snatched from any American city and built in Singapore, everywhere there are orchids—in every foyer, in every room, on every table, tucked in napkins on trays, delivered with the morning papers—there is nowhere to go, nothing to do, that does not involve orchids, always the same sort of orchid.

To be fair to Singapore—a city that offers no real reason to be fair to it—the mood has changed. They are now rebuilding the old buildings as quickly as they can. Chinese merchants and Malay traders are being moved back into reproductions of the shops that they occupied before they were decanted into modern blocks. Bugis Street is being rebuilt—rebuilt somewhere else, for its original site is now the headquarters of the Urban Transit Authority. The Tourist Authority feels the need to recreate some local colour and no doubt a Bugis Street Authority will be created to do just this. The days when you had to kick the pipes in Raffles Hotel to start the flow of water are long gone. The days of the old Bugis Street—a street closed to traffic, opened to food, and the world's greatest form of theatre: the accident of large numbers of people enjoying themselves. Tables all over the pavement, tables all over the street. Food that crosses the borders of the Far East. Nothing that you could not buy in that street, nothing, I suppose, that you could not sell. Packed with travellers, drinking, eating, laughing and, very much later, tears and fights. The nightly parade of transvestites, quite beautiful in their way, posing for photographs with the diners, poking fun at drunks who perhaps did not realise that the beautiful girl they hugged had more to her than met the eye. A visit to Bugis Street was an event. Nothing really to do with the buildings, it was about people—not special people but special I suppose because of their ordinariness. A drunken sailor standing on a table pouring beer over himself. How can you rebuild this? Better let it go.

To wake after a night flight to Australia and to look down on the blue fingers of Sydney Harbour, its white Opera House and grey steel bridge, a city of clean air, a dry city with roofs poking like red pimples through its greenery, a sight that caused some great figure visiting from Europe to exclaim to the press at the airport: 'My first impression of Sydney?—Impetigo.'

Life is about the humans who each play their various roles; when their actions are set in a sterile efficient surrounding, the wonder and the beauty goes from their performances. It is not a matter of surprise that the perfect city, the ambition of the renaissance world, is portrayed empty of a human population.

By the mid-1970s, I had learned that rule of conservation, knocking down bad buildings while keeping the unusual, the bizarre and the beautiful and always trying to give my new buildings a human scale. I also set about actively restoring existing heritage buildings. First in Perth, where the former Bishop's House was restored to its original glory and, at the same time, three houses in Mount Street, as well as the 'Gingerbread House' in Fremantle, so-called because of the architectural feature created by the use of patterns made with different-coloured bricks. Later, twenty or so old pearling masters' homes in Broome were restored: it was, I believe, these old buildings that started my love affair with the North-West.

೭ಀ

In truth, looking at Western Australia from a distance, it has become clear that the place is getting out of balance. Conservation has become too dominant and practised in the wrong places. While the Government hurries to transform the vast empty spaces of Australia into National Parks that people are not allowed to visit, where conservation is most needed, however, amongst Western Australia's historic buildings, it is barely practised at all. The people live in a land and the people must be served by that land, but equally the people must realise that if they abuse their land, that land can no longer serve them. We are merely life tenants of this planet and it is worth remembering that we have a full repairing lease with that tenancy agreement. The transportation system of Western Australia is still, by comparison with other places, primitive. This, however, is a considerable advantage, for now is the time to integrate the use of sea, air, road and rail. Western Australia is a State, so its transport system not only should be thought of in the context of a State. When travelling north to south, railways are not an option, travel by sea extremely limited, travel by road still primitive due to the lack of good hotels, and travel by air expensive. Travelling west to east, railways are inefficient and slow, by world standards; road travel is limited, travel by sea is also limited, and again, by air, expensive. This all must surely be wrong. Australia cannot develop until efficient railways link all the State and territorial capitals. Urban railways must be made competitive with cars and lorries, small airlines encouraged, and the excesses of large airlines curbed. Airports need to be built to allow aircraft to carry freight from north to south and, in particular, overseas. The population should be encouraged to spread rather than to mass in one spot. Isolation in a modern world should not exist. The cost of creating a proper transport system may seem prohibitive but the alternative is a brake on prosperity and a terminal act to the quality of life in Australia by confining people and the means by which they earn their living into a series of small spaces.

II

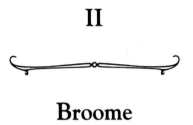

Broome

5

It was John Adams who first took me to the town of Broome in north-west Australia in 1974. John and I had decided to get out of town. I wanted to visit Kalgoorlie because I had heard there were large quantities of old farm equipment lying around the place. I had started a collection of farm machinery and was keen to discover a neglected source of rare pieces. John, however, knew that if I travelled to a new town, I would likely buy something. 'Kalgoorlie,' opined John, 'is far too hot. Let's go to Broome, it's by the sea.' I also collected seashells at that time and, being a cautious man, John preferred that the 'something' be a small shell rather than a gargantuan tractor or plough. He knew only too well that it would be his task to organise this monster's travel to my house in Hampshire.

That day we lunched in Broome, the guests of the local chemist, David Hutchinson, and his wife, Thea. I enjoyed the atmosphere of the town greatly. It was, I believe, love at first sight and I did, indeed, buy some seashells in Broome. I bought them from Barry and Kerry Sharp. Their shop was a disused part of premises that belonged to a local butcher, a man often suspected of cattle rustling. It was filled with disused fishing tackle, old anchors, giant clams and diving suits. Also displayed among all this was Kerry Sharp's collection of shells. In a flash, I was on to this collection—was it for sale? Under no circumstances would she sell her shells, despite the efforts I made over the following years to persuade her to the contrary. For the time being, however, I rummaged around among piles of coral and eventually came up with an Aboriginal carving. This carving was of a barramundi; it was about 70 centimetres long, painted with ochre, a dull red. Spots were made on this wooden fish by flaking off pieces of the timber's surface, leaving patches of unstained wood exposed. I made my purchase and then Kerry produced a small parcel of shells and offered them to me at a reasonable price. I bought these as well as the wooden fish, at which point she gave me some other decorative shells. I always enjoyed the company of Barry and Kerry Sharp: when I bought a home in Broome, we became firm friends. As for Kerry's shell collection, it was offered to me after her death and became part of my collection which I subsequently sold to Chris Mitchell, who worked for a number of years at the Broome Zoo.

In January 1981, the year after I married Romilly Hobbs, we set off for Australia. I had determined to take Romilly to Broome, so we arrived there towards the end of that month. Again, we had lunch with the Hutchinsons and their son, Tony, in the same Chinese restaurant. John and Liz Adams were with us, as were John Taylor, an architect, and his wife, Sue. Michael Szell, a well-known London fabric designer, who designed and worked on the fountain in the driveway behind 190 St George's Terrace, was also with us.

The town of Broome was empty. It was the wet season, and the temperature was several degrees below that in Perth. Despite that, the myth that the north-west of Australia is a hellhole of heat in 'the wet' still persists. The climate in Broome, though, is quite different from the rest of the North-West. Cool breezes blow across Broome's peninsula, one way in the morning and the other in the evening. Often the summer temperature in Broome is considerably less than that in Perth.

In any case, air-conditioning has changed the whole business of living in the North-West. Now, with better communications and facilities—the Internet, faxes, mobile telephones, regular air flights, sealed roads, hospitals and medical attention—what was once a remote and unbearably hot area has now become an accessible and pleasant place to live.

ॐ

At the time of my visit with Romilly, the golden rain and tulip trees bloomed, the frangipanis scented the air and the flowers of the bush were bright. There were no tourists and the locals were lounging in the sun on the beach, a twenty-kilometre beach that is among the most spectacular in the world. Cable Beach, which owes its name to the fact that it is where the international telegraph cable, completed in 1889, came ashore, is six kilometres from Broome on the ocean side of the peninsula and is Broome's main tourist attraction, apart from the Japanese graveyard where generations of pearl divers are buried, most of them killed in the course of their work. Who could not love this lazy place with its ramshackle buildings and eccentric population?

The old buildings of Broome fascinated me; raised on stumps, so that cool breezes could circulate around them, with only latticework to separate them from the outside world. I loved their spacious verandas and long sloping roofs of corrugated iron. In the hot days of Broome's summer, these houses, cooled by slowly revolving fans, made pleasant habitations. Newcomers to Broome, however, preferred air-conditioning and pile carpets and, as a result, these homes had become neglected. Timber in the tropics does not last if left to its own devices; unprotected by paint, rust consumes corrugated iron.

After lunch, Romilly went to Cable Beach with the Taylors, the Adamses and David and Thea Hutchinson. I set out with Tony Hutchinson and Michael Szell. We drove around the dirt roads that were Broome's streets, looking at the old pearling masters' houses that stood among the mango trees with bare earth around them. I was very taken by these houses, built by boat builders for men who sailed boats. One we came across, on the corner of Louis and Herbert Streets, had the sign '4 sale' outside. We knocked on the door, first Michael, then myself. No answer. We called and then we shouted. Yes, the house was for sale, the owner's wife told us. Her husband was at the hotel, but he would come back in an hour. Could we return?

The house belonged to Jeanie and Peter Haynes. Jeanie was cooking lights for the cat when we arrived at her front door; Peter was spending lunchtime and much of the afternoon at the Continental Hotel, or Conti as it was called in Broome. Jeanie, a pillar of Broome society, was president of the historical society and much else as well. Peter, her husband, had been a pearling master and shire president, a man much respected in the community. He was famous for having eluded the Japanese at the fall of Singapore and then making his own way down to Australia by small boat. Peter Haynes was, as were a number of Broome's citizens, inclined to come up with schemes that were close to pure fantasy; he made a highly entertaining drinking companion. The property had been on the market for some time and my interest was unexpected but extremely welcome. The house was large and rambling, and well-kept inside, where a considerable amount of polishing had clearly gone on over the years. Outside, however, the timbers of the old building were showing their age. As for the garden—or yard, for there was not a flower or plant in sight— that was filled with the remnants of Peter's career as a pearling master. The earth of the yard was bare and bright red, but you could not see it on account of heaps of corrugated iron, old and rusting anchors, coils of cable and a whole lot of equipment the purpose of which I was completely unaware. This, however, was the scene that greeted Romilly on her return from the beach. As I told her that I had bought a house in Broome, her face fell. When she saw the Haynes's backyard and smelt the noxious odour of the boiling lights, her face became a picture of misery. The place's only redeeming features were the vast mango trees that grew out of the heap of rusting iron and rotting timber.

Despite Romilly's misgivings, I bought the house. We signed the contract, drawn up by the bank manager, in the bar of the Roebuck Hotel, so named because of its proximity to Roebuck Bay. Roebuck did not graze its shores, rather it was named after HMS *Roebuck*, the ship commanded by Sir William Dampier, a man the British might call an explorer but the rest of the world a buccaneer. In 1699, Dampier was on his second voyage to New Holland, as Indonesia was then known, when he dropped anchor off the southernmost part of the Kimberley coast of Western Australia. We were intrigued as we arrived at the Roebuck Hotel to see a line painted on the street, parallel with its veranda—'No drinking past this line' was printed in large letters on the pavement. Inside was a sign that advertised a 'Hairy Arse Competition. Judging on Sunday'. John Adams, my lawyer, checked the contract and, as a round of drinks was delivered, he asked, 'What's this about a cinema?' 'Oh, you have bought that as well,' was the bank manager's reply. The Sun Pictures, now advertised as the oldest operating cinema

in the world, became mine in this way. John had been right: I do tend
to buy things when I visit towns for the first time.

I did not see my new house in quite the same way that Romilly and
my travelling companions saw it. To me, the house was a wreck—
smelly, tired, falling apart—but it was a lovely house and, standing
restored among a grove of giant mangoes, it would be wonderfully
romantic. You could find that kind of house described in a dozen
Somerset Maugham novels. The Haynes house became my home. I set
about restoring it and, over a period of years, I added a freestanding
kitchen, a drawing room and double-storey bedroom, bathroom and
dressing room for Romilly and myself, as well as a Chinese tearoom and
a treetop bedroom in the garden. Nowadays, my former home has been
turned into a small hotel.

The Sun Pictures was really no more than a spacious timber shed,
with rows of deckchairs to accommodate the customers and ceiling
fans lazily moving the hot night air of Broome during films. Between
the audience and the screen is a stretch of long grass. On exceptionally high tides, the sea came into the picture house and flooded this
stretch of grass. The local airport is behind the cinema and the
planes of early evening flights out of Broome often appear over the
top of the screen, the screech of the engines blotting out the film's
soundtrack, the plane's lights dazzling the audience. There can be
few places in the world more exotic and extraordinary to watch a film
than the Sun Pictures.

For me, it was love at first sight when I visited Broome. I loved
the colours, the freshness of the air and, above all, the laziness of
the place. When I lived there, I found Broome to be wonderfully
romantic—the buccaneers still seemed to wander the town's streets.
Pearls were sold in the town's bars: a pearler would pull a handkerchief from his pocket, not to blow his nose but to show the pearls tied
in its corners. At that time, I used to buy property in the Pearlers
Rest Bar of the Roebuck Hotel. The drinking there began at about
ten in the morning. The days were hot and everyone rose early. Most
work was done by the time that people in Perth took their morning
break for coffee. The system for drinking in the Pearlers Rest was

53

easy. The customers stood at the bar, placing their money in front of them. The barmaid decided whose round it was and took the appropriate amount of money from the pile in front of that customer. After a multitude of beers, the dealing began. A property was mentioned and then a price; an ordinance survey plan was produced and the price debated; a deal struck. John Adams, who had not drunk alcohol at that stage, drew up a contract of offer and acceptance on the back of a beer mat; both parties signed this contract and the land was mine. It is hard to prove but I am sure that I was sold property by its owners just so they would have a beer-mat contract.

Soon my family company and I owned a great many properties in the township of Broome. The architecture of the town was as architecture nowhere else. The old buildings were ungainly and all the better for that. It was not only their shape and size, however, that interested me, but also their colours, often garish in the bright sunshine of the North-West. It was how these buildings related to the people who lived in them that attracted not only me, but also many of the painters who have portrayed Broome's streetscapes. In time, I discovered that you can restore buildings easily enough if you have the will to save them, but you cannot convincingly place the patina of age on new timber.

⌘

It was only a question of time before I became fascinated by Broome and my vision for that town's future. My every move, my every investment, was dominated by the desire to change a tired old town into a modern tourist resort without destroying the soul of the place. It has been my experience in Australia that old homes restored to their original condition only attract speculators who, seeing something beautiful, set about changing them into buildings that are commercially useful. This happened to the houses in Mount Street in Perth that I had saved and to many of my former properties in Broome; it is not an edifying spectacle. This, however, is not an argument for allowing buildings to rot, rather an observation on the attitude to conservation in Western Australia in the 1990s.

In time, the idea caught on that money could be made out of

development in Broome. New developers came to town, supermarkets were built and shopping arcades. A town with previously one of the highest records of unemployment in Australia has become prosperous. In all such schemes, there are losers, and in Broome it is the old people who have lost. The town has changed beyond their recognition. Change, however, was inevitable—I just happened to realise what was going to happen because I had seen the same phenomenon before in other places, and it was my intention to try and make the change happen in as orderly and civilised a manner as possible.

There can be no doubt, however, that the scale of my efforts at conserving buildings in Broome has altered the general attitude to architecture in that town. While the old buildings may well have been changed in both their appearance and usage, the new buildings that have gone up in the last decade have, at least, paid lip service to the style of Broome's distinctive architecture. It must be remembered that without a contemporary use an old building is of no more use than an empty bottle, decorative perhaps, but useless. Today, however, the coastline of the Broome peninsula is not cluttered with concrete towers and the other effluent of a tourist boom. No building taller than a palm tree is the rule. It will be interesting to see if that rule stands firm when the commercial pressure is really on. If, indeed, that rule can be kept, then the town will have no choice but to spread, and then it will be the time for satellite towns to appear further up the Dampier peninsula. Each of these satellite towns should be surrounded by an expanse of bush, each of them set back from the sea's shore. Communications will then become a problem and the answer to that problem will, of course, be a railway. A railway that links towns and then links these towns with villages on the coast, villages with small populations that supply the access to the sea that tourists and residents both will demand.

ൟ

Mrs Wing's restaurant was a long, brick building that might, if it had not had tables and chairs in it, have been mistaken for a warehouse. The food, however, was wonderful, quite the best food in town. Today, Mrs Wing has moved to another brick restaurant and the good food moved with her. Even inside this brick shed, to the casual diner, the original building did not seem like a restaurant, for it was not unusual to find a dozen tables occupied and nobody eating. Service was extremely slow, largely due to the fact that Mrs Wing also ran a takeaway. Since customers are more inclined to walk away if there is a delay in food they are waiting to take home than if there is a delay in service at a table, where they are settled with a bottle, takeaway customers were given precedence. The seated customers did not seem to mind, however, for Wing's was as good a place to play cards as anywhere else. Men and women drank, children became fractious and the evening wore on. As a result, I suppose, of plenty to drink and little to eat, fights broke out. These fights would have been objection-able in a restaurant in Sydney, or in any of the other State capitals, but in Wing's in Broome they only added to the general enjoyment of those waiting to eat. It was, I suppose, a tribute to Mrs Wing's cooking that so many were prepared to wait for so long to eat her food. The menu was copious, but there was plenty of time to study it before making up your mind. The item that caught my attention, however, was 'Chicken Wings'. What exotic dish could this be that Mrs Wing had dignified with her own name? What dish of oriental fantasy had Mrs Wing invented? I asked the surly waitress, a waitress so surly that if I did not attach that adjective to her name, I would have to apolo-gise to anyone else whom I have ever called surly. She was a young girl who was working at Wing's before setting off on the next leg of her journey around Australia. 'It's chicken,' she replied. 'I know that, but how is it cooked?' 'Fried.' 'Fried' did not seem to have a ring of the exotic Orient. Watching my bewilderment, the girl explained with a considerable touch of sarcasm, 'It's bits of chicken.' As I was about to question her further, she began to flap her arms in the manner of a chicken that was hyperventilating. At the same time, she emitted loud cries of, 'Wings! Wings! Wings!' My question died in my throat; this dish owed nothing to the culinary imagination of Mrs Wing.

My mistake, I suppose, underlines the great cultural divide between those used to eating at restaurants in great cities and life in the outback of Australia; the waitress had merely pointed out my inadequacy. Later that week, Romilly and I returned to eat at Mrs Wing's, in fact, at that time when in Broome, we nearly always ate at Wing's. The waitress took her time coming over to our table and when eventually she did arrive, she gave me a look of total contempt. Romilly had obviously decided to humour the beast. 'Hello', 'How are you?', and that kind of remark, ending, on looking around the restaurant and seeing it empty, a good-natured 'Which is the best night here?' Quick as a flash, the girl replied, 'Monday.' Romilly fell into the trap. 'Why is Monday such a good night?' 'Because no-one comes here,' snapped the waitress, and then headed for the kitchen.

After an interminable wait, during which time I felt certain she had taken time to eat her dinner, the waitress reappeared. By this time, one other table was filled by a pleasant-looking family. Father, mother, two boys who seemed to be aged around twelve and ten respectively, a small girl who looked about six years old and a babe in arms. The waitress headed for them straight as a well-aimed arrow and, as it turned out, just about as deadly. 'It's a long time since I've seen you,' she said to the man. His wife looked surprised, but said nothing. 'I've never been here before,' the man protested. 'I recognise you,' the waitress accused. 'But I've never met you before, I don't know you. I know I don't know you.' The man's wife began to bridle and then, as the waitress pressed home her attack, 'That beard's a good disguise but it's your boots that have given you away,' she rose in anger. The waitress turned and headed for the kitchen. The woman slapped her husband, gathered up her children and left. Romilly and I sat and waited for someone to take the order for our dinner.

6

Perhaps it is the weather in Broome that makes you feel so good. The inhabitants of that small north-western town rise in the morning to a clear blue sky. 'Oh, hell,' they say to each other, 'it's another perfect day.' On the other hand, perhaps it is the heat of the wet that makes the people of the North-West a trifle eccentric. Whatever, be it their eccentricity or the boredom of good weather for most of the year, Broome is a place where I always found laughter. Joy, tragedy, success, failure, they all have their funny side and in that remote place, I discovered that it was the humour that people looked for. The tale of the town's baker who, finding an Aboriginal had broken into his bakery, sought the man out and shouted at him in a thoroughly abusive fashion. As the baker caught his breath, the Aboriginal replied, 'You are only saying these things to me because I am a blackfella.' 'Hold on a moment.' The baker turned, picked up a barrel of flour and tipped it over the Aboriginal. 'Now,' said the baker, 'you are a white fella.' He then continued to curse the poor man.

Almost the first day after I had moved into my house in Broome in the winter of 1981, I set out to find Paddy Roe, an important Aboriginal elder. His address had been given to me by Mary Macha, a considerable expert in Aboriginal art and other matters. Paddy lived in the Aboriginal camp at the end of Dora Street. The camp was composed of tin houses with corrugated iron roofs and no glass in their windows. Beds were laid out between these huts, iron beds with old mattresses. In the centre of the camp stood a large shady tree, the earth all around it bare and red. An old man was sitting beneath the shade of this great tree carving a mother-of-pearl shell at which he peered intently through old, misty eyes. His hands and bare feet were gnarled and knotted, and he wore a pair of shorts and an open check shirt. An old man of considerable dignity, he took no notice as I approached.

'Can you please direct me to Paddy Roe?' said I. 'Patrice,' he replied. 'Patrice, Patrice,' he kept insisting as he climbed into my car. 'Patrice, yes,' I replied as he directed me along the wide red earthen tracks that were then Broome's streets. First left, then left again and right, straight on—his directions were mostly given with hand signals. Every time I tried to speak to him, he replied, 'Patrice, Patrice,' and urged me on with frantic movements of his hands. In time, we passed a low white building; its most impressive aspect a sign describing it as a hospital. 'Stop, stop,' the old man said and jumped out of the car, quickly disappearing into the hospital. It cannot have been more than a minute or two before he reappeared, fitting a hearing aid into his ear. 'That more better,' he announced. 'I can hear you now, my patrice were dead.'

I enquired where Paddy Roe was to be found. 'Paddy Roe,' he replied, 'no worries,' and he took me back to the encampment where I had first met him and went off among the tin houses. Soon the old man reappeared from between a pair of tin homes and with him Paddy Roe. A man of commanding presence, Paddy wore a wide-brimmed hat that shaded his eyes. Arms hanging at his side, baggy trousers held in place with a wide leather belt, his face broad, with generosity in his eyes, he had a gentleness about him as he spoke, his mind as quick as his hearing. In that first meeting with Paddy, I felt the man's great strength. Paddy often seemed a simple man. I doubt, however, that there is any aspect of his character that ranks akin to simplicity. I knew him well for seventeen years and I was endlessly fascinated by how his mind worked. In the days that we first met, he was an Aboriginal leader of consequence and his manner carried the natural authority of a true leader, an authority that comes not from money or privilege, appointment or position. Paddy Roe's authority came from within the man himself.

At the time, I did not realise that the old man I had come across in the Aboriginal camp was Joe Nangan, or 'Butcher Joe', as he was called by the locals. Joe Nangan was a considerable artist who worked in crayon on sheets of paper taken from an exercise book. He recorded the myths and legends of the Kimberley. His pictures have an immense power that comes from an age-old people and the giant landscape that surrounds them. They are not the paintings that have caught the popular imagination, the abstractions of ceremonies long performed, nor are they the work of an artist urged on by art advisers of European stock in the pay of the State. These pictures are, however, in the European tradition, and they record the traditions of the Broome Aboriginals. Small, serious works, they would be categorised as primitive art. They are not eye-catching, flamboyant paintings, useful to a Western interior decorator to hang in a socialite's drawing room, but small, well-considered works whose primary purpose is to record tradition as that tradition is seen by the artist. In this, they succeed wonderfully and, in their success, they have become important works of art.

Joe Nangan and Paddy Roe were partners: Joe would dream the dreams and Paddy would make the costumes for the small corroborees that they performed. Paddy is not of pure Aboriginal blood, and had been taken from his mother as a small child to be reared by the State. It became a driving force in his life to recover the traditions of the Aboriginal people and somehow to be a bridge between black and white Australians. Paddy patiently guided me through a quagmire of traditions and rivalries in Broome, endlessly explaining why a particular mound or group of trees was important to the Aboriginals, and telling me why, when faced with the same proposition, one person would behave in a particular way and another would behave in the diametrically opposite fashion. Paddy is a serious repository of Aboriginal history and tradition. His face would break into a wide smile and then he would quite literally slap his thighs with delight as he burst into laughter at some memory that tickled his sense of humour.

Paddy Roe carved small wooden lizards. As the new lizards were finished, he would bring them to sell in my shop at the zoo, that I had recently opened. 'These little fellows keep breeding,' he would say as he broke into laughter at his joke. 'What will you have to drink, Paddy?'

'I'll have just an orange juice.' And we would sit in the shade and gossip. Over the years, most of Paddy's relatives worked for me in one form or another; fine, strong young men, often leaders in their community. In the days when I first went to Broome, there was little crime, nobody locked their cars, homes were left open. There were only drunken fights and a bit of grievous bodily harm; theft was unknown. Sadly, as the town grew and access to the outside world became easier, the curses of that world came to Broome as well as its benefits.

I can recall leaving Mrs Wing's Chinese restaurant one night to find three men beating up a fourth on a vacant lot. They had him on the ground and were kicking him. Happily, the police arrived at the same moment as myself. As the constables sauntered towards the combatants, the fight broke up, the four men moved on and the police left. Out of sight of the law, the fight began again and soon the fourth man was back on the ground again, getting another good kicking. Dr Reid, for some time the town's doctor, once told me how he had treated Aboriginals with injuries to their heads that would have killed a white man. The women used to fight with heavy sticks, smashing them together and destroying any part of the human body that got in the way. Dr Reid used to treat hands where the knuckles had been beaten to pulp. Dr Reid was a considerable, if controversial, figure. He became Shire president, a position roughly equivalent to that of an English mayor.

Right through the 1960s and 1970s, the town of Broome hibernated—there was little happening there. It wasn't that the inhabitants were naturally lazy, just that there were very few jobs available. In the wet, the grass grew and the people of Broome moved around on bicycles: cars were a menace, I was told when I first arrived in Broome. A bicycle could be thrown down in the long grass and it disappeared, but a car was another matter—everyone knew where you were. Often, when I received telephone calls from England, the calls would be put through the local switchboard and the caller informed of my whereabouts. In Broome in those days everyone knew everyone else's business or, if they didn't, they invented it.

❧

In fact, so quiet was the place at that time, the only serious crime, apart from grievous bodily harm, was a bank robbery—that and a bit of cattle rustling. The bank in Broome was robbed by two men on bicycles. The teller was so shocked that the money was handed over without even a murmur. The thieves left the bank's premises and, climbing on to their bicycles, pedalled like mad up the road towards the Continental Hotel. As soon as they were out of sight of the angry bank employees, who by then were searching for a policeman, the thieves ducked into the mangroves that grew along the shoreline. Hiding their bicycles, they waded through the mud and mangroves until they were opposite the Continental Hotel. It was their plan to return to their hotel rooms, wait a few days, and then quietly leave town with the loot. All went well until they crossed what passed as the Continental Hotel's foyer. Normally, the receptionist would have paid these villains about as much attention as she paid the other customers: service in the North-West was merely a concept in those days, one so foreign to the nature of those who worked in hotels that it was barely, if ever, put into practice. Leaving dirty footprints on a recently cleaned floor, however, was another matter. 'Hey!' she called. 'What do you blokes think you're doing?' The thieves took no notice, which infuriated the receptionist, and a ferocious argument ensued. The receptionist, whose anger was, to say the least, considerable, called the police. For the sake of wiping their boots, the thieves found themselves in Fremantle jail. Strange as this tale may seem, a far stranger matter occurred the night the fire brigade were called out to a serious fire. There was not a lot they could do about it, however, for the building on fire was the fire station and the fire engine was safely locked away inside it.

⁂

While Paddy Roe put on small corroborees, Roy Wiggin, from the Bardi people of One Arm Point was, of this genre, a true Diaghilev. I had over the years become very friendly with Roy. He had a dream about an epic journey made by his father and he was determined to turn his dream into a corroboree. The Aboriginal corroboree is not a sacred or secret ceremony; in fact, its character is not too different from Italian nineteenth-century opera. These corroborees are often filled with tales of heroes, triumph and tragedy. A popular corroboree might be performed for many years; an unpopular corroboree does not make it past its first performance.

༄

I arranged with Roy Wiggin to put on a performance of his own corroboree. However, as so often with Roy, there was a problem. He had lost his totems. These totems were held in the hand and helped to differentiate between one performer and another. They took the place of costumes and moved the narrative of the drama forward. Roy Wiggins needed money to make new ones for the performance. I arranged with Roy that I would pay him a generous sum for each totem that he made. I would own the totems and look after them, and he and his performers could have the use of them whenever they were to perform. Roy saw this deal as a regular source of income; whenever he was a little short of the ready, he turned up with a bundle of totems. By the end of our association, Roy had sold me over three hundred of these wooden frames with coloured wool stretched between nails, much as a spider makes a web. The totems, like much innovative art, did not cost a lot to make—just the price of some balls of coloured wool, nails and a small quantity of timber. The totems for this corroboree were truly objects of beauty, the variety of designs endless. The time spent making these totems could not have been too great either, it was the idea that really counted. The inspiration for the designs was a dream Roy had about his long-dead father's experiences during a fishing expedition from One Arm Point. In his dream about his father's journey, Roy had seen tide races, whirlpools, dangerous rocks, islands, sharks and dugongs, birth and death—a drama on an all-embracing scale. Cecil B. de Mille would have been proud of Roy Wiggin's production.

As the number of totems accumulated, the day of the performance drew near. I had arranged that the performance should take place at six p.m.; dinner would be served to the performers afterwards. Despite a delayed start, Roy Wiggin's new corroboree was a triumph. His brilliant totems are now in the Australian National Maritime Museum in

63

Sydney. As objects that draw their inspiration from the sea, they could not find a better home.

⸎

Each winter in Broome, there is a festival that lasts about a week. These fairs are jolly events, attracting large numbers of people—concerts, exhibitions, parades and other events fill out the week's program. This festival is called the *Shinju Matsuri* or 'Shinju' for short. It was never a traditional event, rather the idea of Dr Reid's family, created to help the tourist boom that the Reids felt, quite rightly as it turned out, was about to hit Broome. At first, the festival was centred around the pearling industry; *Shinju Matsuri* is Japanese for 'Festival of the Pearl'. Timed to coincide with the end of the pearl harvest, the festival used to include a race between the various luggers belonging to the local pearling companies. The race was discontinued; some say it was discontinued because the wife of a visiting notable, having drunk too much beer, fell overboard. The fact that the pearling companies had given up their picturesque luggers, which were prohibitively expensive to maintain, in favour of modern craft, seems a more likely explanation for the demise of this elegant event. Soon after this, however, the pearling industry and its festival drifted apart. The pearlers got on with their pearling and Broome's tourist authority got on with its festival.

During the festival week, an evening market is set up on the town's oval with stalls selling food and 'local' handicrafts. As is the way in even the most remote of places, these local handicrafts are far from local; handicrafts that are, in fact, manufactured tourist rubbish. The festival is a multinational event, with Malays, Japanese and Chinese, as well as European Australians and indeed the Aboriginals who preceded them all in their arrival on Australian shores. One of the dealers at the evening market was a smart young lad of Aboriginal descent. His sales technique was lent a certain urgency by the discomfort of his broad feet, which were encased in narrow, pointed shoes imported from Italy. One year, he had the idea of selling what he called 'real Chinese jade'. The Chinese community in Broome is prominent, and, after conferring with his colleagues, a respected member of that community shuffled up to the Aboriginal lad. He pointed to the jade and said: 'This one Kimberley coloured stone.' At this, the crowd melted away. As the Chinese went back to his group, the lad ran after him and seized him by the shoulder and shouted, 'Listen, do I tell people what you put in your long soup?' Then he walked off with as much of a stride as his shoes would allow. Having considered the situation, the Chinese shuffled back to the lad's stall, and, striking an inscrutable pose, announced: 'This is pure Chinese jade. Absolutely pure.' What he knew, and what the lad knew but the crowd did not, was that the secret ingredient in his long soup was Actifed syrup, which normally serves as a well-known international cough mixture. The world being the way it is, they had reached a necessary accommodation with each other.

By tradition, one of the events at the festival was an art exhibition. Local painters exhibited their work, a judge decided who was to come first, second and third, and small prizes were presented. Shortly after I arrived in Broome, I was asked to judge this exhibition. The year before, I had mounted a show of Sidney Nolan's early work in the town's library. The paintings, all from the late 1940s and early 1950s, came from my own collection and that of the University of Western Australia. All of these paintings, and there were about twenty of them, depicted the outback and the buildings of its small towns. As a result of this exhibition, opened by Sidney Nolan and the Shire president, Dr Reid, the committee of the *Shinju Matsuri* had come to the conclusion that I knew something about art. It was the tradition that the work winning the first prize was bought by the Shire and hung in the Shire's offices. For the previous two years at least, and possibly three—my memory fails me on this point—the wife of a Kimberley station owner, a pastoralist, had won the prize. Her paintings were talented but academic, high quality narrative pictures of station life and landscape. On the day of the judging, I spent several hours looking at all the works on show which, as you might expect, were a motley group. Some good, some bad, some talented, others lacking both expertise and talent. Only one painting, however, stood out. It was a dark and moody picture, a painting of near genius. A painting of the landscape in its abstract form, torn from the landscape. It was clearly streets ahead of all the others; in fact, streets ahead of any painting that I had seen at that date in the North-West. The first prize went to the gloomy landscape, the second to the station owner's wife, and I went home to have lunch.

By mid-afternoon, the Shire president and town clerk were, metaphorically speaking, knocking on my door. When calling on a person in Broome, it seemed the habit just to walk straight into his garden and not finding him there, to walk into his house. Would I change my mind about the first prize? 'Why?' I asked. 'Well, people have complained. It does not have a frame.' To my undying shame, after a short discussion, I swapped the order of the first and second paintings. It was a small thing, or so it seemed at the time; why should I care who won a local art competition? If the locals felt so strongly about a painting not having a frame, why should I explain that most of the great paintings of the previous twenty years did not have frames and that the sculptures of the same period were more often than not without bases?

That night my shame was compounded, for as I sat with Romilly and half a dozen friends in Mrs Wing's Chinese restaurant, the eventual winner of the Broome Shire art prize approached and presented me with a bottle of wine in recognition of my appreciation of her talent. This tale of weakness on my part would have passed from even the deepest recesses of my memory had it not been for the fact that the picture I had demoted was by a certain Jimmy Pike—an Aboriginal painter of colossal talent. Unbeknown to me at the time of the art competition, Jimmy Pike was serving a sentence in Broome jail for murder. Now generally considered one of Australia's most important painters, Jimmy Pike is a man for whose work I have a deep respect. In fact, I would go further and state that I regard his work as outstanding among both Aboriginal and European painters in Australia. One of the few Australian artists who has an international reputation, his work is found in many important collections including several State galleries and the National Gallery in Canberra. His work is also represented in many private collections in Europe and

America, and he has exhibited in Japan, France and Britain. During the last years of the 1980s, Jimmy Pike used from time to time to visit my zoo to sell me paintings. He has also recently had a highly successful show at the Rebecca Hossack Gallery in London.

Jimmy Pike spent his earliest years living a traditional Aboriginal nomadic existence in the Great Sandy Desert. As a teenager in the early 1950s, he and his family joined one of the last migrations out of the desert to the European settlements in the north. Settled on a cattle station near Fitzroy Crossing, Jimmy learned the trade of a stockman, only beginning to make prints and to paint while serving his sentence for murder in 1980. Released in 1986, he returned to the desert and set up camp with Pat Lowe, an English-born writer of considerable ability. Their life together has been recorded by Lowe in a series of extraordinary books including *Jilji Life in the Great Sandy Desert*, and the surreal work, *Jimmy and Pat Meet the Queen*, where Jimmy takes the Queen on a tour of his desert country and explains to her the problems that beset the issue of land rights.

7

In the late 1980s and early 1990s, the momentous events in Eastern Europe and the black comedy of people collecting lumps of the Berlin Wall seemed very remote to me as I walked down Cable Beach, the most north-westerly point of Australia, where people collect old bottles and remarkable seashells instead. Early most mornings, I would walk down Cable Beach with a man who, in the vernacular, would be described as 'my mate Snowy'. Short, stocky, fair-haired and blue-eyed, Snowy County was born in Melbourne. Rough and tough as Australians come, he made his way around Australia working in mining camps and construction sites, eventually finding his way to Broome. His tales of those days are truly horrendous: of 'bullfighting', where men get down on all fours and, racing towards each other, crack heads; of parties where all the guests arrive with a bottle whose contents are poured into a dustbin, stirred and then drunk; of fights and other escapades in camps where he worked.

Snowy makes Crocodile Dundee look like a suburban Sydney car salesman. Snowy County is a pearling master or, rather, the part-owner of a pearl farm that produces the very large and beautiful pearls that are sometimes seen around the necks of the world's most beautiful women, pearls of gem quality. But for every thousand pearls produced, there are only two or three that the pearling master will describe as 'gem'. Whether they are baroque, grey, pink, golden or white, with a deep, deep, lustre, rarely is a cultured pearl from Western Australia smaller than ten millimetres in diameter; the largest is the size of a damson. Some years ago, when Snowy was starting his pearl farm at Deep Water Point, he regularly drove the three hours down the track to Broome for supplies. On one occasion, the back of the truck was full of cardboard boxes containing the plastic baskets used in pearl culture. Sitting beside him was a young Japanese diver who was chain-smoking and casting the cigarette butts out of the window. 'It's hot today,' Snowy remarked. 'Very hot,' replied the diver, taking off his shirt. 'Bloody hot,' said Snowy, taking off his shirt as well. 'Very, very hot,' replied the Japanese, taking off his trousers. Now Snowy is used to hot weather but, before long, both he and the diver were bumping along in their underpants. It was a rough track, in fact, it is flattery to describe it as a track, and as Snowy slowed approaching a particularly deep ditch, the cab was engulfed in a sheet of flame. The pair of them jumped out and ran into the bush— or rather what was left of the bush after a fire the previous week. Shortly after Snowy had explained to the diver, in language that tended towards the crude, that it is not a good idea to throw lighted cigarettes out of a moving vehicle, the truck exploded.

Having got that off his chest, Snowy addressed their problem, which was that they were twenty kilometres from their camp, on a road that only they used, with no water, no hats, no shoes and only two pairs of underpants between them. Snowy took off his pants, tore them into strips and tied them to his feet. The diver did the same and they began to trudge through the bush. The temperature was 46 degrees centigrade, and after about eight kilometres, the diver lay down in a saltpan to die—Snowy's best efforts couldn't move him. So Snowy walked on, sometimes over rocks that were so hot that you could fry eggs on them—and then grill the bacon in their reflected heat. Eventually, Snowy reached the camp, put his head in a water trough and then called for help: 'There's a bloke out there on his back in a saltpan. Throw some water over him and bring him in.' After an experience like this, nothing could make the price of even the most beautiful of pearls seem more irrelevant.

Snowy was first my companion and my guide; later, my friend; and, after a while, my business partner. In all these roles, his behaviour was impeccable which, I may say, is not a tribute that I can pay to most of the people who played in those roles during the 40 years that I visited Australia. Snowy is the most congenial of men; he has a tolerance of the failings of others that would make a saint feel proud.

That I am an erratic driver Snowy has remarked on from time to time, and I suppose that I would be completely incompetent in the bush alone. However, with great patience, Snowy taught me the rudiments of driving, living and behaving in the bush. On our first journey together in the outback, I did not really understand how life operated in the bush. It was almost midday when I got my vehicle bogged down in a riverbed—I had not listened to Snowy's advice on how to cross seemingly dry rivers. Snowy and Charlie Diesel set to work with a winch and, using the second vehicle, pulled the bogged truck out as I set to work on lunch. Oliver Ford, our close friend and travelling companion, who even in those days suffered from weak lungs, sat panting in the heat under a tree with Romilly. In time, I finished my lunch and Snowy his task. 'Well,' say I, 'let's get on,' and off we drove. Snowy never murmured a complaint at missing his lunch. It was only that night as we camped that he explained that it might be wise if we shared some of the tasks and also shared our lunches.

✺

After Snowy settled in Broome, he became the Shire foreman and assistant to the Reid family at the time that Dr Reid was the Shire president. The Reids always had some cunning plan or other, which was likely to benefit only their family, and Snowy was often carried along in their general enthusiasm. It was all understandable, because the Reids moved as a clan and wherever they were, that is where the fun was to be had. Snowy joined with Rod Reid and Peter Kinney in a venture to establish the pearl farm at Deep Water Point, a place a great distance from human habitation on King Sound. The peninsula of Deep Water Point is a couple of kilometres long, rocky with rough bush and pandanus palms growing on it. Together they carved that farm out of the bush, breaking a track through the tangle of untouched vegetation, laying a pipeline for water over miles of uneven country and building accommodation for their work force at the pearl farm. Peter and Beverley Kinney were local Broome people who ran a very successful clothing store; Beverley was of Aboriginal–Chinese descent. When I arrived in town, the Reid's main plan seemed to be that they would sell me as many of their holdings as possible at prices advantageous to them and then decamp to Cairns. This plan, as it happens, suited me rather well. Snowy, however, became a victim of their desire to sell. Snowy's friend Peter Kinney had died of cancer and Beverley, his widow, had taken over his shares in the pearl farm at Deep Water Point. Rod Reid wanted to get out and, as Beverley was clearly not going to buy Rod Reid's shares, that left Snowy as the only avenue for Rod Reid's exit.

It was a hot Saturday and I had lunched well under the branches of the vast mango tree that provided the roof to my open-air dining room. Snowy wandered into my garden and joined me. I offered him a drink and put a freshly opened bottle of wine between us. We talked of many things and slowly the afternoon passed into early evening, empty wine bottles accumulating on my dining table. Then Snowy told me of his problem—he had at lunchtime given Rod Reid a cheque in payment for his shares in the pearl farm. As a result, on that Saturday evening, Snowy was the proud owner of two-thirds of a pearl farm, knowing that on Monday when his cheque was presented, he did not have the funds to cover it. Would I like to buy Rod Reid's shares from him? Filled with enthusiasm and wine, I answered, 'Yes.' The money only needed to be in Snowy's account by Monday morning. On Sunday, I rang my lawyer, John Adams, who said that I was mad. Later on, John bought a minority share and did very well out of it, but no matter. At the time, both Snowy and myself were considered a pair of mugs, lumbered with a pearl farm that was going nowhere—even Beverley Kinney must have had her doubts about the venture because a short time after my initial purchase, she sold me most of her shares.

There was a problem with the pearl farm, but it was one that was easily overcome. Nick Paspaley, whom I knew slightly as I had bought pearls from him in Darwin, was coming as my guest to lunch during the America's Cup races in Perth. Few people know more about running pearl farms than Nick Paspaley, and few people in the pearling industry measure up to the level of efficiency and integrity he has achieved. He was the obvious choice to run our farm and happily he agreed to take on its management. For a number of years, things went smoothly and profits rolled in. Self-confidence is, however, a dangerous friend. The farm ran so easily, its results we regarded as a triumph: 'Surely it is easy to run a pearl farm,' we told each other. Then one year the crop failed and, as is the way with pearl farms as the crops tend to go in pairs, the crop failed the next year as well. These twin failures hit me at financially the worst possible moment. John Adams, who had for years looked after my affairs, left for the Supreme Court to take up the post of Master, and Russell Chapman, my accountant, took over John's role. There were many differences between Russell Chapman and John Adams, and this is neither the place nor the time to rehearse them. Suffice to say that while John ran the pearl farm, he never had any desire to be a pearl farmer—he was wedded to the law. Russell Chapman, an accountant, was different; his desire to be a pearl farmer became increasingly obvious. Under his management, the pearl farm did not run easily. Snowy County was unjustly removed from its day-to-day management. I discovered that, although I had 58 per cent of the pearl farm's shares, I had no more say in how it was run than the other partners who mostly had 3 per cent each. At John Adams's suggestion, I had sold shareholdings to these people for an injection of cash into the company of $25 000 each. In most years, the dividend that they each received exceeded $100 000 and the capital value of their holdings multiplied many, many times. Most of them contributed nothing of any consequence to the running of the farm; indeed, it is fair to say that the majority of them regarded it as a fine place to take a holiday. In the final event, after a deal of coming and going, in 1996 I sold them my shares. The behaviour of those friends and acquaintances in the last years of our partnership in the pearl farm was, if they ever take time and think about it, of a standard that was less than acceptable.

Snowy County, however, behaved with honour, dignity and generosity, and showed not the slightest trace of greed throughout that whole unpleasant period. The pearl farm made a difference to Snowy; it changed him from a man of simple means to an extremely rich man and he deserved every penny of that profit. Snowy moved from a shed to a fine house on Broome's Pearlers Hill—then nearby to the 'old Male house', named for its previous owners, which he has restored so that it has become the finest residence in Broome. Snowy, however, is not changed by wealth—he is still the same kind, companionable person that I knew when we first travelled in the outback. Always a traveller, Snowy visited London and stayed for a time with his friend in a guesthouse that my family owned, not a hundred yards from the Houses of Parliament. One night, returning home by taxi, they were opening the front door when the taxi driver, believing them to be a pair of burglars, called out, 'What are you two up to? Blokes like you don't live in a house like that.' If they are Snowy County, they do.

⸱⸱

Many of my guests who came to stay while I lived in Broome found difficulty in coming to terms with the difference between the safety of the township and the dangers of the bush, as do most people who visit the North-West. Albert Roux, the proprietor of Le Gavroche Restaurant in London's West End, master chef and patron of a whole generation of young chefs, who have run restaurants in places as disparate as Yorkshire in England and Sydney in Australia, was among the most delightful of my visitors. Despite the fact that he was on holiday, he was generous with his time, cooking bouillabaisse for 25 of my guests, the soup made from the fish that he had caught that day. Apart from being a great chef, Albert is an accomplished fisherman. I sent Albert and his wife Monique on a trip into the outback with David and Lita Young. At the time, Lord Young was Secretary of State for Trade and Industry in the British Government. The culture shock of the bush threw them a little at first, but by the second night Albert was cooking crocodile steaks over a camp fire. They told me that these were delicious, and I can well believe that to have been the case, although the quality of that particular meal would have owed more to the expertise of the chef rather than the natural taste of the meal's ingredients.

Lord Young and his wife came back from their jaunt in the outback filled with confidence, not realising, I suppose, that their trouble-free travel in the bush was due to the skill of those who looked after them.

A few days later, they set off alone in a four-wheel drive along Cable Beach, a safe enough place in all conscience. We expected them home at about six-thirty and when they had not returned by eight-thirty, I was beginning to get worried. A search party was in the process of being organised when the couple appeared, covered in mud from head to foot. It seems that, encouraged by the beauty of the scenery, they had driven to the far end of the beach where their four-wheel drive became bogged down. Inexperienced in handling such vehicles, their efforts to drive out of trouble only made matters worse. Soon the tide was on the turn, a tide that comes in at the speed of a galloping horse. The afternoon was hot and their efforts to dig the vehicle out became desperate. Luckily, a local, driving from the settlement at Coconut Wells to Broome by way of the beach, helped them out. That this man passed by was a chance in a thousand; had he come an hour earlier they would not have been there, and an hour later he could not have passed for the tide. The Youngs would have been faced with walking home through some pretty rough bush, while my four-wheel drive rotted under five metres of salt water. Despite this unfortunate incident, the Youngs seemed to enjoy their stay in Broome. Later, back in Britain, for some time they spoke a lot about their adventures.

My eldest daughter Jane, staying in Broome, set out with a friend to go north to the mission at Beagle Bay. The road up on the Friday was busy. Many people in Broome go camping at weekends and the coastline from Broome up Cape Leveque has dozens of popular places to stop. My daughter and her friend decided to return to Broome on the Sunday afternoon. Soon after they set out on their return trip, their four-wheel drive broke down. They had committed the cardinal sin of travel in the outback: they had not told anyone when they were leaving, where they were going or when they might be expected back. The road had been busy on the drive up Cape Leveque, so logic dictated that those cars that had driven up the Cape must return down its only road. However, they had not realised that the next day, the Monday, was a bank holiday, and so most cars would be returning on that day. It was then that they made another mistake: they left their vehicle and started walking, expecting to get a lift, but no cars came.

The weather was stiflingly hot, so they drank some of the Coca-Cola that they had brought, instead of water, and ate some of the salted peanuts, which was the only form of food they had with them. They got hotter and thirstier and still no cars came. In the north, you must never leave your vehicle, however unpromising your circumstances; it is the only place that anyone will ever find you. Those used to the bush will take oil from the vehicle's sump and paint a cross or a circle on the vehicle's roof; lay tarpaulins around the vehicle; light a fire with the spare tyre to make smoke—anything to attract attention from aircraft that may be looking for you. Conserve your energy, conserve your water supply, sit and wait—those are the rules. Luckily for my daughter, she and her friend were in the end picked up by a passing car. They were, however, seriously dehydrated by this time and had the car not passed, they might well have perished.

Another couple who almost came to grief in the bush were my guests, Nicholas Barker, a painter, poet and excellent furniture designer who trades under the name of Alvis Vega, and his wife, Liza Bruce, a highly talented fashion designer who is also extremely beautiful. Neither Liza nor her husband is stupid: they have both spent time in New Mexico and are familiar with empty spaces. Nicholas was born and brought up in East Africa during the Mau Mau emergency and is familiar with the bush. They allowed themselves to be persuaded by my gardener, Ronnie, to set out on a drive to Coconut Wells. Even in those days, the road or track to Coconut Wells was frequently used and was by local standards of rather good quality. Perhaps that was the reason why their four-wheel drive got out of control—Nicholas had found the driving easy, perhaps too easy. Suddenly, the vehicle began to slide on the sand and turned upside down. Nicholas and Liza were relatively unhurt; Ronnie has had trouble with his back ever since. A moment of overconfidence could have ended three lives. Such an accident could have happened, of course, on a suburban road near Sydney or Melbourne, but there the facilities are easily available to bring help. In the bush, however, it's just a matter of waiting until someone comes along.

When I bought my home in Broome, I already had a garden for it in my mind. I dreamt of that garden, working in Perth; I thought about that garden, travelling by aeroplane, busily setting out the plans of it in my mind. Cardboard match covers were used as sketch pads, paper napkins became plans and plant lists. The idea of a tropical garden had me in its grasp. Turning through notebooks and old files long put aside as I researched this book, I came across a description of my gardener's dream, written in the year that I bought my house on the corner of Broome's Louis and Herbert Streets. I include it here not to show what I achieved, rather to give the spirit of what I intended to achieve. It went thus:

Take red sand, hot winters, plants . . . Add water and mix—in weeks you have a subtropical garden. This region of Western Australia (the North-West) gives reality to the phrase 'instant gardening'. Clumps of strelitzia and canna lilies spread, blooming within days of planting; palm trees grow well over two metres in one year, mostly between December and February. Speed is everything in the tropical heat. The philosophy of gardening by extraction really counts.

The garden clippers give way to the crosscut saw. Paths are overrun, clumps merge, the violent colours of heat spring up where they are least expected. Carefully considered colour schemes can be destroyed in a week, while masterpieces, those brilliant accidents of gardening which we see creeping up on us in Britain, appear and vanish in a month. Bougainvillea, a delicate plant in the British hothouse or lightening the landscape of the French Riviera, grows thorns of savage temper and dreadful accuracy when fighting a bi-monthly pruning, curling great ropes grow into nearby trees. Their gentle colour has a violence which is almost invisible against the midday sun but reappears in the early evening in bright colours that match the sunset.

After the excitement of frangipanis, baobabs and African tulip trees, a monotony sets in. Gardening is done, the thing is made, flowers are perpetually in bloom—always this great mass of green.

For a gardener from Hampshire—who takes for granted four to five hundred varieties of old-fashioned shrub roses, bulbs that flower in ranks from March until December, each different, and a hundred and thirty varieties of snowdrops together— what is there to do in this hot climate that happily kills most of the plants we know?

At Broome, I would start with ferns planted in clumps— different shades of green, different textures of green, different shapes of green. There are tree ferns, staghorn fern and elkhorn fern, with their stately fronds; calf's foot ferns, bird's nest ferns, club ferns, moss ferns, *Paraceterach muelleri*, *Lindsaea microphylla*, *Asplenium simplicifrons*. I planted upward of thirty different varieties of ferns in the ground. All them have to be planted in deep shade under the mango trees, which are part of a subtropical orchard: pawpaws, bush lemons, rambutans, custard apples, guavas, passion-fruit, lychees, peach mangoes and pomelos.

There's a clump of bananas, colossal growers which drink gallons of water, and a palm garden hedged with Darwin palms, coconut palms (plant these away from people, the falling coconut can be deadly), the miniature date palm, travellers' palm, *Livistona muelleri*, *Liculnalea orandis*. The water garden is to have the blue, night-scented waterlily, the water hibiscus with a red flower the size of a cherub's trumpet, water lettuce, *Pistia stratiotes*, *Lotus nelumbium*, and several varieties of flax. Water irises could also be tried but they probably would not survive the climate in Broome. The water hyacinth *Eichornia crassipes* would grow wonderfully, but there would be little thanks to the gardener who introduced it to this part of the North-West, for further up the coast, inland from Wyndham, the waterways are clogged with it.

Around the house there are to be gardenias five feet high and covered with blossom; lilies, the Singapore lily, *Agapanthus africanus*; and ginger plants, Kahili ginger, torch ginger, shell ginger. Around the water, swathes of bamboo, and frangipani trees, the evergreen native, the deciduous pink and the yellow tamarind tree, Cape lilacs, hedges of oleander, hibiscus and bougainvillea. Smaller in scale are the plastic plants, two or three varieties, all brightly coloured and just like their name.

Candlestick plants (*Plectranthus certendahlii*), so often seen in florists' jungles, look quite different massed in a garden without their plastic pots and instructions on how to water tied to the stalks. *Monstera* curls and grows into the trees, useful in the shade. A thicket of heliconias, mixed in colour—if only it were possible to buy the jade vine in Australia, a plant that really fulfils a tropical expectation, pendulums of turquoise parrots' beaks. Perhaps in time a plant will be imported; it would certainly grow at Broome.

In the summer, winds come with the rain, six feet of it in over two months, so the garden needs protection and, as the house is set back fifty feet from the road on two sides, the verges have to be planted with a thick hedge of Australian natives, with wild-sounding names like waratah, wattle and bush oleander. These are all extremely hardy and will withstand wind and drought. Among them is the boab, the symbol of the region, a great, fat, bottle-shaped tree with nuts much prized by the Aboriginals for carving, and equally prized when carved and sold to the tourists. For water, there is reticulation for ten months of the year from a bore in the garden for two months' rain. All these plants must have water, lots of water.

The road itself has to be lined with frangipanis, planted in 40-gallon oil drums with the bottoms knocked out. These drums speed growth and protect the plants from the multitude of dogs and careless drivers (Broome is infested with both). Then there is a rock garden. The rocks barely need plants: the shapes would put new life into many a sculptor, coloured in red—and such a red. What to plant in this rock garden? Cacti, orchids, *Paphiopedilum* from Thailand, a group of *Angraecoids*.

Of course, there are the orchids—in the ground (*Lycaste stanhopea*); on trees (*Cattleya oncidia*); dendrobiums, particularly the Australian native, *Dendrobium speciosum*, with its long tongue of white bloom; and in tree stumps, *Cymbidium suave* and the black orchid, *Cymbidium canaliculatum*. These last are two of the three cymbidiums that will flower in the heat. The third is *Cymbidium madidum* but I have not been able to find it yet. Everywhere there are orchids . . . and then there are the bromeliads. Did I suggest that a subtropical garden could become boring? Surely I never wrote such a thing.

I fought the land around my house to build the garden of my dreams. I acquired fine orchids, *Cattleya* and *Dendrobium* in France, and native species in Sydney and Perth. Transported to Broome, I planted them in pots, fixed them to trees, even planted them in the earth. Water was the problem, not the quantity of the water, but the quality of that water. Still I persevered. I improved the water, but Broome is a seaside town and, in those days, without a great deal of foliage. I believe many of my orchids were killed by salt and wind. There was a gardener of sorts, hired to look after them while I was away. He had no feeling for orchids, nor much else; he knew the jargon but there was not a trace of green in his fingers. I did better with the ferns; they grew well for a while. The palm trees were a triumph—they grew so quickly that it was not long before I had to remove them, for they were too large or the white ants had got them. In fact, it began to occur to me, after about seven years of failed gardening, that I was growing the vegetable equivalent of caviar and feeding this delectable and expensive stuff to the local insect population.

I gave up on my efforts to create a tropical garden and settled for a yard with a few fine trees. The idea was still with me, however, and I did grow orchids with considerable success at my zoo, where I had skilled staff who were regular in attendance when I was not there. My dream of Broome as a garden became a reality, despite the failure of my dream garden in Broome, the town is now conscious of trees. At first, I planted boab trees in Broome, brought from the bush. There was considerable disturbance about this idea; the people of Derby were certainly upset. Derby was the boab town, Broome had the beach, so why did they need to steal the boabs? Well, it wasn't Broome that stole the boabs, it was me; and in any case, I did not steal them, I merely moved them a few miles and very fine they look in Broome, now that they have grown into stout trees with plenty of foliage. The problem with planting trees in the township of Broome, during the early 1980s, was that an element of the population used to tear the branches off them. Any horticulturist knows that it is better to transport a tree when it's young. Young trees improve at a far greater rate when they are moved than mature trees which lie dormant for some years after transplanting. It is, however, a lot harder to pull the branches off a mature tree than a young one and damn nigh impossible to pull branches off a full-grown boab tree.

వ

In those days in Broome, there was a small group of people who opposed almost everything that I did on principle. I was the successor to the Reid family, Public Enemy Number One. The Reids were very commercially minded and often sought to change the status quo to their own advantage. And, as far as these people were concerned, I was the same. It is true that I was in favour of development but not the sort of development that the Reids had in mind. I was cast in a role similar to a famous gunfighter who had come to town. The local would-be politicians of the Left needed to try their hand at destroying me to enhance their own reputations—they needed to outdraw me in order to win fame. The irony of all this was it never occurred to me, nor, I suspect, to them, that such a game was being played. In the end, it was the pilots' strike and the overwhelming recession of 1989 that put an end to my activities, not the machinations of the Labor Left. As happens from time to time, the airline pilots in Australia were looking for better pay and conditions. Normally, this matter would have been resolved without too much trouble. However, Bob Hawke, the prime minister at the time, had other ideas. This was a splendid opportunity for him to discipline a white-collar union, and he grabbed it with both hands. The pilots struck and the Federal Government stayed firm on its original position. Emergency aid was made available by the Government to Perth and other State capitals. No provision, however, was made to help those who lived and worked in the North-West.

As for the political situation in Broome, much as the place may seem to change, in reality the situation stays the same. The small group that opposed me still clamours after power, a prospect that they do not fully understand, for power is given by the people and, when they have a mind, taken away by the people. An almost invariable rule in politics is: if you desperately want something, you seldom get it. The people mistrust those who try too hard and so, in the end, it is the people who withhold office, the prize for which ambitious politicians strive. So it is in all democracies, so it is in Broome.

Accustomed to living in a town where anyone who has a few bucks sets about multiplying them, usually at the expense of the community, these people were naturally suspicious of my activities. Try as I might to explain that my motives were to make the place that I had chosen to live in better, rather than worse, it made no difference. Understandably so, because my motives were not only beyond their experience but also beyond possibility of belief. As an Irish diplomat once said to me as we were drinking in the bar of London's Garrick Club: 'Innocence is a difficult position for a person to improve on'. How true these words are—trying to convince this small but eloquent group that I meant their town well was a fruitless task.

An outlet for this group's opinions was *The Broome News*. The Reids had run one of the previous editors out of town. However, as I could see no reason to be hostile to this journal, I provided it with subsidised accommodation. Criticism I can take. I believe in a free press and a diversity of opinion: a catch-phrase that has always appealed to me is, 'To irritate is to stimulate'. However, *The Broome News* printed hair-raising stories of my activities, to the point that I began to believe that I was a masochist, helping these people to attack me. In the end, I resolved to fight them—I had tried helping them. I had supported their Botanical Garden Society, always a critic of mine, and I had housed their journal, *The Broome News*. Finally, I had to recourse to law in order to put a stop to some of the wilder rumours that circulated about my activities. How much more productive it would all have been if we could have worked together. As I look back on these arguments, I see quite clearly that these people were well-intentioned: they were not competitors, trying to sabotage my projects, merely people who judged what I would do in the light of what others had done before me. There is, I suppose, a similar scenario in many Australian boom towns—a dominant force trying to bring about development and a group of concerned citizens trying to maintain the status quo.

In the end, those in favour of development tend to win, for the simple reason that development brings jobs and jobs bring prosperity. Both jobs and prosperity are believed by most people to be beneficial. This is true, but only up to a point, for towns, both large and small, are about people, and when the town changes so the people change. While the town may be the better for change, there is now doubt in my mind as to whether the people are really better off, other than in a material sense. With growth and size comes crime; with wealth comes poverty; with business activity, sealed roads and neat municipal gardens and parks. Hand-in-hand with these obvious advantages come traffic and air pollution. The streets become dangerous places, homes have to be secured. People lose the privilege of knowing all the people that they meet in the streets; they live among strangers. Had the people who opposed my ideas for the development of Broome thought all these things through, or were they just playing the game of cutting down the tall poppy? Certainly I was motivated by the certainty that Broome would never remain the same paradise I found on my first visit. The growth of tourism in Australia and the newly created access to the town limited as it was, both by road and air, would see to that.

After years of combat, my opponents finally won. In the event, their victory was of great benefit to me. By their victory, I refer to their success at frustrating my efforts to build an airport, which, had I succeeded in constructing, would have opened in the face of the largest financial downturn in Australia's history. While both my opponents and I can take some comfort at the outcome of our battles, the failure to provide the Kimberley with an international airport will in time be seen as an act of treachery perpetrated by a timid Government and the project's opponents.

8

I had not been long in Broome before I discovered that Australia was giving away land—well, almost giving it away. All you had to do to receive a ten-acre block, slightly over four hectares, was to tell the Government what you wanted to do with it. If no-one else wanted the land for a similar purpose, then you paid $10 000 and the land was yours. Well, almost yours, for you were contracted to develop the land. Development in the early 1980s in Broome meant that the land had to be improved; improvements constituted erecting a fence around it and building a shed on it. Only then would the Government give you the freehold and you could do what you liked with the land, within the local planning laws. Laws which seemed to me, at least, to be extremely flexible and largely decided upon in the Pearlers Rest Bar at the Roebuck Hotel.

The snag was that this land was at Cable Beach, six kilometres from town, adjacent to the magnificent beach but, at that time, a long way from the population of Broome. Many years later, however, this initial disadvantage became the land's greatest advantage. I decided that I had better have some of this land; I qualified for a grant because I was a resident of Broome. I have always enjoyed keeping animals, so I would start a zoo. As it turned out, getting the land was the easy part. The fight with the bureaucracy of Western Australia to obtain a licence for a zoo was far more difficult. It was the first of many fights that were to follow in the next twelve years.

My first experience with the wildlife authorities of Western Australia did not fill me with a deal of optimism in the matter of getting the licences that I needed to operate a zoo. The first Christmas that Romilly and I spent in Broome was a strange affair for us. Christmas in our minds was a time of chilly weather and family gatherings. Here, we were on our own, the weather was stinking hot and there was not a member of our family within 10 000 miles. Christmas lunch was spent at the Mangrove Hotel, in those days a low building with a central block of concrete walls with iron girders supporting its corrugated iron roof. Parts of this hotel had been purchased when the British closed down the rocket ranges at Woomera, then transported to Broome and added to the hotel's two wings; bedroom wings with about five rooms in each of them, wings that contained bedrooms of the lowest order. It was in the Mangrove Hotel that the Reid family celebrated their Christmas and we were their guests. We all assembled at about twelve o'clock, drank a lot of beer and then sat down to lunch along with about 50 other locals, who had paid to join the banquet. If Romilly and I had any nostalgia for a traditional British Christmas, that nostalgia was about to be sated in full. First, a course of melon filled with a sweet wine. Then turkey, fully trimmed, followed by ham with parsley sauce. Then plum pudding with a white sauce, something between custard and brandy butter. Mince pies and cheese followed. None of it had been cooked in quite the right way; it all lay heavy on our stomachs. The Reids, however, were generous hosts and whenever they gathered there was plenty of fun, so, in spite of the uninspiring food, we enjoyed ourselves.

At home on the corner of Louis and Herbert Streets, we stretched out in the sun beside our pool. The heat of the afternoon was incredible and soon I was dozing fitfully. 'Are you Mr McAlpine?' a voice enquired. I awoke with a jolt and there standing beside me was a fine-looking young man in a white shirt, shorts and long white cotton socks. 'I am from the wildlife department,' he announced with some glee. 'You have broken the law.' The delight in his voice was barely suppressed. I was a little confused, and asked him what on earth I had done that broke the law. 'It's the parrots,' he replied. True; I had, while in Sydney some months before, entered a pet shop and bought a pair of sulphur-crested cockatoos. I had arranged for these birds to be sent to Broome just after my arrival a week or so before Christmas. This operation had all gone according to plan. The only fault in the whole thing was that nobody had told me that I needed a licence to keep a parrot—or any other bird, for that matter. 'What are you going to do about these parrots?' the young man asked. 'Get a licence, I suppose,' I replied. That was not good enough for this enthusiastic civil servant who had taken the trouble to dress up on Christmas Day for, it seems, the sole purpose of dressing me down. I was treated to a half-hour lecture on wildlife licensing—a strange performance, I believe, because the birds that I owned were only a pair of pet shop parrots who sat in a birdcage exchanging bird calls with a couple of hundred of their cousins infesting the trees of my garden and eating the mangoes that were just on the point of being picked.

Exhausted by the heat and enthusiasm for his authority, the young man eventually left, muttering threats of dire punishment about to descend on my head after the Christmas holiday, when his colleagues in Perth returned to work. He was clearly destined for high office in his department, having caught an offender parrot-handed, so to speak. For my part, I rang my friend John Roberts. 'What's all this about parrot licences?' 'I haven't the first idea,' he replied. 'I'll ring Ray and ask.' The Ray in question was Ray O'Connor, premier of Western Australia. In those days, John was as ignorant of the protocol for owning birds as I was. Today, he owns one of the finest collections of birds in Western Australia, with many breeding successes to his credit.

Later, I discovered that in Western Australia there is virtually no activity the mind can conceive of that does not need a licence. As well as needing a licence to keep parrots, a licence is needed to export them from one state to another. The exporting of birds from Australia is, however, strictly forbidden, indeed, smuggling specimens of Australian flora or fauna can bring a fine of up to $200 000. Once I observed the law in action at Perth airport. A seemingly innocent man with a scruffy leather case was queuing to check in his luggage for a flight with Qantas when a hand fell on his shoulder and a voice ordered him to open the case. The tone of voice left no doubt that the man was a criminal, and so he was, for inside his case were at least 50 parrots, each with its head and tail sticking out of a cardboard tube. 'How was he spotted?' I asked the Qantas clerk. 'Somebody squawked,' he replied drily.

∽

The matter of the parrots passed over and life went on in Broome at a rather different pace from that set by the wildlife official. In the evenings, Romilly and I sat on Gantheaume Point smoking and watching the sunset. The sun, a great red ball, dropped below the horizon and, as the dusk began to gather, it seemed that all was over. Then, quite suddenly, the world seemed to catch fire. The sky turned red and the rocks at Gantheaume Point added that colour to their own bright red. Even the sea began to glow and as the redness left, the sky turned first yellow and then the deepest black. On a particular night of a particular month, when the tide was just right, we watched the stairway to the moon on Roebuck Bay. As the moon came over the horizon, every ripple on the mudflats across the bay became a step in that stairway. Nature in the North-West is bold and strong, sunlight sucking the colour out of everything, and darkness, or at least dusk, making the colours of the bush grow again. Often we would sit on the veranda of our home and watch the electric storms in the distance light up the night sky. These storms made the world's greatest firework display. Often people spoke of rain. 'It'll be an early wet this year', but in the early 1980s, the rain never came, unlike a few years ago when Broome had over 50 inches in twenty-four hours. 'The frogs are croaking, the wet will be early this year', and still the wet never really came.

Tales of Roebuck Plain flooded, the township of Broome water-logged, and still no wet. One year, the weather just became hotter and hotter. It was as if we were all in a pressure cooker. Then the wind got up and soon the buildings were shaking, palm trees tried to imitate croquet hoops and the heat just seemed to increase. Then rain, a burst of rain, that rattled the tin roof of the house and flooded the garden. Then it was all over. We had been on the edge of a cyclone. The pindan, the semi-arid country of the region, sucked up the moisture like the most effective blotting paper. The township of

Broome was green again, the red dust washing from the leaves of its trees and plants, the air cool, fresh and wonderful.

⋄

In time, I was given my grant of land, ten hectares, and I was in the zoo business. Why would anyone want to open a zoo in Broome, all the officials asked? There are so few people in Broome to visit a zoo, surely anyone who opens one must be mad, these same officials thought. My line of approach was rather different: Broome has exactly the right climate for most of the birds that I wished to keep. To mollify the officials of Western Australia's wildlife department, I hired a curator from Perth Zoo to run the establishment in Broome. A pleasant-enough person, this man was an expert on snakes. At first, the birds that I wished to keep were the common local parrots, the mammals, banteng oxen, donkeys, water buffalo, camels and dingoes. Much later, I discovered that the Broome climate is perfect for the endangered antelopes of North Africa, such as the addax and the scimitar-horned oryx, which bred in Broome like the proverbial rabbit.

As was, of course, inevitable, after a while we found that the first ten hectares were too small for my purpose and more space was needed. As the zoo grew, so my plans for what the zoo might become grew. And those plans grew at a speed that was disproportionate to the reality of the situation. Another ten hectares or so were acquired from the Government. Still the zoo grew and still the plans multiplied. New and more exotic animals, new cages, vast aviaries and large paddocks. Lakes and ponds, forests and deserts—these ideas streamed from my imagination. I needed another 30 hectares; the animals needed space and I needed more animals; a railway, I imagined, would run around this zoo. The authorities in Perth allocated me the land, for by now my zoo was a great success. Often reported in the media and well-thought of by zoo authorities across Australia, the zoo was also a considerable tourist attraction and source of employment in Broome.

The land became mine, but at a price. The token payment that I had made when I acquired the initial lot changed into a realistic payment for my second lot, and for my third and largest lot, the price had increased beyond all expectation. By that time, the land at Cable

87

Beach was no longer considered a rural subdivision distant from Broome, rather prime land for tourist development. The price of my new lot was over half a million dollars, a price rise influenced by the area's new affluence—an affluence caused largely by myself, for I had taken the Reid family's old caravan park, complete with its acres of septic tank, and turned it into an extremely attractive international hotel. While I was the victim of my own success, the scale of my zoo was the result of nothing more or less than my own folly. However, the narrative moves forward with too great a pace.

The first ten hectares of land that the zoo occupied was just behind the sand dunes that edged Cable Beach. Opposite my zoo was the Reid's caravan park, which could best be described as squalid. My zoo, grandly named the Pearl Coast Zoological Gardens, was, however, far from grand, just two parallel lines of cages and half a dozen paddocks. At least I had started, and possessed a licence to own and display animals, the only such licence for over 1200 kilometres in any direction. To extend the collection was, indeed, another matter. It was only after a lot of argument that I acquired permission to own a dozen or so black buck and a pair of dingoes. Black buck come from India but are to be found in a feral state in the Hamersley Range, dingoes almost everywhere in Australia. The precautions that had to be taken under the terms of my licence to make sure that the dingoes did not escape made the average high-security jail seem like an open prison. Sure enough, however, the dingoes did escape. When questioned, no-one knew how they had got out. It seemed to me, however, that their escape had the assistance of humans. In the event, they ate a couple of my black buck and were recaptured while still at lunch. Their capture was no hard task, as my zoo manager was in the habit of taking them for a walk on a lead every afternoon. These dingoes were as tame as any pair of dogs walking with their owner in a city park.

At about this time, there was a lot of talk about Lindy Chamberlain, who was accused of murdering her baby. She had been convicted and sentenced to jail. Her defence had largely centred around the plea that a large male dingo had committed the crime. The jury did not believe her story, as a blood-stained coat, a vital piece of evidence, was missing. Dingoes do not attack children and certainly would not kill a child, experts testified at her trial. The incident took place at Uluru (Ayers Rock) where the dingoes are quite used to human contact. Many of them are fed by tourists and have lost any fear of mankind. Some years later, the bloodstained coat was found at the foot of the Rock, the sentence overturned, and Lindy Chamberlain set free. I was relieved when she was released from jail, for I had always been convinced that the dingo was the guilty party. At the time, many people thought the whole incident quite bizarre and the controversy about the role of the dingo still causes considerable argument whenever the subject comes up. Many strange things, however, have happened at Uluru.

I can only record that my dingoes, while tame as house-trained poodles, became manic when they saw small children. Animals that would take sausages from my hand and then lick that hand afterwards, would, when young children approached their enclosure, snap and bark, tearing at the earth and the wire fence with their teeth and claws. At first, I did not believe the father who told me that his baby girl had been frightened out of her wits by animals that were tame when he approached them, but became intensely hostile as soon as she joined him. The reaction of my dingoes came as a surprise to me but it seemed to support Lindy Chamberlain's story. I thought no more about this until I read an article in an English newspaper about some British tourists who had been attacked by a dingo only a few metres from a camp site on Fraser Island, off the coast of Queensland. It seems that the dingo attacked without provocation. Dingo attacks on Fraser Island are no longer rare and tourists are routinely advised to be careful around them. If such dingo attacks could have been presented as evidence for the defence in the Lindy Chamberlain case, I doubt very much that the jury would have returned a guilty verdict.

There can be little doubt that the most dangerous of all wild animals are those that have lost the fear of mankind. From time to time in northern Australia, there are crocodile attacks. In 1971, when crocodile numbers were down to about 5000, hunting them was banned. While a protected species, the great crocodiles of the North had little to fear from humans, each year becoming an ever-increasing threat as tourism brought more and more people to the immensely beautiful lagoons, inlets and coastal rivers that are their territory. By 1999, the crocodile population had reached over 60 000, and the Northern Territory decided to lift the hunting ban and allow the first legal crocodile hunt to take place.

∾

Zoo-keeping is a learning curve; there is no expert who knows it all. When in the world of zoos and zoo-keeping, always expect the unexpected. As I set out my zoo, I made the enclosures, both for mammals and birds, far larger than was necessary. People who come to zoos do not understand that animals and birds are largely territorial, seldom moving outside of their own territory. I made the cages and enclosures in my zoo larger than they needed to be, not for the sake of the animals but to make people feel better about visiting the zoo. The downside of this was even when the number and variety of my mammals increased, I used to get complaints from people who had walked around the whole place without seeing any animals. The same, of course, was true for the birds, whose cages were filled with natural foliage. To see animals and birds in these conditions, you need to stand and watch until your eyes get used to the natural camouflage of the enclosure's inhabitants.

At first, I worked in my zoo, setting up cages and creating landscapes with rocks and trees. I enjoyed the physical work and was delighted with my small collection of animals and birds. Each evening at sunset, I would walk around the enclosures looking at all the creatures, many of whom were hand-tame. I fed many of the birds with the bird food from a bag that I carried. Soon, however, the collecting instinct took over. More bird cages were built to house a growing collection of birds. The feral donkeys went and scimitar-horned oryx came. These wonderful animals with, as their name suggests, horns shaped like Arabian sabres, were bred at Marwell Park Zoo in England. John Knowles, the proprietor of that zoo, then became my consultant, guide and conscience in all matters zoological. He visited Broome on several occasions and, between visits, we were in constant contact by telephone.

By this time, my first manager had left, and Ross Gardiner, formerly employed by the Western Australian Government department responsible for wildlife, had replaced him. Ross was not an expert on snakes or, for that matter, much else, but he had a wide knowledge of wildlife and considerable natural charm. In time, we did have snakes in the zoo. Not just the occasional trespasser, such as the python which slipped through the wire of a birdcage, ate the occupant, then found its bloated body prevented it getting out and so became a prisoner. Such snakes were either released in the wild about sixteen kilometres away from potential dinners in my zoo or consigned to the zoo's collection. Only once in all my years in the outback did I come across a snake in the wild. On that occasion, both the snake, a two-metre king brown, and myself were taking a walk. The king brown was wriggling its way up a path and I was meandering down the same path. Neither of us was taking much notice of the world in general, so we were really only a few metres apart when we noticed each other. I might have been expected to stand alert, my stick raised ready to strike, the snake to coil itself, equally ready for action—in the event, both the snake and myself turned tail and ran like hell. A snake that found its way among the audience at Broome's Sun Pictures was less lucky than the snake of my passing acquaintance, for this unfortunate python was delivered to my zoo with both its head and its tail sticking out of the same end of a short length of scaffold tubing. The rest of its body, some two metres of it, formed the loop that stuck out of the tube's other end.

It's easy enough to catch a python. They bite but their bite does not kill. In the roof of my house at the corner of Louis and Herbert Streets on Broome's Pearlers Hill, I had a python. This snake served a useful purpose, keeping the building clear of rats. Once a week or so, the python would catch a rat, usually in the early hours of the morning, and a struggle would ensue. The snake would wrap itself around the hapless rat and would crash and bang against the corrugated iron roof as it twisted and turned in its attempts to consume the rat. After a quarter of an hour's racket, all would go quiet. Visitors were frightened out of their wits by the disturbance above their beds. It is hard to tell really which was the more shocking—falling coconuts that hit the tin roof with an explosion, or the rattle of the feeding snake.

The consequences of playing around with poisonous snakes can, however, be severe. If you are foolish enough to interfere with them, they are certainly capable of doing you a deal of harm. Swan lager, the locals believe, is a great help when bitten by a king brown. You must, of course, have two cans of it: you drink the first and if you have time to drink the second, you will probably survive. A welder working at the zoo was engaged in cutting up piping into equal lengths when he saw a king brown about three metres long scuttle into a pipe, having been disturbed. Hoping to catch the snake for my collection, he tied a sack over the end nearest the snake's head, then he warmed up the end of the pipe at its tail with a blowtorch. The snake moved into the sack, so the welder tied the sack's neck with wire and picked it up. Unfortunately, there was a hole in the bottom of the sack and a very angry snake lost no time in passing through this hole and biting the man on the ankle on the way out. In moments, his leg turned black. Luckily there was help nearby and the hospital only five minutes away by car. He was two weeks in that hospital, suffering considerable pain in both his leg and his head. Without the hospital and expert attention being nearby, the welder would not have survived.

Broome is not a place known for snakes, in fact, they are almost a rarity around the town. On the other hand, around Go Go Station, situated on the southern outskirts of Fitzroy Crossing, a hamlet on the Fitzroy River, it is a different matter. During the dry at Fitzroy Crossing, they pile beer cans around the trunk of a tree. In the wet, the pile of empty cans, which by this time has reached the higher branches, is washed away by the flooding waters of the river. Not much else happened in Fitzroy Crossing in the days when I first went there, except regular fights when the hotel was closing for the night. On the occasion that Romilly and I stayed at Go Go Station, we were told that they shot eight king browns that day around the station homestead. The daughter of the station manager told us that the day before she had killed two king browns with the one shot. 'How did you do that?' I asked. Like all newcomers, I was eager for information, especially when that information involved animals as romantic and dangerous as snakes. 'They were copulating,' the girl replied.

After a year or two, the amiable Ross Gardiner left to engage in the tourist industry, a job for which he is well suited. If I were to take a trip into the outback, I cannot think of a more entertaining guide to show me its wonders. His position as manager was taken by Graham Taylor, an aviculturist from the Queensland–New South Wales border. Graham brought with him an assistant, Eddie Pszkit, a man who had a way with birds. With this team, I set out on what was to become the largest and most sophisticated expansion of my zoo.

Administrative offices and residential accommodation for the zoo's staff and their families were built, as well as a veterinary clinic and separate kitchens for the preparation of animal and bird food. A breeding complex and a whole series of new aviaries were constructed. One of the largest aviaries, over 100 metres in diameter and 50 metres high, had timber walkways, a considerable waterfall and a rainforest. It also had a microclimate that was over ten degrees cooler than outside. It was truly spectacular, and housed a collection of pigeons: the bleeding-heart pigeon, the Torres Strait pigeon, and the white-fronted ground dove. The Pearl Coast Zoo had the largest collection of macaws in Australia. There was also a collection of finches— Cuban finches, blue-faced parrot finches, long-tailed grass finches and star finches—and a good selection of waterfowl. In the grounds of the zoo, I built a lake with a surface area of over 13 000 square metres and, with it, a series of smaller lakes, ponds and waterways. Bustards and brolga cranes walked at will. Over 15 000 trees were planted in the zoo and goodness knows how many shrubs and plants. A dozen sorts of pigeons, finches and parrots perched in the trees, insectivores and honeyeaters— and the ugliest bird in the world, the tawny frogmouth. My parrot collection expanded until I had almost all the Australian species and most of the varieties and subspecies. The lake in partic-ular was a great success. As the country around Broome is dry for most of the year, with few waterholes, wild birds flocked to my zoo—I used to say that seventy per cent of my stock were volunteers. Even the kangaroos and wallabies tried to break in rather than break out. Raised timber walkways were built throughout the zoo so that tourists could cross it without disturbing the animals.

Graham Taylor, who had a remarkable talent for putting together a most amazing collection of birds, spent many hours on the telephone being passed from breeder to breeder on the rumour of a rare species. In time, he managed to acquire a trio of palm cockatoos. Palm cockatoos are not uncommon among the rainforests of Queensland, but are virtually non-existent in captivity. These birds, however, were still of breeding age, so it was a considerable excitement to us when one of the hens laid an egg. We placed this egg in an incubator and reared the offspring to about six weeks, when it died. A few weeks later, the male bird also died. About three weeks after the death of the male, the female laid another egg. This egg was again placed in the incubator and while we were waiting for it to hatch, the female also died. In time, the egg hatched and we reared the chick by hand, again to about six weeks, when it, too, died. These birds were worth $20 000 each so there was a considerable financial loss to be taken into account. That, however, was a small thing by comparison with having such a spectacular success snatched from you not once but twice. The parents were old, it was a gamble anyway, one that no reasonable person could have expected to have come off, but those who breed animals and birds are not reasonable people. The last of the trio of palm cockatoos travelled with Graham Taylor to his home in northern New South Wales. Graham and the palm cockatoo had become quite attached to each other. Graham would put out his tongue and the bird would scratch the tip of it with its extremely large and powerful beak.

Breeding at the Pearl Coast Zoo was not always a tragedy. One of the most exciting moments for me, when I arrived in Broome, was to visit the breeding complex. In the nursery could be found literally dozens of small chicks, all in different stages of development—some naked, some nearly fully fledged. Eddie Pszkit's wife would be feeding these chicks from a dozen different mixtures, using a narrow spoon to drop food into their extended crops. The greatest triumph that Graham Taylor and Eddie Pszkit had at my zoo was to breed the red-browed fig-parrot. Found in the coastal rainforest of the Queensland tropics this parrot is one of three subspecies of fig parrot in Australia. The breeding of the red-browed fig-parrot at the Pearl Coast Zoo produced valuable information that may have helped save the very rare Coxen's fig-parrot that was threatened with extinction at that time. Graham and Eddie could get these parrots to lay eggs, then the birds would sit and hatch them, only for the chicks to die after a few weeks. Even when they were hand-reared, the chicks died. Hand-rearing a chick the size of a small fingernail is no easy matter, but it was not the feeding that was the problem, it was the food. Avi-culturists believed that these parrots eat the small figs from a variety of figtree usually found in the Queensland rainforests. They are often seen feeding on these trees and they gobbled up that tree's fruit when fed in captivity. It was, however, not the fruit that the birds were after, rather the larvae that grew inside the fruit. The solution to rearing the young was simple: add protein to their food. After this, we bred several fig-parrots, both in the nest and by hand-rearing.

Pelicans flew into the zoo's lakes and even jabiru storks, along with thousands of migrating birds. Eight million of them come from Northern Europe, leaving a European winter to join in an Australian summer. They land on the beaches of Broome and then move inland to the seasonal deposits of water. In the sky above the zoo, black, whistling and Brahminy kites could be seen, and ospreys were regular visitors. Among the injured birds and animals brought to the zoo were a pair of osprey chicks. They were reared by the zoo's staff, and for a season would swoop out of the sky to take the food held out for them. After that season, they moved on. Birds came and birds went; always there was something wonderful to see. Both white and glossy ibis made their home at the zoo. Royal spoonbills came, along with great egrets, Pacific heron and straw-necked ibis. Lesser frigatebirds, their red chests inflated, wheeled in the sky and, swooping, took fresh water from the lakes. Eyton tree ducks, black duck, white-eyed duck and grey teal all came in the season. Marsh sandpipers, sharp-tailed sandpipers, common sandpipers, green shanks, grey-tailed tattler, bar-tailed godwit, black-tailed godwit and the black-fronted dotterel, all waded in the marshes at the edge of the lakes. In these marshes lived reptiles and lizards, amphibians, burrowing frogs and two species of tree frogs—desert tree frogs, green tree frogs.

All came as volunteers to my zoo. The only species that did not come in great numbers was humans. Sadly, the visitors to the town of Broome, of whom there were each year increasing numbers, did not share my enthusiasm for animals. New plans were hatched to attract the tourists. A large complex was to be built to house primates. Tourists love primates—they can stand and watch an ape for hours on end. They don't, however, seem to get the same pleasure out of watching a brolga crane or a spotted bowerbird—tourists are curious creatures. Some of the varieties of marmosets from South America were installed; cheetah arrived and settled into their fine enclosure. Our ostriches bred, but once again we had trouble with the offspring. Searching for food in the pindan, the earth of the Kimberley, the young ostriches used to swallow a considerable quantity of this earth, which went solid in their intestines and destroyed their digestive systems. The Australian cassowary is a fine-looking bird but a poor display for the tourist; it tends to hide in the thick bush of the rain-forest enclosure. A bird that is both formidable and highly dangerous in the wild, the cassowary must be handled with great care. Cassowaries are short-sighted, attacking when they hear a sound rustling through the bush, pushing trees aside with their heads that are protected by a huge helmet or lump of bone. These birds have a savage kick and their claws are capable of tearing out a human's stomach.

John Knowles supervised the selection of the mammals and their transport. An expert in the field of conserving endangered species of mammal, he took particular trouble to make sure that we not only imported mammals that would thrive in the climate of Broome but also prepared the correct habitats for them before they arrived. He has earned my undying admiration for the patience he demonstrated in his dealings with the officialdom of both Canberra and Perth. A

Boeing 707 was hired to fly in addax, red lechway, sitatunga, nyala, nilgai, greater kudu, gemsbok, Grevy's zebras and Congo buffalo. Banteng cattle, Asiatic water buffalo, black buck, rusa deer and hog deer were acquired from within Australia, as were various varieties of kangaroo and wallaby. One of the rarest species of Australian wallaby, the nail-tailed wallaby, was indigenous to the land where the zoo was built. The climate of Broome was perfect for them and they bred well. My zoo was at last becoming an ark, where breeding stock of the some of the world's rarest antelopes could live in isolation away from disease and, more importantly, poachers and warfare.

The zoos of the Australian capital cities were generous with both their advice and their stock. Melbourne Zoo sent us a pair of pygmy hippos on breeding loan. The RAAF flew them for me to Broome. Unfortunately, someone with a curious sense of humour told the military personnel concerned with this operation that the hippos ate cream buns, and a large quantity of cream buns was included on the aircraft's manifests. News of these cream buns reached the ears of a parliamentarian in Canberra, who made a considerable fuss about the whole affair. His efforts to cause trouble, however, came to nothing. Not only was the RAAF engaged in an exercise of conservation by moving these hippos, they had good reason for apparently doing me a favour.

During the war, a Spitfire had crash-landed on some mudflats near Walcott Inlet, some three hundred kilometres north-east of Broome. The RAAF wished to return it to Melbourne where it would be restored and put on public display, since Spitfires these days are even rarer than pygmy hippos. The RAAF's problem was how to get the Spitfire from the mudflats to a point where a low loader could transport it to an airfield. John Adams and I had the answer: we owned the only landing craft in north-west Australia. We did a deal—the RAAF delivered my hippos, we lent them our landing craft, and the aircraft that brought the hippo took away the Spitfire.

Some years earlier the transporting of a tapir from Melbourne to Broome had not gone as smoothly. Ross Gardiner and his assistant had been despatched to Melbourne to collect the tapir. The animal was loaded into a crate made by the Melbourne Zoo's carpenters and the crate put on the back of a trailer. It was about a three-day journey from Melbourne to Broome, travelling mostly by track, via Alice Springs and the Tanami Track. For the first two days, all went well. Then the tapir decided to break out of the crate—whether the crate was badly made or the tapir too strong for it will never be known, nor, indeed, will the reason why it took it into its head to escape. A tapir cannot be allowed to roam the Australian bush; despite its chances of meeting a mate and breeding being somewhat remote, the officials in Canberra just would not stand for it. Ross Gardiner had no alternative but to shoot the tapir and bury it. The zoo's staff and I had waited with great anxiety for the much-delayed arrival of the tapir and it was with considerable sadness that we learned from Ross Gardiner that the animal had been killed. Whether you run a farm or a zoo, the old adage, 'Where you have livestock, you have dead stock' is equally true. It did not seem to matter whether that dead stock was large and rare or small and common, the sense of failure was always the same.

One of the most attractive Australian mammals is the wombat. This cuddly creature has never achieved the same popularity as the koala. The wombat's habitat, a deep hole in the ground, is probably the reason for this. It is a lot easier to feel well-disposed towards a cuddly animal that spends its time sitting in a tree munching eucalyptus leaves than to an animal that spends most of the day deep underground. The wombat, however, has a better nature by far than the koala, which is inclined to scratch and bite when handled, quite apart from covering the unwary handler in foul-smelling urine. At my zoo, I had a pair of wombats—at least, I thought I had a pair of wombats. Their cage was carefully constructed. It was a large cage roughly 30 metres square, with full-grown boab trees in which resided a flock of Torres Strait pigeons. The floor of the enclosure had been excavated to the depth of over a metre and heavy steel mesh laid all over it, cut carefully around the roots of the boab trees. The earth was then put back, and a pond, a large waterfall and a stream built. The overall effect was most attractive. The pigeons flew around the aviary and rested in the spreading branches of the boab trees. A boab is a fine tree for putting in an aviary, and it transplants well even when full grown. Indeed, where boabs have stood in the way of road construction and have been uprooted, thrown into the bush and left lying on their sides, they have been known to take root and to continue growing in a horizontal position. Boab trees also have the advantage that they seldom grow over eight metres in height.

The wombats arrived and were introduced to their cage. At first, they sat around and sometimes played with each other, then they began to dig. We were all very pleased about this, as digging showed that the animals were really settling in. Then for days on end we did not see the wombats. The daily, or rather nightly, ration of food was still disappearing and I was coming to the conclusion that the only way we could see the wombats during the day would be to build a tunnel for humans beside the tunnel that the wombats had built and put observation panels between the two. Before I embarked on what would no doubt have been a most costly exercise, I thought we should see where the wombat tunnel ended. A fire was lit at the tunnel's mouth and the smoke was sucked straight down the hole, which clearly meant that the tunnel had another entrance. Nowhere could we see smoke in the park, so one of my staff climbed on to the roof of the cage, which was about ten metres high. He saw smoke all right— a plume of smoke much as a campfire might make on a still day rose to the heavens about half a mile away. My wombats had escaped; they were long gone and we had been feeding an empty cage for some months. Their food, I suppose, was taken by rats and mice but the wombats were never seen again.

⤝⤞

We used to get a number of calls to help birds in distress. This other function of the zoo, as an animal first-aid post, was one of the most exciting aspects of the whole venture. On one particular day, Des Higgins telephoned from Waterbank Station just outside Broome. The weather was dry and his waterholes were drying up. At one waterhole, there was a mass of ducks stuck in the mud. Graham Taylor immediately sent out some of his keepers to help. In the waterhole, there were about fifteen or twenty centimetres of slush and then just mud. The feathers of the ducks were all coated in mud and they could barely move, let alone fly. The problem, however, was easily solved by a good washing. To their surprise, the men who went out to help the ducks noticed that what water remained in the water-hole was boiling with the movement of fish. They thought that the fish would be mullet, which are common in the waterholes of the North-West. So, having brought the ducks back to the zoo for the necessary remedial work on their plumage, the staff returned with their fishing nets. The fish, however, were not mullet as expected, but rather good-sized barramundi. Twenty or 30 of these barramundi were subsequently released in the zoo's lake where they grew and also bred. At feeding time, they were summoned to the pavilion on the walkway in the centre of the lake by someone banging a metal bucket. The sight of these barramundi being fed, each fish now weighing about nine kilos, was quite spectacular. All went well with the barramundi until a wet when a small crocodile escaped from the nearby crocodile park and found its way into the lake. There was considerable consternation when a visitor to the zoo, Nick Paspaley, the pearl farmer, spotted this young crocodile, which was growing rapidly on a diet of barramundi. That crocodile, I am bound to record, took quite a deal of catching. No-one was particularly keen to get into the water in case the small crocodile's big brother was somewhere about.

∽∝

Looking back, I sometimes ask myself which bird was my favourite, and which mammal. Each time, the answer is different. In the end, I suppose, it is the eclectus parrot, a variety where the female wears the smart red clothing and the male a simple green jacket. I love these parrots because of their size, their dignity and their humour. And which mammal? The answer is simple—it has to be the scimitar-horned oryx. Whether they are standing, racing across a paddock, or sparring with heads down and horns locked, they are things of beauty, elegant and, oh, so terribly grand.

9

It was the pilots' strike and the subsequent recession that brought my zoo to an end. I had dreamt too much and brought too many of those dreams to fruition. The time came and it all had to end. It was sad to end it, but the story would have been far sadder had the zoo never been built in the first place. My ambition to set up an ark to save a number of endangered species may well have failed but, even so, every effort in the fight to save the wildlife of our planet is worth something in the overall scheme of things. While my ambition was thwarted, the fate of living creatures remains one of my paramount interests. When I think of the Pearl Coast Zoo, I smile. Although I failed to create something of lasting value, what I did create gave value to the lives of those involved in its creation. A quotation taken from the last pages of Lord Haldane's memoirs sums up his personal philosophy, and seems appropriate to my situation on the closing of the Pearl Coast Zoo. Haldane, a considerable figure from the first half of this century, a statesman, philosopher, minister of war and Lord Chancellor of Britain, wrote:

The best that ordinary mortals can hope for is the result which will probably come from sustained work directed by as full a reflection as is possible. This result may be affected adversely by circumstances, by illness, by misfortune or by death. But if we have striven to think and to do work based on thought, then we have at least the sense of having striven, with such faculties as we have possessed devoted to the striving. And that is in itself a cause of happiness, going beyond the possession of any definite gain.

As for the animals whose existence I tried to safeguard, my efforts were but a drop in a vast ocean of need.

At the time that my zoo in Broome opened, there were disturbances and civil wars in Africa, and the Middle East, a place not unfamiliar with warfare, was a tinderbox waiting to be ignited. For centuries past, man has fought over its fertile valleys and deserts, has built monuments and then destroyed them. Towns and cities have been consumed by warfare and rebuilt in the image of the conqueror. Great cities have been destroyed by earthquakes, peoples destroyed by famine and pestilence. In the heart of this region lies Basra, the site of the Garden of Eden, the site of the beginning, perhaps, of life on earth. What is certain, however, is that the valleys of the Euphrates and Tigris rivers meet here, valleys that are the flight path for millions of migrating birds, birds that journey from Europe far into Africa, birds that travel each year from Russia to northern Australia, birds as diverse as the white stork and the small warbler. While man is ingenious enough to rebuild and improve upon destroyed architecture, and his hands are supple enough to replace broken artefacts, he has, however, no means of replacing a lost variety of bird or beast.

The desert area of Iraq is of particular importance in nature, as it is the meeting point of European and Arabian species. The brown bear, seldom found now in Europe, the Arabian wolf, and many other interesting and beautiful animals and birds can be found here. One of the ironies of the destructive attack upon Kuwait by Saddam Hussein was the disastrous consequence of the action necessary to remove him. This area, where allied troops fought Saddam Hussein's army, was one of the few places in the world making great efforts to repair some of the ravages of the twentieth century by restoring locally extinct species to their original habitat. A small group of the extremely rare Sommering's gazelles, along with the animals in the Old Botanical Gardens of Kuwait City, were shot by Iraqi soldiers. However, the real tragedy is the loss of the plans by the Kuwaiti Government to establish a national park along the border with Iraq, a park where it intended to reintroduce the Houbara bustard and the Arabian gazelle, a desert reserve to which many of the species now extinct in this region would return. It must be hoped that when the rebuilding of this region begins, these plans will not be overlooked when the Kuwaitis construct new motorways, hospitals and schools. Reservoirs of these rare animals need to be established not only in Kuwait but around the world in places not given to regular wars.

In Saudi Arabia, the government has set up a centre for the conservation and breeding of many of the endangered species native to that country, with the intention of returning them to the wild. In this centre, there are well over 1000 of some of the world's rarest animals: sand gazelles, Arabian gazelles; the Saudi dorcas gazelle, extinct in its habitat; the Saudi wolf; and the Ruppell's fox, a small and rare sand fox. Then there is the Arabian oryx, the most beautiful of these creatures, an animal thought to be the mythical unicorn, for when seen in profile, its long, sweeping horns seem as one. It was an animal hunted for 3000 years by desert warriors, yet it survived. But no antelope, however agile, is equipped to withstand the advent of the automatic rifle, and the early 1960s saw its demise outside captivity. The research centre in Riyadh has prospered, and the number of these rare animals has increased. There are several zoos with important collections in Israel, and the Tel Aviv University Wildlife Research Centre has done much work for conservation, and still cares for many rare animals. In Oman, meanwhile, repatriation of desert antelopes has started. There is now a wild population of the Arabian oryx, the descendants of captive-bred animals returned to their habitat. Another population of this elegant animal is in Jordan, and there are plans for a reserve on the Jordanian–Saudi border. All of this work goes on in one of the world's most volatile regions.

These animals are in great danger. In the early 1960s, small groups of antelopes were caught and taken to zoos in America and Britain: the addax, short-legged, beige and corkscrew-horned, now thought to be extinct in the wild; the Dhana gazelle, long-legged and long-necked, of which less than a thousand remain; the scimitar-horned oryx, another antelope extinct in its natural habitat. The subsequent civil war in Chad and the famines that sprang from it, combined with high-powered military rifles, have proved the wisdom of this action. These zoos have become a Noah's Ark for these animals, places where they can be bred and studied. London Zoo is one of the organisations active in this field, and has an almost unique expertise in combining field work and research. Zoos are no longer animal prisons; in their modern form, they can be havens of safety. The scarce resource of these rare and extremely beautiful animals, spread among zoos on a planned basis, means that neither disease nor war will ever destroy them completely. Man being the aggressive beast that he is, it is unlikely that the war against Saddam or, for that matter, any other war, will end all wars. We had better take good care of our zoos so that they at least can take care of the world's birds and animals after terrible carnage, and play their vital role in the rehabilitation of our planet.

I believed that Australia had a vital role to play in the conservation of the wonderful antelopes that are endangered. Sadly, we never managed to import either the Dhana gazelle or the Arabian oryx into Australia, but we did bring in the scimitar-horned oryx and the addax, both of which are extremely rare. They are now to be found in Australian zoos in considerable quantities. It was, I believe, the memories of my visits to Kenya and East Africa at the beginning of the 1970s that inspired me. In those days, black rhinos were plentiful while the white rhino was endangered and rare. Within ten years, the situation changed. By 1980, the exact opposite was the case—the white rhino was plentiful in zoos, breeding well and being returned to the wild, while the black rhino was in danger of becoming extinct. It was always my ambition to set up a breeding colony of black rhinos in Broome. In the event, this was not to be; this ambition, like so many of my ambitions, was to be unfulfilled.

It must be fairly obvious to anyone who has ever read a newspaper that a large part of the world's wildlife is in considerable danger. Just how bad this situation has become is not always apparent. All of us know of the dangers to the black rhinoceros in Africa and to the tiger on the Indian subcontinent. Fewer people may realise that there are today around 911 animal species on the critical danger list (this figure

comes from the recently published Red List of the World Conservation Union). When you compare this figure with the 1265 species
that have been lost in the past 400 years, it shows that the rate at
which we are destroying the wildlife on our planet has speeded up
to a point where it has become dangerous. The figures produced by
the World Conservation Union are indeed frightening. In 1994, it
appeared that 18 per cent of mammals were endangered. More
complete figures now reveal the real figure to be 25 per cent. And it
is not only animals that are in danger—23 730 species of higher plant
life are threatened. If you include all plants, 13 per cent of the total
number of species is in danger of disappearing.

Sadly, the main cause of the situation is not so much the changing
climate of our planet but rather the changing habits of its human
inhabitants. The clearing of forests and the polluting of rivers and seas
are some of the causes. Surprisingly, the inhabitants of this planet
most endangered are fish, reptiles and amphibians. There is always,
however, the argument that our lives are not much the poorer for the
loss of the world's dodos. Indeed, there are many who take the view
that it is one thing to talk of conserving tigers, for instance, when you
live in the leafy suburbs of a great city, but quite another if the tiger
that someone else has conserved has just eaten your only goat. While
most who read these statistics will be shocked and probably sympathetic to the plight of the animal world, few will actually do anything
about it. These were the grand thoughts that were in my mind as I set
up my modest zoo in Broome.

In northern Australia, the ban on crocodile hunting changed the
habits of the estuarine crocodile. This is a creature that can grow to
nearly nine metres in length and move as fast on land as in water. It
seems to have known about the ban that protected it, because now it
has little fear of mankind. In truth, you can upset the balance of
nature by conservation quite as easily as you can upset it by destruction. While the subject is immensely complex, it is not the first difficult problem mankind has had to face—with determined effort, the
Americans managed the inconceivable and put a man on the moon.

Unfortunately, stemming ecological change does not offer the same international prestige as landing on our nearest planet. It is as if the great nations of the world were suburban businessmen proudly polishing their cars on a Sunday morning in front of their houses, in full view of the neighbours. Unseen in their kitchen sinks, the unwashed dishes from Saturday night's party join the general dirt and deterioration of wild and careless living. People do not march in the streets on wildlife issues, yet they will sit glued to their televisions watching a documentary that shows how some branch of the animal kingdom is about to be extinguished. They will picket ports to stop the live export of domestic animals; the treatment of veal calves was one of the most emotive issues raised in Britain in the past five years and caused far greater interest than many of the terrible tragedies involving humans.

There is little public interest, however, in the fate of the Galapagos tortoise, despite the fact that this animal was one of the creatures that led Darwin to his theory of evolution. People are occasionally motivated to complain about zoos that mistreat animals, but fortunately, bad zoos are becoming fewer and good ones are at the forefront of animal conservation. In such environments, rhinos, tigers, bears, antelopes and wolves can be saved. It is in zoos that they are being bred with the idea of repatriating them to their original habitat. While all this is good, it not the final answer—that lies with governments. Politicians, however, move slowly, and not at all unless they are pressed. Meanwhile, only wildlife organisations can explain to the people why they need to care. The following paragraphs are how I described the closing of my zoo in the first volume of my memoirs, *Once a Jolly Bagman*.

The Australian summer of 1989 was over. It had been wet, the trees and foliage of my zoo had grown well, all looked splendid. The winter, which is Broome's peak tourist season, looked as if it would produce a bumper crop of visitors. Then the Australian airline pilots went on strike. The winter season was lost, instead of 50 000 visitors, my zoo received a few hundred. Days went by and no-one came to look at my birds and animals and, what was worse, there was no way to send the surplus birds that we bred for sale to the aviculturists of eastern Australia. That year we successfully raised 700 endangered birds, plus many other common varieties. At their moment of triumph, Graham Taylor and Eddie Pszkit, his assistant, were faced with a desperate situation that was neither their fault, nor within their capacity to correct.

Graham and Eddie performed the closing of the zoo as efficiently as they had built it up. No bird or animal was put down; all were placed either with other zoos or collectors. It was a great sadness to me to see the zoo that I had physically worked on in the early days, and certainly spent all my free moments planning, come to a close. Despite the fact that I would far rather have succeeded in what most people believed to be a mad venture, I do not regret it for one moment, because in a small way my zoo helped to change the attitude to zoos and captive animals all over Australia, and the rare antelopes and zebras I imported have become foundation stock whose progeny will breed for generations to come.

10

Shortly after I started my zoo in Broome, I decided to build a hotel, not the usual sort of hotel found in the North-West, something rather different. It was my intention to create a hotel that had all the modern comforts, yet still played homage to the traditional style of building in Broome and its multicultural heritage. If it was to attract an international clientele, this hotel would need a particular touch of European chic.

A friend of Romilly's and mine was, by profession, an architect. She is a Greek, indeed, a very beautiful Greek, who goes by the name of Aphrodite Gallengha. Aphrodite had never worked in Australia before but, nevertheless, she jumped at the opportunity to take this commission. Together with Peter Arney, of Oldham Boas, Ednie-Brown, the architects who had carried out all my work in Perth, she set about designing my new hotel. Aphrodite was to do the conceptual design; Peter Arney and his colleagues were to carry out the detailed work. As a team, they worked well together, and the first stage of what is now the Intercontinental Cable Beach Resort was soon under way. My partner in this venture was an agency of the Western Australian Government. The hotel comprised a central block and about 50 cottages built on stumps with lattice walls, settled in a recently planted tropical garden complete with streams and lakes. To construct this garden, fully grown trees were moved onto the site and a team of gardeners set about planting them and literally thousands of plants. A large swimming pool and several tennis courts were also built. The hotel was opened by Peter Dowding, then the premier of Western Australia; the majority of the guests at the opening were Broome people. It was a magic evening, hot, balmy and lit with flares. It seemed as if the hotel had arrived by magic; there was nowhere like it within a thousand or more miles.

Before long, it became apparent that the hotel could not stay this size; it needed to become larger if it was to have a chance of making a profit. Three new wings of studio rooms were added and a further wing with luxury suites. Two more restaurants, several more tennis courts, a health club and another even larger swimming pool were also constructed. The décor of the hotel was provided by two talented women, Joan Bowers from Sydney, who imported artefacts and architectural elements from India, and Judy Barratt-Lennard, a Perth decorator of considerable taste and talent, who provided furniture and furnishings from Indonesia. At the same time, I set about acquiring a large collection of Australian paintings, mostly by local artists. In the hotel's cottages there are about a hundred crayon drawings by Joe Nangan, and in the suites, works by Sidney Nolan, Elizabeth Durack and Humphrey Price Jones. Aphrodite pulled all these disparate collections together, and we had a hotel of a most unusual and interesting design.

Business took a nasty turn with the pilots' strike and the Government agency was not half as delighted as it was on opening night. It was then that I took a decision that cost me dear. I gave them their money back regardless of the fact that our association had been short and the hotel was then worth a fraction of what it had cost. In a difficult situation is it is often easier to carry on alone than with a partner who is unhappy; it is, however, a folly to pay three times what half a hotel is worth when on the edge of a giant recession. The airport that had the Government's backing was never built. It is also folly to rely on governments, unless you have their signature on many bits of paper and, even then, the chances of them performing are not guaranteed.

The hotel, the zoo, the airport and other tourist ventures were all part of a carefully considered plan—the airport had been the linch pin of that plan. What had once been a serious business strategy, now had the feel of an incredible gamble. Customers in Broome were what I needed, more and more of them, yet Broome was a long way from the Australian market. Still struggling to get the existing airport made international in the face of a sponge of bureaucracy, I set out to publicise the hotel, which was then called the Cable Beach Club, and my zoo. In truth, the people who came loved both of them, but not nearly enough people came. This publicity campaign was greatly helped when the Variety Club of Australia planned to end its annual cross-Australia motor rally for classic cars in Broome. My family company decided to enter a car, a 1963 Humber Super Snipe. In order for this car to cope with the bush tracks from Burke to Broome, it needed some modifications. Sergeant-major Mike Hanlon arranged for volunteers from the Australian Army, Karratha 22 Construction Squadron, to provide a hundred hours of their spare time. A second Humber Super Snipe was acquired and its parts used to make one serviceable vehicle which was fitted with heavy-duty suspension and a fridge to keep the necessary refreshments cool. The finished vehicle was painted in garish colours. I already had two expert bush drivers and mechanics, Snowy County and Charlie Diesel; all I needed was a third. In London, I was dining with the prime minister, Margaret Thatcher, and her family, when I mentioned this project. In a moment, Carol Thatcher had volunteered her services as the third driver. Six months later, Carol, Snowy and Charlie set off along with 200 or so other entrants from Sydney's Bondi Beach, in pouring rain and great razzamatazz. The bash was a great success, enjoyed by all those who took part in it. As a result, the Cable Beach Club received a considerable amount of publicity, not only in the press but on television as well.

Achieving publicity, however, for a middle-sized, up-market hotel is not an easy matter. By far the best form of publicity for such an enterprise is by word of mouth, so I set about getting Sydney's society to visit Broome. To this end, I hired Primrose Dunlop, an expert in this field and a woman who knew everyone who was worth knowing. She did a splendid job and slowly the trickle of wealthy people coming from Sydney to visit the Cable Beach Club in Broome became a stream. Glen-Marie Frost and her husband, Bob, were also invited to visit Broome—Glen-Marie has always been a highly successful Australian publicist.

As a result of the publicity that it received, over the following years,

Broome and the Cable Beach Club became host to a large number of celebrities. The recession, however, got deeper, interest rates rose remorselessly and, in the end, the Cable Beach Club and the company that owned it, Australian City Properties, were sold at about the same time that I closed my zoo. Some years later, I sold my house in Broome and left to live in Italy. My attitude to the Pearl Coast Zoo was one of deep commitment. I did not open that zoo casually, nor did I close it on a whim. I also had a deep commitment to, and enthusiasm for, my other ventures in Broome. Perhaps this piece, taken from notes in my library, explains my approach to people, places and possessions, rather better than anything else that I have written:

At ten o'clock on the 16th May 1990, Sotheby's will begin to auction the contents of my house, West Green, near Hartley Witney in Hampshire. The accumulation of the last sixteen years of my life and a number of objects from the previous 25 years will disappear in almost a 1000 lots and two full days of selling.

The eighteenth-century furniture of the Grand Saloon, the minerals of the mineral room will be sold alongside the collection of over a hundred mocha ware mugs. These mugs, with white and blue bands of colour around them, were used in nineteenth-century pubs to drink beer. On all of them are the chocolate marks that give them their name—marks made by the craftsmen spitting their chewing tobacco at the damp glaze, strange marks in the shape of trees. Wives used to say to each other, when their husbands returned late and a little less than sober, 'He was very tired last night—he's been lifting too many trees.' The collection of garden implements from the sixteenth century to the modern, with its star attraction, a horse-drawn lawn mower complete with leather coverings for the horse's feet, to protect the lawn, will go. So too the shepherds' crooks in the hall, the stuffed birds in the master bathroom, all English birds. The bric-à-brac of my life, collected and hoarded, each individual piece of great importance to the collector.

The mugs, the minerals, the garden implements—they went somehow with the house and now I need a new home with a different feel, harder, emptier, sharper. I am a nomad from a nomadic stock, setting little store in possessions. Anxious in their pursuit, casual in their disposal, I love many things and hate quite as many. No work of art, however wonderful, is a substitute for its creator, or of more consequence than the meanest man that would destroy it. Why sell all? To rid oneself of the chore of making a choice, to make a different style of life, to win the freedom to choose again.

The collections gone, dispersed. What is left? Snowdrops in the garden, over a hundred different varieties, a collection; hellebores, carpets of them in profusion, and roses, old garden roses, perhaps 400 varieties—the record of all these plants and their planting was lost in a fire. There are follies by Quinlan Terry, some built, some, as in all interesting gardens, only on paper, and others only in the mind. And the garden itself, shaped and cared for by a human being, by chance called Mr Mann—sadly, now dead. A garden, I hope, in the spirit of the first owner of West Green, a certain General Hawley, a man who fixed the motto: 'Do as you feel inclined' above his door. Hawley used to visit his friend across the common. One night, after they had dined well, Hawley picked up what he believed to be a lantern for his walk home in the dark. Out in the cold night air, he was pursued by a terrible screaming; the faster he ran, the worse the screaming. Fearing the devil meant to collect his soul that night, he ran faster and even faster—until he fell into a ditch where he stayed till morning. He woke to find that he was clutching his friend's caged parrot.

A garden with the ghost of Hawley's dog; a garden haunted, so word would have it, by Highland pipers come to be revenged on Hawley, who led the cavalry at Culloden. They are as likely to be playing Hawley on as opposing his charge, for more Scots fought on the side of the English than on the side of the Scots in that battle. There are even tales of buried treasure. Many people have lunched there: drunk well, I know; eaten well, I hope; enjoyed West Green and its contents, some more than others. I remember a man who came to lunch. He held the party enchanted by his words; he made two jokes and all the room laughed and laughed. He made a third and there was silence. I mentioned this to him later and, far from embarrassment, he expressed delight. For he had, he said, an audience capable of discernment and it is the bad jokes that one should remember—failure is somehow funnier. It is often that your true friends are not the most brilliant people that you meet and is often a triviality rather than a great event that changes your life.

After Sotheby's have knocked down the last lot and the marquee is gone, the garden swept, there will still stand the obelisk that commemorates the life and work of Mr Mann, the gardener. It bears his portrait in stone, my prize-winning goose between his legs, his hand on the obelisk with his back to the garden and all it might have been, thinking perhaps of what might be. Do I regret leaving? I suppose that I do have a regret at leaving West Green—it is that I should have picked the snowdrops last year.

A few days after that auction, my home was blown apart by a terrorist bomb. I feel today much the same way about the demise of my zoo as I felt about leaving West Green. In all my life I have been blessed with a multitude of advantages, and the greatest of these go hand-in-hand—an incurable curiosity and a never-ending optimism.

III

Travels in the North-West

11

As I was spending much of my time in the small township of Broome, it was inevitable that I should succumb to an urge to travel, an urge which has been with me since I was a small boy, an urge that I inherited from my father, a man who was endlessly boarding ships and aircraft to visit faraway places, a man who would jump on a train just for the pleasure of travelling. Many of my journeys in the North-West have been described in *Once a Jolly Bagman*. Here I shall fill in a few gaps in some of those travels and describe others in far greater detail.

One day in 1982, half a day's journey out of Broome, Romilly, Oliver Ford and I were driving along the main road to Port Hedland just short of Sandfire and we turned left into the bush. Shortly after the turn-off, we came across a bunch of cattle being driven by men on horseback. The cattle were moving at a leisurely pace in the afternoon sun; it seemed such a peaceful sight that we stopped to watch them for twenty minutes or so. Men and horses moving as one gave credence to the centaur of Greek mythology. Later that night, we stayed at the Ironclad Hotel in Marble Bar. This town has some fine old administrative buildings from the turn of the century; they are red brick and fort-like in appearance. Marble Bar also has the greatest range of temperature of any town in Australia; freezing cold in the winter to baking hot in mid-summer. Happily, we were there in the spring when the temperature was about as pleasant as you could imagine. The town—though the place is barely worthy of the designation 'town'—is named after a reef of spar that runs across a series of small waterholes. This reef was thought by the early settlers to be marble when, in fact, it was the much rarer material, spar. We, in the fashion of ignorant Europeans, expected to find in the Ironclad Hotel, a long bar topped in marble with a couple of dozen dour outback characters drinking at it. How wrong could we have been. We found the inhabitants of Marble Bar to be, in general, extremely friendly, ready to offer information on the place and its history, and eager to tell us about the delights that we would encounter on our journey south.

Some years later, I recommended to John Kasmin, the London art dealer, that he visit Marble Bar. His description of what he found varies from mine, largely because he spent most of the night drinking in the bar of the Ironclad Hotel which, incidentally, is named after the first ironclad warships, not the fact that it is built of corrugated iron. Kasmin sat and drank and watched two others drinking, a man and a woman. The man kept knocking the woman off her chair. Each time she climbed back onto her chair, he knocked her off again. Kasmin, believing that such behaviour was disgraceful, tried to bring it to the attention of his neighbour at the bar. 'I'm deaf in this ear,' the man replied, 'and even if I wasn't, I wouldn't want to hear anything that you have to say.' Kasmin, a creature of continental Europe, likes to affect the attire of a French lorry driver when travelling. He stuck out like a sore thumb among the drinkers in the Ironclad Hotel.

Another half day on and we were in desolate country. The countryside around Newman has the feeling of a wasteland—burned landscape, burned trees, burning sun and rocks. Newman itself is a mining town, a town in a brown wasteland. It is as if someone has put a glass dome over the whole place, for it has rows of detached houses with green lawns and cars parked in their driveways. With its supermarket and urban shopping centre, airconditioning and ice-cream parlours, Newman could have easily been removed in its entirety from suburban Perth. Beside the track we came across the carcass of a sheep. Perched on the dead animal's head was an eagle tearing at the sheep's brains with its beak, the skull held firmly in its claws. For several hours' travelling, we saw neither man nor beast, only birds of prey circling in the savage blue sky. We stayed that night in Meekatharra, a town about which Malcolm Fraser's wife made some disparaging remarks while campaigning with her husband, the then prime minister. These remarks were picked up by the local press and the poor woman had to return and make a public apology. Meekatharra is not much of a town; it has an airport and a railway station, the end of the line from Perth. It is a town for shipping cattle and sheep.

๛

As we became more experienced in the art of travelling in the outback, we avoided the small hotels of the townships that we passed through, sleeping instead in canvas swags. No tents, no shelter—just the stars above us which, in nights spent in the desert, were stars as I have never seen them before. They started on one horizon and cluttered the night sky across to the other horizon. Among them was an almost continuous parade of shooting stars. I was always so excited I did not sleep more than an hour or two each night. My wife Romilly always said that she would never share a swag with a man who kept his boots on. However, despite missing the pleasure of having Romilly near me at night, I judged it safer to sleep in my boots in case I needed to get up in a hurry which, indeed, was the case on that first night on the Tanami Track, when the heavens opened and rain came down in sheets. When we travelled, I took a heavy calibre rifle with me, mostly in case we got lost and needed to shoot something to eat. After our first journey, we had become more cautious and took Snowy County and his mate Charlie Diesel with us as guides. The desert around the Tanami Track is flat, lacking even sand hills. It is not desert in the accepted sense of the word, as the earth is red pindan. Pindan, the earth of north-western Australia, is as hard as rock in the sun, but in the wet its mud is like quicksand. The scrub that grows in this land is straggly and, at first sight, seems easy enough to drive through—in reality, it is easy enough to get lost in.

Always an early riser, I usually woke before first light in the bush. Snowy, who barely slept, was already dressed and joined me in breaking sticks rather noisily in an attempt to wake the others. Failing to achieve this, we would usually build up the fire, cough a bit, drop billy cans and then make tea with as much noise as was possible.

119

In this manner we would have the whole group awake by first light, usually shortly after four-thirty. I liked to be under way by five and get a good four hours' driving in before breakfast. On our trips, I drove the Toyota Land Cruiser with Romilly and our other companions, while Snowy and Charlie Diesel took it in turns to drive a Toyota truck. Charlie Diesel's real name is Helquist; the 'Diesel' part is a Broome name, earned in the years he lived there by his ability to fix almost any defect in the engines that powered the pearling luggers of the 1970s. Charlie is a genius when it comes to diesel engines, a talent that he demonstrated like some great magician. On one occasion when one of our trucks broke down, he gathered us around the vehicle, opened the bonnet, gave the engine a considerable tap with a hammer, then signalled to Snowy to start the vehicle up. The truck worked perfectly and we had no more trouble for the rest of the journey.

Charlie Diesel's home was Melbourne, where nowadays he runs a highly successful business erecting and repairing the cranes used in the construction of the city's skyscrapers. Travelling with us across Australia was, for Charlie, a break from his business life.

Often when I was crossing Australia, either by truck or by air, I visited Alice Springs. On my last visit there in 1996, I found the town was rather different. The land around Alice Springs had the green tinge about it that a rainy season brings. I looked out as my Ansett flight made a long, low approach to the airport. I had not been to 'The Alice' for nearly five years. It seemed that nothing much had changed: there were no new houses to be seen as we flew towards the airport, no new roads. All appeared much as before, the low hills that hide the town, the satellite tracking station with its white domes and dishes bright in the sunshine. Only when I climbed down the aircraft's steps did I begin to think I had come to the wrong place. A sign said 'International Airport', and that is exactly what I saw. Gone was the collection of tin buildings stitched together that passed for a terminal. In front of me was a modern airport building—there was no longer a grubby bar with grubby customers where sweat and stubble mixed with ice-cold beer: the flies had gone as well. The cafeteria could seat a hundred and needed to, for planes arrived every few minutes instead of once or twice a day. Like most airports these days, the terminal at Alice Springs has become a shopping mall. Gone are all those men with jaws like set squares and hands like shovels, with floppy hats and a pocket knife at their belts. Gone are the women in their ill-fitting dresses and straw hats. The days when the population of 'The Alice' came to the airport for a beer and to wonder at the miracle of flight are long over. Today, the airport population at Alice Springs mainly consists of pushy German tourists and excited Japanese on a quick flip around Australia. The Germans study maps of the outback and straighten the creases in their canvas shorts and bush jackets, sending ordinary mortals reeling as they turn and strike them with their back-packs. These Germans are as well-equipped for a day in Alice, en route to Uluru, as if they were setting out for several months in the outback; indeed, they are far better equipped for the outback than are the men and women who have lived there all their lives. The Japanese at Alice's airport spend their time and their money buying clothes and Aboriginal artefacts, didgeridoos as long as themselves and paintings by the desert painters. As for the Aboriginals, apart from those who sell their products, they seem to have disappeared, blending in with the other denizens of the outback who now all wear ties and suits.

⚓

The airport at Alice is not the only aspect of Australia that has changed. Across the Tanami Desert along the Tanami Track, past Rabbit Flat on the way to Hall's Creek, you will, if you make a detour to the north, come to Turkey Creek. It is not much of a place compared to the standard set by the terminal at Alice Springs—just red earth and tin huts. But Turkey Creek, for all its lack of modern facilities, is the home of Australia's most exciting school of painting. It first came to fame when Rover Thomas, one of its citizens, repre-sented Australia at the Venice Biennale. His friend Paddy Tjamati was another of Turkey Creek's painters who broke away from the idea of simply reproducing tribal patterns on canvas. These two artists painted the landscape of their country on dismembered tea chests.

121

The works were used in the Krilkrill, a variation of the corroboree. Since the days of Paddy Tjamati and Rover Thomas's early efforts, a great deal of attention has been paid to the work of the painters from Turkey Creek. The painters of Turkey Creek are, however, not the only painters in that part of the Western Australian outback. A few years ago, a group of painters from Fitzroy Crossing exhibited their work in a Perth gallery, artists with wonderful names like Stumpy Brown and Jimmy Bent, Butcher Cheval and Peanut Ford. Their work was received with great acclaim and now fetches good money in the world's sales rooms. These artists from the small bush townships paint their country, its myths and its reality; they paint with great passion and perfect simplicity. In the words of Honey Pulikati, as she describes one of her paintings: 'This is a river behind the station at Yungngora in the rain time. After the rain, the water lies around in purra [billabongs]; we catch fish in these small waterholes, as the waterholes dry up they get caught—they cannot get back to the river.' It's all a bit like that for her people.

⁂

On another trip, Romilly, Oliver and I were driving the 2400 kilometres from Perth to Broome by the inland route through Meekatharra, Nullagine and Marble Bar. We stopped in the near-ghost town of Cue with its wonderful Victorian buildings, the gold all gone and most of the people with it; the bandstand in the main street long without musicians. On that trip we were novices and we nearly perished. It is a strange fact about travelling in the north-west of Australia, a land of low scrub that comes right to the edge of the track, but you see no animal life, or rather you rarely see animals and birds. We had travelled for two days and not seen a kangaroo; indeed, Oliver Ford began to doubt their existence. I felt I had let him down badly in this matter, for I had told him that the whole place was stuffed with kangaroos. So when a group of emus crossed the track, on an impulse, I turned off into the bush after them. We chased the emus in our Toyota Land Cruiser for a few minutes but we soon lost them, then, in an effort to return to the track, we could not find that either. Oliver was the tallest among us by some measure, so he climbed on top of the vehicle, but he could see nothing, just bush. The path we had made through the bush, a wide track it had seemed, was now invisible, the saplings back in place, the ground rock-hard, no tyre marks could be found; we were truly lost. We searched and searched and in time happily we discovered that we were only a few metres from our original road.

◦⃜◦

In 1983, a party of us travelled from Cairns to Cape York. Romilly, her father Tom, Snowy, Charlie Diesel, Oliver Ford and I, along with Stephen Fay and Olga Polizzi, travelled by truck and four-wheel drive, fully loaded with equipment. As we set out from Cairns, a rough town in those days, a place with one modern hotel, an airport and little else of significance, we communicated between the two vehicles by two-way radio. The night in Cairns had been uneventful, just one fight in the local hotel, but that was almost over when we arrived. We stayed in Cairns's new international hotel, a small barren place with few other customers, recently opened. How it has all changed. Cairns is now a large thriving town filled with tourists and those who serve the needs of tourism. We drove along the coast road, a sealed road edged on one side with the sea, a brown sea, not the bright blue sea to which we were used, and on the other with cane fields, mountains in the distance as their backdrop. We were in no hurry, stopping first at the Hartley Creek crocodile farm, then at a bird park. The bird park had a fine collection of local birds—the small, red-browed fig-parrots were of particular interest to me.

Soon we came to Port Douglas. I had heard of plans to build a spectacular hotel there and was interested in seeing the place. Many years later, in the mid-1990s, I returned to Port Douglas. The hotel had fulfilled its cycle: it was built, received great applause for its beauty and subsequent success, became the subject of a scandal, was sold once and now was for sale again.

Years ago, when I first visited Port Douglas in Queensland, Port Douglas was not there. At least, not in the sense that it is today. There was a church and a graveyard filled with the names of British pioneers—names that came from places as different as Cornwall and

Scotland. The Central Hotel, a fine Queensland building, stood on Macrossan Street, notable in those days for two monuments, one to the pioneers who settled Port Douglas, another to the local men who died in the First World War. It took a minute to see all that was worth seeing and I drove on excited by the prospect of the Daintree Rainforest and Cape York.

On my return to Port Douglas since, it had changed out of all recognition. Even the church has left the graveyard and it now sits on the foreshore beside the marina and the shopping centre that boasts shops with names like Louis Vuitton, Ralph Lauren and Loewe. The Mirage Hotel has been built with vast blue lagoons that double as swimming pools. A small railway runs past the town's resorts to a station complete with turntable at the marina. The marina is the *raison d'être* for the commercial explosion that has taken place. From here thousands of tourists are transported by high-speed catamarans out to the platforms on the Great Barrier Reef where they putter around in glass-bottomed boats, snorkel and dive on that extraordinary mass of gloriously coloured corals, teeming with fish of all sizes.

The place is a spectacle, Port Douglas's passport to fame and prosperity. A prosperity almost entirely due to the fact that it is the closest part of Australia to the Barrier Reef. Great palm trees line the roads around the town, palm trees with massed ferns growing up their trunks, manicured golf courses abound, lawns and hedgerows are neatly clipped. The whole effect is of a model town, but a town that could be anywhere where the weather is hot and water plentiful. A Japanese restaurant seems to have been removed from Japan, a Chinese restaurant from China. A restaurant called the Nautilus in Murphy Street, where the food is delicious and the atmosphere seductive, with coal braziers to warm you as you dine in the open air, could have been taken from the Bahamas or Florida or, for that matter, Los Angeles.

In Macrossan Street near the Pioneer Memorial is Club Tropical, a modern building disguised as a cave whose bar offers a drink called a 'Comfortably Numb'. Club Tropical also serves a 'Bushman's Breakfast', which is a very large plate of bacon, scrambled eggs and snags, as they call sausages in this part of the world. I felt quite numb after working my way through this confection. I am afraid that, judged by the standards of Club Tropical breakfasts, I am a pretty pathetic bushman. Opposite Club Tropical and its exotic décor is the Iron Bar Restaurant, a bush restaurant conveniently placed for those who might otherwise travel the bush for years without finding such a place. Their specialties included the 'Bob and Dolly Dyer's Seafood Platter', 'Pig Iron Bob's Steak Royal', 'Squizzy Taylor's Bank Rolled Chuck' and the 'Bradman Steak'. I asked what form the 'Bradman Steak' took, only to be told that it was a very large one. 'Skase's Crab Bounty', also on the menu, appears to be a reference to the fact that Mr Skase built the Mirage Hotel and left in a hurry, leaving large debts behind—the 'C' of Crab is perhaps meant to be a 'G'.

Far more delightful than all the other delights of Port Douglas is the Sunday market. Like all the weekend markets that abound in Australia, this one sells the same goods as the tourist shops of Australia on week days. But, hidden among the dross of tourist clutter and handicrafts, there are a few real gems. The stalls that sell orchids, for instance; these rare and wonderful plants are there in plentiful supply. Many on offer were species from the forests of northern Queensland. The fruit stalls sell exotic fruit like sapota or chocolate pudding fruit—which really does taste just like chocolate pudding. The governor's plum was for sale, too, a bitter fruit with the highest content of vitamin C known to mankind, while the most exotic item was wattle seed ice-cream.

As I left, I watched an Aboriginal playing a didgeridoo the size of an Alpenhorn. Didgeridoos are now sold all over Australia; even some of the Aborigines of Western Australia, who have no culture of playing these instruments, sell them, only they don't bother to hollow them out. However, the aspect of this demi-paradise built by Australian men and Japanese money that interested me the most was the proliferation of government agencies offering counselling.

In 1983, we wasted little time in Port Douglas. At this time, I was convinced that Broome in Western Australia was to be the recipient of the tourist boom. I was wrong, of course; Broome in those days was totally isolated, served only by internal flights. Cairns and the towns of the east coast are served by both a railway and good roads; Broome merely by a long, empty road. It is the railway that makes the difference; masses of people can get to a place cheaply by railway. Now that the coastline of New South Wales and Queensland is fully developed, the railways are finding a new role. The Eastern & Oriental Express—whose sister company runs luxury trains from London to Venice, then on to Bucharest and, finally, to Istanbul, as well as a similar but even more luxurious train from Singapore to Bangkok—now runs a luxury service from Sydney to Cairns and on into the rainforest. Travelling by the luxurious trains of the Eastern & Oriental Express is a far easier way of seeing the countryside than travelling by truck and four-wheel drive in a cloud of grey bull dust.

Our next stop was Cooktown, a place where under different circumstances I might have stayed and never moved again. A town filled with giant mango trees, a town built on a gentle slope to the sea. Its single-storey and double-storey houses have corrugated iron roofs and sit on stumps; latticework abounds. In Cooktown, there was a small museum of local history and artefacts. I have never returned and I have no idea what the place is like today, but then it was to us a place of pure magic. We should have lingered there but I insisted that we needed to make our way to a place where we could make camp overnight, for I did not want to have to spend a night in the rainforest. It was all a bit ridiculous really, because a better camping site than Cooktown would have been hard to imagine. However, as we were still at the beginning of a journey destined to take us more than three weeks, I felt that we had to press on through the Daintree rainforest. As we travelled by ferry across the Daintree River, we searched the waters in the hope of seeing the cousin of the giant crocodiles that we had seen performing in the croc farm outside Cairns. There we had seen apparently comatose crocodiles come to life and jump four metres in the air to take a proffered chicken. Flat empty waters break into turmoil as a crocodile six metres long is disturbed and springs to attack—the cause of his disturbance usually a long bamboo pole.

The going was hard once in the rainforest. Badly built tracks, deep ruts and mud slides had made travelling almost impossible but we pressed on until we came to Weipa in the mining country. In the event, we never did get to the top of Cape York; rather, we turned round and came down the other side of the peninsula, making our way around the Gulf until we came to Arnhem Land. At the Roper River crossing, we were supposed to pick up our permit to enter Arnhem Land, but as the permit had not left Katherine, we had to go there to get it. Arnhem Land is set aside for Aboriginal use only. It has a high degree of self-determination in how it conducts its affairs. The use of permits prevents this attractive and romantic place being overrun by tourists—in this way, the Aboriginals who live there are able to carry on their traditional lifestyles without unwanted interruptions and interference.

Back in Western Australia, the Bungle Bungles, situated just south of Lake Argyle, look like the curled rope beehives of the nineteenth century, but on a magnificent scale. When I first visited the Bungle Bungles it was like coming across a deserted city, rising out from endless kilometres of scrub. Travelling in the bush is often a series of long, lonely drives with only nature for company that comes to an end as the sun drops. To stand in the bush on a rise, looking out to see nothing, to hear nothing but to feel as if every rock and plant is watching, listening, waiting for you to speak—no wonder people fear this beautiful place.

❧

The towns of the bush are isolated from the general run of life, populated with inhabitants who specialise in the unusual. Towns like Wyndham, hot as hell in the summer, cool and perfect in the winter. Road signs that promise paradise when all they deliver is hell. A hot, hard place is northern Australia, a place that is now only part tamed by airconditioning and mobile phones. Towns with grand names are more likely to be no more than a cluster of houses, a hotel and a shop or two. Somewhere north of Tobermory, we stopped for fuel and a meal. A youth, perhaps in his early twenties, filled our vehicles with petrol. He smoked as he did his work. We, for our part, stood well back and prayed silently, wondering how many more trucks he would fill with petrol while smoking before an untimely end came to him. When he had finished, I asked the youth a question about an art deco building the other side of the dusty track. 'That building, has it been closed long? 'About twenty years,' he replied. 'Closed because business was bad?' I asked. 'No, business was good, they just moved away.' Down what passed as a street was a hotel. 'Can we get a meal here?' I asked. 'If you wait a few minutes,' came the reply. We waited some 30 minutes in a bar filled with workers from the Main Roads Department. As a bell began to toll, these men raced for what passed as a dining room, a shed with wooden trestle tables and benches. Post-haste we followed and secured six places on benches at a crude table. The waitress, a giant of a woman with a bristling moustache, advanced towards us. We were a great curiosity to her. 'What would youse be doin' 'ere?' she enquired. 'We've come for dinner,' I replied. The waitress's expression was one of pure contempt. 'There's boiled cabbage and beef,' she announced. The Main Roads men were getting restless; we were clearly getting between them and their evening meal. 'Can I see the menu, please,' I innocently enquired. Before the giant could speak again, Charlie Diesel whispered, 'Run for the trucks.' Snowy, Romilly, Oliver and my father-in-law were already in the street. I followed them as fast as I could into the trucks and we were away. A few miles on we stopped, and I asked, 'What was all that about?' 'She thought that you were taking the piss out of her. At best, she would have beaten you up, more likely the whole mob of them would have set on us. They have to live with that monster; upset her and they don't eat.' It is true that as we left I had noticed the Main Roads men come pouring out of the canteen like a swarm of angry wasps.

᭳

Among all the dangers in the outback, the waitresses in small towns are the most fearful. In the north, the people rise early and get on with the day. We arrived in Derby at about 5.30 a.m. and walked into the local hotel, not the smart new brick construction with a swimming pool and an abundant supply of air hostesses, rather the atmospheric hotel just down the road. 'What do youse want?' Once again, it was a waitress. Once again it did not occur to her that we might be visiting her restaurant in search of food. 'Can we get breakfast here?' I enquired. 'Are youse off the street?' she replied. In time, I discovered that this meant that we had not spent the night in the hotel. There was only one other couple eating breakfast. I walked over to a table by the window. 'Youse can't sit there.' 'Well, where can I sit?' 'Over with them. I'm not dirtying a table just for youse.' And so it went on. Small town after small town—friendly people, hostile waitresses. Is this just me, I wondered, or is it a phenomenon of rural Australia that I have discovered? Far better to eat Snowy County's main roads stew at a campsite, to sleep under the stars, wash in streams when you can find them, and share a basin of precious water when you cannot, than to suffer the taunts of these outback dictators and eat their foul food.

After a heavy storm the night before, we were driving down the Tanami Track in 1983 on the way from Broome to Sydney. It continued to rain constantly that day and we were bogged down several times. Further on down the Track, we helped tow a low loader with a V8 bulldozer on it out of the red mud of the pindan by hitching both our vehicles together. It was a spectacular sight to see these two small vehicles pull this great lorry and its even heavier load out of the pindan. When the low loader moved, it came away like a cork out of a bottle of champagne. A night in Alice, four days and nights in the Simpson Desert and the Channel Country and we reached Burke.

After Burke, the driving was boring, the weather wet and cold. Mid-morning, we stopped to visit the zoo at Dubbo, which had been completed not long before we arrived there, and a fine zoo it is, built to accommodate some of the larger mammals from Taronga Park Zoo in Sydney. These great beasts—hippos, rhinos, elephants, giraffes and the rest—can be seen in their large paddocks from a series of small car parks as you move around the zoo in your motor vehicle. The place was all very new when we arrived there; lots of concrete and some tiny trees. Now, I suppose it has matured, the trees grown high and the concrete hidden. The rain fell around us with a solid consistency; the animals sought shelter as best they could. The weather was cold and, try as they might to reproduce Africa, the planners of Dubbo Zoo had produced a landscape which the weather changed into one not so very different from that of northern Europe.

While I was interested in the zoo's layout and its animals, the whole thing seemed terribly unsatisfactory by comparison with the hot red earth and sunshine of my zoo in the North-West. Dubbo itself is not an exciting town and when it rains, it is not a place that encourages you to linger. We sought somewhere to eat breakfast, without much success, so we carried on to the Blue Mountains, with its high peaks, forested slopes and chalets that seem to come from the turn of the century. On hairpin bends, we looked down into deep valleys with small farms resting in their folds. Farms that had post-and-rail paddocks, with horses and cows. Once again, there was something terribly European about the whole place. I had not come all this way to visit Switzerland or Liechtenstein. I did not care a lot for the Blue Mountains. I am a desert man, not a man of the mountains. I have always suffered from vertigo; I really disliked the narrow curling roads that wound their way through these mountains and I abhor panoramic views. Too much all at once is never good, has always been my thinking. Driving through the suburbs of Sydney, two trucks in convoy recently arrived from the deep bush, we felt so superior to the automatons who drove to and from their work each day amid dreams of golf and sailing. We, after a week, were men and women of the stars and sands, the camp fires and the bush. At the Wentworth Hotel, the doorman greeted us as if we had just arrived in a stretched white Mercedes and our laden trucks were hastily despatched to the hotel's garage.

⸜⸝

Sadly, this was the last trip that we made with Oliver Ford. He died on 17 October 1992, killed by emphysema. He died suddenly while standing in the Great Hall of his home at Lacock—in his later years, he was hard to entice from there. Virtually retired from his business, he devoted his time to his garden, and a remarkable garden it was. Oliver had a certain touch with gardens. His reluctance to travel may well have misled those who knew him only in his last years, for he was in fact a great traveller, not by any means a tourist, but a real traveller who undertook long journeys. He was the most congenial of travelling companions, filled with humour, seldom grumbling, although he in fact disliked foreign food, preferring steak and chips to curry and the other concoctions of the Orient.

In Singapore once, after four days of Chinese food—I am addicted to Chinese cooking—I asked Oliver where he wished to dine. He chose a Japanese restaurant, one specialising in *teppan yaki*. I was a bit surprised at this, but he ordered only chopped steak and quietly bemoaned the missing chips. One night we visited the old Bugis Street. This street was pure theatre. It was filled with tourists who in their turn became part of the spectacle that tourists came to watch. These were the days of the Vietnam War. There were soldiers and sailors who, as the evening grew late, drank and sang; local musicians and vendors came, as the audience, lubricated by Singapore beer, became generous with their money. Then began the parade of the transvestites—soon they were all muddled up. Sailors, tourists, and transvestites, all on the most friendly of terms. Oliver and I were watching all this when a transvestite sat on his lap. 'I am a pretend Mary Poppins,' this exotic creature announced, though how he came to that conclusion eludes me, for a more far-fetched version of that demure creature would be hard to find. Oliver protested, the transvestite kissed him on his bald head and set off to find new pickings. The soldiers and sailors were all drunk, the tourists began to go home, the pimps became more insistent, fights broke out, bottles and glasses smashed. We headed for our hotel. As we climbed from the trishaw, Oliver, offering to pay, found his wallet had gone. Pretend Mary Poppins had not been quite as innocent as she wished us to believe.

Oliver Ford was direct about his life: 'Camp as a row of tents,' he often used to say, and to a female client who boasted of her Queen Anne dining-room chairs: 'My dear, I have more chance of being Queen Anne than those chairs.' But this was the stuff of London. I also knew him in the Australian outback where there is red dust and bogged vehicles. When I remember Oliver, it is not fine curtains and grand houses I think of, but the Tanami Track, the banks of the

Diamantina River and the Simpson Desert, sleeping on the sand in a swag under the stars, more stars than in all the heavens put together. He was to my wife Romilly and I, a good friend.

゜

It's strange driving in the outback, you see long stretches of bush that all seem the same but, in fact, change every quarter of an hour that you drive. The change is subtle but definite. There are areas of what seem like total dereliction, then areas of immense beauty, beauty on a scale unequalled anywhere in the world. It is no surprise that Aboriginals believe that God is in the land. Gorges with pools of water, dark and seemingly bottomless, rock walls that climb into an endlessly blue sky. No cathedral constructed by mankind has this dignity, nor this beauty.

When travelling in northern Australia, it is nature that wins the day, the nature of Australia, the world's oldest continent—the strange paradox is that people the world over refer to Australia as a new continent. Its people are so direct they make Americans appear tactful. I am, if nothing else, a collector, I will go to great lengths in putting together a collection. On the face of it, the Australian outback would not seem a promising place for collectors, but the reverse is true. One of the choicest of my collections is to be found there. It consists of the work of man and of nature, combined to form a culture unique to this continent. But before elaborating, let me dispose of some of the more familiar Australian collections that I am not referring to here.

Australiana, for instance. This means acquiring an object—any object—that has a kangaroo or an emu on it: jugs, tins, odds and ends. This is not collecting, it is accumulating. Nor do I mean Aboriginal art, though a tradition that is several thousand years old has produced objects that range from the incredibly beautiful to the mundane. I do not even mean the great painters, like Arthur Streeton of the early twentieth century, or those other twentieth-century Australian masters, Sidney Nolan and John Olsen.

The collection I admire the most was put together by God. I am thinking of the big pieces, not of the smaller natural objects—the incredible range of shells on the coastline; the amazing fossils, sometimes opalised to produce objects that would do credit to a Renaissance court jeweller; the birds; and the pearls of unequalled size and lustre. The collection I am thinking of—the masterpieces of nature that enrich this continent—contains no objects that can be held in the hand or placed in a cabinet: the vastness of the Simpson Desert; the waterfalls on the Prince Regent River; Uluru, carved by the wind and rain to a shape that, from the air, looks like a great red sleeping dog; and the Bungle Bungles, those recently discovered domes that rise from the earth like papal crowns, bejewelled with the bright green hanging gardens caught in their crevasses.

In the gorges in the Kimberley you stand alone yet always sense someone else's presence. It could be an Aboriginal behind the bush, or God—you take your pick. In the Wittenoom Gorge in the Hamersley Range are high rock faces that leave an impression to compare with Indian temples or Gothic cathedrals. These works of art were created by the heaving of the seabed and the chiselling of the wind. The collector stands in awe of their greatness and wonders whether any gilt-framed canvas will ever seem the same again, whether any man can reproduce such great beauty. Reproductions, however, like the memory, fade.

∽

Photographs in tourist brochures are delightful, but they fail to tell the truth about this hard land in northern Australia, where drought and famine are commonplace and there is seldom a feast. A place where there is either no rain or too much rain. When rivers flood, water spreads for hundreds of kilometres, it is a beautiful but inhospitable place. For the first white men to cross the continent, coping with nature meant cheating death.

12

I did not only travel in the north by truck, I had journeys by boat and aeroplane as well. I often made boat trips from Broome among the humpback whales that migrate along the coastline, watching from a few metres away as these extraordinary animals rose out of the water and then sank back, heading for the depths. Turning again, they broke the water's surface, rising out of it like missiles, only to fall back again, sending spray in great quantities all over our small boat. I used to go fishing, but after a while I had no desire to continue for we caught too many fish, sometimes as many as 60 or 70 in a morning. Once while we fished, my daughter Victoria was both holding a line and reading a book. She caught three large red emperor fish on the same line, almost without realising it. Later on, while we ate lunch, she swam in the picture-postcard sea beside our boat. Lunch finished, I threw my line over the side and caught a sizeable fish. After a considerable struggle, I brought aboard a cod whose body must have been the size of Victoria's. I write 'must have been', for the body had been taken by a shark and only the head was left. Flying over the islands east of One Arm Point, I watched a vast shark lying in the tide race, moving lazily from side to side in order to catch the fish that were forced towards it by the tide.

୶୶

When I first arrived in Broome, Siggi Halter was among the people to whom I was introduced. Siggi was the local charter pilot in Broome. Siggi flew me over large parts of Western Australia and the Northern Territory. On one of these flights we flew to the Bungle Bungles; it was not possible, however, to land near the Bungles. This was the first time that I had seen these curious mountains and I was deeply impressed by the scale of the whole place. They seemed to stretch for miles. As a result of my cursory visit, I was left with a strong urge to return to the Bungle Bungles. We flew on to the Argyle diamond mine. I had never seen a diamond mine before, not least from the air, and I was a bit disappointed with the experience. The hole was impressive mostly for its size, which I suppose is a great deal bigger these days as the mine was then only just getting started.

Lake Argyle, however, was another matter. Siggi began to take the plane down until we were less than 30 metres from the ground when we crossed the southern shore of the lake. The land on the run-up to the lake was swamp-land. Flocks of birds, many of them pelicans, rose into the air as we passed over them. Still Siggi allowed the plane to lose height until we nearly touched the surface of the water. It was an exhilarating experience: the bright sunlight, red hot above and cool water rushing past below. The edge of this artificial lake was trimmed with dead trees rotting in the water that had killed them. Many of the trees were stained white from the excrement of the birds that used them as a lookout in the never-ending hunt for fish. As with the Bungle Bungles and so many of Australia's natural curiosities, it is the scale of Lake Argyle that is so impressive. One other matter sets Lake Argyle apart from all the rest and that is the fact that the lake is man-made—man-made and eight times the size of Sydney Harbour. It is a waterhole that will one day help to dramatically change the north-west of Australia. A few years later, I was taken on a boat ride across Lake Argyle and had a close look at its islands and the rare rock wallabies that live on them. Siggi lifted the nose of our aircraft and we shot over the narrow dam that holds back Argyle's waters. Up into the sky and round the township of Kununurra we circled, coming in to land at its suburban airport.

The next time that I visited the Bungle Bungles, we were able to land. Once again, Siggi flew me there and on arrival we dodged between mountain caps. These mountains were boils on the ocean floor millions of years ago. Forced up by volcanic activity, they now form a curious mountain range, with palm trees growing where their roots can find water, making small rainforests among these mountains in the desert. We landed nearby and walked or clambered as best we could in the heat amongst the inhospitable rocks. There are now tourist facilities at the Bungle Bungles, but when I first went there it was a wild and savage place, where an explorer with a camera had caught on film what seemed to be shots of the long-extinct Tasmanian Tiger as it ran between the rocks.

Often, animals, in particular birds, are believed to be extinct and are then found again. Such birds are the night parrot and the paradise parrot which is, as its name implies, one of the world's most beautiful parrots; both were believed to have been lost to the world. While travellers tell with certainty of places where the night parrot can be found, only rumours keep occurring that tell of the paradise parrot. Indeed, one rumour suggests that an aviculturalist from Queensland knows where the paradise parrot is to be found in the wild, while others suggest that certain aviculturalists have this bird in their collections.

Once, in London, I was invited to lunch by the Royal Geographic Society. Their premises, near the Albert Memorial, are truly wonderful, filled with the memorabilia of exploration. Lunch was already served as we sat at the small round table, about six of us. I finished my first course, a salad of some sort, and, as my plate was removed, I noticed beneath it a small brass plate. It read: 'Upon this table in the house of his friend John Arrowsmith FRGS, David Livingstone worked out the geographical records of his missionary travels in Africa'. The subject of our discussion over lunch was a projected expedition to explore the Kimberley around the Prince Regent River and the Mitchell Plateau, an area to the north-east of Broome. The next year, in 1985, a team of 40 scientists arrived at what they described as the last great, unexplored wilderness in the world. While every day flora and fauna disappear from our planet, it is also true that every day new flora and fauna are discovered. This expedition discovered a great number of new insects and many new forms of plant life. While the Prince Regent River is sometimes visited by tourists who take their boats right up to the waterfalls, it was once the site of a tragic accident. A party of young people swam

The Parmelia, Perth

amersley House, Perth

The fully restored Bishops House, Perth

Cable Beach Club, Broome

The Pearl Coast Zoological Gardens, Broome

Dancing with a brolga crane at my Pearl Coast Zoological Gardens

My wife Romilly, by the McAlpine Oval in Broome

Albert Roux, putting the finishing touches to a wonderful lunch, in my kitchen at Broome

The dining room under the mangoes at Broome. Romilly is on my left and my daughter Skye is in the foreground on the left.

Myself and Snowy County with the pearl harvest

Myself, John Adams, John Roberts and Dennis Cully at the America's Cup Ball

Margaret Olley dancing, after a dinner party at
Joan Bowers' house

The last remaining trick from a youthful
repertoire as a conjuror

Myself and Margaret Olley at Joan Bowers' house

Myself and Romilly at Margaret Olley's house

Myself and Joan Bowers at Margaret Olley's house

Dining with John Olsen and Joan Bowers before John's retrospective at the National Gallery in Melbourne

Dining with John Roberts

ashore; two men climbed the falls while the girls stayed behind on the rocks. As the tide came in, so did a crocodile. One of the girls, Ginger Meadows, a young American model, was taken by that crocodile.

Mitchell Plateau, on the other hand, has very few visitors despite there being an airstrip there. Once I sent a small party of guests to this remote place for a picnic, Siggi Halter flying them there in a light plane. As they ate their lunch, a helicopter arrived carrying a survey party from an oil company. 'What are you lot doing here?' they asked my English guests. 'Just having a picnic,' one of them, Dame Shirley Oxenbury, replied. 'Do you always come to places like this for your picnics?' the surveyors enquired. 'Oh, yes,' replied Dame Shirley. No-one lives within hundreds of kilometres of their picnic spot.

◈

The Ord River leads from Lake Argyle to the sea, some sixty kilometres from the dam, and empties its water into the Joseph Bonaparte Gulf. The town of Wyndham sits on the estuary that feeds that gulf. At low tide, the great mudflats of the estuary are empty, empty, that is, except for crocodiles; at high tide, the swirling waters are filled with danger. I had been to visit a man in Wyndham who bred finches, and I often bought stock for my zoo from him. This man kept a 5-metre crocodile as a pet in a mud hole in his garden. There is not much to see in Wyndham—the town sits broken into three parts: 12-mile, 6-mile and Wyndham, in the shadow of a great red rock. At the time I first went there it boasted a meatworks and a racetrack. Crocodiles lay on the mudflats around the meatworks; seen from the jetty, they looked like so many maggots lying on a rotting carcass. Today, the meatworks has closed and the town has a crocodile farm instead.

Once, I travelled down the Ord River in a tin punt driven by a small outboard motor. I had been to see Carlton Hill Station and my companion was Susan Bradley, the flamboyant shire president from Kununurra whose husband, David, was the local vet who also owned that station. Susan thought that I might like a trip on the river, some barramundi fishing and a night in the bush. There can be no doubt that I enjoyed myself thoroughly as we moved at a leisurely pace down the Ord River. The banks of the river were low, the depth of the water shallow and the width of the river not great. Bushes grew along the banks and as we passed the Bradleys' station, we could see the cattle grazing in the distance. The sun shone and it was an idyllic lazy afternoon. We fished for barramundi and caught several of a good eating size. As for crocodiles, we saw only a few and those that we saw seemed for all the world to be sound asleep. When we climbed into the punt, I had noticed that the boatman carried an automatic shotgun and a box of cartridges loaded with buckshot. After an hour or so, I concluded that he was just of a cautious nature. That night, we dined on grilled barramundi, slept well on the riverbank, and in the morning returned the way we had come. I asked the boatman about the crocodiles. He told me that he had seldom had any trouble with them until the week before, when he was filling a large metal billy can with water from the river and a crocodile sprang from nowhere taking the can instead of his hand and his arm.

Some months later, I had cause to be in Kununurra looking for a site to build a hotel. Hiring a helicopter, I travelled the length of the Ord River. Given the advantage of height over the clear water of the river, I could see what lay below the surface. The whole river was swarming with crocodiles, mostly of the extremely large variety. There they were lying on the river's bottom, waiting for a meal to come their way. As I remembered that pleasant afternoon with Susan Bradley, the memories sent shivers down my spine. When all looks so peaceful, it is easy not to take the crocodiles seriously. I took them so seriously, however, that when I bought a site at Kununurra—as part of my strategy to build a chain of hotels between Exmouth and Darwin—I chose a caravan site on the upper stretch of the river, where there are supposed to be no crocodiles. Heaven alone knows why this should be the case, unless the presence of so many people has driven them away. My wife Romilly and our friend Lucy Nelson, a tall, svelte blonde, swam there and came to no harm. Happily, they had not seen the crocodiles in the lower part of the river.

Crocodiles were, however, always on my mind when we travelled in the outback. Always cautious, I asked a station hand who sold me fuel on a trip from Broome to Darwin by the Gibb River Road—which is in reality a stony track: 'Are there any crocodiles in Bell Gorge?' He replied with considerable contempt for my obvious temerity, 'No.' And then he added, 'Well, only Johnson River crocs.' These are small crocodiles about a metre long. 'Will they bite me?' I asked. 'Only if you step on them,' and then, 'I would bite you if you stepped on me.' Never take chances with crocodiles in the north of Australia, there is no such thing as a harmless crocodile. The extraordinary thing about people and crocodiles is that people seldom realise the risk they take with these animals. While flying in a helicopter, I have often seen a family lying in the sun or fishing on a riverbank while behind a nearby bush is a crocodile. Such families always seem oblivious to the crocodile's existence. The curator of birds at San Diego Zoo once told me that he had tried keeping birds and crocodiles together. Over a period of a week, most of the birds vanished, so he kept watch to discover what was happening. It was not long before he saw a crocodile rise out of the water to take a bird in flight four metres above it.

When I flew up the Prince Regent River a few feet above its surface, it was the same. The crocodiles, some of an immense size, could be seen as they slept below the greenish water. Or did they sleep? The saltwater crocodile is a mammal unchanged for forty million years, the finest killing machine that God ever invented. I asked Siggi whether it was safe to fly so low. 'No worries,' he replied. 'I've done a lot of this in the jets of the German air force.' The jets of the German air force, I pondered, are specially equipped for low flying, whereas in a Cessna you do it by eye. We flew among the thousand islands of the Buccaneer Archipelago. One of these islands is quite spectacular: in its middle it has a considerable lake with two inflows for water from the sea. As the tide rises, water rushes in through these narrow channels until the lake is filled. When the tide drops, which it does in a matter of minutes, the lake begins to empty, squirting water out through the narrow channels. These waterspouts shoot high above the water level of the sea and extend about a hundred metres from the island on either side. The Buccaneer Archipelago must, with its whirlpools and waterspouts, be one of the most beautiful pieces of ocean anywhere in the world. A thousand or so islands dotted in a bright blue sea, whose water is so clear that, from the air, its giant fish are easily visible.

On one return journey, we stopped at Karratha for fuel. While the plane was being refuelled, my companion, Clodagh Waddington, and I took a car into town, or rather to the dock where we were shown heaps of rocks with carvings of fish. What was different about these rocks from other rocks that we had seen with fish and snakes carved on them, was that an attempt had been made to terrace some of them. Only remnants of this terracing remained but terracing it appeared to be, nevertheless. Our guide regarded this terracing as highly significant for, despite being unable to date it apart from the fact that it was very old, this terracing proved that the Aboriginals at some period had taken an interest in gardening or agriculture. Some years later, when I visited an island in Collier Bay, we found pits filled with stones which were used by the Aboriginals to grow yams. The stones collected the moisture from the air and watered the yams which grew longer as they tried to reach the water at the bottom of the pit. When the yams were fully grown, being planted in stones made it all the easier to pull them out of the ground.

⚜

Darwin is a city that I have always enjoyed. When I first visited it in 1980, it was a strange mixture of modernisation and the culture of the Australian outback. Houses built of timber and corrugated iron that were spared by the terrible cyclone, Cyclone Tracy, that devastated Darwin on Christmas Day 1974, rubbed shoulders with modern office blocks and hotels. Trucks just out of the bush jostled in the traffic with the latest models from Mercedes-Benz. The outback trucks, which have extensions from their exhaust pipes fixed to their driving cabs which allow them to cross fairly deep rivers, always seemed to carry a jumble of baggage, with dogs sitting atop, swags and other equipment piled on the flat body behind the driver. In Darwin, you could walk out from a modern hotel fitted out to a very high standard and into the local hotel bar with characters as rough and ready as they come. Once walking down the mall in Darwin, with my middle daughter Victoria, I came across a character who threatened to fight anyone who came his way. Luckily, someone had knocked him over by the time we came near. The shops of Darwin sold useful goods as well as fancy stuff, very fancy stuff. My youngest daughter Skye was about five when I first took her to Darwin. Skye fell in love with a bridesmaid's dress that must have been intended to be worn during a Greek wedding. For a few dollars, I bought this exotic confection for her. Happily, in time she grew out of this extravagant dress and now has developed a sharp eye and good taste in the matter of fashion. Usually when I was in Darwin, I called on the shop that sold Aboriginal arts and crafts, never leaving it without a pile of packages to be sent home to Broome.

∽

In the early 1980s, my friend Barry Sharp and I visited a number of places in the Kimberley. Barry's shop had changed dramatically since the day that I first visited Broome. Gone was the old butcher's shop; Paspaley's Pearl shop stands there now, as smart a shop as you would find in the main shopping streets of any of the world's capitals. In fact, today in Broome there are a number of jewellery shops selling diamonds from the Argyle mine and pearls from the coast around Broome, set together to the highest professional standards. In fact, it is no romantic exaggeration to state that the pearls available for sale today in Broome are better than those in any other place except, perhaps, Paspaley Jewellers shop in Sydney, where you can find at least their equal. Barry and Kerry Sharp's emporium of the mid-1980s, however, was not as grand as the Broome jewellery shops of today. It was, nevertheless, a fascinating place. Kerry's collection of shells had grown since we first met and now were carefully displayed in smart showcases. A stonefish, one of the most deadly fish in the North-West, rested in an aquarium waiting in vain for some creature to step on it as a preliminary to becoming its lunch. Sea snakes curled and twisted in their own aquarium, surrounded by baskets of shells and trays of souvenirs made from shell. Hung on the walls were skulls of sharks, their large and deadly teeth bared for all to see, along with Aboriginal artefacts, the shells of turtles and sawfish snouts. Needless to say, Barry also sold pearls. He also had a number of mother-of-pearl pubic shields, which were hung around the waist on hair belts by the Aboriginals during some of their ceremonies. They were mostly carved with geometric patterns. Some, however, were not used in ceremonies and were carved with fish and sea-going mammals. 'Butcher' Joe Nangan carved a number of these pubic shields, as did a gentleman called Sampi.

Once I saw a pubic shield carved with the image of a motor car that would now be a rare vintage item and, in the days that the shell was carved, must indeed have been an even rarer sight in the Kimberley. These early innovative shell carvings, that depicted the artefacts of the civilised east of Australia on the traditional ceremonial equipment of the north-western Aboriginals, interested me very much indeed. Asking Barry Sharp if he had seen such carvings, I was delighted when he replied in the affirmative. He had seen a mother-of-pearl shell with an aeroplane carved on it; a bi-plane, probably from the 1920s. The next day we set off for One Arm Point and the Lombadina Mission where this wondrous pearl shell was reputed to be found. One Arm Point is near the tip of Cape Leveque, a place of rocks and boiling water as the seas race between small islands. On our way to One Arm Point, our light plane passed over a promontory into the sea that surrounds the Buccaneer Archipelago. Below us was a beach with sand as white as the paper used in this book. We flew low over a creek where a giant crocodile, at least six metres long, lay visible beneath the shallow water. Not far from the coast, we saw a school of whales which seemed to be playing rather than travelling. As we approached the rough landing strip at One Arm Point, I could see the lighthouse and a few habitations that are now used to house tourists who visit the place.

Our landing was bumpy but safe, and soon we were met by a truck whose Aboriginal driver greeted Barry like the friend that he is to the Bardi people, who live nearby. After a short but rough drive, we arrived at the settlement. Barry introduced me to the Aboriginal who owned the mother-of-pearl shell and, after considerable discussion, he offered to show it to us. We followed him to his home, a corrugated iron building raised off the ground on short metal posts. Most of two sides of this building consisted of glass louvres, although much of this glass was broken and the rest so caked with dirt that you could see neither in nor out. The Aboriginal owner asked us to wait while he went inside to fetch his famous possession. It was then that the strangest thing happened. As Barry and I watched, a long arm came out from between the glass louvres and moved towards the ground, then its hand dug around in the loose earth below the building. Finding what was sought, the arm, the hand and a carved mother-of-pearl shell were retracted through the window into the house. In a moment or two, the owner of the pearl shell joined us and, unwrapping a piece of old newspaper, he produced a brand-new, carved pearl shell. True enough, the shell did have a carving of an old bi-plane on it, but it was not the shell that I sought. As a matter of politeness, I bought that shell and several others that its owner had carved.

The mother-of-pearl shells that I bought at Lombadina were different from the carved shells that I had bought at La Grange Mission, where the carver told me that each of the geometric patterns used in carved mother-of-pearl shells was a 'key'. (A sign of identification is what I believe he meant.) In any event, he was quite clear that each pattern was the property of one man and that no-one except that man's heirs must carve that pattern. Generally, carved mother-of-pearl shells come from the coastal regions of the North-West and are then traded to tribes living more towards the centre of Australia. The tribes who buy these shells believe that carved pearl shells have the power to bring rain; scrapings from the shells are thrown into the air during rain-making ceremonies. As a result, the carved pearl shells that you might find in Alice Springs, for instance, are much smaller and of far greater religious significance than those found in and around Broome, where they are used merely in dance ceremonies and for trade.

❦

Carved mother-of-pearl shell is also used in love magic and is regarded as having a powerful effect. While, to a person of European descent, all of this may seem strange and quite barbaric, it is worth remembering that Doge Dandilo, a thirteenth-century Doge of Venice, used to eat each day scrapings from a narwhal's horn. He and his contemporaries believed both that this horn came from a unicorn and that to eat it guaranteed long life. Doge Dandilo led his Venetian troops at the sacking of Constantinople—at the time he was well into his nineties and blind, yet he was still first over that city's walls. This was an exploit that must have been due to something, but I doubt if it was eating the scrapings of a narwhal's horn. His successors to the position of Doge, no doubt impressed by the effects of this horn on Dandilo, decided to try the same diet. The city's government, however, fearing for the complete destruction of their rare and immensely valuable 'unicorn's horn', banned the practice. The much-scraped narwhal's horn can be seen today in a small room, up a narrow staircase to the right, just inside the main entrance to St Mark's Cathedral.

⌘

Shortly after our visit to One Arm Point, Barry Sharp and I travelled to Kalumburu to visit Father Chris, then the priest at the mission. Kalumburu in its day was a model of what a mission should look like. It had a fine herd of pedigree Brahma cattle and bred fine horses as a result of a gift of a stallion from brother monks in Spain. The mission buildings were laid out in an orderly fashion and its approach was along an avenue of massive mango trees. The place was clean and its gardens produced a whole range of vegetables. In the late 1970s, however, the Government disapproved of the church running these missions, believing instead that the State should take over the running of them and that the education the monks provided should become part of the State education system. The natural discipline that the Catholic religion gave these missions deteriorated into the unruly mould of so many State-run organisations where bureaucracy has killed initiative.

Chris Saunders at Kalumburu, along with the priests at other missions, now played the role of parish priests, responsible only for souls; the fabric of the place was looked after by the civil servants. Despite the change at Kalumburu, Father Chris did a remarkable job and became much admired for his work. Barry Sharp and I arrived by plane with Siggi Halter at its controls. It was a lovely afternoon. I had never met Chris Saunders before. Tall, physically fit, with a strong but gentle face, he is a man of natural authority. He was at the landing strip to greet us as we walked from the plane, offering us tea, which we accepted with enthusiasm. We sat and talked. Barry obviously knew Chris well and clearly had a great respect for him. In time, I was shown around the mission, and I bought two small examples of the art works that the local Aboriginals had made—Wadigji figures, the strange painted images that are almost human in appearance, people from outer space, with helmeted heads showing only eyes, their mouths entirely missing. In the centre of the mission there were a number of round concrete tanks about six metres in diameter. In these were kept small crocodiles, which I imagine had been hatched from eggs found in the river estuary nearby. The crocodile is a strange creature. I once watched one hatch; slowly it bit its way through the leathery skin of its egg. The egg was held by Malcolm Douglas, a considerable expert on crocodiles and the owner of the crocodile parks in Broome. Malcolm told me that the first instinct of a new-born crocodile is to attack whatever comes its way. True to his words, the crocodile, with only its head out of the shell, sank its teeth into his finger. Time passed quickly at Kalumburu, and at the end of a congenial afternoon, Barry Sharp, Siggi Halter and I all flew back to Broome. We crossed low over Walcott Inlet, the surrounding stretch of countryside an area with which I was to become deeply involved.

A few years later, in 1996, Father Chris became Bishop of Broome. His appointment was greeted with great joy by the people of the Kimberley. His diocese is an area of two million square kilometres with only 29 000 souls in it. Over 2000 people turned up for the ceremony in Broome. The service that marked the episcopal ordination of the Most Reverend Christopher Alan Saunders, DD, Bishop of Broome, was for me both a sad and happy occasion—sad to see the departure of Bishop Jobst, happy because the new bishop was Christopher Saunders. The new bishop's predecessor in the Diocese of Broome was a man of considerable standing, relentless in his fight to improve conditions in the Kimberley for Aboriginals and whites alike. Bishop Jobst was a fine, handsome man with steel-grey hair and piercing blue eyes, and a back as straight as an iron fencing picket. Many tales are told of Bishop Jobst—whether these tales are true in their entirety is a matter of conjecture, but they give the feel of the man, if nothing else. On one occasion, while visiting the minister of education in Perth, he made a forceful case for more funds to help with Catholic education. The minister had determined to say 'No'. Bishop Jobst, however, had in his mind that the only answer that was acceptable was 'Yes'. The meeting dragged on and on, the bishop giving no ground. After some time, the minister announced that he had to leave in order to catch a plane. The bishop replied that he would accompany him. I suppose that the minister put up with his arguments as they drove to the airport, imagining that he would be rid of this troublesome priest when he boarded the plane. When that moment arrived, however, the bishop went on board the aircraft with the minister and took the seat beside him. Such was the fame of Bishop Jobst that none of the flight crew batted an eyelid at this behaviour.

Bishop Jobst, I believe, along with Charles Court and a few others, was one of the great advocates for the people of the North-West and the Kimberley at a time when they and their country were regarded by most politicians in Perth as a regrettable nuisance. The Bishop's exploits with aeroplanes were almost as notorious as his art of lobbying politicians. It was his habit to start his aircraft in its hanger, then let the throttle in to take off from a standing start. Once, impatient at idle aircraft staff, who were delaying his take-off by lingering when they were supposed to be fuelling his plane, he took off anyway, coming down out of fuel in the bush somewhere short of his destination. On another occasion, he asked two nuns who were his passengers to hold the throttle while he swung the propeller. Perhaps they were unclear about how they were to hold the throttle or maybe there was just a misunderstanding. In any event, the plane and the nuns went off without him. Mercifully, they crashed at the end of the landing strip and no-one was hurt. Flying with the bishop, Barry Sharp told me, was like accompanying the pilot of a Stuka bomber on a dive-bombing mission. The bishop would approach an airfield and then point the plane's nose towards the ground. Their seemingly endless dive would terminate in a sudden levelling of the plane and a hectic landing.

چ

Bishop Jobst is a fine and good man, who often visited my house in Broome and Romilly and I became very fond of him. On one occasion, over lunch in Broome, he asked if we had ever met the Pope. The answer was 'No'. Bishop Jobst then asked if we would like to meet the Pope; the answer, of course was 'Yes'. Romilly and I thought no more about this conversation until a month or so later, when the invitation for a private audience arrived from His Holiness. That spring, Tom Stephens, the upper house member in the Western Australian Parliament for Broome and the Kimberley set out from Australia and joined us in Rome for this great occasion. The weather was perfect as we presented ourselves to the Swiss Guard at the Vatican's Gate. We were passed from hand to hand along the intricate maze of the Vatican corridors; each guide who took charge of us was rather grander than his predecessor. Finally, a tall and extremely elegant Italian in a tailcoat, white tie and with a heavy gold medal hanging around his neck, took us in a lift to a large and sparsely furnished waiting room. We sat on straight-backed chairs and watched television, which seemed totally out of keeping with the dignity of the room. After a few minutes, the gentleman in the tails turned off the television and a group of Papal officials entered. They ignored us and began a discussion about how the Pope should pronounce my name. Romilly, who is fluent in Italian, explained their conversation to Tom Stephens and myself. It went like this: 'McAlpini', 'No, Alpini' . . . 'Perhaps Alpino'. Then a bishop who had not spoken before said, 'He will just have to sort it out for himself.' The Pope, who spoke perfect English, had no trouble at all with my name. It was a wonderful experience to meet this man who has done so much towards the destruction of communism. I came away with a feeling that he was tired and old, but he had given his life to God and, while it might well have been the inclination of another to retire, His Holiness knew that he had to continue in his arduous task until his end. I felt that I was in the presence of a goodness that I had never come across before. As we walked from the Vatican, we barely spoke: all three of us were greatly moved by the experience of that morning.

We lunched in a restaurant, Piperno's, in the heart of Rome's old Jewish district. We ate simply and then returned to the Vatican where we met an Australian priest who took us below the crypt where the popes are buried, into the Roman graveyard where we saw St Peter's tomb. Legend had always identified the spot; nobody, however, knew for sure if it was the true tomb of St Peter. The tomb was excavated during the Second World War. The Church, believing that the war would mask the outcry if, in fact, it turned out to be the tomb of an unknown man or woman, took the opportunity to carry out the exhumation. In the event, the skeleton was male and matched both the known characteristics of St Peter and the manner of his death. Despite St Peter's having been built long after the graveyard was covered over, the tomb is exactly beneath the hole in the centre of the Cathedral's dome. Again, it was a moving experience, being so close to the roots of a great religion. Later, as we came out of St Peter's, we visited the tourist shops and, like the millions of pilgrims who come every year, we bought our souvenirs.

༺༻

It was on one of my trips in the Kimberley that I was first seriously affected by the disease that was to require me to have heart surgery. There had been problems before. I passed out on a plane on the last stage of my return from a visit to China, and I had passed out during the opera at Glyndebourne. Carried from the auditorium, I was laid out on the floor of the foyer and for some reason the first aid attendant had taken my trousers off before going to get help. Just after I had come round, a flood of people who had been watching the opera joined me. I felt rather silly lying on the floor wearing a black dinner jacket, a bow tie and no trousers. Doctors had told me that there was nothing much wrong with me except I was overweight. Then one Sunday night, after a long and heavy lunch in the country, I had travelled to London. At about eleven thirty that evening, after I had been asleep for about an hour, I awoke feeling sick and suffering from what at first I took to be indigestion. In time, I decided that it was my heart. Romilly disagreed with me, saying I had drunk and eaten too well which, of course, was also true. The next day the doctor confirmed her opinion, adding that I had a hiatus hernia. At a London clinic, I had tests for this hernia, which confirmed my doctor's opinion. A packet of pills was the cure. I left his office much relieved.

In time, I left as usual to spend the English summer of 1987 in Australia. I did not feel well as we drove from Broome to Darwin through the Kimberley. Along the Gibb River Road, which was barely a track, are a number of small lakes and waterfalls in rocky country inaccessible by motor vehicle. We—my two eldest daughters, two girlfriends of theirs, Romilly, Snowy, Charlie Diesel and myself—decided to walk to one of these lakes, called Bell Gorge. That morning we had breakfasted in Derby just after six, in an outback hotel with outback staff and outback food. In this type of hotel, it was, as I have written, quite normal to be asked to share a table to save dirtying another tablecloth. There were enough of us on this occasion, however, to warrant a table to ourselves. I ate a plate of kidneys and bacon covered in brown sauce, fried bread, potatoes, beans and tomatoes, toast and marmalade, all washed down with a mug of coffee. The sun was hot as we walked to Bell Gorge down a steep slope, climbing over rocks until we reached the water. The girls stripped off their clothes and stood under the waterfalls; Snowy and Charlie swam in the clear water of the small lake; I sat on a rock feeling short of breath and sick.

For some days my left arm had ached. I believed that the pain came from my posture at meals, that my chair was too low or my table too high. As we set out to climb back to our vehicles, I lagged behind. I felt pain in my chest and was violently sick. Snowy came back and helped me. We all put my illness down to a heavy breakfast and the hot sun. I drove on and two days later, after two nights sleeping in the bush, we reached Darwin.

When we returned to Broome it was to a political battle over my idea of building an airport. A public meeting was called and I had an overwhelming majority of 1200 to six, or something of that order. A petition in favour of the airport was circulated, and was signed by over 2000 of Broome's inhabitants. Then it was back to London and to a difficult Conservative Party Conference at Blackpool.

At the Party Conference, I felt tired and ill. On the Monday after it, I visited my doctor who arranged for me to see a heart specialist the next day. Foolishly, I missed the appointment and it was the Wednesday afternoon before I met with the heart specialist. By Thursday, I was in the Wellington Hospital having an angiogram. The best artery that I had leading to my heart was working at 40 per cent of its capacity; the worst, at 10 per cent. 'Do not even get out of bed,' the heart specialist told me. 'I want to get a really good surgeon, and I want him to operate tomorrow. He will need to be fresh; this is going to be a long job.' I was, on the whole, rather relieved by this news. At least I knew what was wrong with me. The next day, Gareth Rees operated on my heart for eight-and-a-half hours. When I woke in the Intensive Care Unit of the Wellington Hospital, I asked how it had gone. 'Six bypasses,' he replied. 'Bloody heck,' I mumbled, and dozed off. The nurses kept waking me. I was desperately thirsty, so they gave me cubes of ice made from lime juice to suck, which I thought a wonderful invention. As I lay I could hear the voices of Romilly and Olga Polizzi, who both sat with me all night.

Romilly slept in my room when I was out of intensive care, and it was wonderfully reassuring to have her there. As it turned out, I had been very lucky, for my activities of the previous year had not been ideal for a person with a heart that was barely working. Later, my doctor told me that it was my lack of exercise that had saved me. 'Had you ever played squash or taken heavy exercise, you would have died of a heart attack.'

13

Pearls, diamonds and cattle are found in the Kimberley, the world's last great unexplored wilderness, now officially explored but, for all that, still a vast wilderness many times larger than the state of Texas. For many generations, the wealth there sprang from cattle. In the Kimberley, cattle stations can run anywhere from half a million hectares in size to literally millions of hectares, and the owners of the largest stations were kings. Their world was well-ordered: the Aboriginals who worked for them received no wages; on the other hand, the station owners provided food and accommodation for their workers' extended families. This they regarded as generous and I believe that they were sincere in this respect. They were, however, clearly without remorse for the fact that they had taken the land that provided their wealth from the very people who were the recipients of their apparent generosity. While it is clear that a number of station owners formed a real and often lasting relationship with the Aboriginals they employed, this was not always the case, particularly with the large cattle companies who were, in effect, absentee employers. They often became the object of considerable hatred. The lot of the Aboriginal was not a happy one, despite the facts that the white fellows brought them education and medicine. They also brought disease, alcohol and the notion of poverty. One cannot deny that this grievous state of affairs happened, however why should it be a bar to a civilised existence in which the Aboriginals play an equal part with their fellow Australians, who currently happen to be all shades of white and yellow?

꿍

Today, cattle stations are close to becoming a liability. The station that my family owned was Roebuck Plains, just south of Broome with

Roebuck Bay on its western side. The man who managed it for me, David Thom, was well-known for his knowledge of cattle and how to handle them. He set out to make Roebuck Plains into a model cattle station. The old hybrid stock were phased out and new pedigree Brahma cattle were imported from Queensland. The ancestors of these cattle originally came from India. They are successful in the Kimberley because they generally have a quiet temperament, unlike the local cattle, and their skin is nearly hairless, thus making them resistant to cattle ticks. Australians like big, red cows whereas the Brahma are a pale tan, white, brown, black or even a dusty shade of blue: a herd of cattle looks so much better if it is of one colour, so we set about dividing our herds into different groups, each of the same colour. The land was fenced, paddocks built with runways between them, to ease the handling of the cattle. Towards the end of the years that my family owned Roebuck Plains, the quality of the stock had risen and the place was prospering. Roebuck Plains, however, was not bought for its cattle or for its broad hectares. I needed a strip of land, just a few hundred hectares out of over 300 000 on that station to build an airport. It would be easier and, I believed, cheaper to buy the whole place rather than to try and negotiate an excision of land from another owner. Despite this, I wanted to make Roebuck Plains into a cattle station to be proud of and on my behalf David Thom succeeded in achieving that very thing. On the station was a dried-up lake called Eda. I am bound to say that when I drove across the station for the first time with the owner's agent, the whole place looked like a dust bowl, overstocked and under-watered. You would never have guessed that Lake Eda had ever existed, although the owner's agent claimed that he had been waterskiing on it during the wet season.

It was David Thom's careful management and the slow build-up of cattle numbers that turned the land from dust to soil-bearing grass. Among the first things to be done, when I took over the station, was to set about building proper accommodation for the station workers; the place was a mess. Indeed, the first cyclone would have taken it all away. At the same time, I decided to fence off Lake Eda and about

8000 hectares around it. It was always my intention one day to move the large mammals in the collection at my zoo from the township of Broome, leaving the zoo containing only parrots, small mammals and birds. In the space of about three years Lake Eda returned to its natural state. Without cattle, the lake held its water or the greater part of it for the whole year. The bush around the lake regenerated the place—in a word, it became a paradise. Now large groups of brolga cranes gather there, jabiru storks stand in the shallows and fish swim in the waters of Lake Eda. Water birds cover the lake in the dry, wading birds come there during the wet. On the coastline of Roebuck Bay that edges the station, there is a bird-watching post. When we pulled down the accommodation at the caravan park that is now the Cable Beach Intercontinental, I gave several of the cabins to the local bird-watching society. A few guests pay each year to watch the migration arrive and these cabins provide their accommodation. There is, however, no season in the Kimberley when conditions are not good for bird-watchers and certainly an evening spent at Lake Eda would be the high spot of such an expedition. The beauty of Roebuck Plains and Lake Eda is that they are only about twenty kilometres from the town of Broome. In the end, Roebuck Plains station was sold in 1994, along with the rest of my family's company, Australian City Properties. Now the great days of cattle over, the meat works in Wyndham and Broome are closed, and the age of the farmer in the Kimberley is just beginning.

The land around Kununurra is prosperous farming country. The road between Broome and the turn-off to Derby and the north is now populated with a series of agricultural holdings. These farms are producing a variety of fruits and vegetables. Their watermelons are formidable—heavy with juice and filled with flavour, they have to compete, however, in the markets of southern Western Australia when they should be sold in the north or exported to Singapore, Indonesia and Malaysia. It is only a matter of time before someone produces pineapples on that immensely fertile soil around Broome. The problem, however, is the distance from the perceived markets in the south, and a lack of speedy transport to the markets of the countries to the north. A modern airport would of course resolve this problem, an airport that could take the large freight-carrying aeroplanes.

⁂

Pearls are another source of wealth in Western Australia. In the waters of the Kimberley almost 80 per cent of the world's cultured pearls are grown. When in Darwin, I would visit Nick Paspaley, a leading master pearler and his family, on occasion buying pearls from him but more often just going to his office and looking at the truly wonderful pearls that he kept in a safe the size of a small room. In fact, Nick treated this safe like a room—hung with pictures, carpeted and complete with easy chairs, a table and a sofa—it was a delight to sit there and watch Nick pull out wondrous pearls from a cabinet.

On one occasion, I watched his year's crop being sorted. The pearls come in all shapes and sizes. There was a small mountain of pearls ranging in colour from steel grey through to gold in all its shades to white and palest pink. There were baroque pearls and teardrops, button pearls and perfectly round ones, literally sacks of them. Then Nick asked if we would like to see a few pearls that he had put to one side. Romilly and I entered his splendid safe, sat down and were served cold drinks, then Nick drew a bag from the cabinet and spilled the pearls onto a velvet tray. The quality was truly incredible. 'Each of these pearls I have picked because I have never seen its like before,' he said. One specimen brought to mind the parable of the pearl of great price—*St Matthew*, chapter 13; perhaps you will recall that parable. I have always known that feeling: finding something for which I would sell everything. It is the instinct by which a true collector can be recognised. This pearl was pear-shaped and 15 millimetres in diameter. Nick called its colour strawberry, but to me it appeared at first to be coloured pale gold, and then changed before my eyes into a pale pink. Every time I moved it between my fingers, the colour changed. After studying this pearl for some time, I asked if I could buy it. Nick took it, looked it over and slipped it back into its bag before returning it to his safe. 'How can you price a pearl like this? This pearl has no price,' he said. Sadly, it was a case of no price, no deal.

154

My first visit to a pearl farm was in 1981 when Romilly and I travelled up Cape Leveque to visit the Brown family, or rather the brothers Brown and their respective families. The Browns' father had come ashore there when, fishing for pearl shell in the Buccaneer Archipelago, he spotted at once the beauty of the place. With his eldest son, Lyndon, he set about putting together a small cattle station and a pearl farm, carved out of the bush. Their cattle were from Africa, big red cows; as Lyndon had told me: 'Australians like big red cows.' The Browns slashed the wattle on their small station and, as a result, young shoots sprang up and the cattle ate a plant that they would otherwise have avoided. Among the rough buildings of the Cygnet Bay pearl farm, buildings that looked as nothing but served their purpose, and were wonderfully situated to take advantage of every breeze, was a tennis court—the grass was bright green among the burnt bush, the surface as smooth as a marble tabletop.

The Browns were friends of Thea and David Hutchinson, the chemist in Broome, who had taken Romilly and I there to stay the weekend. Alison, the wife of Bruce Brown, the younger brother, was a schoolteacher, and a party of schoolteachers and civil servants arrived after lunch on our first day at the farm. Lyndon Brown hated schoolteachers and civil servants alike and, what is more, said so. He and his wife stayed at home; the rest of us went to play rounders on a saltpan just down the coast. I hate any game that includes a ball except perhaps billiards, and I am none too keen on billiards, so it was not much of an afternoon for me. Next day it was tennis; things were beginning to look desperate as far as I was concerned. What on earth would we do next? Swimming, I supposed. I hate swimming and particularly I hate swimming from beaches, the sand gets between my toes and no amount of washing will get it all out. 'Can I possibly see some pearls?' I asked Bruce Brown. 'Sure,' he replied, and we went into his bedroom where he pulled several plastic buckets from under his bed. These buckets were covered with dishcloths and filled with pearls. 'Do you want to sell any of these pearls?' I asked. 'What else would I do with them?' he replied. Romilly and I chose about fifty baroque pearls of the sort that the pearl farmers call tornadoes. They have a band around their widest part and this band is replicated on each side of the pearl's centre in an ever-decreasing size. These tornado pearls, when of the best quality, are by far and away the most beautiful of the Australian pearls. For some time they were quite common; today, they barely appear at all. Their absence is due, I believe, to the greater expertise that is now used in the growing of pearls. The casual attitude of the Browns to their pearls and to every manifestation of authority was, I found, quite refreshing. That night, Romilly and I wandered along the beach at sunset and all was perfect in a paradise that hides a multitude of dangers. The next day, we drove back down the sandy track to Broome leading our small convoy of two cars. The bush roads now held no terror for me and I was driving with a new confidence and I believed considerable skill, when the car skidded out of control and away into the bush. I was lucky that it did not turn over or hit a tree; I was also lucky that there was a car following to help me back onto the track.

The pearl farm at Deep Water Point that Snowy County, Rod Reid and Peter Kinney started, and which I owned most of during its formative stages, now prospers. That farm was a ramshackle affair to begin with. Soon, however, we improved the accommodation and now it is a fine-looking place. The theory of management that I have always applied is to give good accommodation to your employees and so be able to employ the best people available. Sometimes that theory works, sometimes it fails. The men and women who spent their weeks there bathed in the sea and played tennis on the court that had been built. Beverley Kinney, ever imaginative, had constructed her own home complete with an outdoor shower built among the rocks. Snowy had a manager's house built in the Broome style; later, he moved out and the farm manager took over this residence. Busy with my zoo, I only visited the place half-a-dozen times. Life on the pearl farm was hard work and the solitude broken only at weekends. During the year, the oyster shells, which were about the size of a small dinner plate, were taken each week from the sea and cleaned. The plant life that is attached to the oyster shell competes with the oyster for the food that floats past. Machines need to be maintained, boats cleaned and repaired: the work is arduous, tiring and really quite boring. Only when the pearl harvest was on, and the work was almost non-stop, was there any excitement about the place.

In the early days of the pearl farm, Snowy spotted a crocodile lurking in the water while the work on the pearls went on. A wary eye was kept out for this creature. Then, for a time, not much was seen of it. A few years later, it, or one very like it, was captured. Its legs were tied with rope and its mouth was bound with electric tape. Immobilised, the animal was put in the spare bedroom of the manager's house and a message sent to Malcolm Douglas in Broome, for he usually deals with recalcitrant crocodiles. That night, the crocodile freed itself and, jumping through a window high in the wall of the building and smashing the glass, took the window frame from the wall along with it on its dash to the sea. This crocodile, clearly not best pleased with humans, has moved further down the coast to a still-peaceful spot.

※

When the pearl farm was just beginning, Snowy used to drive down from Deep Water Point in his truck, the pearl harvest in cotton sacks under his seat. He would arrive at about breakfast time and empty the sacks on my breakfast table. My guests were truly amazed at the heap of pearls amongst the platters of fresh fruit. Nowadays things are done differently. Snowy no longer runs the farm, and pearl robberies have become a regular occurrence on the Cape Leveque Peninsula. There are no more breakfast-time displays of casual affluence, rather a hurried trip with the pearl harvest to a bank's vault. At the time of writing, five Broome men are in the dock charged with the theft of between half a million and two million dollars' worth of pearls. The police allege that these men systematically raided a pearl farm 150 kilometres north of Broome in the Buccaneer Archipelago, and that about 1700 pearls were removed from the pearl shell at that farm. Their operation was carried out using a two-metre-long fibreglass boat. No pearls have, however, been recovered. In the light of this and other robberies from pearl farms, plans are in train for a squad of police to be set up to deal with the theft of pearls, similar to the squads that protect the gold-producing industry. Pearling in and around Broome has changed over the years from something akin to a profitable hobby to a multimillion-dollar industry, an industry that is one of the largest employers in north-west Australia.

Sadly, pearls are not the only things that thieves in the North-West see profit in stealing these days. Recently, two men have been charged with stealing dinosaurs' footprints. Cut from the rock about 38 kilometres north of Broome, these footprints are from a stegosaurus and are believed to be 130 million years old. The traditional owners of the area, where these footprints were, have not unreasonably asked the Western Australian Government to limit access to their land. No doubt this will be yet another firebrand thrown onto the smouldering issue of land rights in the North-West.

In truth, the only answer is for the Government to step up supervision of these remote and immensely beautiful areas to stop the criminal vandals who will plunder them. If the Government believes it worth the cost of protecting the pearling industry, an employer of much labour, then it should definitely spend the funds to protect the material wealth of a growing tourist industry in the North-West, an industry whose value will one day far outstrip that of pearling. Closing land is not the answer: the Kimberley is no longer the greatest unexplored wilderness in the world; it is part of a modern, industrialised continent with all the advantages and disadvantages of that status. Human footprints in rock have also disappeared from the Lombadina area, 180 kilometres north of Broome. These stolen footprints will, without a doubt, find their way onto the world market for fossils, a market which is of such a scale that the chances of either the five-toed stegosaurus footprints or the human footprints ever being recovered are somewhat remote. While Joseph Roe, the representative of the Goolarabooloo people, quite rightly, wrote to the State's Premier, Richard Court, this sorry affair is not, however, an Aboriginal matter. It is a matter that should deeply concern all Australians. Richard Court should act speedily to set up the necessary safeguards for valuable natural specimens located in remote parts of his State.

Diamonds are another great source of wealth in the Kimberley. So far, there is only the Argyle mine operating, which produces about one-third of the world's diamonds. There are, however, many aspiring diamond tycoons who search for, and seldom find, the fortunes that they seek. For many years, I have held the view that alluvial diamonds must be hiding in the prehistoric rubbish under the sea off Roebuck Plains, rubbish that was part of a river bed. Roebuck Plains was once such a river, a river vast in size that is now removed and become the Fitzroy River, its mouth a hundred metres wide in the dry, 160 kilometres wide in the wet, its waters having risen up to seventeen metres in past wets. My own experience of diamonds is somewhat limited. I did, however, discover in a casual conversation with a member of the Oppenheimer diamond family that they had spent literally hundreds of millions on searching for diamonds and only found them in any quantity once. Apparently, all their best mines have been found by independent prospectors. It was, therefore, with hope in my heart that I agreed to a proposition by Des Higgins, as independent a prospector as one is likely to come across in a long day's march.

Des Higgins was a gaunt man with a considerable gap between his front teeth. Ross Gardiner, the gentleman who once ran my zoo, was of the opinion that the gap was caused by drinking from a stubby of beer when his truck went over a bump while travelling at high speed. For myself, I prefer to believe that the gap in his front teeth was natural, a sign given to him at birth to show his luck with money and, I hoped, with diamonds. The Higgins family lived on Waterbank Station, which had the township of Broome along one of its boundaries. For years there was tension between the Higgins family and the Broome Shire Council. The town authorities coveted the Higgins' land and, to my certain knowledge, it has taken them over twenty years to lay their hands on it. The Higgins family is, to put it mildly, eccentric, a family who are their own men and women, a family that, like myself, has a strong distaste for bureaucrats and all things bureaucratic. What was theirs, they regarded as their own, and they didn't want others interfering with it or trying by bureaucratic means to take it from them. Mrs Higgins is a fine woman and a strong Catholic, much involved with the Church and charity. A naturally kind woman of strong principles, she and her family have had more than their share of tragedies. Des Higgins, a brilliant raconteur and entertaining companion, often used to call at my zoo for a beer. On one occasion, he told me of a skeleton he had found in the desert; the length of the skeleton was about three metres. Allowing for exaggeration and the natural lengthening of the body as it decomposes, this skeleton had undoubtedly been that of a very tall person. It is with some regret that I write of never having made the journey with Des to view these remarkable remains. Des Higgins, who sadly is now dead, spent much of his time in the bush, grading tracks for the Main Roads Department, going to places that few of the inhabitants of Broome had ever heard of, let alone visited.

One day, Des sat down on my veranda and, accepting a beer, began to explain that the reason for his visit was not just social. As he talked, he leant forward and tipped what looked like four small lumps of grizzled glass onto my table. 'Diamonds,' Des announced. He had found diamonds which, I am bound to say, came as no surprise to me at all. 'Where?' I asked, and Des began to explain. After five minutes, I was lost in the desert somewhere to the west of Halls Creek. The diamonds, however, were far away from there, hiding in the rubble of the rocky outcrops of the Caroline Ranges. During the next half an hour, Des and I did a deal: we would go fifty-fifty on the diamond mine and, in return, I would give Des a set of new tyres for his truck and enough petrol to get him back to the find. Then I would contact diamond companies and set about turning our claim into a fortune for both of us. The diamonds were, in fact, real diamonds. The mineralogist who looked at them was of the opinion, however, that they came from South Africa. This could be explained in part by the fact that Des had a previous partner in this deal, a man of dubious reputation who had been in litigation with others who claimed the land he regarded as his, and which now both Des and I regarded as ours. The diamond business, however, did not come to me with the same basket of luck that I had received when I bought a share of Snowy's pearl farm.

While most people believe the name of Broome to be synonymous with pearls, for many years when Broome was mentioned, people spoke of the place in terms of Diamond Jack and the stolen diamonds. During the war when the Japanese invaded Indonesia, the Dutch authorities put all the diamonds that they had control over in an aeroplane in order to get them to safety in Australia. This plane, piloted by a Russian, was shot down off the coast of Cape Leveque near Carnot Bay. None of those aboard were aware of the fortune that their aircraft carried, in the form of £250 000 in diamonds, packed in a parcel the size of a cigar box. By chance, Jack Palmer, a beachcomber, was passing in his lugger. While four members of the party on board died, the pilot and some of the plane's passengers made it ashore. The pilot despatched two of them to fetch help and, after another brush with the Japanese, help came in the form of two RAAF planes which dropped supplies. When the wreck of the plane was searched, no diamonds were found. Jack Palmer handed in some diamonds but nobody believed that he handed over all of them. For years afterwards, diamonds began to turn up in the Kimberley, and so began the legend of Diamond Jack. For myself, I have often imagined, as I walked along Cable Beach in the first light of the morning, that I would stub my toe on the largest pink diamond known to mankind.

Despite the fact that our diamond mine never materialised, I was well-disposed towards Des Higgins, although never a week went by without some person or other warning me about his character. The aspects of his character that others found so inconvenient, I greatly admired. He was a simple man: if you treated him well, he would treat you well in return. While he may well have been a simple man, towards the end of his life Des Higgins had the most memorable of experiences, an experience that was far from simple to explain in any rational sense. Staying in a motel at Kununurra, he woke after an hour or so of sleep. In the corner of his room was a blue light. Imagining it to be the television or some other electrical device, Des turned off all the switches in the room but still the bright blue light would not go away; in fact, it began to get brighter. Des was quite perplexed at this, so he got up and left the room. As he did so, the blue light began to fade. After smoking a few cigarettes on the motel's veranda, Des decided to go back to bed. As he entered the room, the light began to glow and steadily it increased its intensity until it was a startling bright blue. I am not sure how or why Des Higgins came to the conclusion that this light was a visitation by the Virgin Mary. Although not a religious man himself, he was clearly influenced by living with a wife who is deeply religious. Greatly impressed by what can only be explained as a vision, Des later visited each of the people with whom he had had disagreements in the past, making his apologies to his enemies. Shortly afterwards, he died at peace with his own conscience and returned to the fold of his God. Whatever you care to make of this strange light that Des Higgins saw, there is no doubt about its impact on him. A man who spent much of his time alone in the bush, it is no surprise that he reacted in the way that he did, for, if ever there was a country truly inhabited by God, it is the lonely wastelands of north-west Australia. It is a place where strange happenings seem not strange at all, a place where the bizarre and the unusual are quite in tune with the nature of the countryside and its people.

⁓

After some years of living in Broome, I began to long for a place in the bush that had less people around. Broome had become my place of business and I needed a retreat from that business. Walcott Inlet at Collier Bay seemed just the place and the land on one side of it, which was called the Charnley River station, became mine in the strangest of ways. In Broome, I had a lady who worked in my garden. She was a pleasant young woman, who in her own way kept my garden tidy and did her best to encourage the few remaining plants to grow. One morning at about 6.30 a.m., this lady asked if she could have a few words with me. It was my habit to rise early in Broome, to bathe and then to take a walk along Cable Beach. This woman caught me just after my bath and before my walk. Her request was quite frankly inconvenient. She, however, was in a considerable state of agitation about something, so I arranged to see her later in the morning. She got on with raking my yard, and I with my daily exercise.

Later, it transpired that her father owned a cattle station of over

32 000 hectares in the Kimberley. His proposition appealed to me immediately. For some time, I had been in communication with the Lands Department looking for a small cattle station. Her father had exactly what I required, which was just as well as he desperately needed to sell his property. Later that day, the young woman brought her father to see me. He turned out to be an extremely pleasant man and we concluded a deal in a matter of minutes. He would sell me his cattle station at Walcott Inlet with any cattle that I could find on the property for $20 000. The station had, to all intents and purposes, been bought sight unseen. With Siggi Halter, I had flown over the property and noticed cattle on it but I was uncertain about its boundaries. Walcott Inlet itself formed one boundary and the Isdell and Charnley Rivers two more, but heaven knows where the fourth boundary was to be found. Situated approximately 300 kilometres north-east from Broome as the crow flies, it is one of the most beautiful pieces of land in the Kimberley, teeming with wildlife. The countryside is wild and wonderful; fresh water is plentiful in the rivers that provide two of the station's boundaries. Fish are plentiful at Walcott Inlet, and it is a place much prized by barramundi fishermen. Ducks nest there, migrating birds come and go as they please. It was exactly what I needed, a small cattle station with three boundaries that cattle either could not or would not cross. The fourth was rugged mountain land that in many parts was as good a barrier as a fence. To add to the advantages of this station, it backed onto a national park. The Charnley River Station was the perfect place for the experiment with my British White cattle.

That afternoon, I rang John Adams about my latest purchase. Surprisingly, he seemed rather enthusiastic and offered to take a half-share in my land. This pleased me, for a partner of Western Australian birth would make life much easier with the authorities. It was my intention to breed British White cattle on this station. The British White is one of the world's oldest breeds, it was brought to Britain by the Romans, and has several characteristics that would make it suitable for use in the Kimberley: the cattle are naturally polled, so they have no horns to damage fencing; they have virtually no hair, so they would not be troubled by ticks; and, while their coats are white, they have a black pigment in their skin that protects their teats, noses and the skin around their eyes from sunburn. In Britain, they will survive the winter on a bale or two of straw, fattening quickly when there is new grass available for them to eat. What is more, these animals are dual-purpose cattle: they produce enough milk to raise twin calves and are sometimes used as dairy cows. As beef cattle, they have a double thigh giving them extra kilos of prime steak. A butcher in England told me that he would pay an extra 50 pence a kilo on the carcass of a British White steer on account of the quality of its meat. Finally, these cattle were by nature extremely tame; even the bulls could be treated like big dogs. In the past, the British Whites had prospered in Kenya and, as I had a herd of these cattle in England, it was my intention to bring stock out to Australia and see how they managed on this remote station.

John Adams and I approached the Minister of Lands to have the station transferred into our names. We attended a lengthy interview where we were told that cattle could not survive on this station. So we produced photographs showing that quite clearly this was not the case. Then I explained my theory about the British Whites. The minister and his staff clearly believed that I was nuts. Indeed, anyone who opened a zoo in Broome and believed that town would grow to become a metropolis must in their eyes be nuts. So the bizarre nature of this new request came as no surprise to them. In the event, they gave me permission to take over the land. After all, John Adams and I had bought it legally and clearly intended to farm the place. For our part, we set about this venture with great enthusiasm, acquiring a landing craft to move cattle in and out of the station, and hiring a drover to muster what cattle he could and to shoot the rest so the station would be free of TB. Finally, we commissioned plans for a station homestead. Then came the rub—what had seemed the land's greatest advantage, its proximity to a national park, turned out to be its greatest disadvantage. Someone came up with the idea that this station should become part of that national park.

About six months after we had acquired the land, all hell broke out. The small group of activists in Broome who believed that the mantle of the Reid family had fallen firmly on my shoulders set about trying to stop me from carrying out my plans at Walcott Inlet. As mentioned earlier, *The Broome News* and the people who congregated around its flag certainly succeeded in irritating me; in fact, they stimulated my thoughts to such an extent that I achieved far more in Broome than had ever been in my mind when I first went there. The irony of this journal and its supporters' attacks on me was that, only some time after the attacks had abated, did I, for totally different reasons, leave the township of Broome. There was no plot, no cunning plan, no hidden agenda to my activities in Broome. These people and their journal were a nuisance, but no more of a nuisance than the sandflies that come with the spring tides in Broome.

On the matter of Walcott Inlet, the writers at *The Broome News*, and others, went too far, one of them stating on the local radio that I was involved in corruption. Faced with such charges, I had no choice but to sue. I won judgements in my favour on all the cases, and apologies were forthcoming. It was never my intention to earn money out of litigation, rather to clear my name. By this time, the West Australian Government was involved. The activists in Broome were insisting that Charnley River Station should be part of the nearby national park, a national park, incidentally, which the nation was not allowed to visit. The ecologists spoke of it as a lung, which is a curious thought when you consider that Australia, being approximately the size of North America, has a population of only eighteen million people. The whole place could be considered a lung under those circumstances. Without doubt, I can accept the principle of lungs in the world, but a land that is nearly all lung reduces this principle to the ridiculous. The people of Australia should be allowed to visit areas such as Walcott Inlet, for a nation must have in its makeup a degree of soul, and the country around Walcott Inlet is nothing else if it is not a place of the soul.

John Adams and I argued that Charnley River Station had been specifically excluded from that park when its boundaries were drawn up. The chairman of the commission had, by coincidence, been Phil Adams, the father of John Adams. The argument lasted several years, with John and I offering to pay and accommodate a manager to protect the Inlet, where poachers had been shooting crocodiles. The Government was adamant. Pressure from the Broome activists gave them no room to manoeuvre. I agreed to abandon my cattle-breeding project, and we offered to give up all except 40 hectares of land in return for permission to put a camp site for tents there so that tourists could visit the national park. This was unacceptable to the Government, for the last thing they wanted was for people to visit their newly extended national park.

In the end, the State Government bought Charnley River Station from John Adams and myself for twenty thousand dollars, the price that we had paid for the place. The venture had cost John and I four or five times that figure, quite apart from time that it wasted. I now predict that, without the shadow of a doubt, it will only be a few years before the Government of Western Australia will be begging a developer to bring tourism to Walcott Inlet and their national park. Not only will they be begging a tourism operator to go there but heavily subsidising that company's activities. It was, I think, the pure tedium of dealing with uncertain and weak governments in Australia that caused me to divert my energies elsewhere. This is written not in recrimination at plans unfulfilled, rather to record how I was dealt with, in the hope that those in authority and their successors might read these words and, realising how badly the North-West has been served, bring about a change in attitude which will allow the Kimberley to truly become a source of wealth for the whole State, rather than remaining a creature in receipt of subsidy.

IV

Politics and Politicians

14

When Margaret Thatcher came to Australia, she was in fact the first British prime minister to do so. But she never came to Broome; despite the fact that her private jet passed right over the town, she is too canny a politician to take the risk of visiting friends at the expense of the British taxpayer. She did, however, come to Perth, staying in my family company's property and private residence, the Bishop's House. She loved Perth and thoroughly enjoyed her fleeting visit to Australia. Her schedule was hectic; her stay in Perth was only for a day and a night. Early the next morning, I was waiting with some of her staff in the kitchen of Bishop's House for her to come down for breakfast. Suddenly there was a series of loud crashes. The security men sprang into action; it was, however, no emergency—simply the prime minister pulling a heavy suitcase down a flight of jarrah stairs.

While Margaret Thatcher was in Perth, I raised with her the matter of Yagan's head. My friend Ken Colbung, one of the most decent people that I came across in Western Australia, was at the time of Margaret Thatcher's visit searching for the whereabouts of this severed head. It was known to be in England but nobody seemed to know quite where. Just before Margaret Thatcher was entertained by the Western Australian Government on her one evening there, I arranged for Ken Colbung to have the opportunity of a few words with her about his search. Afterwards, she told me that in principle she was sympathetic to the idea of returning Yagan's head to Western Australia, where the rest of his body was buried, but she could not do much until the head was found. In 1995, more than four years after Margaret Thatcher left office, Yagan's head was discovered. The

Conservative Government was still in power in Britain and, although I was not by any stretch of the imagination *persona grata* with the prime minister, John Major, I was definitely on speaking terms with several members of his cabinet. I set about trying to get Yagan's head repatriated, without, I may say, any success at all. After many unsuccessful private approaches, I decided to write of the British home secretary and the fact that I had found him reluctant to do anything about this matter. At the time, I was a columnist in the *European*, a newspaper which served as a perfect forum to liven up the debate. I took the matter into the public domain and I reproduce the piece that I wrote here:

It is seldom that a writer gets the opportunity to record a tale that involves a severed head and a British government minister, so I will not miss the opportunity. The severed head is that of Mr Yagan and the member of her majesty's government is Home Secretary, Michael Howard.

Yagan was born in Western Australia in 1810, twenty years after the British first colonised Australia. His father was Nyoongar chief Midgegooroo. An important leader of the Aboriginal community, Yagan soon came into conflict with the British authorities.

Despite the murder of his brother and execution of his father without trial, Yagan was generally well-disposed towards the settlers who had arrived in his land. He helped them find food on occasions when otherwise they would have starved. However, after a series of retaliatory attacks on the British following the slaying of various members of his tribe, a price was put on Yagan's head.

Bounty hunters captured Yagan but he escaped. He was then pardoned, but before long was again in trouble with the new arrivals. He was deemed outside the law and again a price was put on his head. Despite his troubled relationship with the authorities, he enjoyed cordial relations with the white settlers. He was murdered, however, while out hunting with two teenage settler friends, William and James Keates. While Yagan walked in front of the pair, they took the opportunity to shoot him in the back of his head and earned themselves a £30 reward [A$78].

That was not the end of the matter. Before he was decapitated, the decorated skin on Yagan's scalp was removed and turned into a belt. Later, his severed head was smoked for several weeks and then sold as an anthropological specimen.

Robert Dale, a British soldier, bought the head and took it back to Britain with him on 29 September 1833. Unable to sell the head at a profit, Dale donated it to the Liverpool Royal Institution, which later loaned it to Liverpool City Museum where it was displayed for some years.

By 1964, the public attitude towards exhibiting bits of other people's bodies in museums had changed and the Liverpool Museum sought permission to inter it in an unmarked grave. For many years, it remained undiscovered in a cemetery.

Ken Colbung, an articulate Western Australian Aboriginal leader, who is a descendant of Yagan, had for years searched to find his ancestor's head. Last year, Cressida Ford, a postgraduate archaeology student at Southampton University, located Yagan's head in an Everton cemetery. It was in a grave beneath the coffins of twenty stillborn babies.

The Home Office was approached and they set in motion the procedure for recovering Yagan's remains. This procedure involved asking all the parents of the twenty stillborn children their permission to dig up the grave. Some of the parents could not be found and others refused their permission. Colbung and his relatives were devastated by this news. They are still attempting to reunite Yagan's head and his body. This issue is of great significance to the Aborigines of south-west Australia, in particular, and to those of Australia in general. To the British Home Office, it does not seem a matter of any importance. They simply say that there is nothing to be done.

Some months ago, I wrote to the Home Secretary and a month or two later received a reply that contained the biggest load of nonsense I have read in years. Yagan was only one of many thousands of Aboriginal and Maori peoples whose heads were taken to Britain and sold as souvenirs. To their credit, many of the museums and institutions that held these heads have since returned them and reputable salesrooms nowadays no longer trade in human remains, although this was a regular practice until just a few years ago.

Usually the problem is finding the rightful owner of the heads to return them to. In this case, however, the ownership is clear. To take these heads in the first place was a barbarous act, but an act committed in a barbarous age. To keep Yagan's head in Britain today shows a total lack of sensitivity for the feelings of Yagan's people in an era when generally we are more attuned and sensitive to these issues. Yet, as far as the Home Secretary is concerned, nothing has changed. There can be no justification for keeping Yagan's head in Everton cemetery while his body lies in Western Australia.

While the removing of Yagan's head from Everton might upset a few British voters and there are no Aborigines voting in the next British general election, it is too much to hope that Howard will do anything about this issue. It seems that Ken Colbung will have to wait until there is a less ambitious and electorally sensitive head of the British Home Office for his ancestor's remains to be reunited.

Two years later, the Conservative Party was destroyed at the polls. Within a week, Ken Colbung came to London and helped the New Labour Government solve all the unsolvable problems of Yagan's head, which only goes to show that where there is a political will, there is always a way. Yagan's head was exhumed and returned to Western Australia in September 1997. In the event, there was a further dispute over its ownership, but this was finally resolved and Ken Colbung's mission completed.

Margaret Thatcher chose me to be the treasurer of her party in 1975. I was a Conservative by instinct and habit. I was never an activist, climbing my way up some party ladder. It was to join Margaret Thatcher's 'Long March' that I went to work in 32 Smith Square, the Conservative Party Headquarters. I am still, by instinct, a Conservative; the habit, however, has now been broken. I am more searching in my enquiries these days as to how the Conservative Party conducts itself. I feel that I have remained much the same in my views, but that the Party has crept away, like some husband slipping from his lover's bed in the early hours of morning to return to his wife. Margaret Thatcher's Long March culminated in 1979 when she became prime minister, with the Conservative Party being seduced back to conservatism from the near-socialist philosophy to which it had been married during the previous twenty-five years. While I am sad that the political ideas of Thatcherism are one by one first reviled and then discarded by those to whom they handed office, I have, however, few personal regrets.

Margaret Thatcher changed my life, as she did the lives of so many other people. I have, however, changed many of my views over the years. Many years ago, I gave up going to the Church of England and, after a long period in which religion played no part in my life, I started attending Catholic churches. I am now a regular churchgoer; I feel better when I have been to church. To me, birth, life and death all seem the greatest of miracles. I am still interested in politics and occasionally active, though most of the time I just write about politics. I write and travel, and am still blessed with an endless curiosity about people, places and things. I live in continental Europe; I revel in the beauty of that place and the vast quantity of man-made masterpieces there. I have, however, after years of looking at man-made beauty, come to believe that it is only human beings who are really important.

⸎

Working in British politics and being closely associated with the prime minister, I expected to attract the attention of the terrorist IRA. Always on the alert at sensitive times such as elections, I sent my wife and daughter overseas. Each night I would sleep in one of three different hotels, choosing among them at random and making the decision only when I was in my car in the early hours of the . morning. When my friend Airey Neave was murdered by the IRA, I was desperately sad. To me, however, they still seemed an abstract threat—that is, until the terrorist attack on the Conservative Conference taking place at Brighton in 1984. The second bomb attack that

I was involved in took place in May 1990. I had left my home at West Green. I had for some years been a specific target on the IRA 'A' list, and West Green was vulnerable to attack. I suppose some instinct encouraged me to move; indeed, I also moved my London residence. A week or so later in my new London apartment, I woke to discover that the IRA had destroyed West Green.

Unpleasant as these two experiences were, they came as no surprise. An incident, however, that did surprise me was one that happened in Australia in the mid-1980s. I had bought for myself an old house in Peppermint Grove, Perth's smartest suburb, so-called because its streets are shaded by huge peppermint trees. This house sat on a double block and was just down the street from John Adams' home. It was my intention to knock down this poorly-designed house from the 1950s and build something better-looking. By chance, while I was waiting on the plans so that I could apply for permission for the work to be done, John set about extending his house. 'Could I and my family borrow your house for a few months?' Without hesitation I agreed, and the Adams family moved in—John, Liz and their son, complete with his nanny. Some weeks later, John and Liz left to visit Sydney for a weekend. On the Sunday night, someone put a fire bomb in the main bedroom and another under John's Mercedes-Benz that was parked in a lean-to at the side of the house. The place went up like a Roman candle. The nanny and child escaped out of a window. The police investigated the attack and could find no culprit. Perhaps, they said, it was a bomb meant for a doctor who lived opposite, who was often involved in acrimonious disputes over workers' compensation. If that was the case, no further attempt was made against him when his enemies discovered that they had bombed the wrong house. As far as I can discover, this attack on my house is the only incident of its kind ever to have happened in Peppermint Grove. Was it an attack by IRA sympathisers? Who knows, and, as far as I am concerned, who cares? I was not harmed nor, indeed, was anyone else. As for the house, it was due to be pulled down anyway. It is only fair to record, however, that I sold the empty block some time later, and that while I was in Perth, I continued to live in the city.

15

Australia is so distant from Europe that in Britain they tend to think of it, if they think about Australia at all, as just an unusual place to visit. A continent of breaking surf with handsome men and women who spend a great deal of their time cavorting in that surf. A land of sheep and cattle, deserts and jungles, populated by that exotic race, the Aboriginals. Seldom do we Europeans remember that Australia is a vast continent strategically placed on the Pacific Rim— an area that despite recent setbacks is destined to become the epicentre of prosperity in the next millennium.

As for their politics, the generality of Europeans know nothing at all about the politics of Australia. When it is explained to them, Europeans find the political system of Australia as incomprehensible as those who are not Italian find the politics of Italy, or those who are not British find the politics of Britain. It takes a considerable effort to explain to Europeans the complexities of a system where the Liberals are really Conservatives, the Country Party is interested in more than country matters, and the Labor Party has spent much of the last ten years trying to jump over the backs of the Liberals to occupy their policies—which they have, in fact, generally succeeded in doing. While I tend towards Labor in Australia, in truth, I would be in a quandary if I had the vote there, as to how I should cast it. The two parties both embrace free enterprise; their policies are so close that, at times, it is hard to tell them apart. While I disagree with particular policies in Australia, I seldom disagree with the overall thrust of either party. A good deal of what Paul Keating achieved, I am sure John Howard, now prime minister, agrees with, for it was John Howard's efforts as leader of the conservative opposition that largely set the agenda of politics that forced Paul Keating and his party to the right.

Paul Keating was a man who had great success at the hustings and who served Australia both as treasurer and then prime minister. I knew him well. I particularly admired this cultured man's use of language in a parliament that is the antithesis of culture.

Paul Keating is on record as having often addressed parliamentary rivals in less than complimentary terms. He is a fine practitioner of the art of verbal violence. Some of the phrases and words that he uses to describe opponents are: 'piss-ants', 'harlots', 'sleazebags', 'perfumed gigolos', 'dummies', 'scumbags', 'gutless spivs'. He even called one opposition member who returned to a portfolio that he had some years before given up, 'a dog returning to eat its own vomit'. Paul Keating turned parliamentary abuse into an art form. In his private life, Paul Keating is an intelligent and cultured man, an expert on classical music and a great enthusiast for French Empire clocks. When I once asked him how he could afford to collect such valuable antiques, he replied: 'Most people buy their antiques when they have been tamed,' by which he meant, found and cleaned by expert dealers who would add a large mark-up. Keating went on, 'I catch them while they are wild.' I firmly believed that Paul Keating would win his last federal election and his government be returned to power. I was totally wrong in this for, despite the fact he is highly intelligent and, furthermore, his government had the courage to carry out their ideas and had the language to sell them to the electorate, he was unceremoniously thrown from power.

Among other Labor politicians I find attractive as human beings is Bob Carr, the victor in the New South Wales election of March 1999. I will quote from a television commercial that promoted his cause during a previous election. He was asked if he would endorse President Clinton's policy of 'three strikes and you're out'. 'No,' Carr replied, 'under my plan, it is one strike and you're out. Why should we give those who commit serious crimes three chances?' Surprisingly, Carr is the most humane of men and leads the Labor Party in New South Wales with great skill and consummate ease. The politics of Australia may well be complicated, but Carr has hit on a truth that would get him elected in any country of Europe. The time has come for people to be treated humanely, not the criminals who prey on them. Bob Carr is a man for whom I have the highest regard. He is one of a small group of politicians in governments the world over who actually takes the time to read a book. Literate and intelligent, Bob Carr is about as interesting a person to spend time with as I have met anywhere. His wife Helena is beautiful, clever and charming.

✤

Sir Charles Court, who led the Liberal Coalition and was premier of Western Australia from 1974 to 1982, believed in capitalism and he believed in his State, and under his administration both flourished. He is a man with a huge personality; dealing with him was a real pleasure, nothing was ever impossible. It was never a question of taking ideas to Charles Court, he was full of ideas himself for developing Western Australia—he only needed entrepreneurs to carry them out. Sir Charles Court, perhaps more than any other man, set the pattern for growth that subsequently ended in tears, tears largely because the government of Brian Burke understood and liked the results of Sir Charles Court's ideas, but failed to understand how they were put into practice. In time, Carmen Lawrence became premier of Western Australia. Billed as the clean hands that the population was told would sort out the mess, in the early 1990s she, with masterful inactivity and frenetic public relations, turned prosperity into an evil word and helped the State of Western Australia and its people not a bit. How strange is the coincidence that it has fallen to Sir Charles Court's son, Richard, to restore the State's reputation.

On my second visit to Western Australia in 1964, I was invited to lunch with Charles Court at Parliament House. He was Minister for Industrial Development and extremely powerful. I was a callow youth who had never eaten oysters before and regarded them as preferable to poison, but only just. Sir Charles was kind to me; he treated me as if I was an experienced businessman, which I most certainly was not. We sat down to lunch in the dining room at Parliament House, and the first course was served. I admired the view, and toyed with a large glass filled with tomato sauce, oysters without their shells and one lettuce leaf. Sir Charles ate his oysters with relish, carrying on a conversation at the same time. For my part, I tried to hide a dozen oysters under a small lettuce leaf. Sir Charles drew no attention to my predicament. I have since learnt that I love oysters and eat dozens of them every time I am in Australia—without doubt, the Australian rock oyster is by far the sweetest and most delicate oyster in the world.

After a long period in office, Sir Charles Court was eventually succeeded by Ray O'Connor, who took the same views about industry and the development of Western Australia but achieved little. Life dealt unfairly with Ray O'Connor when he became premier, for he inherited the tail end of Charles Court's government. A large bluff individual filled with apparent goodwill, I felt that Ray was more interested in having a good time than governing Western Australia. I first met him at lunch with John Roberts. John had invited the premier to lunch in order to introduce me to him. As a side attraction and to impress me, he had also invited Dennis Lillee, who was currently playing in a test match in Perth. The lunch was the greatest of fun—John Roberts, a brilliant raconteur, was far more impressive than O'Connor and Lillee put together.

◆

After the days of building Western Australia during Charles Court's premiership, and the fun of Ray O'Connor's administration, came the new energy and enthusiasm of Brian Burke. The new premier, the leader of the Labor Party, believed in enlightened socialism, a mixture of free and State enterprise, a partnership between the State and its entrepreneurs. For a time, this seemed to work. Then the inevitable happened—the functionaries of the State began to behave like entrepreneurs, using the apparently bottomless resources of the State as a bankroll. The days of scandals and the crash in Western Australia will never be forgotten by those of us who ran businesses at that time. Western Australian entrepreneurs, sighting gold to be mined through the incompetence of the bureaucrats' political masters, set off to have the lion's share of that valuable substance. 'It was,' said one senior civil servant who had disapproved of the whole venture, 'as if they were taking grain from blind chooks [chickens].'

Despite all that has been said and written about Brian Burke, the premier at that time, I have never believed him to be a dishonest man. While I know full well that honesty is like pregnancy in that you cannot be a little bit pregnant nor a little bit dishonest—in both conditions, you either are or you are not—I still contend that while Brian Burke may have committed questionable actions, he was and still is, at heart, an honest man. He believed that certain aspects of how business was conducted in Western Australia needed changing, and he was right—they did need changing. Brian Burke believed that Western Australia could be set alight in a frenzy of commercial activity and that, from this activity, profits could be made for individuals and the State at the same time. The State could then use its share of the profits to finance the social policies that he deeply believed in.

Brian Burke sincerely believed that all this would be good for his State and, up to a point, he was right. Like a number of other politicians, he also believed that Western Australia's success would do his career no harm. By the time the excitement of the America's Cup was at its peak in 1987, he was suffering the hangover that comes after the high of success. Sitting next to my wife Romilly at lunch in our pavilion on the dock at Fremantle, he explained that each morning he just wanted to pull the bedclothes over his head and stay in bed; that he would rather watch 'Play School' on television than go to the office. Given this honest assessment of his own mental state, it is not entirely surprising that Brian Burke got himself deeper into the muddle that finally disgraced and sent him to jail. His crimes were not the crimes of a criminal; rather they were the actions of a man whose life had run away from him. He had been surrounded by people who genuinely believed that they could fix things and, while doing this fixing, could take a cut for themselves. Brian Burke's fate was not the well-deserved end of an habitual criminal, rather it was the final scene in a play where he unwittingly played the fall guy, while believing all the time that he was cast as the hero.

᪣

Peter Dowding, who succeeded Brian Burke as premier of Western Australia in 1988, was a highly intelligent politician who did the best he could, but the cycle of disaster was too far advanced for him to be able to take the action that was needed to reverse it. Try as he might to unravel the relationship between business and government in Western Australia, the task was beyond him as, indeed, it was beyond anyone else. However, Peter Dowding understood the North-West in a way that Brian Burke never could; Brian Burke could never understand that complicated place which seems at first sight so terribly simple. Peter Dowding was enthusiastic about my plans for a new Broome airport and, had he survived as premier, I have no doubt that it would by now be built and operating. Like his predecessor, he never seemed to hold against me the fact that I was a senior official of the British Conservative Party working for Margaret Thatcher. Brian Burke had appointed me to chair the newly formed Aboriginal Enterprise Board, an organisation whose object was to finance Aboriginals who would rather start small businesses than stay on the dole. We bought boats for fishermen, tractors for tractor drivers, lorries for hauliers and put up money for several arts projects. It was fascinating work and I enjoyed it immensely. We never really got all the financial backing from the Government that we were promised but I was quite used to that happening in Western Australia, so no matter.

It was, I believe, a conference in Davos in 1989 that did for Peter Dowding's premiership. He had asked me to join the Western Australian delegation and help in the effort to promote the State. His team at that conference, despite carping criticism from home, did a splendid job of selling Western Australia, an effort that was rendered worthless by the change of power in their Government. Peter Dowding was right to go to Davos, for the only painless way out of Western Australia's financial problems was colossal inward investment, and the conference at Davos was one place that might have generated such investment.

However, back home in Perth, the newspapers and the gossips were busy. They claimed that Peter Dowding and his new wife, a delightful Scandinavian, were living the life of Riley in Davos—fine wines, food galore, important people, in fact everything that the rest of the cabinet back in Australia were not getting. It was all untrue, of course, but jealousy feeds on jealousy. In Australian politics, the end for a marked premier is a quick one. His enemies laid their plans while he and his close allies were out of the country, and those enemies struck soon after his return. The truth, of course, was rather different. We were quartered in an adequate but modest hotel; Peter and his delegation ate modest meals, listened to tedious speeches and sold the idea of investing in Western Australia to whomever they could get to listen. I paid my own expenses and I took my lunch in the best restaurant in town. It has always been a principle of mine that if you want to collect honey, go where the bees are. Likewise, if you want to sell something, go where you will meet the people likely to be able to afford the goods that you are selling. On the last night, I took all the staff who were helping the delegation out to dinner at a restaurant where I knew the family of the owners. It was a riotous evening, ending with the hard core of the revellers and myself listening to a bagpiper in the restaurant's kitchens at one o'clock in the morning. The staff who served that delegation were kind and decent people, fine representatives of their State and their nation. Their attitude to life was so terribly different from the air of false sophistication affected by so many of the delegates from other nations at that conference. I had the most wonderful time that night.

Peter Dowding is a man whom I have always liked and still do. He once said to me that I had all the assets that were needed to succeed in Western Australia—energy, enthusiasm, capital to invest and the entrepreneurial spirit to invest it. Only one aspect of my situation was missing—I was not a Roman Catholic. He is a man with a sharp but dark sense of humour. When I first met him he was married to Jill, a fine-looking Aboriginal, a woman whom I always found to be extremely pleasant and who, along with Peter, introduced me to a community in Broome that I would otherwise never have met.

༄

Carmen Lawrence succeeded Peter Dowding in 1990 and almost immediately appointed a Royal Commission, which, at great length, investigated the whole affair of the State's dealings with individuals. She was almost immediately dubbed 'Dr Feelgood' by the Western

181

Australian press. Her approach to politics was one of: 'I'm honest; you are safe in my hands'.

I worked fifteen years for Margaret Thatcher; four years as a columnist for Eve Pollard, the editor of the *Daily Express*; and for the last ten years I have worked for Min Hogg, at *World of Interiors*, as editor-at-large and a columnist. Working for all of these three women has been a most enjoyable experience as far as I am concerned; in fact, at the risk of appearing prejudiced, I would rather work for a woman than a man any day of the week.

Carmen Lawrence was, however, something else. On one occasion when she was a minister, I had a most unsatisfactory meeting with her. I entered her office. 'What do you want,' she asked. 'Nothing,' I replied, and then explained that I had come to offer the State my collection of 700 pieces of Australian furniture, much of it from the first settlement. I wished to form a trust and what I needed from her was a building in which to house this collection, a building where the public and tourists could conveniently view it. The local officials had suggested the disused customs building in Fremantle. I needed the Government to put the building into the trust, and I would put in my furniture and the money to restore the customs house. Carmen Lawrence's reaction was totally negative; she obviously had a deep suspicion of anyone who had any sort of project which could be considered altruistic. As a result of her premiership, nothing much happened in Western Australia. Soon the people did not feel good any more, throwing her out on her ear at the next State election.

After Carmen Lawrence went, her legacies to Western Australia of both the recession and the Royal Commission stayed. Her attitude to business in Western Australia could not have been more different than that of Pam Beggs, a minister in the Western Australian Government who applied commonsense to every proposition that was put to her. A distinctly feminine and highly intelligent woman, Pam Beggs was a great asset to Western Australia during its troubles. I only wish that there had been more ministers like her.

In Australia, I am, I believe, a Labor Republican, while in Britain, I am a Conservative Monarchist. I find no problem with this apparent split in my personality. The monarch is thoroughly good for Britain and should continue, if only for the reason that if the monarchy goes, the British will have Ted Heath, Roy Jenkins or even Norman St John Stevas, now Lord Fawlsey, as President, and that would be intolerable. The monarchy, on the other hand, does nothing for the Australians. Take the simple proposition of a state visit to another country. The Queen goes there to sell Britain, and often her visit will be timed to coincide with British trade missions. The Queen is the Queen not only of Britain and Australia but also of many of the Commonwealth countries. She does not, however, promote Australian trade interests in that country or anywhere else or, for that matter, the interests of any other country that she is Queen of, except Britain. The monarchy is a thing of the past in Australia; Australia will never truly be a nation while the monarchy lasts there. Britain, on the other hand, could easily cease to be a nation should the monarchy finish.

A large part of the population of Australia is either indigenous, comes from places that have no connection with Britain, or descends from people who have no connection with Britain. Australia's multicultural society should be the country's greatest pride. As Britain has drawn closer to Europe over the last 25 years, its ties with Australia have become looser. How strange it is that the citizens of two countries ruled by the same queen should need to have visas in order to cross each other's borders. How strange it is that Australians are restricted from living and working in Britain, when French, Germans, Italians and other Europeans can do so freely, and that there are restrictions on Britons who wish to live and work in Australia, ruled by the same queen. The situation as it exists is clearly nonsense. The overwhelming need in Australia is to find a unity of purpose. Slowly the differences with Australia's indigenous peoples are beginning to be resolved. The second and equally important stage in reaching that unity of purpose is that Australia should become its own country, owing loyalty only to the citizens of its own continent. The way to achieve this is for the Australian people to move without delay towards becoming a republic.

Never a day goes by in Britain that we do not read about the monarchy's attempts to prepare itself for the twenty-first century. A new, streamlined monarchy seems to be the order of the day; a monarchy that will fit in with a Europe of a single currency and, indeed, most likely, a European federal state. Regardless of whether or not Britain joins a single currency or a federal Europe, she will be affected by both events. The trappings of pomp and title from the past must be cast off in a new egalitarian world. Already the new Labour Government is actively reforming the House of Lords, a matter that I regard as a tragedy, but such is the fashion of the age that this will be done. With the millennium fast approaching, change is in the air. What better time for Australia to make that change? It is, after all, not such a dramatic change as might be feared, for already an Australian represents the Queen; let that person in future represent Australians. As for the Commonwealth, an organisation that often does good while giving respectability to dictators and sometimes murderers, the Queen will stay as its head, as she has said, for as long as it wishes her to fulfil that role. A nation does not need to have the Queen as its monarch to be a member of the Commonwealth, so Australia as a republic can retain its position in that important forum.

One evening, a year or so ago, I dined with Di Jagelman, a well-known beauty and a famous Sydney hostess, at her home. The dinner, as you might expect from such an accomplished hostess, was as near-perfect as it is possible to get. There were only three other guests, one of them, Malcolm Turnbull. Like everyone else in Australia, I had heard of Malcolm Turnbull and the Australian Republican Movement. Knowing little else about him, apart from his involvement in an incident that took place in my London club, the Garrick, I was not well-disposed to him personally, despite the fact that I have been advocating for many years that Australia should become a republic.

The unfortunate incident at the Garrick Club was during the Spycatcher trial in which Malcolm Turnbull represented the author and former MI6 agent, Peter Wright. It seems that Malcolm Turnbull was sitting on a lavatory behind a fine mahogany door while the British Lord Chancellor was using a urinal and, at the same time, regaling other members of his club who were also in the cloakroom with the intimate details of the trial. Something that he said was subsequently used to advantage by Malcolm Turnbull. Members of the Garrick Club, who at that time included some of the most influential politicians and journalists in Britain, were extremely put out by the use of what they considered confidential information. Malcolm Turnbull no doubt was not aware of the Garrick's rule that all conversations on the club's premises are regarded as private; not under any circumstances are they to be repeated outside the club. The Garrick Club has this rule so that members and their guests can speak with complete freedom, knowing that what they say will remain confidential. As a result, the Garrick is the place with the most interesting conversation in London. Malcolm Turnbull does not strike me as a man who would let what he might regard as the arcane rules of a London club stand between him and success in a court case. The late Michael Havers, a charming man, held the post of Lord Chancellor towards the end of his life. An amusing man, he was totally indiscreet in his conversation and I suppose paid the penalty for forgetting that, although he held the highest law office in the land, he was also a politician.

The dinner at Di Jagelman's was, from my point of view, a great success. Whether this was because of her skill as a hostess or Malcolm Turnbull's charm, I do not care to make a judgement. My misgivings about his behaviour at the Garrick were quickly forgotten and I left confirmed in my belief that Australia should be a republic and happy that Malcolm Turnbull was a leader in advocating this state of affairs.

ఌఙ

At the time that I was first in the Kimberley, the attitude of many Australians towards Aboriginals varied from the condescending to the downright aggressive. There was considerable anger that the Government seemed to set the Aboriginal people apart. It was generally believed that an Aboriginal could arrange finance to buy a car with the utmost of ease, whereas a white man would be turned down. These new cars, it was said, were driven through the bush by drunken

Aboriginals, who in the course of time wrecked them. The evidence to support this idea was the number of wrecked cars that seemed to litter the landscape. Any Aboriginals that I came across, however, took considerable care of their motor vehicles. It was much the same with drinking. Aboriginals as a generality were believed to be drunks who lived on social security and were not in the habit of holding down even the meanest of jobs, that is, if they could summon up the energy to get such a job in the first place.

This was not at all my experience. Over the years that I lived in Broome, I employed many Aboriginals in posts as simple as gardeners and as responsible as bird and animal keepers. My general conclusion is that the Aboriginal of the Kimberley is much the same as the white man of the Kimberley; like the curate's egg, they are good in parts. As, indeed, if we search our consciences, we all are—we all have our own talents and our own failings. The job of employers, however, is to get the best out of the people they employ, not to casually bar from the chance of employment whole sections of the community with opinions based on race or creed. As for drink, there are drunks in every community, but, unfortunately, they tend to hang around hotels and public places. As a proportion of their numbers, Aboriginals, considering their situation, have no greater number of alcoholics among them than do the Americans or the British.

The Catholic Church in the North-West, led by Bishops Saunders and Jobst and assisted by Fathers McKelson and McMahon and many others, has played a vital role in the reconciliation between the black and white populations. There can be no doubt that, viewed from a distance, the lot of the Aboriginal since the white occupation of Australia has not been a happy one. Equally, many of the traditional pastoralists genuinely believe that they dealt charitably with the Aboriginals in the past. Time, however, has moved on and charity has become a despised word. Rights are the nature of today's ethics. To give to someone what is theirs by right should not be considered an act of charity. In the growth of a nation, history tends to be amended. If true unity is to be found in a nation, it is important that historians continue to search for the truth of that nation's history. When that truth is found, it is important that the political and religious leaders of that nation accept it, using this valuable truth as a guide for future actions. Only when Australia searches for, finds, and accepts the truth of her history, is there any chance of national unity. Australians should be searching for, finding, and accepting that truth, in the full knowledge that, without unity, it is a travesty to call their continent a nation.

The days of Stephen Hawke and Tom Stephens fighting for Aboriginal rights are over. The battle, however, can barely be considered to have been won. The fight goes on, for today the attack on minorities still exists; it is just perpetuated in a far subtler form. It is well that politicians like Tom Stephens, the member of the Upper House for a large part of the North-West, and Ernie Bridge, who really care about the population of the Kimberley, still carry on the fight against a bureaucracy working 2500 kilometres away. They have helped change the opinions of some of even the most recalcitrant of those who live in the North-West.

In my first memoirs, *Once a Jolly Bagman*, I wrote that I was sure that a great deal of what John Howard would do as Prime Minister, Paul Keating would like to have done. The reform of Aboriginal rights carried out by Keating during his term as prime minister was, in my opinion, one of the most enlightened pieces of legislation in Australia's history. I wrote that John Howard would be the man to finally resolve the Aboriginal problem in Australia. In this, I was wrong. This new volume has given me the advantage of hindsight and I am able, thank goodness, to reassess those words. In short, John Howard has destroyed the integrity of Paul Keating's Aboriginal land rights legislation. As a matter of political convenience, legislation has been passed in Canberra that Aboriginal leaders believe robs them of 90 per cent of the benefits of Keating's bill. In this, I am inclined to agree with them. John Howard has found a formula that pleases the National Party and many of the Liberal Party's supporters, but takes away most of the rights that the Aboriginals struggled for. It is all fine and dandy to say that the Aboriginals will still have the right to use the disputed land but not the right to own it. How ironic this all is

187

when you consider that ownership with legal title is a European concept, while the right to use land by tradition, in this case, is an Aboriginal concept. Yet the white migrants to Australia have put so much emphasis on legal title that now the Aboriginals will not settle for anything less. Paul Keating might have refined his legislation on Aboriginal land rights but I am sure that he would not have neutered the legislation in the way that John Howard has. Law, however, is only one aspect of this matter. More important by far, is the attitude of the people.

I have known John Howard for many years, first meeting him in the early 1980s when he was in Malcolm Fraser's government. He was at the time the federal treasurer. Intercontinental Hotels and my family company were trying, desperately, to build a new hotel in Sydney. At the time, the State Government in New South Wales under the premier, Neville Wran, was bending backwards to get this project under way. It had offered us a site, the old Treasury building, a fine example of Australia's heritage that was currently being used by the Transport Department. It was, I am afraid, in a shocking state of repair. State office workers on the whole are not the most congenial tenants for a heritage building. We had the finance, the hotel operator, and were all set to go; only the permission of the Foreign Investment Review Board (FIRB) was needed to allow us to get our planning permission and to start work. For some reason, the FIRB appeared reluctant to give this permission. I had met with the chairman of the FIRB privately. By a fortunate coincidence, he was the uncle of Alison Brown, the wife of Bruce Brown, the Cygnet Bay pearl farmer. On my visit to the Browns, I had mentioned my frustration in Sydney, and Alison had telephoned her uncle and a meeting was arranged at the FIRB's office in Sydney.

The meeting itself was a strange affair. I arrived at four o'clock in the afternoon at the city building that housed the FIRB. The twelfth floor was where I had been told to attend, so I took the lift to the landing outside the FIRB's office. I then found that the door was locked and the office seemed unoccupied. Disappointed, I was about to leave when an elderly and immensely courteous gentleman got out of the lift and, greeting me, unlocked the office door. If these offices had seemed empty, it was because they were empty. The old gentleman turned on the lights and airconditioning in what turned out to be an extensive suite of offices. We sat opposite each other in heavy leather upholstered easy chairs, entirely alone and each with a plastic cup of water, then we discussed my problem.

I was told that there was only one man who could help me and that was John Howard, and that he needed to vary the guidelines that directed how foreign investment was dealt with. It was on this occasion that I learnt the difference between guidelines and the law. The law is a rigid thing—you are either acting legally or illegally. A clever lawyer will often find a way around a law, allowing you to act legally but still act against the intention of that law. Guidelines are, however, different; there is no convenient way around a set of guidelines.

In Canberra, John Howard received me well; after all, I was a senior official in the party that formed the British Government. After a pleasant-enough conversation about Margaret Thatcher and her policies, we got down to business. In short, there was no way that the guidelines could be varied. Despite the fact that unemployment was high in Australia and this new hotel would create over a thousand jobs, still there was no way that the guidelines could be changed. They were the rules, did I not understand this? Of course, I understood that they were the rules, but governments make rules and only very foolish governments do not change them when circumstances have changed. At that time, I was lobbying anyone who I could lay my hands on and among those I lobbied was Philip Lynch, a cabinet minister in Malcolm Fraser's government. Philip Lynch lived just outside Melbourne on the coast. His home was most elegant, and his wife both beautiful and charming. He had in his garden a hedge that made a profound impression on me. So large was this hedge that on the occasion of my visit, three men were clipping it. During lunch in his home, we talked of my problem and he agreed that it was a problem made by bureaucracy rather than a problem caused by principle. Philip Lynch was very kind to me: he took up my cause and the problem was overcome. In the event, the Sydney Inter-Continental has been nothing but an advantage to Australia, playing a large part in achieving Sydney's aim to become the venue for the next Olympic Games. The fact that this hotel was for a time owned by foreigners seems not to have mattered at all.

∽

As for Australia realising the geographical reality of her position and accepting that she is part of a group of Asian continents and islands, John Howard has allowed the insidious lobbying of a certain Pauline Hanson to make all the running on that front. In the following pages, I will come to Pauline Hanson in some detail. At the last federal election, Hanson's party was almost wiped out. That, however, is not enough. Had John Howard destroyed her intellectually when she first emerged, none of us would have ever heard of her again. It was not that John Howard could not have destroyed the arguments that this woman made, rather that he chose not to destroy them, hoping, I imagine, that they would destroy themselves. In this, history will judge him and I suspect the terms of that judgement will be harsh.

If John Howard has one overbearing disadvantage, it is that he is too nice. A cultured and kind individual, he has all the talents for politics. It is just that, while he relishes the chase, he holds back from the kill. One aspect of John Howard, is, however, totally beyond question, and that is his honesty. At a time when Howard was in government, his brother Stanley and his wife came to lunch at my country house, West Green. We were a party of about twenty that day, including my partner in the pearl farm, Snowy County, and his mate, Richard Ballieu. Introducing Stanley Howard to Richard Ballieu, I remarked that Stanley was John Howard's brother. 'I know your brother very well,' said Richard. 'We own a lot of housing sites together in Broome.' Stanley went white at the idea that his brother was involved in property with this rough-looking character. In fact, Richard Ballieu comes from a highly respectable family in Melbourne; he just happens to look a little on the rough side, but no matter, Stanley Howard was speechless. I let the silence hang for a moment or two and then explained that the John Howard I referred to was

Australia's prime minister, while the one that Richard Ballieu referred to was the magistrate in Broome. I have never seen a man look as relieved as Stanley Howard did at that explanation.

It would be churlish to leave the subject of Australian politics without just a mention of Malcolm Fraser. It always seemed to me that Malcolm Fraser is just the stretched version of the British prime minister, Edward Heath. Neither of them are true conservatives; both of them led their parties into opposition. Purely as an insight into Malcolm Fraser's political judgement, I will recall a night during the 1983 British general election. It was in Annabel's, the fashionable London nightclub, that I met Malcolm Fraser. Most nights during elections, I went there after a day's campaigning to collect money for the Conservative Party. Sitting in the bar near the door to the restaurant where I could buttonhole likely donors, I smoked a cigar and drank mint tea. At about one in the morning, in comes Malcolm Fraser. We greet each other briefly and then, without a moment's hesitation, he launches into a dissertation on how he had studied the polls and the political situation, coming to the conclusion that the Conservatives would lose by a mile. Protesting that he was wrong, I offered him a drink, only to be stuck with this Jeremiah for some half-an-hour. Luckily, he was distracted from politics by someone he knew from Australia. When they got up to dance, I went home to bed. A few days later, despite Malcolm Fraser's gloomy predictions, the Conservatives won the election, gaining the largest majority they have ever achieved. It is, however, fair to write that, in 1978, when our political prospects did not look so good, Malcolm Fraser sent Tony Eggleton, the general secretary of the Liberal Party, over to Britain, to give us some advice. Tony Eggleton arrived, bringing with him a videotape of the Liberals' famous election broadcast, 'Memories'. It was this tape that set the pattern of the Conservative party's advertising that summer. Like the Australian Liberals, we went straight for the jugular and the following year won a victory that put the Conservative Party into power for eighteen years.

As a rule, I am generally well disposed to politicians, even when I disagree with their politics. Among the politicians that I have never met is Pauline Hanson. Of this I am heartily glad for I detest her policies, which are not really policies at all, rather a hodgepodge of statements and ideas of a despicable nature. She has no place in these memoirs, however, because her words are likely to affect the future of Australia, a country of which I am inordinately fond. I have taken space in this book to explain why I believe her words and her policies to be so destructive to the future of Australians, regardless of their race or colour. On the Statue of Liberty that stands on Ellis Island at the mouth of New York's harbour are engraved the words: 'Give me your tired, your poor, your huddled masses on your teeming shore'. For many years, the world did this, and America grew great. Australia, by comparison, adopted a rather different attitude to immigration. White was the colour of the game and when white people from Britain were in short supply, disgracefully, young orphans were transported without telling them where they were going or why they were going there.

In America, the penniless immigrant's sons and daughters became doctors and scientists. In Australia, if you were a scientist or a doctor, you could come to live here. The rich rather than the poor were welcomed, poor and white perhaps, but poor and black—never. Those days are long gone but this attitude to foreigners lingers on, and among those foreigners are numbered the indigenous Aboriginal population. This is an attitude that is deeply ingrained into the psyche of a small part of Australia's population. Sadly, this attitude is from time to time adopted by a politician, then taken up by the press and displayed in all its racist horror.

Pauline Hanson's words were first heard by a world unfamiliar with the niceties or, rather, nastinesses of Australian politics. Unaware of how Hanson has been ridiculed by both the public at the polls and the cartoonists in the media, the world still remembers those words, and suspect that the feelings they express lie dormant in Australia's subconscious.

Australia, however, is a free land, a democracy, and Hanson is entitled to her views. John Howard could not have been expected to silence Hanson; he could, however, have been expected to show the

Australian electorate the shallow quality of her views. Her proposals for the Australian economy were ludicrous, such as a special bank giving loans of 2 per cent. This idea, in a country where the interest rate is a considerable multiple of that figure, was destined for spectacular failure, a formula for jealousy and corruption. She also supported tariff barriers, in a country that lives by its exports. Such measures would only bring retaliation from Australia's trading partners.

All of this is obvious to anyone with eyes, ears and a brain in between them. Just as is the canard that if a finite number of Australians can live well, due to the minerals that are dug up, the trees that are cut down and the other natural products of Australia that are exploited, then to increase the number of its inhabitants will lead to all living less well or, for that matter, the canard that there would not be enough water if the population is dramatically increased. Water is only a matter of engineering, as has been shown in Israel. Australia has never really grasped the possibilities of becoming fully populated in the same way that America is fully populated. This is Howard's mistake; it is the task of a nation's leader to lead that nation to a prosperity, not just to preside over the division of a prosperity, most of which exists largely due to the benevolence of nature and God. To 'deal with' Hanson is merely to operate in the currency of her own language and to hasten progress towards the kind of state that Hanson advocates. Happily, the Australian electorate had the good sense to 'deal with' Hanson and her followers at the polls, humiliating them and, for a time, rendering them and their successors politically irrelevant. Pauline Hanson's words, however, have been said and the poison remains in the Australian national bloodstream. To demonstrate, on the other hand, the great benefits that will come to Australia from massive immigration on the scale of nineteenth and early twentieth-century American immigration makes Hanson irrelevant. It offers to the Australian people a prosperity, a power and a culture far beyond their wildest dreams, thus removing Hanson's poisoned words from the conscious memory of the nation. Only when this happens will Australia fulfil its true destiny to replace America as the most stable, prosperous and powerful nation on earth.

In time this will happen, whether Pauline Hanson and her colleagues like it or not. It will happen, regardless of the apathy of Australia's politicians, for this under-populated continent will be filled by immigrants regardless of what care she takes in defending her boundaries. How much better that Pauline Hanson and John Howard should turn their minds to ensuring that this influx of immigration is carried out in an orderly manner. How much grander they would be, remembered as the founding fathers and mothers of a truly great nation, than as just a pair of politicians who merely stood and bickered as the inevitable course of history approached.

V

Collectors, Dealers and Artists

16

All my life I have been a frustrated shopkeeper. I love the idea of owning and running a shop. After many years, I have, however, come to the conclusion that I am rather better at buying stock than selling it. To be a successful shopkeeper, you need a reverse talent to mine. It's not that I do not enjoy selling or, indeed, that I am not personally good at selling. When my wife Romilly had a grocer's shop in London's Covent Garden and subsequently in South Audley Street, I would occasionally go and encourage her customers to buy. Without an undue lack of modesty, I believe that I was rather good at selling groceries. The customers used to go away with a myriad goods that they had no need of, let alone any intention of acquiring when they entered the premises. Romilly's shop, started before we married, bore her maiden name, Hobbs. It was a leader in its field, way in advance of tastes current in the late 1970s. Romilly only sold her shop when I became ill with the heart condition that culminated in a sextuple bypass operation. It was to her a considerable sacrifice to give up the business that she had started in order to look after me, and I am deeply grateful.

Shops that I ran myself over the years include a bookshop, an antique furniture shop and a premises that sold curiosities and antiquities. For some reason I love not only shopping, but, more so, the shops themselves. I am tempted to open a shop almost every time I see a promising premises with a sign indicating that it is to let. It is a great joy for me to sit in shops—to watch goods being bought and sold is to me a great excitement. Over the years, I have sat in dozens of galleries and antique shops around the world, gossiping with their proprietors and this, I suppose, is how I came to learn about antiques and paintings. It was certainly where I learned the trade of dealing and the principles that apply, whether you are buying and selling land or Greek sculpture. Traders are, by nature, enthusiasts; they like to trade because that is what they do best, and the activity of trading gives them pleasure. True traders may be able to walk away from particular offers, but they cannot walk away from the activity of trading. Therefore, experienced traders are life's easiest victims. Never try selling jewellery to a jeweller, for the jeweller will know its value down to the last cent; offer it instead to a picture dealer who knows it to be valuable but not its exact worth. When the goods on offer reach a price where they appear to be a bargain, the picture dealer will have no alternative but to buy. It's is in the blood, nothing can be done about it. Expert and as hard as nails at their own trade, a dealer will become putty in your hands when enticed into a transaction involving goods of whose value the dealer has only a notional idea. Dealing has provided me with immense pleasure over the last 50 years.

Given my predisposition towards owning shops and knowing that I am a better buyer than a seller, it is not entirely surprising that when I came across Joan Bowers in Sydney I became her business partner. Joan imported Indian art and artefacts. She is an enterprising woman who, when in India in the 1970s, saw the possibilities of selling the goods that they made there in Australia. Her shop was a delight; it did not matter whether it was in bronze, marble or wood, Joan's eye was impeccable in the choices that she made. In time, she was importing large chunks of India's demolished buildings to Sydney. Joan had developed a passion for India, she was fascinated with it, and adopted initially two small Indian children, a boy and a girl, and then later a second girl.

Only married recently to Stephen Bowers, she and her family acquired a larger house in a rather unfashionable suburb of Sydney, a suburb where the gracious old buildings had become ruins, their gardens repositories for rubbish. Stephen Bowers, who was an architect by profession, cleaned up the house and the family moved in. Joan was young, enthusiastic and happy with her Indian family.

For the best part of 20 years, the name Joan Bowers was synonymous with India. For me, her emporium was one great confectionery shop, with rows and rows of goods as delectable as sweets and cakes. When I called at Joan's shop, which was at least twice a year, I found nothing that I did not want to own. When I visited Sydney, I camped in her premises. I loved the atmosphere, I loved the social whirl that surrounded the place. For Joan's impeccable eye could not only spot just the right architectural details, textile, deity, doorway or pot, but the right people as well. Joan Bowers' taste is in humorous people. It does not seem to matter to her where they come from or who they are, she collects characters with as much unbridled enthusiasm as she scoured India for that perfect piece. It was the lunches and the parties, the table gossip and the casual generosity of her hospitality that made her shop a point of pilgrimage, the genius of her ability to put disparate objects together, to show them in a different light, that made her shop an outstanding success.

In the early days when Joan first opened her shop, fascinating and wonderful objects were plentiful in India. Joan never bought masterpieces in the pompous sense of the word; her interest was in the beauty of the work that came from the villages. She did not strip India of its heritage, rather she promoted the brilliance of its indigenous arts. Joan knew an India that tourists and dealers tied to a hectic itinerary could never find. For her, choosing her stock was never a matter of filling a container or knowing that she could sell a particular piece. She bought what she liked and only what she liked.

☙❧

Joan regularly made buying trips to India and usually stayed at the Rambagh Palace Hotel in Jaipur, where the manager was in the habit of calling her Mrs John Borris. He was, however, not the only member of his staff to be involved in a misunderstanding where Joan was concerned. A waiter at the hotel had become her friend and regularly took her home for meals with his wife and family in their village. On one occasion, Joan knew that his wife was absent and was somewhat surprised to be invited to dine there. She refused the invitation on the grounds of etiquette, leaving the waiter bitterly disappointed. That night, she dined instead with an English couple who were also staying at the hotel. During dinner the waiter approached Joan, telling her how much he loved her. She in her turn told him not to be foolish. Later that night, the same waiter returned and apologised for an apparent misunderstanding. Needless to say Joan was greatly relieved. The waiter then set about explaining the misunderstanding, telling Joan that he did, indeed, really love her. It was, he explained, she who misunderstood his words. Joan replied sharply to him, telling him to go away, but there was no stopping the man. The fateful words burbled out of him. 'I desperately need to see you without your clothes on. I mean you no harm. I love you so much, I would not lay a finger on you. I only want to see you without your clothes on and to prove my good intentions, I will have another waiter watching while I look at you.'

♣

When I met Joan, she was living in Paddington and running a very successful shop at 1 Paddington Street. Unfortunately, her partner in the shop, now dead, was not the easiest of people. Joan was in some distress about this during a visit she made to Broome. She was travelling with the Frosts and it was after some discussion under the mango trees in my garden that I and our mutual friend, Bob Frost, decided to go into partnership with her and take over her partner's interest. They all enjoyed their time in Broome: the weather was, as always during the winter season, perfect. Bob Frost is the most amicable of men, quite apart from being an extremely able accountant, financier and property developer. His role in the partnership was to make certain that a strategy for Joan's shop was in place. All went well at first but the troubles came and, as troubles will, they came all at once and from the most unexpected quarters. The landlords terminated the lease on the Paddington Street premises. Trade was brisk and the shop was now without a home. Joan, naturally enough, was in a considerable state at this turn of events. It had been decided for us that we should move, but where would we move to? Rents were at that time in Sydney at their highest, and good premises hard to find. Joan set out to explore and identified a warehouse that we could convert. For my part, I was in hospital undergoing heart surgery. We borrowed money and bought the premises freehold for $2 million; then we borrowed more, $500 000, to pay the builder.

All seemed fine at first, then came the recession of the late 1980s. Business dropped like a stone and the bank began to talk of calling in our personal guarantees. In time, with the recovery of the Australian economy, Joan refinanced the business and bought me out.

My business venture with Joan gave me endless pleasure but absolutely no profit. Joan's shop flourished and so it should have done, for she is an immensely talented woman of whom I have always been extremely fond. In time, of course, that recovery in the Australian economy began to flag and the financial situation among the Asian countries made trade uncertain. Joan sadly, but wisely in such circumstances, decided to close the shop, to close the doors of her emporium and 'retire' to India. As usual with Joan, she closed her shop as she had opened it, with great style and some of the best stock that she had ever owned.

The closure of Joan's shop, I must confess, left me with a tinge of sadness. However, our lives are so ordered that all things come to an end—good or bad. Joan Bowers' emporium of Indian Art and Antiques was high among the best of things in Sydney. These paragraphs are not an obituary to the demise of the most stylish of shops, rather a celebration that this shop and its predecessors under Joan's management existed at all, existed when Indian art was virtually unknown in Sydney, let alone Australia, and existed at a time when 'taste' of any sort was as rare as hens' teeth. Joan Bowers and her shop had both taste and style in profusion. Twenty years on, the world has changed. Joan's imitators are commonplace and the perfect object is harder to find.

The whole event had, from my point of view, been highly expensive. It was, however, a salutary lesson on the subject of buying in at the top of the market and waiting for values to recover once that market has dropped. The moral of my story is that one should cut one's losses when business dealings begin to go wrong and you are unable to put them right. Waiting for events to change your fortune is a fruitless and folly-ridden exercise, more an exercise in conceit than business management. A number of years ago, Earl Macmillan, the former British prime minister, well-known for his cunning and mastery of political tactics, was asked by a young politician what he should be aware of in his political career. The old master replied, 'Events, dear boy, events. It's always events that bring you down.'

\~

Bob Frost is a polymath, a thinker and a doer. A man with a fine eye for art, an acute nose for business and a most entertaining companion, he is married to Glen-Marie North, an able and flamboyant publicist. After the considerable setback he received from his London colleagues, he set about rebuilding his career, while Glen-Marie's went from strength to strength. Their wedding was the talk of Australia. Unfortunately, I was unfamiliar with Australian weddings and did not realise that the appropriate dress for four o'clock in the afternoon was a dinner jacket. Arriving only just before the bride (I was delayed over lunch with Sidney Nolan), I was surprised to find all the other male guests in dinner jackets and black bow ties. I was in a pale beige linen suit with the garish pink and green Garrick Club tie. Trying to slip into a back pew was no solution to my problem. An usher insisted that I sit in the front row with the bridegroom. The walk down the church between rows of expectant guests was a terrifying experience. The bride entered with an assortment of bridesmaids: Sonia McMahon, widow of a former prime minister who had arrived in an ambulance and walked with a stick; Di Kirby, an ex-model; and Jane Walker, Glen-Marie's general factotum. Happily, Glen had given each of them the material for their dresses and left the design to the individual concerned.

No sooner had the parson passed the ring to the bridegroom and he had slipped it on the bride's finger and given her a considerable kiss, than she turned to the congregation and proclaimed: 'He gets the glamour, I get the money,' at which the congregation broke into rumbustious applause. The reception was a lavish affair at Barford, one of Sydney's finest historic mansions owned by Barry and Wendy

Loiterton, the former owners of Hayman Island. The caterers came from Hong Kong and a maypole stood in the centre of the marquee, its pink ribbons trembling in the evening breeze. On each table there was an ice sculpture that slowly melted during the course of a very warm evening. Even these melting sculptures, however, could not dampen the high spirits of the guests. Primrose Dunlop, who was sitting next to me, drew up her skirts high on her thighs and threw her shapely legs across my knees, as from nowhere a photographer appeared and recorded this extraordinary sight for the Sydney newspapers. As the night drew on, the wedding reception seemed to gather momentum rather than to slow down, memorable is a poor word to describe this occasion. Outside, the streets were lined with hired limousines; there can have hardly been a limousine left to hire in all the metropolitan district of Sydney. Later that week, I watched a video of the whole event; one moment of that wedding sticks in my memory. As the camera panned to the right, an anonymous voice was heard to say, 'Move over to the right, Susan. That's where the press are.'

It was Joan Bowers who introduced me to Margaret Olley, a considerable painter who has been portrayed at one time or another by most of Australia's great painters. Margaret Olley has a brilliant eye, and the Oriental Collection at the Art Gallery of New South Wales has often been the beneficiary of its selections. A generous woman, both with her purchases and her hospitality, dining in Margaret's house is an occasion to wonder at. It is, in fact, not one house but two or three houses with a carefully planned but overgrown garden. Room after room of objects that she has collected from different continents and cultures, a dead bird and a few dying flowers preserved for use as models in a painting among them. Room after room of her paintings, all in various stages of completion. On the first visit to her house, it is almost impossible to understand the geography of the place. While guests sit in comfortable but tired easy chairs, balancing drinks on their knees—for there is absolutely no place to put down a glass, let alone another object—Margaret cooks in a tiny, untidy kitchen. Called to the table, guests are confronted with tablemats of an erotic nature and a meal that would delight the most discerning of gourmets. The conversation sparkles in much the same way that Margaret herself sparkles. Time flies, and when the polite time for the guests to leave has long passed, they begin to drag themselves away, then linger at the door, delaying to examine some marvellous object, not noticed before amongst the carefully arranged jumble. At last they leave this enchanted place, a house where time has stood still, where culture and pleasure, kindness and joy still mingle.

&

All my life I have been fascinated by dealers and their dealings. At heart, however, I am a collector, a collector of people like Joan Bowers and a collector of places and things and, above all, moments that remain in my memory. Not many years ago, Sotheby's gave a dinner party for many of the leading wine writers. The meal was extraordinary, and so it should have been, for it was cooked by Michel Roux of Le Gavroche. The wine defied belief. Let me record the list: Champagne Krug 1982, followed by Haut Brion 1961 en magnum; Margaux 1953 en magnum; Latour 1952 en jeroboam; Mouton Rothschild 1949 en magnum; Lafite Rothschild 1945 en jeroboam. All this was finished off with Chateau d'Yquem 1970. I asked the excellent gentleman from Chateau Latour why he chose the 1952 vintage, and he replied that Chateau Latour was famous not just for making great wines in great years, but for making good wines in bad years.

This just shows there is no such thing as an absolute value, a point wine illustrates as well as anything else. Christie's at about the same time also asked me to drink some of their fine vintages and, since I was in a wine mood, I waxed lyrical about the merits of wine. I remarked that I had seen a bottle of Cheval Blanc 1949, a superb wine, sold for £600. The lady on my left attacked my enthusiasm for this bargain: 'What extravagance!' 'But,' said I, 'we have just looked at a beautiful Cezanne due to fetch £10 million. If you were to buy that painting, it would cost you about £5000 a day in interest. You could buy a lot of wine for that.' 'Rubbish,' she replied. 'You drink your wine and it's gone. I still have my Cezanne.' Rather weakly,

I suggested she must have worked out a way to take it with her when she had gone.

But the truth of the matter is that there are many types of collecting, and two are the collecting of the tangible and the intangible. Each is, I suppose, legitimate, each for quite a different sort of person. Of course, there are plenty of collectors who understand neither one nor the other.

చివ

It is impossible to move in the extraordinary world of collectors and traders without coming across a good many art dealers. While I personally have never held this view, art dealers are often thought of as shady characters at best, likely to be downright charlatans, ranking in public esteem a little above criminals and politicians. This negative view, however, has a profound effect on the way the customers view their trade. It is amazing the way they feel that a dealer is obliged to give them a bargain when they buy a picture. Yet they do not feel a similar obligation to pay, delaying settlement for months on the assumption that the dealer probably made too big a profit anyway. They ignore the fact that dealers in art are no different from motor manufacturers when it comes to covering the costs of their business. Worse still, if the artist's work has failed to prosper, the customer often returns the painting to the gallery, usually in a large car driven by a chauffeur, along with a complicated message about changing the colour of the dining room walls and a request for the refund of the £200 paid two years earlier. The message ends with the news that the chauffeur will wait for the cheque. In this hostile environment, art dealers often discover that, no matter how competitive the business, they need each other.

Despite many tales of dealers' cunning and, sometimes, downright dishonesty, I have always trusted art dealers. One or two have stretched the truth but, by and large, it is a world in which honesty prospers and dishonesty gets its just reward in the end. When I was collecting American abstract expressionist paintings in the early 1960s, I made many of my purchases from Leslie Waddington, the owner of Waddington Galleries. Friends described me as quite mad, but Leslie helped me build an important collection of paintings and sculpture, and when events dictated that they be sold, his help was invaluable. Dealers and collectors are actually good for each other, for the combination of professionalism and enthusiasm is formidable.

But there are occasions on which even the shrewdest dealers can be of no help to the most inspired collector. It is, I am afraid, impossible to be both a buyer and a seller at the same time. The dealer must quote a price and the customer must decide whether or not to buy. During the mid-1980s, one particular dealer, after staying with me in Broome, set off after the big hitters among the collectors of Western Australia. The Perth collectors were at that time among the most active in Australia and were well-known for paying the world's highest prices, in fact, they actually liked to pay the highest prices. My friend, however, pitched her prices just a trifle on the high side, even for the wild enthusiasm to buy paintings that then prevailed in Perth.

She was keen, young, with a nicely turned ankle and immaculate grammar. When she came across a fine painting, it was not by chance, for it was her trade. One day, she sought out a nineteenth-century picture of horseracing in South Australia. It was not a picture that would become the subject of a scholarly article by Denys Sutton in a literary art history magazine, for example, *Apollo*, nor would it find itself on the pages of *The Burlington* magazine. It was for the collector whose taste runs more to horses than painting, and who lives in Australia. The painting was, after its fashion, a masterpiece, and was one with a ready market among the wealthy racehorse owners of Western Australia. But that made it a one-hit picture: fail with it in Australia and it is yours for life. Our dealer hesitated. Maybe it was natural caution, but she struck no deal. She did not buy the picture, but she did acquire a photograph of it and reached an understanding with the owner. Our dealer would journey to Australia and offer the painting to a client, not, I must add, a client known personally to her, but a client who collected on such a grand scale that he retained his own agent who cared about such details as authenticity and provenance.

By chance or intent—we shall never know for sure—this agent was bypassed and an appointment made with the grand client. Australia is a long way from Britain by anyone's standards, and as the kilometres passed in the dark, unsleeping hours of a night flight, the beauty of the painting grew in the mind of our dealer. So did the price: the photograph was shown to the client and a price of £225 000 asked for the painting. 'You mean dollars, my dear?' said the client. 'Pounds,' she replied. 'Not a penny less,' echoing the words of Jeffrey Archer, the writer of popular thrillers. 'Such a price,' said the client. 'Impossible.' 'But such a picture,' she replied, 'so early for Australia. It is so rare . . . such a chance . . . there are, of course, many other distinguished collectors . . . came to you first . . . admired your taste, acumen, judgement.'

She deployed all the blandishments of her trade; all the flattery that turns a bicycle's handlebars into a Picasso. Having finished her recital, she returned the photograph to its envelope but, as she made to go, the client asked to see the photograph again. He returned it to her once more. 'My dear,' he said, 'I'm afraid I have bad news for you.' 'But the painting is of great quality,' she said, thinking that he did not admire it. 'Indeed,' the client said, 'any ten collectors would have this painting in the rustling of a cheque. The painting is all that you say it is, perhaps even more. No, my dear, the bad news is that I acquired the work last week.' 'Impossible,' she gasped. 'No, my dear, quite possible. And for only £125 000.'

The moral: you must not sell what you do not own. Every collector who has sprung a dealer's careful trap may squeal with delight at this story. Everyone who has bought a silver dish or piece of porcelain that was not quite what it purported to be on the day of purchase may celebrate in the knowledge of a dealer caught. Or pause and weep, for the great dealer—and this dealer may one day be great—is the friend of the collector. Through this friendship, the dealer becomes the collector's other half, his twin in collecting, as keen to form a collection as the collector, use such a dealer. The young lady's mistake was not the price she asked, which showed courage; it was the caution she revealed in not buying the painting in the first place. A dealer's profit is a payment for skill. In this case, our young dealer did not display sufficient skill and lost her profit.

Among the many strange beliefs held by even the most sophisticated of people is the one embraced by London dealers in the 1980s that the newly rich of Australia were an easy mark—kookaburras there to be plucked. This belief lacks logic: if a man has just made a large amount of money through his skill and shrewdness, he will surely be among the hardest of people to take it from. Nevertheless, stories abound concerning both these tycoons and the optimistic dealers of London.

∞

This is the story of three men: a prince, a tycoon and a London dealer known for the touching honesty with which he restores furniture. The dealer is a man who scrapes every vestige of the kindness of time from a piece of furniture and returns it faithfully to its bright new condition. Now this man had a prince among tables in his possession, a table fit for a prince, so when a large slice of the wealth of Australia walked in and inquired about the price, it was only a moment before a deal was struck. A night or two later, the dealer dined with a real prince, Prince Charles, who mentioned, as I suppose princes do, that he required various fine pieces of furniture, among them a table. The solution to the supply of the table was obvious: here was a Prince, the dealer had a princely table, and the deal was struck again. The table was delivered to the Prince, and the Australian's cheque was returned. After all, a peasant must give way to a prince. This, however, is not how Australian 'peasants' view these matters. Lawyers were called. There was acrimony: to sue or not to sue. The dealer was confident: an Australian would not have the temerity to sue a prince, surely? The Australian viewed this matter with refreshing clarity. Later, I dined at this table, perhaps even a king among tables, in Australia, where it is now settled.

The moral of this tale is that antiques can be sold only once, or rather, to only one customer at a time, regardless of the temptations of the second offer. If an object you once owned is sold and sold again for ever-increasing sums, don't think about it. The important price is the one that was paid to you. As for the profit that accrues to others, smile and take pleasure in the evidence of your own good taste.

∞

Collectors with great wealth are different from other collectors. The habits of most collectors vary from nation to nation, but for those who inhabit the stratosphere, there is an international taste that varies only from time to time. It makes no difference whether the seriously rich live in Tokyo, Paris, London, New York or Sydney, they collect the same objects: the French impressionists and French furniture, although these have now been joined by works from modern European artists and, in some cases, the abstract expressionists. All are symbols of wealth, and the wealthy fight for them. Witness, for example, the battles over the last three paintings by Vincent van Gogh to appear in the salesroom. They were purchased by mystery buyers. Much later, one at least of these mysteries was solved. The purchaser of Van Gogh's *Irises* was Alan Bond; the price he paid is still the world record, although the painting is now in the Getty Museum. The prices that these Van Goghs fetched appear even now truly remarkable, considering the provenance of many of them.

It is only six decades ago that the elder Gimpel, whose son founded the Gallery Gimpel Fils in London, left Holland with a bundle of Van Gogh's paintings. At the French customs, he was stopped and asked what they were. 'My own work,' he replied. 'I am taking them to Paris to see if I can sell them.' 'I think you will need good luck,' replied the customs inspector, whose attitude at the time perfectly reflected the buying public's view of the works of Van Gogh. Since then, France has adopted Van Gogh along with Picasso, Dali, Giacometti and a host of painters and sculptors from other nations. The French promoted them and, in the fullness of time, this chauvinistic approach to art paid handsome dividends when the volume of interested money increased at a rather greater rate than the availability of masterpieces by desirable dead artists.

Collectors, however, will go on buying what they like, and that is usually a reflection of where they come from. Each nation tends to buy its own art—the French buy French art and the Germans buy German art. The Canadians and Americans seldom buy anything other than work by native artists; the Americans have a very strong market in American art. The French, who invented the word *chau-*

vinisme, practise its meaning in the extreme. Let us take the case of a shrewd French collector on whose walls hung works by Monet, Manet and Renoir. In his private gallery, he had a large and magnificent Turner on an easel. His guests would declare it was a great work and ask who painted it. The collector would reply that it was attributed to an English painter named Turner, but added that it must be a fake, because no English artist painted that well.

⚭

The market for Australian art is in Australia, among Australians, with the exception of those foreigners who visit Australia and fall in love with its landscape and its people. These visitors may not even be collectors when they arrive. Usually, however, after their first visit, they leave as I did, clutching an Australian painting, only to return and to buy yet another and another. Even before I lived in Broome, I had become interested in Aboriginal culture. On my second visit to Australia in 1965, I acquired a number of bark paintings. These, however, were of no real quality. The enthusiasm for trading in this kind of painting had not yet really caught fire. It may sound perverse, but in the early 1960s, when the work of Aboriginals was not much sought by collectors and tourists, their work was harder to acquire. It is only after the idea gets around that a particular genre of painting or sculpture is likely to become valuable that much of it comes onto the market. Worth remembering also is the fact that the number of Aboriginal painters and sculptors working in those days was minuscule by comparison with the number active today. There can be no doubt, however, that the imaginative quality of their work is now far greater than it was 30 or 40 years ago.

When I moved my home to Broome, it was all different for me. I was no longer tied to acquiring my collection from the Perth, Melbourne and Sydney dealers, or at the London salesrooms where Aboriginal artefacts occasionally appeared and were knocked down for a pittance. Among the first people to help me with my collection was Father McKelson, a remarkable man, conversant with several Aboriginal languages. He introduced me to many of the artists who carved stone heads. The Kimberley and Broome were the source of a great deal of creative activity by Australian Aboriginals and I was spending much of my time at the heart of it. The carved mother-of-pearl shells worn as pubic shields fascinated me. They, along with the painted shields and boomerangs used in dancing, were objects that I had never seen before.

Mary Macha, who still deals in Aboriginal art and artefacts in Perth, has been to me for many years a guiding light in all matters Aboriginal. Mary Macha, now well on in life, is a fine-looking woman, with eyes that look straight at you, never blinking. In a conversation with her, there is no subterfuge—Mary tells it to you just as it is. She is a woman blessed with the patience of Job and this, combined with her obvious honesty, made her the perfect person to deal with Aboriginals. When the market in Aboriginal art and artefacts began to open up in the early 1970s, Mary was a driving force in its development. In 1971, she had begun working as a project officer for the Native Trading Fund, established to market Aboriginal craft in Western Australia. In 1973, Mary continued with this role for the Aboriginal Arts Board of the Australia Council. It was about this time that I first met Mary. Her enthusiasm was infectious, her knowledge considerable and, quite apart from these qualities, she saw the need for Aboriginal artists to record their cultures. In the goods that she dealt in, Mary always maintained a strictly observed level of quality. She fought fiercely against the 'Let's make a few bucks' school of thought, with its production-line mentality. Mary was consistent in her attitude that only those with talent should become artists. She did not subscribe to the view that because Aboriginal art exists, all Aboriginals are artists—any more than all Chinese are brilliant at business, or all Italians expert lovers. This selective approach to arts and artefacts was dramatically different to that practised in other parts of Australia.

By May 1979, Mary was conducting intensive art and craft courses, assisted by her husband. Part of an adult Aboriginal education program, these courses helped Aboriginal artists identify the best materials to use in their work and the best techniques for using those materials. One artist, Mingelmangau, seeing the large canvases of Robert Juniper, wanted to work on the same scale. Without a great deal of difficulty, Mary persuaded me to commission six large canvases by this artist. In the event, I believe that only two or three of them were delivered. The first of them hung in the foyer of the Australian Bank building on St George's Terrace, a property development that I had undertaken. Often when I was in Perth, I would visit Mary at the gallery that she ran on St George's Terrace. It was through her that I obtained the most interesting pieces in my collection. One of the most unusual aspects of Mary's character was the way that she was determined to maintain equity between the artist and the collector; she had a determination to see that each deal she orchestrated was fair to both sides.

It was Mary who first introduced me to the work of Rover Thomas and Paddy Tjamati. They created a corroboree, Paddy Tjamati doing the dreaming and Rover Thomas doing the painting. The pictures, painted on large panels of plywood, the panels having been taken from crates, were carried on the shoulders of the dancers. A television crew from the BBC came to Turkey Creek to film this corroboree. They set up their cameras and lights opposite the dancers and their painted boards and started to film, at which point the choreography of the dance dictated that the dancers turn around. In time, the camera crew moved and set up their equipment on the other side of the dancers, just in time for exactly the same thing to happen all over again.

It is hard for those used to European culture to come to terms with the partnerships that often create Aboriginal art, in which the dreamer owns the right to the image and the painter owns the right to the way that image is portrayed. The boards first used by Rover Thomas and Paddy Tjamati were the tops and sides of tea chests; later, small boards were used, either square or rectangular. Irrespective of their size and shape, these boards are directly in the tradition of the painted dance boards of north-western Australia, long, plank-like objects painted with ochres and chalks.

In search of Aboriginal art, I travelled many thousands of kilometres in the North-West. Mary Macha sent me to Bathurst and Melville Islands, located about 80 kilometres north of Darwin in the Northern Territory. The home of the Tiwi Aboriginal people, the islands are often simply known as the Tiwi Islands. They are very different from the Kimberley; they are tropical islands with tall hardwood trees, their timber heavy as lead and hard as iron. I flew there in a light plane, landing on the short runway of Bathurst Island. Arakike-Apuatimi Declan, whom I had come to see, carved the hardwood timber with an old bayonet from the last war. A small man, slightly built, he was in his early sixties when we met. He was relaxed as he showed me his work, but as he talked about it, his enthusiasm became electric. We sat, we talked and finally we came to a deal. From Declan, I acquired the rights to all his work for the next three years; from me, Declan acquired a brand-new Toyota Land Cruiser. It was a good deal and we were both delighted. An art adviser of that region tried to change the terms of the deal later on. People such as that man could neither understand nor approve of people like myself who valued Aboriginal work at a proper price. According to Ronald M. Berndt, Emeritus Professor at the Department of Anthropology at the University of Western Australia, the artist Declan, like many a Tiwi, was adventurous. He travelled into what he would have regarded as foreign parts, and also worked on the luggers.

Darwin, for instance, was virtually a Tiwi outstation, even though many other Aboriginals from a variety of different cultural backgrounds were also there. Near the Bagot Road Aboriginal settlement, some Tiwi people were buried and their graves were complete with their mortuary posts. Many Tiwi were also employed on Aboriginal Army settlements or attached to other military, naval and air force units in varying capacities. Declan was amongst them.

The village on Bathurst Island is an attractive place, its buildings well-spaced and its gardens lush with tropical plants. There is a thriving pottery as well as a workshop where fabrics are printed; these ventures are now highly successful. As outside interest in Aboriginal art increased, Declan commenced producing for non-Aboriginals. He was among a number of Tiwi working through the medium of carving and painting; others are making decorated pottery of a high order and screen-printed fabrics. The collection that I acquired from Declan not only included the traditional Tiwi carved burial posts but also carvings of humans and animals. There were also a number of bark paintings in this collection, a number of throwing sticks, spear points and some saw-shark noses, all of them highly decorated with coloured stripes and dots. Many carvings and poles made by the Tiwi people were shipped from Darwin to my home in Broome. Sadly, shortly before Declan completed his contract with me, he died. Declan was not only an admired carver and painter, he was also an exceptionally gifted singer and dancer. A dignified gentleman, he died of cancer in 1984. Sir Sidney Nolan wrote the following words as a foreword to a catalogue of Arakike-Apuatimi Declan's work: 'Painting is an extension of communication. As such, it's pure, difficult and wonderful. Declan's work is all of these. In doing this, he utilised his own heritage, its unique shapes, designs and imagery, in an innovative manner.'

The collection that Declan made for me was sent on a tour of regional art galleries in Australia after his death. My appetite for Aboriginal art at that time was immense; even today it matters not a lot to me whether the work is old or new, traditional or innovative, or in wood, stone or fibre. Baskets and feathered ornaments, small carvings or large carvings—I love it all. I felt an energy in the work of Aboriginal artists that excited me as I had not been excited since I first came across the abstract expressionist painters of New York in the early 1960s. I do not truly know to this day whether that excitement came from the works themselves or the spirit of the countryside and the people who made them. In the event, where that excitement came from is immaterial, for an object that passes on the ethos of the person who made it and the place where it is made is surely a true work of art. The communicating of a distinct and unique feeling is what art is all about.

∽∾

I find that I am drawn to collect above all else the art and artefacts of the country where I am living at the time I make that collection. So it was with Australia. For some years, I had noticed that the antique shops in the cities were filled with stripped pine furniture. Every vestige of paint and patina destroyed, its wood laid bare, clean, fresh and lifeless. By chance, I came upon a dealer before he committed this calumny on a fine softwood dresser. The colours of this dresser were truly wonderful. It was, I suppose, at this moment that I was taken with the idea of collecting bush furniture, but only examples in their original state. All the while begging and cajoling dealers to resist dunking their stock in the acid tank, my collection began to grow. Graham Cornall, a Melbourne dealer, was the chief supplier of this furniture and in the end he played the part of curator to my collection as well. Once bitten by the bug, my collection grew apace. Soon I was collecting the jarrah tables, chairs and wardrobes of Western Australia, and then the fine furniture of Victoria and New South Wales. The collection grew and grew. Wooden toys were added and then a deal of colonial pottery joined the furniture. The beautiful sat side-by-side with the bizarre among the 700 pieces that formed my collection of Australian furniture, a collection that was chronicled by Graham in his excellent book, *Memories*, which I published.

In the 1980s, I was in Australia and enjoying its orgy of self-indulgence. Hardly a week went by without a sale of Australian paintings, furniture and pottery. There was also bric-à-brac, which is described as 'Australiana' and includes anything with an Australian trademark stamped on it. The enthusiasm for anything Australian seems almost boundless. Of course, this was exaggerated by the Bicentenary celebrations in 1988, a great Australian party with parades of tall ships and Aboriginals who came to protest but who, like the rest of us, enjoyed a good party as well. The Bicentenary celebrations were accompanied by a significant number of cultural events devoted to Australia's history: her way of life, her marine biology, her ships, her trains, and, indeed, a warehouse devoted entirely to her bric-à-brac. The Bicentenary not only made the multinational inhabitants of this country supremely aware that they are Australians, but also aware of their land and its art. To a random collector, all this may appear to indicate a glut on the market. But the real collector knows this is not the high point of a market, rather the beginning of a better one. Opportunities like these only occur once every two hundred years or so.

The line between rarity and obscurity is very narrow. In time, the great works by Australian painters such as Sir Sidney Nolan, John Olsen and Russell Drysdale will rise in price because they have quality above and beyond their Australianness. The best prices of nineteenth-century cedar furniture and First Settlement furniture of colossal originality will rise in price along with the best pottery. The price of bric-à-brac will remain constant and, in some cases, drop right away, only to revive and drop again in the years ahead. There is a lesson here for the discerning collector: spot a nation whose prospects are good—there will be plenty in the next two centuries—and buy the product of its people. As the country becomes rich, so will its people. And as they become rich, they will collect the work of their forebears. The shrewd collector, however, will already have discovered the value of these trappings.

✦

The art world abounds with stories, many of them cautionary tales and rightly so, for there is a great need to be cautious when moving in that world. Here are three stories about the dreadful effect on talented people of three great human failings: pride, greed and jealousy. They are sad stories because each of these failings destroys, slowly but with absolute certainty, its victim.

First, pride. There were two Bond Street antique dealers of great repute. Their shops were opposite each other. They were adversaries; their rivalry took the form of uttering mildly deprecating remarks about the other's stock. 'Too brightly painted', or 'Too highly gilded', one would say of a piece in the other's window display, and each was so proud of his own stock that he could not bring himself even to enter the other's shop. One of these dealers acquired a bow-fronted commode of such beauty and quality that it might have been made by Chippendale himself. This commode stood in the back of his shop and eventually attracted the attention of a discriminating Knightsbridge dealer, who bought it. By a remarkable coincidence, just as it was being delivered to his shop in Knightsbridge, he received a visit from the other grand Bond Street dealer. 'What a piece,' exclaimed the latter when he saw the commode. 'What's the price?' The

Knightsbridge dealer contented himself with adding a modest profit to his purchase price—he doubled it; after all, he had owned the piece for only a few hours and here was the possibility of a quick sale.

'Where did you get it?' asked the Bond Street man. 'I'm afraid I cannot disclose where I acquired it,' replied the Knightsbridge man, a trifle pompously, 'but I can tell you that I'm frightfully pleased with it and if it is of no use to you, just let me get it into the shop and with one telephone call, I'll be able to sell it.' At this, the Bond Street man threw himself between the commode and the shop's front door. The removal man stood by, uncertain whether it was coming or going. 'It's mine,' cried the Bond Street man. 'Load it up again and deliver it to my shop. At once.' It is questionable whether he would have displayed the same enthusiasm had he known that this great commode had sat for months in the back of the shop across the road at half the price. He did not know, however, because his pride had not allowed him to cross the road and look. So he paid instead.

Next, greed. There was a shop in Mayfair that dealt in arms and armour. It was a paradise for small boys, although I am bound to say that when I grew up, I lost none of my enthusiasm for that emporium. One day, the owner was away at a country sale and left an assistant in charge of the shop. Shortly after 3 p.m., a well-dressed man, obviously possessed of a few quid, entered the shop. The assistant did not know much about arms and armour, but he did know a rich drunk when he saw one. The customer began to enthuse about a pair of pistols, cocking them, pretending to fire them, pointing them at passers-by in the street, and indeed, making a proper nuisance of himself. As he did this, the assistant noticed that their price tag had become detached. It read £750. When the well-dressed man asked the price, the assistant told him £1500. 'Done,' was the reply and, having written a cheque on the spot, the gentleman left, taking the pistols with him.

On hearing this story when he returned to the shop, the owner, an honourable man, was not impressed by his assistant's enterprise. He telephoned the customer that same evening at his home and said that a terrible mistake had been made. The pistols were not really for sale but, since the fault was entirely his, he would be grateful if the customer would return the pistols and take a cheque for £3000 for the inconvenience and embarrassment. But greed, fed by the deep suspicion of the truly ignorant, had taken root. 'It's no good trying that one on me,' the customer said. 'If you have undersold them, that's your bad luck, a deal is a deal. Sorry.' Puzzled, the dealer kept the money, but more importantly, he retained his honour. Both his honour and his profit had been kept intact by the customer's greed.

Finally, the worst of these failings, jealousy. This story took place in Melbourne, where a dealer had the good luck, some might call it skill, to turn up a cedar bureau bookcase of Australian manufacture and to recognise it as possibly the earliest known piece of Australian furniture. It was quite fine; not a masterpiece, but its extreme rarity made it much sought-after by Australians. The find was a triumph. It was a triumph, however, spoiled by the behaviour of a rival dealer in Sydney specialising in Australiana. This competitor spent a good deal of time debunking the man from Melbourne and his bureau bookcase. He did not offer any evidence that the bureau bookcase was not what the Melbourne dealer claimed, indeed, his argument came down to this: if the bureau bookcase were any good, it would be in his shop in Sydney. He was jealous, and it was destroying him. This story contains a moral for dealers everywhere: it is better to spend time improving your own understanding than to waste time knocking the competition.

If you are a dealer and a customer reveals that he has bought an object elsewhere, and you know that it is half the quality and twice the price of one you have yourself, the best thing is to smile and say, 'Very nice; indeed, wonderful. Very good of its kind.' You must never—please, never—discourage a collector. Especially, never discourage a child who collects, even if that collection is as mundane as pebbles from the beach. One in three adults in the Western world collects something, while in America the overwhelming majority of children have up to eleven different collections each. For a dealer, every child that collects may one day become a customer.

❧

My first shell collection came from the beach at Bournemouth in

England. Like other little boys, I found these pretty, useless objects irresistible and took them, covered in sand in a plastic bucket, back to the hotel and washed them in a basin—to the distress, I suppose, of the hotel's maids. In those days, it was my firm belief that small fish were born from seashells. I did not realise that the seashell is a mollusc, an entity in its own right. My second collection, enriched by the shells I got from Kerry Sharp, grew in leaps and bounds, not least from shells washing ashore that I found while walking each morning along Cable Beach at Broome. Cable Beach is uncluttered by surf-boards or beach umbrellas. The air is fresh with the smell of bush plants growing in the dunes. Sea eagles coast above the beach and migratory wading birds that, like me, have flown in from northern Europe, rise in clouds from the gentle surf. The sea is a highway for migrating whales and a resort for turtles and dolphins; on the beach, phalanxes of seashells glisten colourfully in the sun. I cannot resist them, though life for the adult collector is not as easy as it is for little boys. Shells gathered in the early morning quickly dry out on the breakfast table. As if cursed by an appalling mystical force, they become dull and lifeless; like the ones I collected in Bournemouth, despised when they lost their lustre.

The glistening gems accumulated by true shell collectors have to be plucked from a reef deep in the ocean or dredged from its bottom. Then, when the inhabitant of this strangely shaped skin is killed and removed, time stops for the shell and its lustre is preserved forever in its pristine state in readiness to join a collection. Collectors, however, must beware the little-known phenomenon of the killer seashell. Some of the cone shells—*Conus textile* and *Conus stratus*, for instance—are among the nine or so varieties that sometimes fight back. These are violent creatures, fish-eating shells that shoot a small dart of poison into their victims. Paralysis and death follow, suggesting that it can be deeply unwise to look down the wrong end of a loaded cone shell. In Australia, paralysis and death are not the only fates that can befall unwary shell collectors. Large areas of the coastline are national parks, and collectors caught plundering the shells are subject to heavy fines.

No laws prevented the early explorers of the southern hemisphere, such as William Dampier and Captain Cook, from bringing excellent examples of Australian shells to Europe, where they were mounted on silver or gold. Indeed, shells from around the world have a place in history: primitive people used them for dress, and Pocahontas, the American Indian princess who befriended the early settlers, wore them as wampum. The nautilus shell is the image of the renaissance and the model for Sydney's Opera House. Hawaiians used the golden cowry as a symbol of royalty; cowry shells have surfaces so smooth and a texture so perfect that they are called *porcelain* by the French, and they are the pride of any shell collector's cabinet. As stamps are kept in albums, so shells are kept in cabinets. As in all forms of collecting, shell specialists have their eccentricities. Some collect freaks—misshapen or discoloured shells—cones, spiked shells or white shells. Some collect giant clams; others, cowries so small that they can be observed only under a magnifying glass and picked up with tweezers. Collectors of Victoriana prize particularly the pretty shells arranged in patterns in boxes made by seamen on long and lonely voyages. The sums of money that pass between a dealer and a collector trading in shells are considerable. Of course, primitive people also used shells for money—the *Cowry moneta* was one of the earliest forms of currency, so perhaps shells are money after all. Perhaps that is why people collect them.

My boyhood interest in collecting seashells was renewed upon my arrival in Australia, inspired by the shell collection of Paul Jones, the Australian botanical painter. I first came across Paul when I found one of his botanical paintings reproduced in a magazine and, as a result, I determined to meet him. A painter of flowers and sometimes shells, he was a man who could catch a moment of nature and commit it to paper with pencil, brush and colour. Not the easiest of people, Paul was given to grumbling at imagined slights and omissions of attention. For three years, he came in the spring to paint portraits of the flowers in my garden at West Green in Hampshire. There are well in excess of 40 portraits that he painted during those three years. I gave them to my wife Romilly and they used to hang in our home at West Green. When we sold the contents of that house, they were almost the only things that we kept. Now they decorate our new home in southern Italy. There is something both timeless and restful about Paul Jones's paintings of flowers. While difficult with people, he was at one with nature. On each of my frequent flying visits to Sydney, I visited Paul. I sat listening to his grumbling conversation and all the time I looked at the beauty that he had caught on paper with his brushes and paints.

Possibly the only advantage of jet lag is that you are fully awake at times of the night when you would otherwise be unaware that there was anything worth waking to see. The last hours of full moon, for instance, as it hovers over Sydney Harbour; the first hours of light before the sun comes over the horizon; the sunrise that paints each ripple on the surface of the Harbour's water and gleams on the shiny arcs of the Opera House. Then there is the freshness as you walk in the Botanical Gardens, a freshness that comes with dawn, a few moments caught between the stifling heat of antipodean night and the blazing sun of day, moments when the birds sing just for the joy of singing. None of this has changed since I first set foot in Australia 40 years ago. None, that is, except the Opera House: in those days, it was just a building site jutting into Sydney Harbour.

In my hunt for rare seashells, at the beginning of that strange enthusiasm, I came across Lance Moore and his shop, which was hidden in The Rocks not far from the Opera House, behind the Sydney Harbour Bridge. Lance Moore sold shells, seashells in a thousand shapes and colours. I say a thousand, but he may well have had ten thousand varieties in his narrow shop. All I know is that there were shells everywhere: great baskets of common shells, rare varieties carefully wrapped in cotton wool and pulled from a drawer filled with unpaid bills and unanswered letters, scraps of paper each with a telephone number or an address on them. A filing system from hell, a bundle of addresses with no names, and names with telephone numbers that no longer answered, would be pulled from a drawer with a shell he was showing a serious collector.

I know little of Lance Moore's background. He seemed once to have been a sailor or at least spent time on ships; clearly, he was a diver and a collector of live shells. I write 'clearly' when, in fact, I do not know, for Lance was to me quite as mysterious as the sponges and corals that decorated his walls. Giant crayfish and crabs of vast proportions hung there too, among the rows of sharks' jaws and turtle shells. His back office was a salon, not of writers or painters, other than Jonesy, as he used to call Paul Jones. No, his was a salon of fisherman, divers and collectors of shells, a salon in which your intellect was judged not by the sparkle of your wit or the depth of your education, but by whether you could put a name to an obscure mollusc. Shells were taken from cases, laid in raffia baskets, lifted and examined, occasionally compared to examples in reference books, but more often name-tagged and put away. Paul Jones sat with a discriminating eye, looking for the perfect example, for he only collected the most perfect of shells which he kept in a single cabinet, each tray a work of gleaming beauty. Cowries were the shells that attracted him the most, but not exclusively, for his collection was wide-ranging, but a rare and perfect cowry visibly excited him. Shells have that effect on those who love them, like the effect that gold, diamonds and pearls can also have. As far as I know, men do not kill for shells, but they come close to it.

Lance Moore had only one leg, and hopped among those gathered in his back room, distributing tea and often cake. He held court at these gatherings, generous with his knowledge, careful with his friendships. Along with the stuffed fish, baskets of shells and various pieces of equipment which cluttered up the space, Lance also had two very large dogs, both of which gave one the impression that they would have been very angry if you trod on them. Lance was in the habit of taking a nap with his dogs under the table in his back room. It was a surprising sight for customers who wandered in, to find a single leg sticking out from under a table. Today, Lance Moore is dead and he holds court no longer; Australia has lost an epicentre of real culture.

∞

I have never forgotten an experience that I, always an enthusiastic collector, suffered as a child. Invited for a day's salmon fishing on the lower reaches of the River Test in England's county of Hampshire, I stayed with my hosts the night before the expedition in order to make an early start for the river. That evening, my hosts had a dinner party, in which I joined, although I was only about twelve years old. The conversation moved about the table until a woman sitting on the other side of the table quite suddenly addressed a question to me. 'What do you do, Alistair, what are your hobbies?' She may not have used my name, perhaps she just called me 'little boy'; I do not remember. The question was innocent enough, but my answer clearly did not measure up to the standard of reply that she expected. 'I collect things.' 'What sort of things?' she asked. I suppose she had expected me to say that my hobbies were cricket or football, or even train-spotting. 'I collect arms and armour,' I responded. At which point, this woman addressed the entire table—there were eleven others apart from me sitting there—'Arms and armour! When I think of armour, it is synonymous with boredom. Armour is the most boring subject that I can imagine.' The hostess, I believe, then changed the topic of conversation, which was not hard because the entire dinner party had been struck silent, expecting, I suppose, that I would burst into tears.

I often think back on my varied career as a collector and my collections. From Australia, I collected paintings and bush furniture, Aboriginal art and artefacts, modern and contemporary paintings, furniture, bush furniture and Australiana, books on Australia and by Australians, seashells, parrots and other wildlife, and not forgetting the historic buildings of Perth, Fremantle and Broome. These were the physical collections that I owned; the experiences that I had while living and travelling in Australia, they are yet another collection. Then there were my collections of ties, marbles, Venetian beads, books, manuscripts, English furniture, garden implements, rare breeds of pigs, chickens, ducks and geese, sheep and shepherds' crooks, nineteenth-century policemen's truncheons, stuffed animals, farm implements from tractors to pitchforks, and, of course, arms and armour. Today, I still collect; currently, only ties, marbles, beads, glass and political badges. I try to keep my collecting under control. Slowly but remorselessly, however, the collection of odd-shaped stones in our house grows and grows.

As I have written, my interest in arms began when I was still a boy. Over the years, my collection grew to include Highland edged weapons, English pistols, long guns and, most particularly, nineteenth-century revolvers. One pair of pistols that I found in England went to Australia. Many years later, I came across them again in the collection of Warren Anderson, the Australian property developer and Colt pistol collector, who sold them in America for £250 000. When I had bought these pistols, I had paid £2000 and sold them for £5000; the first dealer to own them had paid the equivalent of £2.50. These pistols took only thirty years to reach the amazing figure that they fetched at auction in America. Warren Anderson kept his gun collection in his historic house, Fernhill, on the slopes of the Blue Mountains. It was certainly the best collection in Australia, and in respect of his Colt revolver collection, was beyond doubt among the best in the world. Tall and built like a brick wall, with a craggy face and a head of blond hair that would do credit to a thatched cottage, Warren Anderson is descended from a Norwegian sailor who jumped ship in Australia.

One winter, I visited Warren at Tipperary, his station in the Northern Territory, bordering on Darwin. With me were John Roberts and Bob Frost, my partner in the venture with Joan Bowers. We flew from Broome in a small jet, landing on Warren's airstrip. The three of us had to share a room. It was a large room but not one of us could be described as small. In the north, I always travelled with a bathplug tied to my car keys with a piece of string. This bathplug was the subject of much comment, not to say considerable hilarity, among the people who knew of its existence. 'Why would you need a bathplug?' I was often asked, usually in the bush a few hundred kilometres from the nearest bath. Well, the answer was simple: the Australians take showers while the British take baths. In my whole time travelling in the north, whenever I came across a bath, while the shower worked, the bathplug was missing. This was also the case at Anderson's station.

We arrived early in the morning and spent the day with other guests, flying across Tipperary in a trio of helicopters. John Roberts sat between Bob Frost and myself. It was the sort of helicopter that has no doors and only two seat belts in the back, so we tied John in with a piece of rope and off we flew, happy as Larry. Then the pilot spotted a cow and, like a Stuka pilot, he dropped our helicopter from the heavens in a sideways dive. Frankly, I was terrified as we skimmed the trees. Tipperary is the most beautiful of places, and we flew from its mountain ranges, across rivers, over rainforests, on to the swampland near the mudflats that edged the sea. It was on the swampland that Warren decided to land. As we stepped out of the helicopter, all around us were the nests of crocodiles. Warren, it seems, is immune to fear; for myself, already frightened by the flight, I was downright terrified by the ground where we had landed and desired nothing more than to be airborne again.

As we flew back to the station homestead, we skimmed the tops of forests, the black and white Torres Strait pigeons rising in clouds as we passed over them. Below us were the nests of jabiru storks with the immature birds staring up at us, their beaks opening wider and wider expecting a delivery of food. The natural wildlife of Tipperary is quite remarkable, both in its quantity and variety. On the outward trip, several members of the party had shot with rifles, out of the open side of the helicopters, a large number of the feral pigs that infest the north. These pigs ruin the countryside, ripping up native growth with their rutting as they search for food hidden in the earth. Because of the massive damage they do to the land they have to be regularly culled. As we returned, I expected to see the line of carcasses that we had left behind us. There was not a dead pig in sight; the crocodiles had in the course of an hour or two disposed of over a hundred of them. As we landed, a group of station hands nearby were handling a bull buffalo, trying to get it from a truck into a cattle race. One of these men had blood running from a bandage on his leg—a bandage is rather a grand word for the covering of what was clearly a serious wound. In fact, he had simply tied a dirty handkerchief around his leg, and that handkerchief was now soaked in blood. 'What happened to you?' Warren asked, pointing at the man's leg. 'That old fellow got me as we were putting him on the truck.' 'You'd better get that seen to,' said Warren, looking at the ghastly wound and then at the sharpness of the buffalo's horns. The man looked at his watch and then replied, 'I'll be finished in a couple of hours, I'll get someone to look at it then.'

The men of northern Australia are hardy men. That night, Warren gave a party. All the workers on the station turned out to eat and drink, and a few of them to dance. Bone meat was the dish that I had for dinner, its bone touching both ears as I tore at its middle with my teeth. 'It's really good for your virility,' one swarthy individual informed me. Without doubt, he did not need much bone meat to pep him up as he lurched from station female to station female. John Roberts and I were frankly exhausted after our day's outing, so we decided to retire to our beds, beds that were the best part of two kilo-metres away. It was pitch dark and we were fearful of the crocodiles we had seen around the homestead that afternoon. They had lain like giant maggots sunning themselves on the nearby river bank. 'We stick to the road,' John instructed. For myself, I could not see how a road was going to protect us from a hungry croc whose tastebuds had been alerted by the scent of the barbecue. Not long after we had set out, a truck's headlights could be seen behind us. 'Good old Warren,' says John, 'he's sent one of the men to give us a lift to our quarters.' As the truck drew level with us, a female voice enquired, 'Wouldn't you two fellows rather be coming with us?' As our eyes became used to the bright lights, they focused on two of the most toothless old hags one might ever meet. If there had been a third, they would have been straight out of Shakespeare's *Macbeth*. John and I looked at each other and then at the hags. 'Oh, thanks a lot,' says John, 'but I think I'll walk, it's a lovely night.' With a serious belch, the driver of the vehicle commented, 'Youse fellows don't know what you're missing.' Then they drove off.

17

Travelling in Australia, or rather urban Australia, which is where ninety per cent of the people live, I am struck by the interest in art—not art in general, but Australian art, particularly nineteenth and twentieth-century Australian paintings in the European idiom. There is hardly a restaurant in Melbourne or Sydney that doesn't hang works by Australian painters. Certainly no bank is without a twentieth-century Australian painting or sculpture in its foyer, or a nineteenth-century Australian painting in the boardroom. The art of France, America, Britain, not to mention Spain, Italy and the rest of Europe, has no place here. The names of the great icons that we Europeans admire are to be found in art galleries but not in houses, office buildings or banking halls. Australians collect Australian art or, at least, the most prudent of them do.

The first Australian artists were visitors from other countries, recording the plants and animals of Australia to show an astonished world what a kangaroo looked like. Convict painters first recorded life in the colonies or, in the case of William Buelow Gould, death in the colonies: heaps of dead game and fish, carefully recorded, complete with blowflies. The first serious school of Australian painting was located in the bush not far from Melbourne at a place called Box Hill, where three painters named Roberts, McCubbin and Abrahams lived in the 1880s. They painted in the style of the French impressionists. They painted on empty cigar boxes because they gave a good texture and surface to paint on—and were free. Abrahams's father was an importer of cigars. He was, incidentally, also grandfather to Sir Denys Lasdun, the British architect and designer of London's National Theatre. In 1889, this group of painters held an exhibition that was called '9 × 5 Impressions'—nine inches by five being the size of a cigar-box lid. Australians, in those days, were clearly not smoking Laranaga Magnums which come in a somewhat larger box. These antipodean impressionists, whose most recent exhibition was called 'Golden Summers', drew a mist of happiness over their harsh and dangerous landscape. Their work is in vogue and fetches great sums.

Australian painting trundled along without arousing much interest among European collectors until the Second World War, when a group called the Angry Penguins emerged. These were painters and writers whose trumpet was a magazine by that name, and who were fighting one of the obscure battles that seem to obsess the art world but which have no relevance for the collector. By this time several artists were painting the Australian outback, but none caught the reality of the bush in the way Sir Sidney Nolan first did in the late 1940s. Nolan's bush strikes fear into the urban population of Australia. He painted the bush where one man never asks another man where he is from, or where he goes to, where laughter is crude and unforgiving and violence equates with humour, where a joke can be made of death. This landscape predates man by millions of years. The bush has resisted almost every attempt by Europeans to destroy it: it has resisted cattle, sheep, mining, litter, and even the demand for Aboriginal bark paintings. This is the hard bush, and Nolan painted it as it is. Many other painters paint it as they imagine it to be: a bush that does not disturb the peace and comfort of a Sydney drawing room.

Arthur Boyd put strength, not into the landscapes, but into his figures—savage brides and beasts and bulls. Russell Drysdale painted soft landscapes with strong people. John Olsen's bush is knowing, lonely and distorted, empty but full of humour. John Percival painted *Demented Swans*, no kidding. As is the fashion, there is also a mass of painters working in the modern idiom, from Tim Storrier down—or on. Slowly, the styles of the painters in European idiom and those of the indigenous people merge, this is art that is conscious of Australia's proximity to the Far East.

Art in Australia takes two paths: there are paintings about the country as a place and as a nation. There is freshness in the sunshine, in the people, in the cities and in the paintings, whether they are good or bad. If you are excited about Australia, you will be excited about its art. I suspect this strange continent creates collectors of paintings. In Sydney, the doyen of the dealers was Barry Stern. While Barry has given up dealing, the Gallery Stern still exists, now run by Dominic, and Dominic's exquisite and catholic tastes make this gallery a good place to start.

The first Australian painting that I ever bought came from Barry Stern. It was of emus dashing across a red landscape—Barry had an eye for a good painting and without doubt was an extremely able dealer. I enjoyed drinking a cup of coffee and catching up on the gossip with Barry when he was in business and I enjoy doing the same with his successor. When Barry moved to Morocco, he left in style with a splendid sale at Sotheby's. One lot in particular amused me. It was of twelve saucers and two cups—clearly designed for the family which keeps a lot of cats!

∞

A painter who has a real sense of humour is Elizabeth Durack. She managed to pull the best joke on the art establishment of Australia and its attendant flock of dealers since Ern Malley, when two young Australian writers, fed up with what they regarded as the drivel published by trendy magazines, fancied a practical joke. With the help of the works of Shakespeare and a dictionary, they wrote a number of modern poems under the name of Ern Malley and sent them to an avant-garde magazine called *Angry Penguins*, which enthusiastically published them. When the truth came out, all Australia laughed at how the art establishment of Europe and America was fooled. Elizabeth Durack, however, is no mere practical joker, rather a serious and talented painter. It was, I suppose, out of a sense of mischief that she started to paint under the name of Eddie Burrup. Three of these paintings were submitted for an exhibition, 'Native Title Now'. With the paintings went a fake biography of Burrup, a name that many assumed to be Aboriginal, when in fact it was that of an Englishman who gave it to a peninsula on the Western Australian coast. Along with the biography was an interview in which Burrup refers to 'the olden day track place where dreaming time . . . bin . . . put'm first time'. Not content with this, Elizabeth Durack also entered one of Burrup's paintings in the competition for the Sulman Prize.

When the hoax was pointed out to him, Edmund Capon, the Director of the Art Gallery of New South Wales and the least pompous of men, merely remarked that artists, like writers, often used pseudonyms. Most of the painters who painted in Renaissance Italy are known by the names of the towns where they originated, rather than by their real names. Go back 600 years and you find painters with curious names such as the Master of the Lily. Edmund Capon was quite right, of course, in his assessment of the situation. In the world of conceptual art, what is taken as a hoax would, in fact, be a complete work of art. Painting, biography, interview and invented name—all part of it. What a shame that Elizabeth Durack did not enter her 'hoax' for the annual Turner Prize offered by Britain's Tate Gallery; she would most likely have won it.

Humour is the key essence of communication. With her humour, Elizabeth Durack, whether she intended to or not, was making a considerable statement. Aboriginal art, primitive art, conceptual art, abstract art, figurative art—is all art and should be judged by the same set of standards. The setting aside of any particular strand or type of art is just misleading, for it is a work's quality that matters, not the style in which that work is painted. Unfortunately, the statement by the director of the Kimberley Aboriginal Law and Cultural Centre— 'We are upset that someone who claims to have an understanding of and respect for our Aboriginal culture should act in a way that can only be interpreted otherwise'—adds fuel to the ever-smouldering fire of prejudice in Australia.

Artists are artists the world over, nothing more, nothing less. Where they come from and the style in which they paint are simply matters of incidental interest; it is the quality of their work that matters above all else. As for the idea that Elizabeth Durack was abusing Aboriginal culture by painting in a style reminiscent of that culture, the notion is ill-founded. Aboriginal culture is one of the strongest cultures in the world, and one from which in the past many people have drawn, Picasso's X-ray paintings, for instance. What is more, many people will draw inspiration from Aboriginal art in the future. Once a culture is discovered by the art world it, of necessity, becomes the property of all artists. There are in the twentieth century a legion of examples to demonstrate this fact. Matisse's use of African tribal art, Henry Moore's use of the sculptural images from the Mayan culture and, not least, the use of European images drawn from European twentieth-century culture in innovative Aboriginal sculpture, painting and music. The people who harm a culture are those who distort its history and invent for it new traditions, in the way that the English destroyed the clan culture of the Scottish Highlands during the eighteenth and nineteenth centuries. The Australian Aboriginals, however, have had their share of this, with foreign best-sellers identifying curious Aboriginal customs as spurious as those allegedly practised on an American writer, in which she was buried up to her neck in the ground. Such ideas owe more to spaghetti westerns and the book *The Songlines* by Bruce Chatwin (now disclosed in his widow's autobiography as more the product of his fertile imagination than carefully researched text) than anything Aboriginal. In the event, however misleading these curious notions may be, they draw attention internationally to the existence of the Aboriginal people as well as to their grand and powerful culture. In the end, this attention can only help those people in a struggle for the recognition of their rights.

No sooner had Elizabeth Durack's hoax hit the news than a publishing company in Broome set up to publish only Aboriginal writing was taken in by a Sydney man masquerading as an Aboriginal woman. So long as there are publishing houses that practice a racial policy and art exhibitions that exhibit work based only on race, there will always be fraud. The argument used by Magabala Books Aboriginal Corporation that it was set up to help Aboriginals who found it hard to get their work published is spurious. There are people all over the world who would like to have their books published and cannot achieve their ambition.

For many years, I have known Edward Capon and I regard him as among the most civilised of humans and a good friend. It was for this reason that in the late 1990s I decided to give not only a large number of works by Sir Sidney Nolan to the Art Gallery of New South Wales, but also my collection of twentieth-century fashion photographs by European photographers and a much smaller collection of photographs by Australian photographers. Among the former collection there is a group of about 70 photographs by my friend, the late Terence Donovan, along with those of his friend David Bailey and others of their generation. In the early months of 1997, Terence Donovan committed suicide; a less likely candidate for that end I could not imagine. Overcome, however, by deep depression from a severe outbreak of eczema and the cortisone that he was given to cure it, he took his own life.

⌘

Whether there for business or to find pieces to add to my collections, I thoroughly enjoyed my visits to Melbourne, finding that city both attractive and highly civilised. When I first went there in the mid-1960s, there were two apparently first-class hotels to stay in—the incredibly stuffy Windsor Hotel, where Sir Halford Reddish always stayed, and the brighter but less comfortable Southern Cross. The food and the beds at the Southern Cross were dreadful. As a hotel, it crossed the spectrum from the garish to the downright uncomfortable, yet it boasted four stars. For my money, I would not have given it any stars at all. However, the Southern Cross did have one asset: it was run by one of the most remarkable hotel managers that I have ever come across. John Carrados had two main interests, racehorses and women, and these interests worked greatly to the advantage of the Southern Cross. The racing crowd met there and there were always glamorous women about, one of the few things to recommend the place. John's personality gave the hotel life—there were people there most of the time, which is more than you could say for the Windsor Hotel which was, as far as I could tell, empty whenever I went there.

My association with the Southern Cross did not start well. The first time that I visited the place, my first wife, Sarah, and a girlfriend were left alone for lunch. I was out engaged on business. When I returned, I discovered two very angry young women. It seemed that they had walked into the hotel's grill room, a pleasant restaurant decorated much like a London club. Seeing no head waiter, they found themselves a table; Australia being the land of self-sufficiency, this seemed to them the right thing to do. Settled at the table, they set about getting the attention of the waiter, who studiously ignored them. Sarah, not being the most patient of souls, summoned the head waiter, who had by this time appeared. Before she was able to complain about the lack of service, he announced, 'You can't sit here.' 'Well, where can we sit?' Sarah asked, and began to move towards another empty table. 'You can't sit anywhere in this restaurant. It's for men only.' This was a concept that was new to Sarah: a hotel restaurant that only served men. She and her girlfriend protested vehemently, only to be summarily thrown out of the Southern Cross's grill room. Sarah seldom returned to Australia, a country that she believed to be hostile to women and, I have no doubt, or so she believed, to her in particular. Happily, Australia began its great change after this and the Southern Cross began to serve all comers, male or female.

John Carrados was among the most amusing of men. He explained to me that when flight crews checked into the hotel, he watched for the best-looking women among them. Then, having noted their room numbers, he called on them with a bottle of whisky. 'Don't you get a lot of rejections?' I asked, for he would suggest to these attractive young women that they share the bottle with him. Then he would stay on a little longer. 'Of course,' he replied, 'but I also get a number of girls who are delighted with my idea and invite me into their rooms.' When John's time at the Southern Cross expired, Intercontinental Hotels sent him to manage the Mark Hopkins Hotel in San Francisco.

It was while I was staying at the Southern Cross that I met and made friends with the art dealer Julian Sterling, who owned an art gallery in the arcade below the hotel. Over the first five years of the 1970s, I bought from him a number of Sidney Nolan's early works, among them *The Dog and Duck Hotel*, painted in 1948, which I had fallen in love with when I first saw it reproduced on a Qantas menu:

Burke dying under a tree, the deserted mine, and a policeman with his head down a wombat hole. Along with these paintings, I also bought *The First-class Marksman*; it is one of the few of Nolan's famous Ned Kelly series exhibited in London and still in private hands.

John Adams, my lawyer in Western Australia, often stayed at my home when he visited England; usually, he slept in the same guestroom. On one occasion in, I believe, 1966, he asked me about the painting that was hanging in that room. 'Is it a copy of Russell Drysdale's painting *The Cricketers*?' 'No,' I replied, 'it's the real thing.' John looked a trifle shocked. 'That's Australia's most famous painting.' He was right, of course; it was then and it still is. I had bought the picture from Julian Sterling for £6000. Its sale was reported in the *Financial Times* as the highest price ever paid for an Australian painting. A few years later, I sold it for £12 000 and was very pleased with the deal. Today, that painting must be worth well over $500 000. I love Russell Drysdale's work and bought several more of his paintings. At his exhibition in London's Leicester Galleries, I missed the chance to buy what I regard as one of his most haunting works, *The Barmaid in Broome*, as I had arrived at the exhibition only minutes after it was sold. I had never heard of Broome in those days, so my judgement was not coloured by my affection for that town. The painting was pure magic, far better than *The Cricketers*. The new owner was a man I knew quite well, but he would not part with it, despite being offered a considerable profit. The picture remained in his collection until his death; afterwards it was sold at auction by Sotheby's in London, along with the rest of his impressive collection of Australian paintings. By this time, Russell Drysdale had died and the prices for his pictures were running into hundreds of thousands of dollars.

Lauraine Diggins was another dealer from whom I bought some wonderful paintings. Imaginative and energetic, she always seemed to be able to lay her hands on just the right sort of paintings, a talent displayed by few in her trade. On one occasion while I was in Melbourne, John Olsen asked me to open an exhibition of his work at the National Gallery of Victoria. To do this was for me a pure pleasure, because I have always admired John's work. At one time

I owned a number of drawings and watercolours that he had done of Broome and its inhabitants. John Olsen and his elegant wife Catherine had fallen in love with Broome, and some years later, after visiting the town each winter, bought a house not far from the town. As for John's paintings, they have a quality and a content that surpasses the natural attractions of Australian painting. His pictures would be as at home in New York or in London's winter light. Somehow, John seems to have caught the light of Australia in his pictures, rather than just relying on the Australian light to be reflected on them. Among the friends that I have made in Australia, John Olsen stands out. I regard him as Australia's greatest living painter. Of the people I most enjoy spending time with, he and his wife Catherine are high on the list.

༺༻

I first met Sidney Nolan in 1978, when he was brought to see me by my friend, the painter and typographer, Gordon House. They visited me at my bookshop in London's Cork Street to ask if I would be interested in publishing Sidney's own poems. The bookshop was laid out like a sitting room, with armchairs and sofas. The books that I sold were extremely eclectic and included twentieth-century contemporary poetry and novels, as well as second-hand and antique books. While the shop specialised in fine eighteenth- and nineteenth-century botanical and natural history colour-plate books, there was, however, another aspect to the stock that I kept at 31 Cork Street. On the shelves was a large selection of *beaux livres*, among them a copy of Matisse's great work, *Jazz*, in a fine contemporary French binding. Works illustrated by most of the great painters from *l'école de Paris* were there. One book in particular, I remember, was a thin book of poems illustrated with four cubist etchings by Picasso. Sidney bought this book for a small price and I have often wondered what happened to it.

Sidney Nolan was very taken with my bookshop and set about taking books from the shelves with a wild enthusiasm, while Gordon House was diffident about the purpose of their visit. 'Sidney thinks that perhaps you don't like his work.' It was not surprising that Sidney should have come to that conclusion because, at the time, I collected abstract colour sculptures, mostly by artists from the St Martin's School of Art. I also collected American abstract expressionists and the colourist painters of the New York school. I have always liked Sidney's work, at least, since I began collecting paintings in the early 1960s. I had in my collection at the time at least three of his paintings. Reassured, Sidney began to talk about his poems and how he would like the book containing those poems to look. The book was to be called *A Paradise Garden*.

A month or so later, I was invited to Sidney's house in Deodar Road in Putney. When I saw the paintings that would illustrate *A Paradise Garden*, I had the shock of my life, for there were well over 2000 of them, small paintings each about 30 centimetres square, that when joined together made up the large painting called *Paradise Garden*. Later, Sidney painted two more sets of these oils on paper, which made up a painting called *Shark,* and after that an even larger painting, *Snake.* These three pictures were huge.

I was deeply impressed both at the quality and the scale of his work for the project, so it was only a matter of moments after seeing these paintings, stacked against the wall of the studio, that I agreed to publish Sidney's poems. Gordon House designed *A Paradise Garden* and in less than a year I had delivery of the copies from the printer. Despite the fact that *A Paradise Garden* was a beautiful book in every respect—no expense had been spared in its production—I was only able to sell a small number of copies. As for the painting of the same name, a work nearly 30 metres long, it was only years later that I saw it all in one piece. Sidney and I, along with Lord Clark and Sir Norman Read, then director of the Tate Gallery, had made a trip to Dublin to see a retrospective of Sidney's work exhibited in Dublin's Agricultural Hall. *A Paradise Garden* was hanging there in all its size and glory. There was no doubt in my mind after seeing that exhibition that Sidney Nolan was a great painter. When he was the director of Britain's National Gallery, the art historian Lord Clark was the one person who realised the importance of Sidney's work. He had been to Australia in the 1950s and could see the paintings in their natural context. While Lord Clark had always held that view, Norman Read went along with it as well after seeing the exhibition in Dublin.

A *Paradise Garden* was, I believe, the most original and impressive book that I have ever published and I very much enjoyed working on it with Gordon House. The fact that it sold rather badly did not stop me embarking on a second book illustrated by Sidney Nolan. Like *A Paradise Garden*, *The Darkening Ecliptic* was a fine publication. With poems written by Ern Malley, illustrated by Sidney, it was perhaps not quite as lavish as *A Paradise Garden* but of that order. However, in common with the first book, it did not sell in any great number. A glutton for punishment, I continued to publish books, all of them illustrated by a variety of artists and on a variety of subjects, of equal quality to the books illustrated by Nolan, with an equal lack of commercial success.

When Sidney first showed in London, his pictures caused a sensation. Many people believed that he was an abstract painter, that it was impossible for landscapes to have the shapes and colours that he painted. While Sidney Nolan certainly understood the abstract quality of the Australian landscape, his colours, however, were true to life. During the mid-1960s, the Art Gallery of Western Australia bought a large painting by Sidney Nolan from Rose Skinner, the West Australian art dealer. Made up of eight panels and called *The Desert Storm*, it depicts the bright red landscape of the Pilbara with a purple storm and is among Sidney's greatest works. Because its colours seemed so unnatural, this was exactly the sort of work that made collectors in England and America believe him to be an abstract painter. The art gallery trustees of the day viewed the painting and Rose told them in all honesty that it was a masterpiece. When the deal was all set to go, there was a snag—the art gallery's wall was too short and the painting far too long. Rose had the answer: the painting came in eight panels, so why not take only seven of them? The gallery trustees agreed and for years only seven panels hung in the Art Gallery of Western Australia. Later, Rose Skinner sold me the eighth panel for £220, never mentioning that it was the tail-end of a much larger painting. Many years later, Cherry Lewis, now the doyenne of the Perth art dealers, tried to have this panel reunited with its fellows.

The trustees of the art gallery at this time seemed content with the panels that they owned, despite the gallery having been rebuilt with larger walls. In time, I gave the eighth panel to the Art Gallery of New South Wales, along with many other paintings and a large collection of photographs. It is my hope that they will lend the eighth panel to the Art Gallery of Western Australia and then Sidney Nolan's work can once again be seen complete.

Cherry Lewis and her late husband sold me many pictures during the 1980s. Their gallery was an intimate space; their stock small but of a very high quality. The pair of them had a brilliant eye when it came to selecting the best of Australian paintings. Quite apart from their ability as art dealers, I enjoyed their company. Often, I would leave my offices at about eleven o'clock in the morning to take a walk and stop by their gallery; at other times, I would visit them at home for a cup of coffee and gossip to relieve the pressure of a hectic day's work in the office. To take time talking to the Lewises was to enter a different world from that of planning permissions, tenants, architects and banks, which made up my day from seven-thirty in the morning to late at night. The Lewises, along with Mary Macha, the dealer in Aboriginal art, were the people who really put the joy into my life in Perth.

I was somewhat perverse in my dealings with Sidney Nolan, for I used to buy his early works in Australia, the ones that everyone wanted, and swap them with him for his later pictures, the ones that nobody seemed very interested in owning at the time. Sidney needed his early work, first as a reference from which to move forward and then to give to the art gallery at Lanyon near Canberra. Over the years, Sidney and I saw a lot of each other. On several occasions, he visited my home at West Green, but mostly we met in my shop or at the National Gallery, where he could usually be found sitting in front of Piero della Francisca's three great masterpieces. On at least one occasion at West Green, I showed him my collection of chickens. It was this collection that caused him to paint a whole series of works entitled *Oedipus*. The strange-looking creatures in these paintings were my rare breeds of chicken; I had at the time over 75 different breeds.

On a number of occasions, Sidney and his second wife Mary came to Broome. Often we would have lunch at the Mangrove Hotel at a table and chairs placed on the lawn overlooking Roebuck Bay. We sat and watched the blue waters of the Indian Ocean, eating quantities of its produce and then we talked. Always we talked, each of us inventing stories more implausible than the last tale told by the other. Other times, we would sit under my mango tree with a bottle of wine and gossip. He told me of his experiences with Xavier Herbert, who was undoubtedly Australia's greatest novelist, easily comparable to Dickens in his robust treatment of social issues. Sidney told how Herbert had taken his hand and squeezed it until he was forced to his knees. 'My legs are filled with steel,' Herbert told Nolan, and then released him so that he could get to his feet again. Sidney felt that Herbert badly treated the local telephone operator in the Queensland town where he lived. She was, in Sidney's opinion, really Herbert's slave, a situation that he found in contradiction to Herbert's socialism. Endlessly, Sidney would recite a story by Herbert about Herbert. He entitled it 'My Grief'. It told of the death and burial of Herbert's wife. Mary tried to stop Sidney telling this awful story but he was incorrigible. As for Patrick White, Sidney intended to be revenged for the slight that White had given him in his auto-biography, *Flaws in the Glass*. (Patrick White had said that Mary moved in too quickly after Sidney's first wife, Cynthia, died. This throwaway comment sparked a feud that ended only in death.) In the event, Sidney's revenge was terrible. He painted a portrait of White as a dog with his hindquarters being sniffed by his homosexual partner. The painting is one of the best works to come from Sidney's brush, and I still own a study for it. Sidney loved feuding and the feuding with White seemed never-ending: not a day passed without Sidney devising some new jibe to launch at White; no press or tele-vision interview was complete for Sidney without the ritual trashing of Patrick White. Each day under my mango tree, Sidney would plot and plan the next move in his vendetta.

Back in England, Sidney Nolan painted Broome. The Sun Pictures, my cinema, became the subject of a masterpiece; my portrait appears on a poster to the left of the picture house's door. The Bungle Bungles again became the subject of another masterpiece, and is now in the collection of John Roberts; there was a series of paintings of the Mitchell Plateau and the Kimberley bush, wonderful pictures on a scale that Sidney had never attempted before. For a man who normally painted cabinet pictures, these pictures were huge. Large pictures were now the order of the day: two metres by two metres, and larger. Larger and larger grew his work and, as the size of the canvases grew, so too did the quality of his work. Like Titian in his old age, Sidney painted relaxed, easy paintings. The agony, the anger, and the despair were gone from his palette. In their place were the colours of a lyrical beauty, each easily finding its place on these vast canvases.

One year in Broome, Mary and Sidney were joined by her son, Percival, whom I commissioned to paint the people and the places of the Kimberley. Strangely for a young painter, he did not catch the way that the Kimberley was changing. His paintings were fine works that caught the violence of the landscapes and the nostalgia of its people but not the spirit of change that was abroad. Sidney Nolan, who had painted all over the Kimberley in the late 1940s and early 1950s—the stations belonging to the Vesteys were often his favourite subjects as they had sponsored his travels there—seemed to me to have no trouble with the way that the place was changing. The mobile telephone, the fax machine, airconditioning, helicopters, four-wheel drives, and all the late twentieth-century equipment that vehicles carry today. Sidney was a modern man: he understood change, delighted in it, and used that change to push his work in advance of many of his contemporaries. Sidney took to the spray can beloved of young German painters in the 1980s like a duck to water. They had made their way to fame through using this technique, but for Sidney it had the reverse effect. Dealers or collectors unfamiliar with the German school, whose work was fetching hundreds of thousands of dollars, saw the use of this style as a sign of laziness, a desire to speed up the time taken to paint a picture. In time, however, some of these works will be considered to be among Sidney's best paintings. The comment 'I really much prefer his earlier work' was always much used about Sidney and, indeed, if Sidney

Nolan was to have an epitaph written for him by the art dealers of Australia, it would be those very words.

Towards the end of Sidney Nolan's life, I commissioned him to paint a series of pictures for an office block on St George's Terrace in Perth. Sidney finished the paintings and attended the opening of St George's Square. These paintings, like many of Sidney's later works, were difficult to accept; I am, however, without doubt that these paintings will one day be regarded as among his greatest works. At the same time that I commissioned these paintings, I arranged for Sidney to carve a dozen marble sculptures for the gardens of the office block. Sidney was just not able to complete them—he made one, the rest remain only as drawings and, somewhere I suppose, there are maquettes for others. Certainly, Sidney was a fine sculptor as well as a great painter; the series of small sculptures that he made in gold bear testament to that and they certainly are among his finest work. Faced with problems from the British Inland Revenue—Sidney had only the vaguest notion that sometimes you had to pay tax—he went into a decline. I did not see him in the months before his death. As the years pass, my admiration for his paintings grows rather than wanes. Sidney was a most unusual man and a great painter. As I wrote in my earlier memoirs, *Once a Jolly Bagman*, when Sidney Nolan died, a joy went out of my life, for I miss him and his company.

As a collector of contemporary art for all my adult life, it is not entirely surprising that a number of artists should have offered to paint my portrait. It was, however, something of a surprise to me when Elizabeth Frink, the British sculptress, now sadly dead, asked me in 1965 if I would let her make a portrait of me in bronze. I turned down Elizabeth Frink's offer.

In truth, I did not believe in people arranging to have themselves immortalised in stone, bronze or paint. In retrospect, I regret the arrogance of this opinion and the fact that Elizabeth, an artist for whom I have a great respect and of whose work I once owned over a hundred examples, did not make a portrait of me. Or did she? For, within a few months of asking if I wanted such a portrait and her offer being refused, Elizabeth Frink produced a life-sized bronze of a naked man. This bronze bore a striking resemblance to me. It was not, as I had imagined, because Elizabeth Frink thought that I might become famous or was a particularly interesting person, nor, indeed, was it because I had become a considerable patron of her work. Rather, she wanted to make a portrait of me simply because I had the right-shaped body. For some years, *The First Man* stood in my garden in England before it was removed to the Parmelia Hotel in Perth. While it was in England, I posed beside it, and it was hard to tell us apart in a photograph that was taken. Elizabeth Frink liked, in those days, to make sculptures of men with well-turned legs, narrow hips and vast, heavy bodies topped with block heads. This description exactly fits her work *The First Man*—and it also fits the way I looked then.

From time to time, Sidney Nolan included me in his paintings. Kinder to me than the Frink portrait perhaps, his depictions of me are slight images that are usually not central to the painting. I also featured on sketches drawn on menus in restaurants while lunching with Sidney. John Olsen drew a brilliant cartoon of me buying an antique Chinese pot. Apart from these occasions and one other, portraits of myself are something that I have never encouraged.

Clifton Pugh's portraits I had always admired and, in a weak moment, I had agreed with myself that if ever I had my portrait painted, I would like him to be the artist. In 1983, I received a letter from Clifton Pugh. He said he would be in London before Christmas that year; could he paint my portrait? A day or so before Clifton's letter arrived, I received notification that I was to be made a life peer. In future, I would have the privilege of sitting in the House of Lords. The announcement of this appointment would be made on 1 January 1984. Clifton Pugh and his wife duly arrived in London a few weeks before Christmas. We arranged that our first meeting would be at my political office in the Conservative Party's headquarters at 32 Smith Square. The Pughs arrived, were shown into my office and I offered them champagne. In those days, the walls of my office were decorated with smaller versions of the giant 48 Street posters that the Conservative Party had used during the recent successful election campaign. One of these posters caught Clifton's eye. It read: 'The Conservatives talk sense even when they talk rubbish'. This legend referred to the ability of Conservative councils to improve rubbish collections. I doubt if I would run that advertisement today, in an age when many of the Conservative shadow ministers are clearly not talking much sense about anything. Indeed, they seldom say anything constructive, confining themselves to carping criticism and snide jibes at a Labour Government which seems to me, for all the world, to behave like the Conservatives; while the last Conservative government, led by John Major, appeared to behave just like the Socialists. No more of that, however, for 1983 was a vintage year for Conservatives and Conservative policies.

Clifton Pugh asked me if I could get him copies of these small posters that decorated my office walls. A week later, I visited him at his house in London, just off Kensington Church Street. He stood before a large canvas on which he had made a collage of the posters that I had sent him. Then he began to paint my portrait on top of this collage. I sat on a bed, facing him, my jacket unbuttoned, the Garrick Club tie covering a small part of a large chest and abdomen. After five sittings, the portrait was finished. When it was delivered by the Pughs to my home at West Green so that I could see it for the first time, it was wonderful. Even my wife Romilly, a stern critic, loved this work. Afterwards, we ate lunch, talked and drank. Then we walked in the garden at West Green; despite the season being winter, the sun shone. It was a perfect day.

For ten years or so, this portrait hung in my home in Broome. When I sold that house, I gave the portrait, along with many other paintings, to the Art Gallery of New South Wales. I found Clifton Pugh, an important painter, to be an amusing companion. It had been a pleasure to sit and talk to him as he worked. When Clifton visited London on that occasion, to paint my portrait, it was the first time that we had met. After the portrait was finished and delivered, we never saw each other again. It is like that with myself and artists. Sometimes enduring friendships are formed, sometimes they just pass in the night. With me, this has nothing whatsoever to do with whether they are great painters or merely painters with a specific talent. My friends are few but they are my friends, chosen carefully for reasons that go far deeper than a mere facility or even a serious talent.

❧

It would be something of a travesty to end this chapter on the art world of Australia without mention of two other people, neither of whom are dealers or artists. The first is Leo Schofield, a man who comes and goes from my life, a considerable wit, brilliant conversationalist and a true Renaissance man. The other is Lucio, the proprietor of the restaurant named after him. Lucio is host to the art world in Sydney and serves the best Italian food outside of Italy. People who genuinely enrich one's life are hard to find. Both of these men have made my years in Australia the richer for their acquaintance and I am grateful to them.

It is almost forty years to the day that I first set foot on Australian soil. By far the largest part of my life has been closely involved with that continent. When I travelled on the *Oriana*, it was the stretches at sea that interested me, rather than Australia's cities. Those days between ports gave opportunities for the pursuit of young Australian women; tall, fit, blonde, I had never seen anything like them in the London of the 1950s. Brown and healthy, clad in the briefest of bikinis, they were so unlike the ladies in large hats and long white gloves of Sydney and Melbourne. Susan and Virginia Campbell were stars in this firmament. We became friends but when we spoke, it was not of Australia; they were interested in London and I was interested in telling them of that place. In all honesty, even four years later, when Sir Halford Reddish made the telephone call that sent me speeding across the world, it was not the prospect of visiting Australia that excited me, rather the prospect of going somewhere and doing something on my own.

It was by chance that I went to Perth and fell in love with that city. Chance chose for me a path to hoe and, as I look back, chance chose a hard path. It would be a trivial life indeed, that after forty years had not taught a lesson or two. In that respect, I believe I learnt much in my days in Australia. When I set out in the early 1960s to start a business, I found the Australian attitude to life refreshing, the Western Australians direct in their dealings. It seemed that Australia was a simple place that had worked for years according to well-regulated and sensible rules. Now I realise how terribly wrong I was in that judgement. Australia and the Australians are more Machiavellian in their approach to life than the courtiers of any Florentine court.

In my early days, just married, I knew nothing of life, yet I believed that I knew all of it. Life and death were strangers to me; birth, divorce, death, all experiences of which I had no knowledge. Young as I was, confidence filled me; humility was a virtue unknown to me. I took life at a run, not thinking about where I should put each foot until it hit the ground. Taking friendship at face value, making enemies lightly. I am, as I look back, surprised that with my simplistic approach I survived so long in a country as byzantine as Australia. In my passion, I was, however, remorseless—and my passion was Australia, Australia and all things Australian. It was this pervasive passion for Australia that influenced my every action and coloured my every reaction, both inside that continent and out of it. The people, the places, the things of Australia—I desired to know them all and for many of those years, my view of life and its individuals was through Australia-tinted spectacles.

I learned during the high days of the 1980s that the end does not justify the means, that there is no short cut to success that leads to joy. I learned in the 1990s that in any life there must be moments of pleasure, joy and excitement, and that these moments are balanced by failure and dismay. If a life does not have its dark gorges, how on earth can it expect to have its high peaks? In Australia, there were for me the lean years as well as the years where I lived off the fat of the land. When I left Australia, my affairs were in an orderly fashion; materially, I left much as I had come. Mentally, however, it was a different matter: I left Australia a truly rich man.

The memories that I have of Australia are but a taste of that wealth. No day goes by that I do not recall some aspect of the

Australian countryside and my heart beats a little faster. No day passes that I do not remember a dear friend with sadness or a treacherous friend with anger, but the anger seldom lasts. I learnt in Australia that scale is important; these treacherous friends are no more than pimples on the chin caused by lavish eating, gone in a week of abstinence. More often, I sit in an Venetian campo or take tea among the crowds in front of Monte Carlo's casino, and chuckle as I remember Charlie Diesel and Snowy County, telling tales around the camp fire in some distant desert. I laugh out loud as I recall the gossip of the Pearlers Rest Bar in Broome. Bitterness is a poison that rots the soul and, in time, the body that contains that soul. Laughter is the medicine that cures all ills. However it may seem, Australia is still the lucky country, lucky in the people who live there, lucky in the beauty of the place. Australia is a serious place, a competitor in the world's economies, yet it is also a place where humour abounds, even though the source of that humour is as likely to be a tragedy as a triumph. There is, however, whatever its cause, always a joke to be told in Australia.

Index

UNH●LYLAND

THE TRILOGY

BY AIDAN ANDREW DUN

SKYSCRAPER

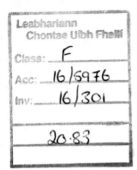
First published 2016 by
Skyscraper Publications
20 Crab Tree Close, Bloxham,
Oxon OX15 4SE, U.K.
www.skyscraperpublications.com

Cover design by Pam Fontes-May

Typesetting by
Chandler Book Design

Printed in the United Kingdom
by Latitude Press

UNHOLYLAND: THE TRILOGY

A love story

Aidan Andrew Dun

For the long-suffering Palestinian people,
for the real Israelis, and for the noble
Bedouin this pebble is cast into the pool
of the continuum of all cultures.

The Bedouin: tribes barricaded
behind turquoise-mountains, unbidden
men, black-blue-and-amber-beaded
hidden-ones; bearded, pagan, heathen
dreamers whose dreams, sand-bedded
don't resemble ours, dreamed (beheaded)
under ceilings: unbounded trackings
atavistic undertakings
dark-sea-crossings of the desert
wanderings among stars unsounded:
these belt-braided and deep-bonded
herdsmen of the universe
dreadlocked nomad-lords of brilliant nights
men who've seen the true Northern Lights.

A note on pronunciation:
The Jewish name Moss, diminutive of Moshe, Moses,
approximately rhymes with the English 'Josh'.

PREFACE

Marie Rambert, my grandmother, took her ballet company all over the world. In 1947 the Rambert toured Australia, in '57 they danced in China, the first British ballet company to do so. Yet Mim (as we knew her) would not take Rambert to Israel; in fact she never herself set foot in that country. An older sister of Mim's had fled the Holocaust from Warsaw and settled there but the sisters did not remain in touch. Even in the fifties and sixties of the last century, when the new state was still riding a wave of world-sympathy after the Nazi scourge, Mim felt for the dispossessed Palestinian people. I know for a certainty that Rambert regarded the situation in the Middle East exactly as that courageous man, Daniel Barenboim, regards it today. And, as a direct descendent of Maimonides (Rabbi Moses ben Maimon, known in Jewish scholastic traditions as The Rambam) Marie Rambert - born Cyvia Rambam in Warsaw - would have concurred with that philosopher's advice to his people when he asked them, in his famous 'Epistle to Yemen', not to allow the sufferings of exile to drive a return to the land of memory.

'Solomon ... inspired by the holy spirit, foresaw that the prolonged duration of the exile would incite some of our people to seek to terminate it before the appointed time, and as a consequence they would perish or meet with disaster. Therefore he admonished and adjured them in metaphorical language to desist, as we read, "I adjure you, O daughters of Jerusalem, by the gazelles and by the hinds of the field, that ye awaken not, nor stir up love, until it please." (Song of Songs 2:7, 8:4). Now, brethren and friends, abide by the oath, and stir not up love until it please.' (From 'The Epistle to Yemen' of The Rambam.)

* * *

My grandmother had a photographic memory for poetry. Night after night, in my late teens, I would lie beside her in the dark until dawn, listening to her recitations of Byron, Dante, Eliot, Baudelaire, Milton. Mim's fervid love of poetry was even more intense than her passion for dance. Whole soliloquies of Hamlet would be succeeded by perfectly memorised sections of Bleak House. Rambert's rendition of Manfred's suicidal meditation on the mountain-verge seemed to lift the old house in Notting Hill high into the freezing, lonely Alps, make it teeter on the rim of an abyss. Even the bombs of the Blitz never shook its foundations like that recitation. Many nights passed this magical way. (Mim was insomniac but when she did manage to sleep, she sometimes suffered a recurrent dream in which the ceiling of her bedroom would very gradually and silently descend towards the floor, threatening to asphyxiate her in a scene from Edgar Allan Poe.) It was during these night-watches and vigils that I first heard - in Russian, naturally - the heartbreaking sonnets of Pushkin, cynical and tender at the same time, the voice of Byron raised to a higher power.

In a sense, *Unholyland* was born in those long nights. My grandmother understood my rebellious nature very well since it conformed to her own iconoclastic spirit, and as I entered my early-twenties, at a time when I was almost completely estranged from the world, going through a savage rite-of-passage from adolescence to manhood, Mim was still my guiding light, my touchstone, my friend. I can never forget that she once even came to visit me in those Dostoyevskian King's Cross derelict houses where my long painful journey to the launch of *Vale Royal* at the Royal Albert Hall began. I have so many memories of this extremely spiritual woman - this wise woman - who could be very tough on those who let themselves down, yet whose warmth, charisma and vision of the human potential for goodness made her so precious.

* * *

Maybe *Unholyland* began to properly crystallize when I understood that one paradoxical aspect of the Palestinian/Israeli conflict would be almost humourous if the broader context of the joke were not so sombre and tragic. Palestinian 'Slingshot' Hiphop (with its Gandhian watchword "Putting down the gun and picking up the mic') is a semi-forbidden artform in some more traditional Islamic societies where it is regarded as decadent and Western-influenced. Yet this same music, with its outspoken poetic message of a people disempowered and defiant, is often at the top of the hit-parade in Tel Aviv, registering with young Israelis, who, it seems, almost at a genetic level, recognize and identify with the voice of the downtrodden and marginalized, the persecuted and the repressed. There came a moment when I suddenly realized that these young Israelis listening spellbound to Tamer Nafar and Dam were responding to that same voice which for two thousand years has bewailed pogroms and persecutions in Europe. And admiring, with Seamus Heaney, the linguistic energy of rap-poetry, the seed-idea of my verse-novel was sown. What if a Jewish DJ should fall in love with a Palestinian girl-rapper?

* * *

It sometimes seems that the issues of the Middle East are so complex and so profound that all the problems of humanity could be resolved if this conflict were settled. But apart from a love-story in which a romantic miracle makes two rival cultures stop and say 'We are just the same', what would it take to find an answer? From the Jewish side it would demand the difficult admission that historical persecutions in Europe catalysed and propelled a colonialist-style takeover in Palestine which culminated in the 1948 Nakba when a million Palestinians were forcibly displaced; and this admission would necessitate amends. An apology would not be enough. The 'right to return' (to a non-apartheid country) would have to be granted to all who have been displaced, and of course these same rights would have to be extended to all descendents of those driven from their homeland in '48. From the Palestinian side a permanent truce and a deep-level reconciliation would require an acceptance that armed resistance, though often extremely courageous, has been useless and even counterproductive, only allowing the occupier to justify his brutal methodologies of control and repression. Perhaps this process of admission and acceptance could be called 'The Way of Water'; since water finds easy ways around obstacles, since water breaks down stone gently over time; because water is feminine, symbolizing flexibility and forgiveness; because water believes, as it flows down any given river, in seeing both sides of every story.

Unholyland begins beside Lake Galilee. Here, my readers will embark with me on a journey into the land of hypothesis and parable. And since we are entering the realms of imagination, and since we are saying goodbye to the solid (but tedious) terrain of actual fact, perhaps I can be be allowed to offer an old far-eastern story as an introduction to my verse-novel.

* * *

A wedding-party was meandering through a riverside town, the groom bouncing like a happy boy among his drunken friends, the bride supporting her mother and father on each arm. Simultaneously in the twilight a funeral procession was making its way riverward, a long column of sombre dignitaries and officials.

(The deceased had been some kind of exalted bureaucrat and was being buried with all the high solemn pomp demanded by his calling.)

The two parties began crossing the river at almost the same moment and the narrow bridge groaned under the weight of so much emotion. The revellers and the newly-weds shrieked like Bacchantes. The bereaved raised a cloud of dust as they slapped their sorry hearts and hung their heads. Suddenly, in the centre of the bridge, the two companies met in head-on collision.

The wedding-guests, intoxicated, jeered at the mourners; the bereaved scowled darkly at the revellers. Neither party would give an inch of the narrow road-deck; but both parties stood glaring at eachother in a confrontational manner.

'Hey, out of the road, make way for life and future generations', shouted a more-boisterous wedding-guest. 'We can't all live in the past, with due respect.' Yet his tone was not in the least respectful, and one member of the cortege, a bulky fellow with a face of stone, bellowed back unceremoniously: 'Out of the way yourself, you jumped-up idiot. You're blocking the passage of a great man to his place of rest.'

Another wedding-guest, imagining (quite rightly) himself described as an idiot, hurled back: 'We're ain't budgin', you zombie. Back-up to the other side of the river and let us through in the name of love. Can't you see these two' (indicating the groom and his bride) 'have some serious business to attend to in the bridal-chamber.'

This raised a howl from the party-animals; while a grim thunderous murmur started building among the bereaved. 'Let's throw these salacious dogs in the river!' said one. 'If we turn their celebration into a funeral *then* we'll understand each other properly,' screamed another, her face contorted with rage.

The best-man had just seized the chief-mourner by his tail-coat's black lapel when a monk stepped onto the bridge. (He may have been a Buddhist monk, he may have been a Christian; perhaps he was a Zen monk or a Muslim zuhd; he might have been a Hasid; the school of his monkhood doesn't matter, it's completely irrelevant. What matters is that the monk in question was a man to whom balance was sacred.) He had seen the fracas developing from a point of observation where he meditated regularly above the river; and now he came gliding gracefully through the crowds - almost like a woman in his movements - the man of God passing through the multitude blocking the bridge.

The humble monk stood before the red-faced ringleaders on either side. 'You can neither of you win this battle. And the whole world will come to a standstill while you try to destroy each other because no-one else can get across the water. I have a solution, if you'll listen.'

His deep calm voice commanded respect. The funeral-goers once more became dignified and silent; the wedding-guests immediately looked happier, less aggressive. (A few took advantage of the lull in hostilities to hang over the sides of the bridge and spew champagne mixed with wedding-cake into the river below.) The monk gestured in his minimal way. And then - without his saying another word - *miraculously* the two parties separated to either side of the road-deck, the funeral-goers to the right and the wedding-party to the left. At a second gesture from the mysterious monk they began to file past each other in opposite directions.

At first they moved in silence, as if amazed by the simple expedient which had saved them from a bloodbath, or as if profoundly ashamed of the fact that they'd nearly come to blows for nothing. But after a while, as they went their respective ways, the wedding-guests once more took up a festive singing of raucous pop-songs; while those who marched toward the burial-grounds on the western side of the river resumed their chanting of those gloomy anthems that remind us of the oblivion we half long for, yet would much rather forget.

BOOK ONE

THE RAMBAM

CHAPTER

1

i

Birthdays: blessings or curses
to be celebrated or dismissed?
Are birthdays 'bout cradles or hearses;
do they remind us we can be kissed
with waters of life and waves of death?
We can all say, in the same breath
'This is the day of my appearance.'
There will come a night of clearance
when we shall extinguish this candle
renounce the fascinating present.
That's when the most unpleasant
contradiction we cannot handle
strikes us directly across the face.
A day of birth is our starting place.

ii

As time races on it leaves
anniversaries, milestones
birthdays, departures (who grieves
not?) in its wake. In monotones
we speak about the Dark One's approach
life's grim joke played; sad reproach
insult of uncertainty and chance;
the way the two-armed beings dance
in shadows, a few lights showing.
Why hellraising and delight
why loud carnivals on the night
when existence is clearly flowing
to oblivion? It may be found
nights are darker underground.

iii

Milestones mean a destination
imply some passage of marked time.
Let's journey to a celebration.
I will give you the sublime
curvilinear of a love-affair
commencing and whirling-afar
to a desert between joy and pain.
(What we feel no one can explain;
while what is known is almost nil.
Some have called it zero, frankly;
and the human mind looks blankly
at the ever-unknowable, still
mysterious. Subtle is this art:
to feel for unity while apart.)

iv

Let's follow an arc of passion
across the skyline of this life:
legendary curve of precision
flashing trajectory of a jackknife
toward a blindfolded victim.
What's that? (Only fiction's whim
remember, only relatively
real, for those of us actively
inching over seat's forward-edge
so soon, though no narrative action
at all, of any description
has moved that aerodynamic wedge
imagination down its track.
See, already there's no turning back.)

v

Our charismatic main-man
transcultural agent, now enters
the arena of the masterplan
where my storyline centers.
Story? The word sticks in saying.
A good friend of mine is playing
the lead-role here, and I object
to depictions incorrect.
Allow me to introduce to you
The Rambam, our protagonist
wordsmith, rap-poet (modernist)
Jewman with a Rasta worldview
gifted as the fire of the sun
straight as the barrel of a gun.

vi

MC Rambam: conceived in Goa
ante-meridiem, at first light
on the beach - what a mindblower -
born to *Dreadlocks in Moonlight*
(Lee Scratch Perry) nine months later.
Dad (Solomon) met Leah (mater)
fugitives both, conscript runaways
from Unholyland, in faraways
India: on the Candolim
coastline of sweet old Konkan
by the Sea which is Arabian
those sands not far from Bambolim.
Baby Moss in tranquil Goan
dawn bawled first dissonant koan.

vii

Danced through childhood to Burning Spear
sang to Bunny Wailer, Ijahman
from day-one till aged very-near
fourteen, when father Solomon
diving into the life Hasidic
stopped the hashish, killed the music
became devout almost overnight.
Moss had to stash CDs out of sight.
Aged ten, to Israel Vibration's
groove he'd boogied in the Galilee,
there was even a home movie:
'From The District Of The Nations.'
(Solomon knew local history
Isaiah 9.1, the mystery.)

viii

On-and-on runs the dancing god
who spins rainforests from sunfire
who breeds in black smoker's mud
the human from the boiling mire
upright, bipedal, brilliant, mobile:
one whose flaming solar smile
superabundant with gold rays
lights-up the world on special days
(nativities of celebration)
who raises dust to protozoa
(making babes on beaches in Goa)
tomorrow's brilliant generation
apart from the men of yesterday
living in a very different way.

ix

Moss rebelled like any son
dethroning the paternal god
invoked that lineal treason
which makes a boy ride roughshod
over rolling ancestral land
hard-won by his father's hand;
took a stand against hard-and-fast
prescriptions of the Jewish past
became a DJ in Galilee
'MC Rambam' his main tag
(sometimes also 'DJ Scallywag')
struggled from his old man to be free.
Solomon was lenient, half-amused
wise enough to be a bit confused.

x

He too recalled wild beginnings
back in the day, way-back-when.
(He'd had his own season of sinnings.)
Conscripted late seventy-seven
just in time for the Lebanon War
he remembered well that Jounieh whore
who'd made him a dangerous man
in her bedroom, on her astrakhan
mezzanine, behind a red silk blind.
Fallen for a Levantine goddess
he'd learned to love under duress
against the internecine grind
the roar and snarl of his Merkava:
lethality-deliverer.

xi

They'd dreamed together of going home
to Galilee, marrying somehow.
Their goodbyes at an aerodrome
made an end of every vow
whispered in love-talk's easy art.
A war-hero with a broken heart
Solomon flew back to Israel
chastened (and initiated) male.
He deserted in eighty-eight
in Goa met Leah on the beach
on the coast of Candolim, a peach
knew at once his great soulmate.
Moss was conceived in ninety-two
our young dude (with plenty attitude).

xii

And so we arrive at the twelfth month
since his last anniversary
at springtime of the hyacinth
in the passing year so cursory.
On the fourteenth day of Nisan
we find ourselves with Rambam clan
(well, not Solomon and Leah
both less than keen on the idea).
Rudeboy Moss is spinning a choon
on his day of birth in coastal glade
sheltered by the eucalyptus shade.
Friends dance, soon a crescent moon
rises over silvered Galilee
shining on that legendary sea.

xiii

Drug-smoke drifts in blue twilight
clouds of aromatic grass:
this party's about to ignite.
The Rambam (with heart of a Ras)
is dropping some substantial dub.
Bass shifts down to regions sub
way below the human spectrum
striking deeper than eardrum.
Now, with impact apocalyptic:
someone (in Arabic) rapping
(sensibilities re-mapping)
flow effortless, fast and cryptic
even more so than usual
for this artform multilingual.

xi

'Who's terrorist? I'm the lyricist
puttin' down gun, pickin' up mic.
Who's terrorist, you're the terrorist
democracy? More like the Third Reich.'
(Slingshot Hiphop from Tamar Nafar
Dam's outspoken demon-rapper.)
Aliyah makes her slim waist flex
in front of Moss, on his record-decks;
twists animal torso round sick beat
chants the hook of this rebel choon
spirals like a sexed-up typhoon
moves her flesh when she feels the heat.
'Moss, babe, do you know what *that* means?'
Right across turntable she leans

xv

Interpretation is pretty clear:
she's seriously into this dude
he's someone she can revere.
She's also had some pretty crude
daydreams about getting stuck
up on mixing-desk… (Wish her luck.)
So she leans across like this
flirtatious Aliyah, cool Miss
Gorgeous, tight blue denim jeans;
big turquoise eyes on fire
burning with carnal desire;
working too behind the scenes.
(From offered reefer get a whiff.)
'Moshe, take a hit on *my* spliff.'

xvi

He has no time for translations
freestyling over another track
on-mic: 'In the Zone of the Nations
hear me now: cut them some slack
in Palestine: One Holyland
is my immediate demand.
Yes, peeps, check me, MC Rambam
pleading with you: Tel Aviv (Goddam)
you bring Israel into disgrace;
in blood-red scrawl on ghetto-wall
in Gaza where the downpressed fall:
'Jewman can't even show his face.'
We used to live side-by-side;
Unholyland is genocide.'

xvii

Several guests in protest leave
SUVs cough, a few horns bark.
They know Moss Rambam to be naïve:
'He's a minority in the dark.'
But tonight in The Galilee
deliverance is breaking-free.
With Greedy Dog from I Vibration
Moss spins from vinyl mass-salvation:
driving song which sends dancers wild
(grinding to its skank in moonshine
putting Zipporah on cloud-nine)
while his existential inner-child
recalls riding his father's shoulder
when he was certainly no older

xviii

Than eleven on this green lakeshore
when I Vibration dropped *Dog* live
in the golden-age, long before
Solomon took his steep dive
into mystic Hasidism;
for his son a cataclysm
since it killed the dub stone-dead.
Moss remembered, still saw in his head
three Rastas moving on crutch-sticks
(childhood polio-victims) dancing
broken bodies balancing
by some act of metaphysics:
three dreadlocks preaching love-and-peace
in the cauldron of the Middle East.

xix

The film (shot by Leah in Hi8)
the home movie *'From The District'*
caught the vibe, ecstatic crowd-state
uplifted dancers, did depict
(at this same gig by I Vibration)
miraculous mass-elevation.
Panning round Arabs and Israelis
(everyone smoking 'Bob Marleys'
with Moss shoulder-high in a dreamscape
with Apple Gabriel, Skelly, Lascelle)
the jerky footage really *did* tell
the whole story on videotape.
Momentarily the Age of Gold
was there for everyone to behold.

xx

Three Rastas from the ghetto-side
wise men in the state of 'Is-nah-real'
singing 'bout mass-infanticide
in Trenchtown's diaspora-ordeal:
endurance in a galvanized box
when the hell of malaria locks
down in long grey rainy-season;
when a tin-shack (blackman-prison)
shapeshifts to a coffin of cardboard.
Moss felt past, present coinciding
(once more Solomon's shoulders riding)
as Lascelle, like Lazarus restored
sang: 'Jus' can't find the way to come home.'
And now, on-mic, Moss chanted: 'Shalom.'

xxi

Ten before twelve he stopped DJing
(brought on Liron through an orbit-scratch)
sideslipped sultry Aliyah saying
brief words he didn't really catch
('Moss, be my partner in crime?')
dodged Aliza: 'Babe, another time'
made it to the waterfront;
trodded north, trying to confront
his demons, calling on his angels
crippled prophets of Rastafari
end-time avatars. 'Jah, why
must there be so-sharp angles
points of difference in the final days
when your people go their separate ways?'

xxii

Soon after one he tracked back to car
run-down beat-up BMW
blackout tints, six-cylinder
coupe, dark gig-horse, no trouble to
maintain (she still rolled a hundred
up the highways, often thundered:
his black 'Bob Marley and the Wailers').
Prayers came: 'No engine-failures
tonight, please, gotta get away;
find Ray' in Natzrat.' (Moss needed
to see a real friend; and proceeded
to drop silver disc in CD tray.)
Firing the engine he cranked the choon:
Greedy Dog under a crescent-moon.

CHAPTER

2

i

A silent engine ticking-over
idling, transmission disengaged
might be compared to mind forever
hovering outside what is gauged
past or future, poised in the present;
suspended, high-powered, heaven-sent;
waiting in neutral for the word 'go'
(which only comes 'adagio'
when a long age has passed at low revs).
Moss sat patiently at the wheel
a good time, getting the track's feel
checking invisible semibreves
in the bassline, lots of space:
Greedy Dog in a state of grace.

ii

Mentally adding a Nepheton
to the Israel Vibration mix
dropping some hardware 808 on
G Dog, introducing rhythm-licks
to the tight groove, he flicked five
gears through neutral in the night, hand-jive
implying that destination
balanced against detention
here, because in no real hurry
(with irresistance meeting fate
in accord with Jah's dictate)
he'd get there tonight, so why worry?
Whatever road he took the same
outcome at the end of the game.

iii

Ideally he'd catch Rayyan
in Natzrat, make the roundtrip
by dawn, sleep-up till noon. Gameplan?
Bound for Nazareth in pirate ship
through the jet-black Galilean night
he'd sail back Sunday with first light.
Rayyan (Palestinian friend
with whom he'd often spend
hours through Nazareth afternoons
talking babes, herbs, rap-poetics
philosophy and politics)
Rayyan was the man for Slingshot choons:
the authority on every new
Palestinian hiphop breakthrough.

iv

Rayyan was the dude in Nazareth
king of the underground side of town.
Light as a feather on the breath
of God, he had the place on lockdown.
If you wanted the *Zahret el Kolch*
other dealers would get you zilch:
Rayyan was, for stoners, the connect.
If you really needed to get wrecked
on that Manali-strain Gold Leb
you wouldn't see where it was at
the whole length and breadth of Natzrat
until you met with that street-celeb:
Rayyan of the heavy-duty toke
Rayyan of the so-luxurious smoke.

v

Client tonight for exactly that
the rare and impossible-to-find
hashish-deluxe sought in Eilat
grown and anciently hand-refined
in southern Lebanon, Moss waited
(smooth engine-power abated
in neutral) ready to embark.
The purring of his beast in the dark
seemed to make the black night warmer;
beneath 'They kill you with tax, I say'
lent the lyrics, lilting away
sweet associations with former
times in camper-van with Mum and Dad
long before times got kinda sad.

vi

Moss felt seriously dejected
on his birthday. (Understandable:
we've not completely rejected
arguments in our expandable
narrative, when at the outset
we discussed what all try to forget:
feeling down on anniversary.
A mean trick of the adversary:
to explode not champagne but trouble
that day – which confounds belief –
when not happiness but only grief
comes in great servings double
from that Mephisthophelean friend
who makes man fear his final end.)

vii

Moss suffered vague misgiving
coupled with nostalgia
waiting at the wheel, reliving
eighteen years by that algebra
where birthdays, in fate's equations
as ceremonial occasions
are represented by x's
(kisses on gifts from both the sexes
not with 'How much do you love me?' signed
yet with such thoughts in the subconscious)
where y's stand for that unjoyous
doubt always in the back of the mind
horror of uncertainty.
(With this life there is no warranty.)

viii

Rolling out of eucalyptus glade
he hung a right, the road to Ma'agan.
(On Route 92 the escapade
begins that is to transform a man.)
At the foot of the freshwater lake
not a single soul remained awake
in the small town he thundered through;
there Leah, and Solomon too
slept as their son passed around
the southern rim of Lake Galilee;
saddened since he could not agree
with tribe on one essential ground:
'Put me up on the witness-stand.
I'll swear-down I hate Unholyland.'

ix

The Rambam was one of those Jews
(maybe not in the minority)
who felt the wrongness of those views
which gave national authority
to a state built on a bad dream:
that nightmare of the Jewish scream
heard in Europe for two thousand years;
that dark river of Jewish tears
sighing down from Russia to Spain
black tributary of grief
raging wildly, beyond relief
torrent swollen with a people's pain.
To him Israel was not legit:
Palestine was stolen bit-by-bit.

x

Paid for at first, truly purchased
properly with title and land-deed
yes, until the Mandate progressed
Britain's geopolitical need
to have Suez under control
as the road to India, the whole
Imperial agenda back then
reflecting global trade-routes. 'Open
for business with nations overseas'
(mechanism most expedient).
Zionism's most obedient
servant beseeches: 'Won't you, please
help yourself to our Protectorate
have your homeland legitimate?'

xi

Ironic: a people expelled
two thousand years in the past
because they could not be compelled
by Roman brute-power and bombast
to venerate a dictator, false
deity, like everyone else;
now returning under guidance
secular, led by grandiloquence;
with no God to give His word
or keep promises in Palestine.
(Why listen to the Arab canine
by European xenophobes slurred
squatting in Israel's birthplace;
why honour his inferior race?)

xii

Dark reflections tortured Moss
gunning silver wheels through the night
past Kinneret-Kvutsa in a flash
cutting westward in night-flight
up backroads, leaving the highway
(winding north Tiberias-way)
through lemon orchards on singletrack
dirtroad, past oak trees pitch-black
in the wilderness, hunched, ghostly
caught in headlights an instant;
passing in dustclouds by deviant
back-ways up to Alumot, closely
located if you went this route
through back-country shortcuts to suit.

xiii

Serpentine turnings in the dirtroad
mounting toward Alumot Junction
spurred The Rambam in go-mode:
switchbacks demanding no malfunction
from the driver who handled the wheel.
Even so, the madman did steal
a glance or two at dark Galilee
spread out below nocturnally:
night-sea, behind and to his right;
with green plantations of kibbutzim -
invisible now - with orchards trim
intervening across line of sight.
(Green because he knew the view so well;
memory is the mind's jewel.)

xiv

At the crest, as the car hit asphalt
the Bimmer's rear wheel driving-traction
sucked Moss back in leather seat: 'Thou shalt
not...' he murmured with satisfaction
talking to himself 'exceed...'
He didn't finish. At high speed
crossing plateau to intersection
his mood of dark introspection
lifted with the surge of his wheels.
There was life still in the black wagon
petrol in the veins of the dragon
(but not enough for the Batmobile's
night-run to Natzrat and back).
Moss dropped x to floor on smooth tarmac.

xv

At the all-night filling-station
next to Highway 767
he got some fan-admiration
from a bro in the kiosk: Aaron
Steinman, working a night-shift;
cool dude who would always drift
across dancefloors as man-of-action
main-mover. After card-transaction
through glass, up-close, Aaron said
'Bruv, seen the news on television?'
Moss glimpsed a flashing prevision
incandescent, filmic in his head.
'Been another bloodbath in the Strip.
A helicopter gunship

xvi

'Lightly attacked from Gaza City
lost the plot, launched laser-guided
Hellfires into flats, not pretty
many casualties, it's so one-sided…'
He broke-off, distant through bulletproof;
yet, in spite of intercom, reproof
sprang fervently in tone of voice
came across with cyclone-force.
Then, vague paternal whisper
Moss heard his father warning
'Don't go this Sunday morning
to Nazareth, my son, be wiser.'
(On forecourt with bass-bin pounding
blacked-out Bimmer stood resounding.)

xvii

Shall our hero still pursue his way
to see his friend under duress?
There are other incentives in play
admit it, come clean, confess
MC Rambam, DJ Scallywag.
You're dreaming of that first drag
on a luxury zoot of Gold
to get you into the sevenfold
heavens of intoxication
climbing the starry Tree of Life
up to the high place beyond strife.
Yet you wait here, in hesitation
trapped. (In our screenplay-for-the-mind
there is one who has to travel blind.)

xviii

Don't continue, reader impassive
if you can't be unambiguously
sympathetic and permissive.
Stop here. Sadly and lugubriously
it's time to pronounce our farewell.
'Go ye rather to them that sell.'
Try to feel for Moss in some way
shattered on the night of his birthday
slumped-down now in black leather
thinking hard, toking a half-dead blunt
wondering about his crazy stunt
in the midst of so-drastic weather.
Should he still go up to Natzrat?
(He sways like some risky acrobat

xix

Who, poised on a cable of steel
suddenly feels an electric shock
through naked soles, surreal
sensation of a crazy spacewalk.
At times like these no wisecrack
no fancy footwork or backtrack
helps one get one's act together.)
Moss is smoking crumbled leather
dried-out sweepings from Algeria
nothing viscous, poisonously-oiled
nothing potent brought from far-afield
but dope really quite inferior.
Up on tightrope balanced - old routine -
he slides from blue-jeans last stick of green

xx

Lights it, suctions-out a long drag;
flicks ignition, slips into gear
(takes another hit on funny-fag)
drops *Garvey's Ghost* - Burning Spear -
in CD tray, smacks down on 'play'
helicoptering over ashtray
spliff the size of a submarine;
pivoting on himself, like James Dean
angled slightly in the driving-seat.
(This is a brer crazily driven.)
Swingin out onto 767
(as hashish accelerates heartbeat)
tonight, God-willing, he'll see Rayyan
the Nazarene, the-man-with-the-plan.

xxi

They say a soul can 'jump the road'
they call it *Kefitzat ha-Derach.*
Moss could never unravel, reload
that night's travelling, roll back
in memory or retrospect
a dangerous, high-speed, half-wrecked
daredevil-drive to Nazareth
the dark night of the mass-death
genocide in Gaza City:
children's bodies on the pavement;
cries of grief, keenings of bereavement
uttered as if for eternity.
The past and the future were uncleft;
The Rambam arrived just as he left.

xxii

They say that when you 'jump the road'
you cease to exist for a time
navigate in another mode
manoeuvre in the sublime
world of the Eternal Now.
If so that was probably how
Moss Rambam made it to that city
Arab capital of Galilee
Arab capital of Israel
living inferno of grief that night
with devastation set alight
for the slaughtered ones who fell
in Gaza, sorrowed-for by fathers
wailed-for and wept-for by mothers.

CHAPTER

i

Climbing into the Nazareth range
passing Mount Tabor on his right
The Rambam noticed a strange
incandescence in the night
over the northwest skyline.
There stars were not crystalline.
The whole northwestern horizon
loomed a dim, smoky crimson.
Along the road from Daburiya
all the way to al-Famaz
the nocturnal panorama's
aspect suggested some great brazier
burning far-off, conflagration
bringing jittery realization.

ii

Taking another shortcut Moss
followed a dirtroad through the dark.
Now the night-sky seemed awash
with fire. Cutting through a park
a vineyard at the city-limits
he hit the first of several hamlets
on the outskirts of al Nassira.
To Nazareth's heart drawing-nearer
outside of Tirosh he stopped:
in headlights making out a crowd
scattering across the dim-lit road;
asked himself now what course to adopt?
People were waving torches ahead
flares and flambeaus turned the shadows red.

iii

Should he go on like a fool or play
things safe, turn round, head back east?
Dropping Dam in CD tray
with volume-dial he increased
the output of his bass-box;
smiling at this crazy paradox:
driving into Nazareth
possibly facing his own death
on his birthday, risking life-and-limb.
(Thinking this he drove into Tirosh.)
Instantly the crowd surrounded Moss.
'Bismillah al-Rahman al-Rahim'
he murmured through his window unrolled
as the crowd engulfed him, uncontrolled.

iv

Moshe Rambam, trilingual
speaking Hebrew, Arabic, English
enjoyed a transcultural angle;
maybe sometimes looked less foolish
where many often seem arrogant
because linguistically ignorant
unable to speak other's tongues
(let alone enjoy another's songs).
The crowd surged forward, strident, angry
steel blades flashed in naked flames.
Fifty young men, shouting ugly names
pent-up to the ultimate degree
slapped hands on the hot bonnet
laid their fists like weapons on it.

v

Yet as window - tinted - rolled down
Dam's *Who's the terrorist?* was pounding.
The crowd, who seemed to want showdown
appeared to find the music grounding.
Someone said: 'This bruv must be cool.
Check that choon, this bro's no fool.'
Then The Rambam offered his blessing
which had the effect of de-stressing
further the mob. Someone said: 'Man, pass.
Go where you're going, Bismillah.'
(Suddenly he looked less a killer.)
And Moss, rewinding black-tinted glass
gunned his BM down the road
giving thanks for the 'area-code'.

vi

As Rastaman The Rambam truly
affirmed all systems based in love;
Jah was unconditionally
revealing One Love from above.
(His creed: 'Good and bad in all races
looking into hearts not faces.'
Moss very often said 'Jah'
but then he often prayed 'Allah'.
He had a deep link with Islam:
his ancestor had been physician
doctor, by royal commission
to Sultan Saladin: that Rambam
who wrote his 'Guide for the Perplexed'
in Arabic, not Hebrew, which vexed

vii

Some who thought inside the box.
Moss Rambam, too, had his own way
his own approach unorthodox;
from the best place in his heart could say
'Bismillah' as a true believer
far from a dubious deceiver).
And now, as he accelerated
his fears were annihilated;
and somewhere in his heart he sang
as he forged through riot-smoke;
and perhaps his ancestor spoke
to him - in Arabic slang? -
as he drove by night into Natzrat
Bimmer gliding like a panther cat.

viii

In Shalom he found a roadblock
manned by the armed Mishteret.
An officer, waving loaded Glock
appeared maniacally upset
screaming at some Palestinians
stressed at checkpoint, pedestrians
cattle-shifting through concrete aisles.
Another policeman was all smiles
since the Machsom Watch was out:
angels who monitor the crossings
because of all the senseless killings;
Israeli women concerned about
daily crushing humiliations
suffered at the roadside stations.

ix

Now Moss could see over the rim
into the bowl which held Nazareth
a chalice smoking with the grim
fire-and-fume of Satan's breath.
The city was pocked with points of light
flickering, exactly like the sight
that greets a painstaking mountaineer
when he feels brave enough to peer
into some half-sleeping crater
(where a dormant cauldron seethes
where a mouth of hell outbreathes)
knowing full well what will come later
(or sooner-than-expected flare)
from that fiery orifice so near.

x

Nazareth was erupting.
Moss passed through the next checkpoint
police only interrupting
progress long enough to say: 'Don't
go in the Old City tonight
near the White Mosque cars are set alight.'
Moss replied 'That woman's pregnant
why must you act so ignorant?'
'Oy, get lost in your fucking hearse.'
The officer, his face a mask
(his M4 carbine, for his task
in life his tool) sent a curse
as Moss vanished in a blur of dust
doing what in life he knew he must.

xi

Up Paulus Hashishi he thundered
as armoured-cars of the Defense Force
out of every side-street lumbered
giving The Rambam no recourse:
he had to keep going straight
up Hashishi, which wasn't great
because he needed to hang a left
into the Old City, now cleft
from downtown al Nassira
by manoeuvres of the army
trying to impose calm on angry
scenes (streaming live on al Jazeera)
all the homicidal aftermath
raging for the Gaza bloodbath.

xii

Forking left onto al-Bashara
continuing to the White Mosque
a burning bus made a barrier
beside a newsagent's kiosk
also in flames, which formed a tower
in a fortress made of pure fire.
Behind the wall of this red fort
a throng of teenagers sought
refuge from rains of rubber-bullets.
Moss felt in his eyes that watering
which comes before the slaughtering
when warning teargas blankets
mobs and multitudes and rabbles
when revolution's cauldron bubbles.

xiii

Rayyan lived in the Old City
very close to the White Mosque
in smaller winding streets certainly
normally zoned as picturesque.
Moss, forking left off al-Bashara
(now his way became unclearer)
felt an iced rush of adrenalin
felt - ghostly - Solomon's tefillin
on his own forehead pressing hard
as, in alleyways his black windows
were slapped, 'played' as if bongos
so whole vehicle rocked and jarred.
Then (crowd surging) something crashed
through windscreen: absolutely smashed.

xiv

The rock that broke to smithereens
the front-glass travelled further.
Amidst the shattered windscreen's
million shards was something other:
red and liquid, warm and sticky
adhering to upholstery thickly.
Moss, slumped, lightly concussed
lay motionless as fire was thrust
through badly-fractured window-plate.
(It seems a moment of sacrifice
in the wars of fire and ice
as through the frosted laminate
what's left of Bimmer's windscreen
comes the comet of the unforeseen.)

xv

So soon the climax of our story?
Unless we have all been deluded
it's dust-to-dust at this point, surely?
Life seems over: canceled, concluded.
That torch melting the passenger-seat
seems the black candle of a complete
cycle, symbol which says 'I burn
one last time, nevermore return.'
That stench of burning leather
mixed with petrochemical reek
is not just belletristic technique:
someone *is* about to smother.
No more Happy Revolutions
round the sun in glad circulations?

xvi

Interior is well-ablaze.
Plastic fumes and petrol vapor
form an asphyxiating haze.
Our young dude, in semi-stupor
half-comatose on the headrest
is about to be dispossessed
any minute of his worthless life.
But look! a hand, holding a jackknife
wrapped in a hijab, smashes through glass
cuts the restraint, severs seatbelt
(as plastic dash begins to melt).
Against sweet stench of leaking gas
The Rambam out of hellfire is hauled;
his early-death has just been forestalled.

xvii

It's Shaza, Rayyan's sister, who guides
him down pavements, pushing through the crowd.
Moss, giddy, on her shoulder subsides.
(Her hand's still wrapped in torn headshroud).
Into the big house of the Shabash
family they stagger, as a flash
lights-up the narrow street behind
(flares in our movie-for-the-mind).
Picture: a large airy courtyard
central to a great stone mansion.
Here's Moshe, man out-of-action
collapsed (with a moonflower on guard)
under white trumpets, in a niche
alone, moaning. Shaza, quite girlish

Gone for help within the house
has known her brother's friend, Rambam
several years, timid as a mouse
liking him, cousin-through-Abraham
though far too shy, innocent and proud
to say one foolish word out loud
let suspicion anywhere murmur.
(To her gaze comes a warm glimmer
when his name repeats at table:
faint, distant and reserved delight.)
Yet everything's so changed tonight.
Like a princess in a fable
Shaza's grown by a few years
in the space of ten minutes, her fears

Overcome by valiance
as if her womanhood began
to shine with lionhearted brilliance
the moment she rescued The Rambam.
Now she comes quickly with her mother
Noor 'Ma' Shabash, and these two mirror
all the tenderness of women
as they, between them, now begin
to restore and resuscitate;
walking the lightly-wounded indoors
guiding him over smooth stone floors
to - beneath a painted ceiling - wait.
Mint-infusions and some aspirin:
and once again Moss wears naïve grin.

Dazed, eyes closed, he hears 'Ma' Shabash
questioning a flustered Shaza.
'How did you…?' 'Well, I heard glass smash
amid the raging over Gaza
looked from my room toward bazaar
down there recognised the old black car
ran out…' 'Yes, I understand, what then?'
'Shush, let me finish! Those angry men…'
(It's that old generational grind.)
Moss opens eyes, above his bed
makeshift, sees angels flit overhead
sees his bredda's face in his mind.
"Ma' Shabash,' he mutters, he begins
'where's Rayyan? Ah, my brain, it spins.'

As explosions rock the timeworn house
Noor 'Ma' Shabash bursts into tears:
'My son's out roaming this madhouse-
city' she cries, expressing her fears
'all night, and now you arrive
frankly more dead than alive:
I can't take it, my age is too great.'
('Ma' Shabash is only fifty-eight.)
Moss Rambam thanks her for her kindness;
light-headedly, too, thanks Shaza
for his life (who, near Mum seems shyer-
than-ever, wounded with awkwardness).
Now he drifts in dream-search for Rayyan
lying here asleep on the divan;

xxii

Seems to visit with his friend
another country full of rivers.
A dream-waterfall which can ascend
flowing skyward, sends hot shivers
up his spine, makes him seem to fly.
(He freestyles, saying a rap-goodbye
to Rayyan who stands alone below.)
Then as the bridge of a rainbow
arcs bright space he sees a woman
her body formed from the cataract
walk-out on the river's level tract
wearing a multicoloured woven
cloud-garment without a seam.
And he walks beside her in his dream.

CHAPTER

i

Underneath a Yohanna ceiling
(where angels transport sacks of wheat
through the sky above Haifa, circling
eternally in high-noon's heat)
Rayyan, sprawled on a green settee
gazing up into a cedar tree
painted by Salib in secco
(a style quite similar to fresco
where mineral pigments blend in egg)
as he waited for his friend to wake
wondered if the mildest shake
delivered to a blue-jeaned leg
were justified. An ugly bruise
over left temple made him pause.

Rayyan and Moss seemed brothers
dark-haired one, about the same height.
Rayyan, perhaps a fraction better-
looking, thought Moss one shade more white.
Both had the strong Semitic nose
driving down their faces - in repose.
As Rayyan gazed up into the dome
whose sunny heaven adorned his home
a European-style cherub
dragged an informative banner
across blue skies of Yohanna
telling the Palestinian Arab
narrative of families like his
who'd commissioned paintings like this

iii

Back in the Ottoman twilight.
He thought about serene yesterdays;
the old times of the Canaanite;
dreamed by poetic pathways
into ages antecedent
when man was simpler and didn't
seem so arrogant and conceited
complicated and self-cheated.
(Rayyan believed the word 'Canaan'
shared its Indo-European root
with that name for forbidden fruit
'cannabis', a linguistic cousin.
The term: 'The land of milk and honey'
for his drug-of-choice made him hungry.)

iv

Suddenly the sleeping man
stirred and twisted, lifting his knees
throwing them out across the divan
like sails trimmed in a contrary breeze.
(The dreamer tacked on a new course
through the ocean of sleep's universe.)
Rayyan called his name: 'Moshe.'
Two blue eyes opened halfway.
A ship of slumber lengthened:
arms went up like a long bowsprit
above the prow, where headsails sit;
and Moss awoke, feeling strengthened
(like a ship when its 'widowmaker'
carries a quickening spinnaker).

v

"Moss, greetz bro, wha's good, bandit?
We've had a mad night of rioting.
We all went up into Natzrat Illit
where we got involved in street-fighting
which is how I picked up *this*:
from the Mishteret a nasty kiss.'
Rayyan rolled his tee-shirt short-sleeved
exposed his shoulder where he'd received
some heavy blow from a nightstick.
Wound, welted, raised and livid
gave an extremely vivid
testament to where some thick
instrument of brutality
had almost caused a fatality.

vi

'If that smack had descended
on ma skull' (Rayyan smiled at Moshe)
'a man's life-story could have ended.
But cuz, you've been through misery
yourself, I know, I've heard from Shaza:
she found you near the local plaza.
Apparently she grabbed a jackknife
from someone in the crowd, saved your life
cut you free when you were gonna burn?'
Can't believe my baby-sister
got you out of there, what a soldier.
Hope she's there for me when it's my turn.'
Moss gazed sleepily at Rayyan.
'Ray', she got me from the frying-pan.'

vii

'Through my windscreen came a stone
like a space-bullet, a meteor.
Lightly-stunned, on backrest prone
man, I was about to be a martyr
till Shaza got me out, what a star'.
Moss groaned: 'Truly, times are bizarre.
Last night, partying by Galilee
on the lakeside ('spected to see
you there, but fully understand)
today, laid up in this nursing-home:
the "Shabash Hospital" of your Mum.
Tell you, fam, it's from novel-land
like the plot of some action-movie
mixing the grotesque 'n' groovy'.

viii

Now that his friend was half-awake
coming out of his coma, switched-on
Rayyan passed him a small seedcake
sesame dusted with cinnamon.
'Bro, if you wanna get *beheaded*
have some confection, bruv, it's loaded.'
Gingerly, Moss took the sliver;
he was used to Rayyan's halva.
He'd eaten many times these slices
ended-up out of his mind
on Ray's spice-cookies, gone moonblind
thanks to his friend's narcotic vices.
'Wha's in here?' 'Nex' stop, euphoria
the land of phantasmagoria.'

ix

Rayyan was a straight-out doper
(though not really in the Western sense)
a Muslim, yes, but a no-hoper
among the orthodox (his offence
to fantasize of heaven-on-earth).
He thought of spiritual rebirth
as getting high with gorgeous women
writing love-songs out of sinning.
Rayyan was a Sufi and a sage
a follower of certain 'filthy' saints
whose work is to remove those taints
which trouble the world in every age.
The young man was a little bit naïve
but who can say what's best to believe.

x

Surely if we know a good pathway
through this labyrinth of shadows
we'll say, in a communiqué
share, in the midst of world-sorrows
promote in some quiet bulletin
the wisdom of our antitoxin.
But we won't force it down people's throats
if others, seeking antidotes
don't like the taste, perhaps, of hashish.
Still: Rastas, Sufis and Green Men
who have the Green Faith say 'Amen'
as they become fabulously rich
in the currency of invention
by the Holy Herb's intervention.

xi

They heard the late dustman's cry
as he wound his donkey through the souk.
They heard a dove in the courtyard fly
with a sigh that left them thunderstruck
though it was lighter than the sound
waves make when they run aground
on the smooth lip of the land
on the infinitely softest sand.
Moss thought of a burnt-out shell
his car reduced to blackened trash.
His ordeal came back in a flash:
its fiery slow-motion bombshell.
He gazed at Rayyan, candlelit:
Jah had dragged him from the snakepit.

They talked of other times and places
(as twilight fell in the Old City)
recalled many names and faces.
Conversation, fairly gritty
veered toward that vexed subject
upon which young men will reflect
doggedly and often, question
frustratedly given expression:
'Why, as individualities
must women be so enigmatic
so bashful and then *so* dramatic?'
They talked of bad personalities:
bedevilment in the beautiful
sweetness in the plain and dutiful.

'Take that Aliyah' Moss was saying
'she's got a thing for me, you know that.
Remember last year, I was playing
riddims when that little spoiled-brat
pulled some sexy stunts. Call me purist:
she's just a relationship-tourist.
Look what Aliyah did to Dekel
man, she gave that brer double-hell:
he was crawling while she laughed.
When she screwed his amigo, Asher
that wasn't blessed, cuz. Shag her?
I wouldn't put my sacred shaft
down there, bredda. She's, like, possessed.
Her beauty makes her think she's the best.'

xiv

'Hear you, bro, but Aliyah can dance…'
Rayyan came back after a pause.
'I'm in love, bruv. Do I stand a chance
a dope-dealer like me, a lost-cause?'
Moss drawled: 'Look out for that one, cuz.
I warn you as your best friend coz
faced by an egocentric demon
disguised as an angelic woman
we're helpless, all driven by the fire
quickly-started, not-so-soon put-out
extinguished, east, west, north and south:
that dangerous wildfire called desire.
Aliyah has no dignity.
(On its own, what is carnality?)'

xv

The cypress in the courtyard swayed
Nazareth appeared to be at peace.
The big stone house, built on the wheat-trade
an architectural showpiece
seemed to settle down in the dusk
glowed a deep silver, its outer husk
polished by the moon now rising
a millstone forever resizing
grinding down the months into days.
Someone knocked at the heavy oak
behind the door someone spoke.
Then Shaza entered, in the moon's rays
beautiful, her black eyes downcast
as through a vaulted doorway she passed.

xvi

Her eyes were fixed upon the floor
yet as she brushed by a stone pillar
the arch above the heavy door
appeared to express displeasure.
It seemed the house itself, amazed
allowed one eyebrow to be raised
displayed surprise at this demure girl
who through her boldness stood, heart awhirl
in the centre of the darkened room.
She wore blue jeans, tight 'n' revealing
but all about her was concealing
as she stood still in the early gloom.
Was this last night's heroine
standing here so shyly feminine?

xvii

'Shaz' went Rayyan 'what's happening
sister, are you good? Look, here's Moshe
in one piece all thanks to your helping
hand in the madness of last-night's fray.'
Shaza nodded at her brother's friend
(awkward as when, at drilling's end
we try to thank the dentist for work
done in a mouth which can only jerk
unpleasantly as it tries to smile).
But Shaz' had something in reserve.
Something flickered in a facial nerve
as from back-pocket she drew mobile
handed it to Rayyan with a nod.
'Check my inbox. It's the hand of God.'

xviii

A second's silence. Rayyan then
grabbed Shaza's phone, hit the screen.
(In blackout of his 'opium-den'
fascia blossomed ultramarine.)
Moss heard a ring-dove calling
her mournful voice rising-and-falling
in her tall green house of cypress
her long cry of painful tenderness
low and melancholy and calming.
Shaza stood in the shadows alone
as Rayyan gazed at glowing phone;
as airy fragrances, night-embalming
drifted from the courtyard to the room:
some sunlit hill's dark-wooded perfume.

xix

'Jalilah's here' Rayyan said.
A smile, but no move to explain.
(The Rambam twists on makeshift bed
as pounding temple shakes his brain.)
Rayyan mumbled 'This is from Jalilah!
How did she come here from Shatila?'
'Smuggled over the border
last night amid the disorder.
Tonight performing you-know-where.'
Shaz' seemed embarrassed, ill-at-ease
in her explanation seemed to freeze
left her last words hanging in midair.
Rayyan handed back the phone
gestured they wished to be alone.

xx

As soon as an oaken door was closed
atmosphere in the room changed
mood was completely transposed:
Rayyan leapt up as if deranged:
'Moss, you will not believe
what Shaz just pulled out of her sleeve.
Slingshot Hiphop has a secret queen.
Bro, she's not even seventeen
but Jalilah's destined for the top.
I heard this young girl a year ago
in Beirut spit her mind-bending flow.
My heart raced, time seemed to stop.
Jalilah's sweet-sixteen-and-a-half:
hiphop genius in a headscarf.'

xxi

'Bro, you need to hear this young girl rap
her flow is in High Arabic.
But think Bahamadia, her zap
lazy, supercool, as poetic
melancholic, funky, on-the-case
in completely another space
to anything you've checked before:
what the Arab world's been waiting for.'
Moss heard only the syllable 'Jah'
for him the name of God Most High
(Israel Vibration standing-by)
attached to the ancient word 'Lila'.
'What does her name "Jalilah" mean?'
'Wait for it, bro: "Splendid One, High Queen."'

xxii

'One hitch tho'.' (Solemn emphasis
introduced a demon, glowering.)
'One glitch, bruv. Tonight you cannot miss
but right now I'm brainpowering
cuz, to think how I can sneak you in.
The club's off-limits to your kin
no Jewman, of any tribe
even Rasta, can peek inside.
Bro, it's in a wasteland location;
me, myself, I hardly know the way.
More secret than Guantanamo Bay
it's under strict classification.'
Moshe said: 'Wha' 'bout disguise?
Trust me, Ray', no one will recognise.'

CHAPTER

i

Over Nazareth the moon rises
mirror of the parallel rays
a crescent moon, the ship of Isis
crossing night's blue-black seaways
carrying variant fortune's freight
increase or decline of fate.
To some she brings velvet fruition
to some, disastrous attrition
the wearing down of all their dreams.
She sails on through trough and wave
from infancy into the grave
through the gulf of golden extremes.
What's she transporting in her hold
for those of whom we have been told?

ii

It is the fifteenth of Nisan
the month of the ripened barley
(in the calendar Gregorian
falling late this year, in early
April, to be more-or-less exact).
The phases of the moon transact;
the life-force leaps in the barley-rows.
And where, from this point, do we suppose
the sad world in springtime is going?
We look around the lie of the land
where harvestings of ten thousand
years have brought gleanings out of sowing
where seven blessings of the Green Man
once raised returns of gold in Canaan.

iii

The fire-mountain is not extinct.
Nazareth smoulders with frustration
her riotous districts interlinked
with cheap telecommunication.
Mobile phones, like ears of barley
buzz with life in her underbelly;
Mashhad and Safafira bubble
in a cauldron of molten rubble.
The tourist-trade has seen a dip:
Molotovs and water-cannons
in Unholyland's environs
(firebombs and snipers) mean 'bad trip'
for the Abrahamic family
holidaying in The Galilee.

iv

Under the moon a car is streaking
fast out of al-Nassira, breaking
speed-limits, velocity peaking
round the one-sixty mark, taking
Highway 700 north
for some secret place setting forth.
In the front-seat the laughing driver
is a skeleton, a cadaver
in sunglasses, dangling a spliff.
Next him sits Rayyan, quite relaxed.
In the back, hardly looking taxed
inscrutable as a hieroglyph
next to Shaz sprawls The Rambam:
here doing the thing which is haraam.

v

A keffiyeh wraps his flaxen dreads
(symbolising dark grains of barley
on a field of white cotton threads).
He looks an Arabic Bob Marley
or some mid-eastern fashionista
sporting trendy yellow blister-
lensed dark-glasses, shielding completely
his giveaway eyes, discreetly
hidden now in wraparound shades.
And what's this on his right temple?
A bandage forms a white trammel
which effectively blockades
all analytic scrutiny:
someone wounded in the mutiny.

vi

Aquaplaning over the skyline
the moon races beside the car
like a speedboat, far behind
dragging a solitary star.
Conversation in the vehicle
travels a three-peopled circle;
Shaza doesn't contribute at all
a pity, she nestles in headshawl
watching a moonboat slide through space
studying small towns in the night
like starclouds passed on a spaceflight.
One by one their flickerings replace
each other, fading out behind
consecutively left undefined.

vii

Moshe's freestyling, excited
tone of voice gives everything away.
Mooncaked and high-spirited
his Arabic's full of gritty wordplay
making Rayyan and the driver smile.
(They reach a canyon, a defile
following a one-track country-road.)
Now a cellphone must download
more directions, a clandestine map.
(Ah, the miracles of Safari
when you're stuck under the starry
night-sky in the train of a mishap.)
Out here still roams the Sand Cat
the Arabian Leopard, come to that.

viii

An email flashes into view
attachment: a hand-drawn map;
they're able at last to follow through
(thanks to the ever-functioning app).
Wilderness has been decoded
to the club they've been back-roaded.
Except no venue's to be seen
just a hillside covered with umpteen
four-wheel-drives and SUVs.
Headlights have to be extinguished
parking-zones are only distinguished
by stewards waving LEDs
to line the motors up in ranks:
cars in metallic phalanx.

ix

Along a stream, by a lemon grove
processing in groups of twenty
they climb on foot - where before they drove -
an incline in the Land of Plenty.
A small cascade descends suddenly
a river tumbling hiddenly.
Now music becomes audible
above the falling water's babble.
A candlelit cavemouth appears.
Bats flit, with dives and quick upswings
feeding on whiteflies and green lacewings:
airy harvest which the hot night bears.
(Shaza pulls her headscarf tighter;
the bats and bugs disquiet her.)

x

Moss feels pulse accelerate
as a lazy dubstep bassdrum
begins to drive, accentuate:
bassline having a tantrum
wobbling about underneath
as if in demonic childbirth
a fire-mountain were stirring
with some terrible recurring
parturition from the deep worldcore:
some pouring-out of black and red
magma from the undiscovered
heart of that living carnivore
men call their mother, far below
down in creation's shadow.

xi

They filter through security:
eight strongmen completely masked
in black, each face, in its entirety
hidden in a headscarf. Rayyan, asked
to step into a dim-lit alcove
is searched as if some treasure-trove
lies hidden in his baggy Levis.
In seams and pockets a sentry pries
looking for the Zahret el-Kolch.
But all the frisking cannot find it
and Rayyan hardly seems to mind it
as men fumble boldly in his crotch.
(That's because *it's* hidden far away
not because our friend Rayyan is gay.)

xii

Spiralling on a long staircase
down through the limestone hillside
all maintain a serious headspace
as they descend with silent guide.
On a deep candlelit landing
observe Shaza secretly handing
something taken from her brassiere
to her brother, druggie brer
the transaction of a split-second.
Now they've reached the lowest level
ground-zero for tonight's revel:
to a glass swing door they're beckoned.
Passing through into Transworld
they find a zone unparalleled.

xiii

The venue is an ocean of sand
with multicoloured islands rising
out of dunes and drifts, a wonderland
futuristic in its devising
a realm from ancient romances.
Warm illuminations, ambiences
uplit scaffoldings and sails of silk
give the sense of an ocean of milk
with islets of luminosity
where dancers move in freeform
through the music's wild sea-storm.
No garishness or pomposity
no strobe, swingfire or traffic-light
make this atmosphere overbright.

xiv

Our trio merge into a dancefloor
surface again ten minutes later;
find a more sheltered, nuanced shore
to chill and lounge on, seeking greater
acoustic insularity.
(Charming dissimilarity
between one and another floor-plan.)
Moss to Rayyan: 'Abdul the Merman
breathes underwater. Yo, this is dope.
Who put this magic cave together
some Palestinian godfather?'
'Nope, a Jordanian philanthrope
Sufi millionaire-eccentric
his purposes quite esoteric.'

xv

'They say there's a fallout shelter
beneath the venue, right under here.
I met the dude one time in Delta
that nightclub down in al-Bayader.
He said he was after "the nonesuch"
I sold him some Zahret el Kolch.
He's interested in plant gateways;
he thinks we're in the last days.
I guess he feels the Iranian
invocation of Azrael;
an A-bomb threat against Israel
justifies this subterranean
experiment in decadence:
pleasure as the only real defence.'

'You've said it yourself: "Reality:
a hallucination brought about
by a lack of drugs." Hilarity
escalates; laughter breaks out
blending with cool electronica.
Byzantine scales drift and flicker
with semitonal tensions moving
subtle, jazzy chord-shifts grooving.
Now on the dancefloors and the islands
(out of the sands rising salient)
on plinths and platforms, radiant
dancers travel in the highlands
jumping sometimes shore-to-shore
island-hopping in rapport.

xvii

Half-niqab screening her lower face
one girl stood out. Both brers tracked her
as she rotated with angel-grace.
Both brothers seemed attracted to her
as she pirouetted to the beat
with understated motions discreet.
Her way of moving clearly expressed
her passion for this music, her zest
for its beauty. She did not say
turning around for all to see
'Ah, people, you must look at me
because I have a special way
because I am the queen of the dance.'
She seemed to say: 'Join me in my trance.'

Rayyan: 'I've seen that babe before.'
Moss: 'That angel feels the groove.'
The brothers pushed to the dancefloor;
both bros felt they had something to prove.
Crossing an ocean of fluorescence
they approached the divine presence;
among the islands closely-chained
dreamed they sailed to paradise regained.
She danced before them; but not alone;
she had a towering amigo
with equally gigantic ego
(apparently) his face carved of stone.
He glared like a sorcerer
looked a cyborg, but scarier.

Rayyan had his wounded shoulder
Moss, a temple still pounding;
they could have left it, acted older
backed off into the surrounding
pandemonium of dancers
without becoming crazy chancers.
Instead they faced the Dark Lord
eyeballed him, fearlessly mirrored
his grim looks and glaring eyes.
Suddenly the cyborg smiled
greeted Rayyan with a mild
expression of cordial surprise:
'Rayyan, you remember me, Aziz.
Shatila of the refugees.

Jalilah's brother. Fam, what's good?
Who's this, your twin? Salaam alaykum.'
The giant gazed at Moss, who stood
like Rayyan, stricken deaf-and-dumb.
Then, in opposite directions
without hearing these warm inflections
both young dudes spun, to find: no one.
Jalilah had fled her chaperone
vanished in the ocean of the crowd
left her admirers and her brother
to make small talk with one another.
And now the music's thundercloud
crescendoed, threw electric darts
into opened minds, awakened hearts.

'Wa alaykum asalaam,' returned
Rayyan and Moss, and cheek-to-cheek
kissed Aziz, though both brers yearned
to kiss a skin more refined and sleek
a complexion of porcelain
not stubbled with facial mane
(where each kiss had a crash-landing).
'Aziz, greets, man. This is outstanding
come over and see Shaz', she's here;
come join us, cuz, you're very welcome
with you, we'll be a foursome.
You remember Shaza from last year?'
(At the words Moss felt the immense
absence of a distant quintessence.)

xxii

Here's Rayyan of the famous smile
opening the gates of paradise
as he gazes at friend Aziz, while
the latter suggests a water-ice
to Shaza, like a gentleman
perched beside her on low divan.
(Naturally, no alcohol's flowing;
atmosphere's more easygoing
thanks to self-control's restriction.)
Aziz rises to get some drinks
takes Rayyan (who to his sister winks).
While Moshe feels the ghost of friction
in the air as Shaza looks at him
gaze unambiguously grim.

CHAPTER

i

To believe: the ultimate crime;
no mystery shall be held dear.
God is forbidden in this time;
science has made everything clear.
Yet every answer from that source
poses ten more questions of course;
and so, probing, edgy and restless
through an empty house which is Guestless
continues. Things slide from bad to worse:
men in white coats give us the jitters
we submit to the atom-splitters.
Man tinkers with the universe
looks for God in a hole in the ground
by reductionism spellbound.

ii

What's the answer? To get stoned
to live in clouds of translation
emaciated and rawboned
like anchorites in contemplation
seeking not analysis
but mysterious synthesis
the marriage of the heart and the world
where inside every flower is furled
the spiral signature divine?
Shall we abandon the machine
leave it, complex and unclean
go back, where's neither mine nor thine
return before it is too late
to the garden of the fiery gate?

iii

Some call the angel of cannabis
random, reckless, unpredictable.
They say her temporary bliss
transports so delectable
lead via sweet narcosis
to the horrors of psychosis.
Is it not we, in our neurotic
cities, who've become psychotic;
are not bedlams and madhouses
built on every suburban street?
Is not every second man you meet
these days a lunatic who oozes
hatred, paranoia and greed
in our jungles of the Devil's Weed.

iv

Take a young man of seventeen
full of talent and unlikely dreams
open, generous, place him on mean
streets at night, where idiot regimes
battle iron gangsters and druglords;
where innocence guiltily applauds
the mobster and the snake with a knife
because at least they live the high life.
Get him zoned on chemical skunk
push him around and play with his mind
teach him to fear what's just behind
his shoulder: some stone-cold fiend on junk.
Then say the influence of drugs
turns dudes of seventeen into thugs.

v

Such arguments appeal to those
for whom the neoteric's dead
who look back fondly to Cairo's
gardens of the fountainhead:
old legendary pleasure-zone
where hashish and *El Kolch* alone
made earthbound citizens
supernatural singers, intense
experience far from this 'everyday';
where, resigned to the condition
called existence, this perdition
all ground to dust is human clay:
Cafour, green palace of the heart
where intoxication was an art.

vi

Cafour. The name weaves a spell
from Baudelaire, Burton, de Nerval
from Rimbaud and his *Season in Hell*.
(Where heaven is just behind the veil
ripped aside by hallucinogens;
where a dirty perceptive lens
is dilated by eastern oceans
opened-up by Egyptian potions
from the high-times of the Caliphate.
(Amplification of Arab myth
became an obsession with
French Romantics and mid-to-late
nineteenth-century Symbolists;
and yet a greater truth persists.)

vii

While Aziz was getting refreshments
Moss and Shaza were engaged
in conversational enmeshments.
The young girl seemed almost enraged
while Moss looked disconcerted.
From time to time he inserted
a word or two when Shaza paused
mid-tirade, which instantly caused
another outburst. Let's overhear
analyse, the subject of their row.
Funny, we were discussing just now
that same question hanging in the air
between these two as they lounge on rugs
spread on sand: they're talking about drugs.

viii

'You and my brother are just as bad
why can't you just get high on life?'
'Shaz, this life is so bleepin' sad
('scuse the language). Sorrow-and-strife
hellfire and evermore internecine
problems right here in Palestine
make this world truly depressing.
One sure way of peeps de-stressing
is through good use of cannabis.'
'Getting high is not the real headache
it's shredded nerves in heaven's wake
when the pothead enters the abyss
after intoxication: that's the problem
that's what I really condemn.'

ix

Shaza said this looking straight at Moss.
'The bad tempers and the demons.'
As she spoke her Macintosh
iphone gave melodious summons
vibrated in her back-pocket.
As she began to unlock it
she gently said: 'To be continued'.
Moss appeared largely unsubdued;
there was much he wanted to say.
'Madness of the work-ethic
makes modern man's spirit sick.'
But this would keep for another day.
Shaza handed over her cell
where on the screen was a marvel:

X

Jalilah's face, three words and a kiss.
'On in five, X…' the message read
there was nothing more than this.
'She's my hero' Shaza said.
'When I first heard her in Shatila
I realized she was a healer
a poet and a peacemaker
a woman and an earthshaker.
She's what the Arab world's waiting for;
a strong calm voice without hatred
a woman dignified yet naked
a beautiful ambassador
for all of us, rapping the truth
in a way that grabs Arab youth.'

xi

Shaza, her gaze full of fire
pointed over Transworld's dancers
to where, on a slightly higher
plinth-island, three pyromancers
played with lights while sound-technicians
checked out mics for two musicians.
One held a mother-of-pearl-inlaid
clay doholla, exquisitely-made
a hand-drum which spoke its name clearly
before it had been touched at all.
Wedging it between his thighs a tall
good-looking African brer merely
brushed the skin with long slender hand
making of the drum his first demand.

xii

As fingers rippled across the skin
the thing came alive and stuttered
smoothly. 'She's going to begin'
was the thought murmurously uttered
by everyone in the venue.
All could see her retinue:
the hand-drummer in black headwrap
covering even eyes, a white cap
just showing above dark spirals;
and another young urban dude
angling a magnificent 'oud
(that friend of ancient pastorals)
so that the soundhole of the lute
faced the mic, now switched to 'mute'.

xiii

A famous choon by Cheb Khaled
his love-anthem to a young girl
came pouring down from overhead
in a psychoacoustic swirl:
Chebba. Three hundred voices gasped
in unison. The drummer clasped
his primordial instrument
between his thighs and softly sent
grace-notes skating over the song;
while oud-man played some high cadenzas
between two of Cheb Khaled's stanzas;
and now the crowd chanted along:
'Waah chebba, ya chebba bent blidi
wayye omnin tadhak khayti.'

xiv

'Young girl, young girl of my town
brothers, when she smiles I see the light.'
Shaza, Moss, Rayyan, Aziz got down
in front of the spotlit island, right
before the little stage on its plinth.
Khaled finished. In his place a synth,
eerie, sounded in the silence.
Then came rumblings of violence
growls of a gunship helicopter
hovering just above the crowd
the turmoil of its props thunder-loud.
Whipping of rotor-blades came harder.
Then emerged a downtempo beat
solemn, heavy, nothing light or sweet.

xv

Breakbeat loped along slowly
heavy, brooding, step-by-step grooving.
Hand-drum came in like some holy
mourner in a death-march moving.
Lights went down, the club went dark;
the oud gave out a three-note cry, so stark
it seized your heart; a synth-bass' massive
frequencies entered, all-pervasive.
Then a voice was heard inside the storm:
'Kfar Saf-Saf, Kfar Farradiya
Kfar Tantura, Kfar Araba
Kfar Tarshisha.' (The voice warm.)
Kfar Fassuta, Kfar Tarbika
Kfar Ayn Ghazal, Kfar Qaddita...'

A murmur went up from the people
as they breathed one exhalation
one long impassioned ripple
as from souls in damnation:
a collective voice of pain
a moan from deeps, a dark refrain.
Moss knew these names out of legend
felt his dreadlocks stand on end.
Lights came up a little; he could see
in half-shadow a young girl's face:
Jalilah stood there with simple grace
chanting the dead hamlets endlessly.
Eyes closed, she seemed asleep;
as she spoke some began to weep.

Of course the world is now aware
how genocide flared in Forty Eight.
As if the whole world had been there
we now know what, until, of late
has been so concealed and denied.
(How the Zionists have lied.)
The Rambam took in every word.
Every village-name he heard
carried its profound vibration.
And because his Arabic was good
he completely understood
Jalilah's next rap-recitation.
(It's given here, in approximate
English, because its power is great.)

xviii

Of course every hip teenaged
kid across Middle Eastern lands
Arab or Jew, anyone engaged
with rap-subculture understands
these words which managed to enchant
(later on) the whole Levant
which transmitted their waves of candour
down the North African corridor.
Yet Arabian MC slang
its dialects and idioms
the nonviolent axioms
of Slingshot Hiphop's cool-gang
don't reach the ipod generation
downloading Western pop-sedation.

xix

So there's an even simpler reason
for translating this famous lyric
which now sent a powerful frisson
(poetry and realpolitik)
through the soul of Moss Rambam
as in fluent wordflow he swam
sensing the drive of controlled rage
in Jalilah's torrent of language;
as awe exploded from his heart
beholding this teenaged girl
head-and-neck concealed in a swirl
her poetic fury off-the-chart!
Something in his chest seemed to shift;
he felt given a real birthday gift.

xx

Yes, a simple reason's very clear:
the truth must be for all to see:
it's time for everyone to hear
the Palestinian history.
We know how Israel was broken
under the Third Reich, forsaken:
Belsen, Treblinka, Dachau
Ravensbrück, Auschwitz-Birkenau.
Yet, dear God, how can it be
that those who suffered Hitler's state
passed Buchenwald's infernal gate
can visit such brutality
upon a proud and innocent race?
(Casting Israel into disgrace.)

xxi

Tears came sliding, burning from his eyes
as Moss Rambam beheld Jalilah
(in blue-jeans, just over pint-size)
apocalyptic storyteller
into a mic unravelling
dark histories, time-travelling
across the Middle-Eastern landscape
telling how the evil day took shape:
the Nakba, that catastrophic
nation-slaying night of bloodlust
which came, another Holocaust
driven by a grim demagogic
cleansing, with a fatal equation:
genocide in the land of Canaan.

xxii

One thought never came to Moshe's mind
(as the helicopter still hovered)
as the rap began to unwind
as the dead were discovered
in their hilltop villages lying
named again and death-defying.
'How could Jalilah, aged sixteen
transmit, in language raw and keen
her traumatized race-memory;
how could a young girl redefine
the agony of Palestine
so truthfully and so tenderly?'
If Moss had let this thought activate
his answer would have been: 'Jah is great.'

Jalilah's Rap

In '48, when hatred of us broke loose
then came platoons of strangers
some who had been neighbours;
like sabre-tooth tigers
carrying automatic rifles.
To hilltop villages came great dangers:
the ethnic cleansing of Palestine.
No use to scream your wife's in-labour;
machine-gun fire raking her naked spine
in the night of the Nakba
sombre second Holocaust:
death-squads for the sons of your line
in your olive-groves the rapings of your daughter.
No truce from that time to this:
ruin and abuse in Unholyland.

That was '48, that was then
Withstanding still, brethren
we throw a mic now upon mic-stand:
Slingshot Hiphop's genocide firsthand;
Palestine's the pain of people holding-inside
a whole country, while others in their land
suntan on stolen beaches of white sand
eating blood-soaked peaches, ripe and red.
Underneath the flag of fear
there's something very wrong here;
Israel, to the truth awaken.
I and I can't get no satisfaction
no, no no, not-at-all, nothing yet:
no human rights, no drugs, no medicine
in the Gaza Strip.

Everything's been taken
I and I forsaken
in Palestine.

So we bring language, redefine superheated
delivered by Arabian MC's undefeated
to the diamond-like whiteness of Tel Aviv;
these words written where the Red House stood
'How to forgive?' (In the days of the Stern Gang
the ethnic cleansing of Palestine.)
When the tortured sang in basements
on Bauhaus Levantine avenues of Tel Aviv
polluted with what is so offensive, I say:
that internecine way. And the displacements
after doomsday left few alive
in the land along the hilltops, on the skyline
where village met heaven yesterday.

CHAPTER

7

i

'Kfar Tantura, Kfar Saba
Kfar Manda, Khirbat Irribin
Kfar Ayn Ghazal, Kfar Araba
Kfar Farradiya, Khirbat Jiddin.'
As the spot dimmed and died an eerie
thought came to Moss: grim reverie.
(Jalilah, still chanting the village-
names, was lost on a darkened stage.)
In the blackout came a vision.
He saw the West Bank settlements'
sinister concrete tenements
(fenced by the chainlink of division
with watchtowers, barbed-wire and arc-lamps)
as replica concentration-camps.

ii

He saw Treblinka and Birkenau
raised again in Ramallah:
terrible fortresses of sorrow
built with the American dollar
by Israelis who, sleeping at night
dream that, somehow, at first light
all the Palestinians will be gone
consigned to oblivion;
who sleep completely surrounded
by an 'enemy' who also dreams
that when the rising sun gleams
the Israelis, steel-compounded
in their mini-cities, guard-gated
all will have been annihilated.

iii

As Moss saw this mental image
lights came up on the stage-island.
Jalilah was gone. In joy and rage
the club exploded with a big hand.
As applause detonated
as appreciation was stated
passionately, the percussionist
became a demolitionist
thundering a long crescendo
on his mother-of-pearl clay drum
which seemed a solar simulacrum
flashing like the dawn-sun which sends slow
pink-gold daylight fanning through the east
faint at first, then fiercely increased.

iv

The black-and-white drum became
shamanic heart of the whole room;
its pulsing seemed now to proclaim
oneness with absolute volume.
Suddenly, at crescendo's zenith
with thunder rolling underneath
the 'blind' man tore black headwrap backward
offered his maniac regard
to just one person in the crowd.
His transfixing gaze was locked on Moss.
Everyone saw this in the hush
that followed after the so-loud
pounding of the hand-drum, amazed
to see how the black man's two eyes blazed.

v

In the path of a narrowed stare
a pencil-beam of fire and ice
laser-powered, Moss became unclear.
Almost unconscious of his precise
whereabouts in the Transworld venue
underground, he seemed to misconstrue
his surroundings, confused timeframe
seemed almost to forget his own name.
Yet everything flared in memory
from the recent wheel of days
from a twenty-four-hour phase
rammed with hallucinatory
transactions and sparks of doing
thrown from his road of pursuing.

vi

Again the waters of Galilee
reflected gold the sun's decline
to the west; again he could see
a water-skier on a tension-line
flying down the lake as if the boat
followed was the solar ship afloat
speeding down the hollowed waves
riding white crests, blue concaves.
He glanced up from mixing-desk:
slant-eyed Aliyah stood there
swaying like the skier, solitaire
so slinky, so statuesque
beckoning. Then, in fascination
Moss saw himself, same location

vii

Seven years sooner - the seven years
significant in his translation -
riding Dad's neck with binoculars
watching Israel Vibration
dropping *Greedy Dog* in Galilee.
Again he was dazzled by the sea
as, on his father's shoulders carried
he felt, in boyhood, somehow married
to the great mystery of the world
balanced on Solomon's strong back.
Then - Kefitzat ha-Derach -
once again he 'jumped the road', hurled
himself by night to al-Nassira
with a void in his rearview mirror.

viii

Again the shooting-star came through
the windscreen with a burning hiss;
again he leant on Shaza, who
like an angel in the abyss
dragged him past the robotic crowd
chanting 'Death to all Jews' aloud.
Flashbacks of fifteen seconds ceased.
(Still two eyes hypnotically released
glittering rays, projected their gaze.)
Then, seized by a muscular black hand
his feet were airlifted from the sand.
Suddenly Moss found himself, in a daze
up on the spotlit island - onstage -
pulled there by the drummer: made hostage.

ix

Jalilah too, taken prisoner
protested without much energy
as the drummer now positioned her
facing Moss, as if some theurgy
some African ceremonial
vaguely matrimonial
were about to be transacted.
All this powerfully impacted
on the audience as it happened.
Not only those at the front
saw the drummer's ritualistic stunt.
Everybody's wild response deafened
as two hands were hand-fasted, made one;
as the hand-drum thundered 'Dun-dun-dun'.

x

Moss stood facing Jalilah onstage
holding her extended hand in his.
Dizzy, still he did not disengage.
(Jalilah tried: the drummer gave a hiss.)
The African joined their hands
as if a bride and her husband's
promises were being exchanged
when a wedding has been arranged
by the stars, when it's been fated.
All around them came raw cheering
which thundered in their sense of hearing
as if some large crowd awaited
outside a festive synagogue
a mosque, a church or analogue.

xi

Moss was shaking, mostly because
he thought he'd been recognized
(freak-out) but with the applause
he calmed down and rehumanized.
(He'd gone into Jewish 'victim-mode'
fleeting paranoia-overload.
Now he felt he could relax
killed that Ashkenazi reflex:
'Oy vey, the Cossacks are coming!')
Now he looked into Jalilah's eyes
anxiously, because of his disguise;
warily, since brain was numbing.
Her gaze - luminous - left him sunblind;
he probed two stars which burned his mind.

xii

Intellectual eyes are bright.
In the human face they blaze
with a great celestial light
eyes of intellectual rays.
(If the eye were not a sun
the eye could never see the sun
blazing with intelligence
source of light which hits the sense.
But darkness in this universe
bereave us all of cosmic fire
since the beauty that we desire
abandons us beneath its curse.)
Moss saw that light which never dies
looking deep into Jalilah's eyes.

xiii

Jalilah, wild daughter of Islam
(almond-shaped soul-windows in surprise
wide-open) stared back at Moss Rambam
clearly trying to rationalize.
The drummer, keeping their hands linked
at The Rambam very slowly winked;
this solemn, priest-like African man
who smiled (as only Africans can)
this brer whose warmth was so tactile
you'd say the sun was in his mouth
shining east, west, north and south
who filled the whole room with his smile.
Then on the sound-system of the club
came a well-familiar dub.

xiv

Israel Vibration's *Greedy Dog*.
'See you in the morning as the sun rise…'
In Moss Rambam's head cosmic fog
lifted, and, in his sudden surprise
he gave a hop and began to dance.
Just one beat Jalilah looked askance.
('The time is dread, O Rasta children…')
And then this beautiful siren
began to move as she'd moved before
when Moss first saw the lovely girl
round her brother spin and whirl
across the Transworld dance floor.
But now she moved in front of him:
one of the cosmic seraphim.

xv

Coincidence is like a window
into Jah's world where all is one.
There is no dualistic shadow;
there simultaneously are begun
and ended in planes of unity
all things above duality.
Now Moss relaxed in acquiescence:
this was meant to be. The Presence
danced before him, what could he do?
Rayyan jumped up from the sand
onto the wooden stage-island
and the brothers in the cool venue
high-fived each other, smiled; while Aziz
pulled Shaza up (giving her a squeeze).

xvi

Up came *Rudeboy Shufflin'* back-to-back
with *Greedy Dog*; Transworld went wild.
The emotion of Jalilah's track
rode on the dub, truth reconciled
with truth and vibe with higher vibe.
(How is it possible to describe
that most abstract of the arts:
music?) *Rudeboy* fused all hearts
among the friends as they danced on.
There was no real need to talk
as Jalilah did a moonwalk;
as Skelly and Lascelle balanced on
their crutches on the video-wall:
the spirit of the music said it all.

xvii

About ten minutes passed in a flash.
Then, for the happy clubbers
(children having a collective splash)
a song of Dimi Mint Abba's
triggered more dancefloor-mania
that music from Mauritania:
The Hassaniya Song for Dancing
so completely entrancing
with huge, subtle bass-drum-throb
its handclap-driven deep-desert sound
in Transworld echoing around
Dimi's voice: angelic half-sob
ecstasy and bitterness in one
her bright ullulations heaven-spun.

xviii

Tidinit and electric guitar
(played by Khalifa Ould Eide
Dimi's husband, another star)
wove through complex yet rock-steady
rhythms, microtonal cadenzas
as Dimi's voice blazed her stanzas.
And then this queen put on her crown:
O Lord, Bring Apartheid Crashing Down
came spiralling, a music sublime.
As the name of Nelson Mandela
was sung by Mauritania's daughter
Moss and Jalilah, clapping in time
had tears in their eyes; and they smiled
at each other: soul-beguiled.

xix

They danced on, not needing to speak.
Jalilah seemed to Moss to capture
all Semitic beauty's mystique:
her face glowing with sad rapture.
'A fir-tree on a northern height
sleeping in a snow-blanket of white
dreams of a palm in Eastern lands
silent, all alone on burning sands.'
Some lines from a poem by Heine
came to Moss (as he looked at her
in the Transworld atmosphere)
seeming somehow to define her.
She glanced at him shyly, eyes still wet:
half-angel, half hot coquette.

xx

He thought of Romeo and Juliet
helpless in love's magnetic-field
dancing in the House of Capulet
their tragic fate already sealed
that very first night of fireworks
(amid flying champagne-corks).
What did Jalilah think of him
he wondered, as he watched her slim
hands floating like doves in flight
gliding to PR's big choon *Sajeen*
(from the nonviolent mujahadeen
engaged in the spiritual fight
where words are the ammunition
where to tell the truth is the mission).

xxi

Jalilah was actually thinking:
'Why sunglasses in the depths of night?
Who does he think he's hoodwinking?
Does he wanna make us think black's white?
Basically he's *wasim*.' ('Good-looking.'
We get the sense that somethin's cooking.)
'He looks a little like Eminem.'
(For Jalilah the *creme de la creme*.)
'But why all the silly camouflage?'
She asks these questions yet she looks serene
dancing to *The Prisoner, Sajeen*:
Palestinian Rapperz in a rage.
(Now two giant hands on the screenwall
make a Star-of-David-handcuff fall

xxii

Broken to the desert floor.)
Look, high tension's not always bad
hey, we've been here many times before.
Love-stories have often been sad:
Layla and her madman, Majnoun;
Romeo and Juliet's honeymoon
over before even started.
Legends of the brokenhearted
belong to all humanity
fill the books and move to tears
millions, who live out their fears
of loving to insanity.
Let's remember that one way to truth
begins with the doomed romance of youth.

CHAPTER

i

Music is a ray from the zenith
its revolutionary wave transforms.
The time of gold returns from myth
when music's electric-storms
and transcultural vibration
(one song from every nation)
create that international language
common to the Aquarian Age.
May that planetary anthem ripple!
But one tedious word of warning
to safeguard the new day's dawning:
'As music is, so are the people.'
Spare us the sound of those songs
which don't address the people's wrongs.

ii

There's the Devil's music too
sugary, plastic and complacent.
It's a helluva hullabaloo
about nothing, ever-nascent
where glitz and fashion overboil
burst from the jaws of the gargoyle
decadence, whose grin is secular.
Music's angelic vernacular.
'Praise the Holy One with joy'
is what they sing out-of-this-world
in the hit-parade of pure gold.
Music is the weapon to deploy
against the mediocrity of hell
when there's no other way to rebel.

iii

We descended into Transworld
imagining a sound-volcano
picturing red-hot detritus hurled
loudly, more forte than piano.
(Thundering ejectamenta
threatened as we tried to enter).
Yet instead of a fire-mountain
we found down there a cool fountain.
(Strange, how we all fear our dreams
coming true, more so than our nightmares.
The worst that can happen? Well, who cares?)
To catch more insubstantial gleams
goldmining, let's go back underground
find the liquid light of future-sound.

iv

Let's have a drink with Shaz and Aziz
with Moss, Jalilah and Rayyan.
Fresh mint would hit the spot. 'Yes, please.'
(Here's that enigmatic African
making assemblage number six.
We know this man, we've heard his licks
driving from a clay hand-drum.)
Time for introductions. Here they come
in Jalilah's low, bewitching voice:
'Shaz', Rayyan… 'Scuse me, what's your name?'
(Hot damn, what a heartbreaking shame.
Does Moss really have no choice?
Must he falsify with his first word
to Jalilah: but that's absurd.

v

Yet his name gives everything away.
Still, deception's somehow a no-no.
What kind of ace-card must he play?)
'The name's Musa.' 'Truly? Good to know.
Musa, meet, from Zambia
Laurence, coolest master-drummer.'
'We linked before, innit Moshe?'
(Did we really hear that giveaway;
did the Zambian just say, in English
MC Rambam's Jewish name?
He leant over, whispered; all the same
he did stun, stagger and astonish.
He knocked sideways our secret-agent;
expression now pretty-vacant.)

vi

A seventh figure joins the group
chillaxing on beanbags on the sand
tall in stature, balding, with a stoop.
See, to Rayyan he extends his hand.
    This is Sajjid, boss of the club.
    Against the music, in the hubbub
we miss his words to Moshe's friend.
(The cast-list starts to grow, distend
    as in the works of Dostoyevsky.
How many more will be introduced
    unexpectedly produced?
        It's risky and it's pesky
    to have characters materialize
all shapes-and-sizes; some in disguise.)

vii

    Sajjid has a proposition.
    Rayyan passes his suggestion
on to Shaza, whose opposition
would be fatal; she sends the question
        over to Aziz and Jalilah
    putting out a social feeler.
(Moss Rambam and Laurence huddle;
    the former plays a paradiddle
on his thigh through loose blue denim
    anxiety evinced by his hand.
        Is he trying to understand
    why the brer wrongfooted him?)
    Answer? Okay, it's democratic;
    all say it won't be problematic.

viii

We're going to a roof-garden
zone two shades more exclusive;
this will surely please and gladden
Sajjid, eccentric and reclusive
not at ease in his own nightclub.
We leave the multicoloured bathtub
where Transworld's dancers revolve
in waves of music still dissolve.
It's three a.m. and cool as hell.
Across the ocean *Paradise Now*
is screening on a sidewall, wow.
We're looking at that gritty farewell
where one must die and one must live
but find mass-murder hard to forgive.

ix

'Yeah, we raised the cash for that flick
the director's an old friend of mine.'
(Sajjid to Rayyan.) With matchstick
probing at his mouth – since cannabine
deposits are gumming up his teeth –
Rayyan has discovered underneath
right molar a large lump of hash
and with a subtle sideways bash
from the toothpick-substitute
he now dislodges the narcotic
as they ascend from the aquatic
dancefloor-levels by a route
complex, labyrinthine, indirect.
'Love that film. Maximum respect.'

x

In the lift. 'That last consignment
really made the camel climb the dune.
Could you manage an assignment
at Delta, next week, sometime soon?'
(This, secretly, in Rayyan's ear
not for anyone else to hear.)
'Sajjid, any friend of Jalilah's
is a friend of this dealer's
you know that.' Elevator's stopped;
chrome door mechanically opens.
Now something comic happens:
twelve dark-accustomed eyes get popped
wide; then everybody squints
against a dawn-sky of fiery tints.

xi

They're in a sort of bubble
made of light, transparently
extending in a streamlined global
canopy of glass - apparently.
'Not glass.' (Sajjid, his undertone
harmonious in the wonderzone
where everyone's silence suggests
they've been thunderstruck, attests
to a transport of amazement.)
'Carbon 60, for architecture
the building-substance of the future.
We're quite proud of this achievement
it's military material
unavailable in Israel.'

xii

'Don't stress 'bout how we got it here
move up close, it's not dangerous;
check the micro-diameter
paper-thin and continuous.'
He grabs bald skull, waves hands in air:
'Made of C60, one strand of hair
would hold the bridge at Istanbul:
nature's superbonded molecule.
We're planning to use it in Gaza
to repair the infrastructure;
then there's the One Holyland venture...'
(Interposingly) from Shaza:
'Sajjid, we really dig your venue
but where do you get the revenue?'

xiii

'S'cuse me if I'm out-of-order
but you aren't Palestinian, are you?
You've crossed red lines here, jumped a border;
you'll be stopped (won't you?) a non-Jew
building subterranean palaces;
The Arabian Nights and *Alice's
Adventures in Wonderland* fused;
your tasteful clubland disabused
free of stroboscopes: disco-deathtraps.
I mean, right now, under our feet
three hundred peeps, synced-to-'da-beat
boppin' to Arabian MC's raps:
how did you set up this place?
Won't they hammer you, get on your case?'

Sajjid stays blessed and unstressed
through the sudden grilling keeps his cool.
(Aziz looks spellbound, seems impressed
as Shaza stirs a social whirlpool.)
'Hey, check out the panoramic view
while I get some mint tea on the brew;
then, all of you, have a sat.
We'll have a proper chat, how's that?'
Jalilah sends Moss a lightning smile
as all drift through the chrysalid
translucent space, curving and fluid
wondering if 'tomorrow's lifestyle'
somewhere in the future, far away
could ever be reality one day.

xv

From the bridge of some science-fiction
ocean-cruiser of times to come
they gaze south without restriction
over a sea of monochrome
lemon-groves in pre-dawn light
pastel-green tinted. Out of sight
somewhere down there is Nazareth.
Laurence mutters under his breath:
'For real, Musa, I heard ya MC
las' summer, down by the Lake;
heard ya drop a verbal earthquake
on the shore of Galilee.
Yes, Rasta, that's why I pulled yah
up on the stage to meet Jalilah.')

xvi

Moss is guided by the shoulder
through the light-filled belvedere.
This morning he feels younger, older.
He surrenders, lets his new bro steer
under the canopy's semidomes
through transparent honeycombs.
Everyone's seated; his floor-cushion
in the circle waits; lotus-fashion
he folds his feet up under his knees
straightens his back, takes a slow deep
breath (thinking of his transcultural leap)
looks at Shaza and Aziz
Rayyan, Laurence and Jalilah
Sajjid (pouring tea) on a kneeler.

xvii

'What we heard tonight says it all.'
Everyone murmurs 'Sajjid, you're right.'
(Laurence winks to Moss as a sheer wall
becomes a prism for the sunlight.)
Jalilah blushes, hangs her head.
'Nah, I tell you, that wasn't said
to make anyone feel big;
what we do here's a mutual gig.
I'm Jordanian, yeah, from Tafilah;
been in Israel ten years.
Five years ago, financiers
from the Gulf, known to me, revealed a
major loophole in Israeli law
opening a tight-closed door.

xviii

'A reform passed through the Knesset
made farmland in the Galilee
a transferable asset
available to be sold freely
because of economic hardship.
Through me, my friends bought a large strip
twelve thousand dunams to be exact.
This morning we're sitting on that tract.
The Sufic interests backing this deal
know the time has come for change.
Our experiments on this hill-range
assume that many others feel
the Zionist-Nazi war-machine
can't be stopped. Love must intervene.

xix

'The West Bank is too traumatized
for our Transworld experiment.
Sadly, there we'd be stigmatized
accused of idiot merriment.
The freedom-fighters, kept in pockets
put their faith in Katyusha rockets.
But however many they smuggle
over the borders, the armed-struggle
is working to their detriment.
Perhaps somewhere near Ramallah
we could try something similar.
But conditions here are different.
Yeah, this club is unusual;
more than a club, it's conceptual.

xx

'No clubs, no cafes in Jericho;
no movie-houses in Ramallah.
(Old westerns filmed in Mexico
used to be very popular
French films, with the odd erotic scene
came sometimes to the silver screen.
The 'Walid' and the 'Dunia'
I remember from sunnier
times before the Occupation.)
Since the days of the Intifada
it's been a hundred times harder.
I've seen a world's obliteration.
Clint Eastwood lookalikes in tanks
enforce the curfews of the West Bank's

xxi

'Hostage cities: Bethlehem, Jenin
Nablus and Qalqilyah.
You can't even buy an aspirin
when they gun you down in Ramallah.
Everyday arrest-operations
armoured bulldozer's devastations
robotic soldiers at nightfall
blasting through your party-wall
moving house-to-house, flat-to-flat
(without venturing into the street
where they'd feel the sniper's heat).
We live like the vulture and the rat.
Favoured races, say Darwinians
survive; but not Palestinians.

xxii

'There's nothing the Israelis fear
more than nonviolent protest.
With Slingshot's thermonuclear
impact we can now weapons-test
a new theory of revolution
test it *now* in the Natzrat region.
That's why I asked Jalilah here
to come down from Beirut, where
as you know, her music is rejected.
In Lebanon, Iran, Syria
hiphop causes mass-hysteria
among respected, well-connected
great ones of the establishment:
to their minds our artform's decadent.'

CHAPTER

i

'That's so diamond-true.' (Jalilah.)
'At school some call me "Filthy Angel"
"Blue Jean Whore" and "Sex-Appealer"
it's one long soul-destroying wrangle.
Sixteen, without nationality
with guns, drugs and criminality
I live in "the country of show-offs"
dress in my sister's throw-offs
watch the kids without any shoes
shuffle through Shatila's ruins;
study the glamorous mannequins
downtown, where the rich bitches booze
with their boyfriends. Sometimes Lebanon
seems to me one vast beauty salon.

ii

'What's the torment in my rap?
My homesickness for Palestine.
I live in a shanty-town rat-trap
remember a paradise once mine.
My girlfriends have *enough* insight
it's my teachers who are so uptight.'
Jalilah's silvery-smooth voice
cracked and broke as she choked twice.
'Backward-looking, they'd strangle me
butcher my words, bury my art
put a bloody spike through my heart.
Idiot schoolteachers tangle me
in argument and admonition
based on the ways of tradition.'

iii

She screened her face with her palms.
It seemed two panels closed around
a painting of some scene from the psalms
where a king's daughter, uncrowned
breaks down and cries beneath a willow
tears of rage descending, long ago.
Shaza felt the boiling chemistry.
'A stranger in your own country
your familiar world's foreign too
you're caught both ways.' Rayyan nodded:
'You must feel, like, disembodied
but your flow, you know, just cuts right through
you're not disorientated there.
Listening to you, yeah, you're everywhere

iv

'Back in your grandfather's Palestine
where on bright days his olive-trees flash;
right here, right now, on the frontline
where grey-grim Merkava tanks smash
through the rubble of the Gaza Strip:
Israel on its Satanic trip.'
'"I leave my hands to the refugees
give my middle-finger to the Nazis
the architects of Occupation."'
Moss echoed Tamar Nafar
Dam's outspoken demon-rapper
poet of excommunication.
All smiled: a brilliant image
from a last-testament of rage.

v

'I know you rap consciously, Rayyan
maybe your friend, Musa, too?'
First rays from the sun just-risen
striking her black headscarf, shining through
the fringe, made complex shadows lie
on Jalilah's eyelids. Neither eye
could meet sunlight openly
vision was indefinite only:
she glimpsed Moss through a nimbus.
Fracturing light played with his features;
bleached them, as when overexposures
leave photographs completely minus
contrast and definition.
She had a flash of recognition.

vi

(Maybe effects of marijuana
additionally destroyed
an illusion of persona
as the sun's dazzling ovoid
played havoc with visibility.
Something - not rationality -
now told Jalilah with blinding
certainty of some pretending;
maybe drug-induced clairvoyance
illuminated the conundrum;
left her with a theorem
difficult of utterance.
As daybreak's halo round him gleamed
she knew this man was not what he seemed.)

vii

'Yo, Sajjid, it's been a cool night
but this ain't right.' (She knew what he'd say.)
'I'm gonna explode some dynamite
a blast of the unexpected, but hey
what's a little semtex between friends?
The fact is I'm a bod who tends
to leap in the dark no-matter-what
with consequences often not
calculated or imagined.
I follow the road impulsively
jump ahead compulsively
before a path has been examined.
The truth is that I'm not really...'
'I know,' said Sajjid. 'You're Israeli.'

viii

'Nah,' corrected Moss, 'I'm Jewish
not Israeli.' Jalilah exhaled
rapidly, observed two bluish
eyes which had been screened and veiled
behind curvaceous yellow lenses.
(Sunlight dazzled ocular sense's
capacity to analyse
colour.) She could catalyse
no thought, felt only premonition's
rightness as Moss removed amber shades.
Now a double game of charades
suspected in her intuitions
ended with the vanishing of night.
Now the truth had come to light.

ix

'Okay, you're Jewish not Israeli;
(Sajjid) 'Any friend of Rayyan's
is welcome to Transworld sincerely.
No Zionist barbarians
naturally get through my door:
I don't want blood on my dancefloor.
But look, my real Jewish friends
my special breddas, the real diamonds
all have visited and chilled:
DJ Te'eni, Hadag Nachash
Mook E and J Kool Habash.
J Kool is a Rasta-rebuild:
Tuff Gong as Ethiopian Jew.'
'Yo.' (Moss.) 'I know J Kool too.'

'Nuff said.' (Sajjid.) 'Right there, another
reinforcement for Arab-Hebrew
rap-culture. J's another brother
rolling with the peace-and-love crew.
We're working with the Serious Road Trip
a British outfit, superhip
eight pantechnicons bound for Sinai
three-hundred Techno-Samurai
taking a transcultural party
into the desert peninsula.
They've got the whole vehicular
thing worked out; not just arty
peaceniks, they're like anti-guerillas
armed with nonviolent formulas.

xi

'If I can get Jalilah papers
an Arab-Israeli passport
she'll go with Palestinian Rapperz;
obviously Aziz will escort.'
Moss couldn't look at Jalilah.
He felt like the dreamland-stealer
snake which plundered paradise
insinuating there to entice.
Suddenly down and paranoid
(Rayyan's extra-strong spicecake
made him supernaturally awake)
Moss felt far from overjoyed.
He glanced at Shaza and recalled
the defensive stuff he'd drawled

xii

Earlier on the subject of dope.
'Ganja makes everything better here.
With dope you walk a tightrope
over the sad abyss of despair:
life's hell.' 'But do you (Shaza'd said)
go to your grandmother's deathbed
stoned as a damn-blasted djinny?
Isn't that disrespectin' Granny?'
He'd struggled back 'The classical Greek
got out of his head at funerals;
imagine synagogues, cathedrals
mosques, full of weed's narcotic reek
the censers fuming amid the tears
in psychotropic atmospheres.'

xiii

Now he didn't feel so certain.
Rayyan's breakfast brownie made him feel
sick in the brain; he saw a bloodstain
suddenly on his right hand congeal.
He looked again: only a sunbeam
red in the dawn, just an early gleam
playing with his mind, making cold jelly
from his nerves. Sick in his belly
he hung his head, listening to Sajjid.
'After Sinai we want a big jam
here at Transworld with Te'eni, Dam
Hadag Nachash, a night of crossfeed
from Arab and Israeli rappers
transcultural hiphoppers.

xiv

'I'd like Alan de Loco
onstage with Arapayet;
I've asked Casa-crew from Morocco
to have Subliminal share their set.
(He was tight with Tamar Nafar
way back). We'll get Yehoshua Sofer
Shadia Mansour, Mahmoud Shalabi
rappin' "R.I.P. Benny the B."'
Moss cut in: 'No one ever forgets
where they've buried the hatchet
so once again they can snatch it
enter a new cycle of regrets.
But perhaps we'll make the madness stop
with the messianic hiphop'.

xv

He shuddered, managed a smile.
'Love your ideas, Sajjid, Jah bless.
Sometimes things seem sooo futile
yet - funny thing in the craziness -
number one in Israel's hit-parade?
Always some hot choon Ramallah-made
in some bedroom, stoned and whacked
with the Cubase software hacked
with the Logic cracked and running
on some antiquated iMac.
Slingshot Hiphop rappers pack
punters into Tel Aviv's stunning
nightclubs: Jewish chicks, Jew-dudes.
All know how every line concludes.

xvi

'They know the flow in Arabic
tongue forbidden on the street outside.
They know every Slingshot lyric
exploring the Palestinian side.
Arab rap from the West Bank
is the sound of a Merkava tank
swingin' turret round in friendly-fire
hitting Israeli kids with truth via
language blazing from underground.
To me, bro, your plan makes sense.
Transworld is in the present tense
the time's come. Still-an'-all I've found
Hebrew rappers chat a bag-a'-breeze
just don't have the expertise.

xvii

Jalilah laughed. 'I kinda agree
but in a day the world can change.
Sooner or later I guarantee
some Hebrew rapstar will rearrange
apartheid and prejudice.
For me rap's built on one premise:
The past is never far behind
you suffer and you speak your mind.
Racism's discrimination
gives black poets the dangerous voice:
they speak because they have no choice
because they face elimination.
I'm the same in Palestine:
I've nothin' left to call mine.

xviii

'Once upon a time the Jews
had a catastrophic story.
To us Palestinians that's news.
We see you in your illusory
superstate of Zionism
promoting your antagonism
towards us, your fellow-hominids.
We'd babysit each other's kids
back in the day according to
my grandmother, old Tamadur.
How brill was that, to be *so* secure.
We had great love regarding you
our noble al-Yahud al-Arab
before you started your landgrab.'

xix

Jalilah looked at Moss a second
he raised his head, met her gaze.
(It seemed to him she clearly beckoned
toward transcendent sunnier days.)
'Yeah, Jalilah, that's well-true
I'm moved to hear it from you.'
She continued: 'I believe
a Jewish rapper could achieve.
He'd have to be incredibly brave
love his people but love the truth
even more. With his badmouth
he might be digging his own grave
but he wouldn't give a damn
he'd spit his wisdom: Blam, blam, blam.'

xx

Moss felt the fear. 'Like Mandelstam
who wrote "There sits a black cockroach
on Stalin's upper lip." Then, wham!
Down came totalitarian reproach
the machinery of repression;
the price of poetic expression
a lifetime in Siberia:
the cockroach feeding on "bacteria".'
All laughed. Moss felt less alien
experienced now a sense of sameness
yet his large eyes betrayed sadness
as he smiled and frowned, pale face ashen.
Laurence winked. Instinctively Moss knew
his black bro had some overview.

xxi

'Peeps, I'm goin' down the hill
to play some hand-drums in the garden.
I wanna feel the sun's goodwill
on my face, laters everyone.
If I stay indoors I'm gonna fold;
see you maybe in the land of gold.
Gotta make the most of the day
gotta catch that transient sunray.
Y'never know: granny Atropos
snip-snip-snipping with her sharp scissors
might clip your braces, snick your sneakers
cut the line you tightrope across.'
The Zambian, his nostrils flaring
with his words gave the space an airing.

xxii

'True say, Laurence. Bro, I remember
last summer's sesh by the lake:
you played a big rosewood marimba.
And sometime round about daybreak
you dropped some burnin' grooves on the shore:
plenty peeps, all wanting to hear more.
We didn't talk but I checked your vibe
proper t'ings you know, Rasta-tribe.'
(Moss speaks English, London-slang.)
'You and Jalilah met Beirut?'
(He switches into Arabic.) Mute
Laurence smiles, lets Moshe's question hang.
'The serpent holds his tail in his jaws;
I'll tell you more when we're out of doors.'

CHAPTER

10

i

A Sunday morning in Galilee.
How long now since that midnight:
Moshe's eighteenth anniversary?
Let's shine a sort of searchlight.
We've already left the unities
far behind: time's strict impunities
have been exposed as non-exempt
have been treated with contempt.
Seven hundred feet below
sea-level we began in the dark;
over destination, question-mark.
That was Friday-night, although
to be precise, Saturday's foredawn
more exactly saw our sequence born.

ii

It's seven o'clock Sunday morning
we joined Moss around nine Friday night:
that's thirty-three hours total, meaning
the unity of time's had a slight
setback on the face of that clock
which measures classically, en bloc;
as in the grim work of Racine
whose fast-moving Alexandrine
drives furiously to that end
foreseen by the tragedian.
(He's no teasing comedienne
who stops and jokes while fates impend.
Before the sun can rise again
he strikes down his defective men.)

iii

As for the unity of space
well, here we've issues to pursue
more tangible. We need to trace
the geographically true
the circumstantially unified
to see if stand unmodified
surroundings and material
to keep a managerial
handle on the substance of the plot.
If zones shift their place, that's not great.
If, while you're trying to relate
the truth of someone's fatal lot
environments metamorphose
it can leave millions comatose.

iv

They get confused, develop a problem
with ever-swirling theme-elements
they fall asleep (we pity them)
just when the Furies' punishments
are promising to do their worst
when blood-vessels are going to burst.
The heights of eloquence fall flat.
Bored readers think 'Enough of that.'
Let's truthfully see how we're doing
scan the contours of location
look high and low - ignore duration -
at least try to see *where* we're going.
Momentum is all very well;
actions must have somewhere to dwell.

v

We're at seven hundred feet
it's about eight in the morning.
(Already things feel more concrete.)
A yellow sun is still yawning
he's only just got out of bed.
Thin quilts of cloud reveal his head
golden-haired, dreadlocked, one might say
at this outset of another day.
Southward are the Horns of Hattin
those twin peaks over Lake Galilee
(just down there, quite faint, do you see?)
where mysterious Saladin
in spite of the True Cross' gleam
put an end to the Crusader-dream.

vi

They would have married Richard's sister
to Saladin's brother after that;
at High Altar he almost kissed her
until the whole grand scheme fell flat.
Coeur de Lion's flesh-and-blood
decided she was far too good
to marry a Mohammedan;
which killed the Lionheart's masterplan
for endless peace in Outremer
that visionary Paladin
that friend of noble Saladin
who found his courage God-knows-where.
(We're speaking about both of them
equal lovers of Jerusalem.)

vii

High in the northern Galilee
from about seven hundred feet
we look south across a lemon sea:
this will be a day of great heat.
It is the sixteenth of Nisan.
(The Barley-month is better than
any in the turnings of fortune.)
Tonight we'll see the Barley Moon
rising from these Galileean hills.
But what's that smudge of sombre smoke
lying on the countryside? Don't joke.
We know Nazareth's Satanic Mills
are burning still down there in hell.
Arcadia is all very well;

viii

Let's not forget reality
in the midst of this romance.
Gaza too's an actuality
further south, in defiance
raging through genocidal nights
encouraging suicidal rites.
(Some don't need suicide-attacks;
they've got atomic bombs, anthrax
F-16s and Merkavas
bio-weapons, psychochemicals
defoliants, atmosphericals
the darker side of the Kabbala's
occult power, the Pulsa D'nura
worst of all weapons: the whip of fire.)

ix

It's Sunday morning - once again -
the air is ozone-rich, ocean-fresh:
in the night there must have fallen rain.
And what of our action's synchromesh?
Have all gear-wheels been lubricated
so that plotline can be related
smoothly and without interruption
without narrative-corruption?
The answer to all that is 'Yes'
though we have a subplot-warning
this beautiful Arcadian morning
(far away from where they dispossess
from where they cleanse and assassinate
far from Hell's Palestinian Gate).

x

Do teenagers cease to fall in love
because they live in a warzone?
When through thin ceilings tanks shove
their spinning tracks, it has been shown
a desperate common drive
to somehow love and stay alive
increases; though some have said
it's more like 'Devil take the dead;
each for each.' Yet that may not be true.
(It's down to who you are, as usual.)
Romantic passions can be mutual
even as the screaming warplanes spew.
Once again and for the last time:
it's Sunday morning. (Not a war-crime.)

xi

Underneath the lemon trees
near that fountain in the shade
isn't that Shaza with Aziz
talking in a citrus glade?
They seem oblivious to the world
laughing and smiling: Shaza's pearled
mouth flashes as her perfect teeth
are revealed suddenly beneath
her sweetly-contoured upper lip
(mimicked by this sinuous landscape
where the skyline takes a sexy shape
drawn by The Artist's fingertip
on the first morning of creation:
this Holy Land of the Incarnation).

xii

They seem at ease in this garden
near the fountain's watersplash.
(Here even wartorn hearts can gladden
as clean waters dance and flash.)
Listen: a dove's plangent singing
above the water's silver ringing.
And what's that liquid hand-drumming
down from some other level coming
rippling from some green retreat
higher in this hillside-garden?
We need to gatecrash this Eden
find the source of that fluid beat
penetrate its polyrhythm
analyse its algorithm.

xiii

It must be Laurence of Zambia
master-drummer of hypnosis
(MC Rambam's saviour)
whose percussion of ecstasis
causes Shaza and 'Big-Man' Aziz
to gently sway in the morning breeze.
(We thought she had a thing for Moss
now it seems Big Aziz is boss.)
They're dancing by the fountain-side
near a feathery tamarisk.
(Would Rayyan like a basilisk
kill if he knew? Up the mountain-side
he's chilling with Sajjid, doing drugs
stretched out on some blue-gold Persian rugs.)

xiv

It's Laurence who, from green leafy cell
taps out a slinky Nubian beat.
(Hamza El Din's *The Waterwheel*
comes to mind, still fresh and sweet.)
Rayyan and Sajjid, as prone as slugs
are trying tinctures, oils, Spark-Plugs
(that's a new type of electric bong
a vaporizer which will prolong
the burning of expensive hashish;
which, with a heat-wand warms the gear
until not smoke but mists appear
blue vapours cool and ready to unleash
dramatic highs, strong hits, for stoners
bent on being mindless free-zoners).

xv

Have we forgotten to account
for anyone? Has anyone gone missing?
We don't seem to have the full amount.
(Now Shaza and Aziz are kissing.)
Action's harmony must be preserved
the unities must be observed
at least where main figures are concerned.
Speaking of whom, what have we learned
about the whereabouts - clumsy phrase -
within this chapter of those two
without whom there is no long view
without whom we're in a haze
hardly more objective than Sajjid
(who, right now's a martyr to strong weed).

xvi

It's clear that Shaza has dumped Moss.
Aziz, Jalilah's bodyguard-bro
is straight, he doesn't mess with hash.
(Shaza got sick of saying 'No'
to spliffs and joints and vaporizers
a long time ago.) Moralizers
from the wrong side of the argument
might think Shaza against enjoyment;
they could be right; that might be fair.
Like many women high on living
Shaza has a basic misgiving
about mind-castles built in air.
She wants something she can seize:
that's why she's kissing Big Aziz.

xvii

Jalilah's wiser, she understands
a little more the evil flowers
men, with their greedy, grasping hands
pluck for aphrodisiac powers
reduce to dust, make into resin
to be happier for a season.
She's been warned, she's heard of Spanish Fly;
she knows Rayyan and Moss get high.
She's concerned for her virginity
yet curious about narcotics
she's one of those rare exotics
with a double affinity.
Loving light and shade just the same
Jalilah plays a more subtle game.

xviii

Speaking of Jalilah and Moshe
the twin suns of our narrative
where, with new developments, are they?
Shall we be conservative
and speculate that they're asleep
in different corners of this steep
sylvan hillside, lemon-groved
honeysuckled and foxgloved?
Perhaps they're in the bubble of light
belvedere, observatory, bridge
that sits atop the sunlit ridge
nodding-off after a crazy night?
Or shall we suggest they're sharing
the orchard? That would be so daring.

xix

This atmospheric garden pleases;
it's like being on another planet.
Here's a waterfall that freezes;
here's a fruiting pomegranate
where, through the dark, a nightingale
sang last night its lyric tale.
Ah, here they are, sharing a joke
it seems, by a Palestinian oak.
Jalilah wears her black-fringed headshawl
Moss has let his dreads hang loose.
(Dove-calls seem to plead and seduce.)
Now they wander by the waterfall
talking where a rainbow over ferns
makes a promise while cool silver churns.

xx

The canticle of falling water
mutes and muffles what they say.
Jalilah, Palestine's own daughter
whispers something to Moshe
son of the antagonist.
Her words are lost in rainbow-mist.
(Is this the land of wishful-thinking?)
Water, cataract-fresh, she's drinking
from his hand to her extended
where the cascade spumes and smokes;
from *that* hand which still evokes
a hatred which has never ended.
(Yet water-sharing is symbolic
where feelings have been vitriolic.)

xxi

'You really have to leave today?'
(This is not the language of conflict
the phrase is spoken by Moshe.)
'I'd love to stay. My Dad's *so* strict
he thinks I'm down in Jezzine
staying with my second-cousin
Haniah; it's bliss to escape
he's always worried about …
He's sweet. But if he knew he'd fall down
stone-dead on the concrete kitchen-floor:
I've never once been away before.
Plus, tomorrow, I'm a school-clown:
got so much Shahaadat work to do
my Baccalaureate stuff. And you?

xxii

'What's your next move? What are you doing?'
Now they're under the pomegranate
where a wood-pigeon is cooing
wooing, over yonder, his grey mate
who glides into the cypress-shade
where a sweet home is being made
high up in the tree of Ferdowsi.
The sound makes the garden drowsy
keening, longing, pleading, yearning.
'Well, I turned eighteen last-week-Friday.'
(Red suns of a grenadine sway
overhead, ripening, sunburning.)
'Trust me, things are looking well-stormy.
Gotta go - like, soon - to the army.'

CHAPTER

11

i

Moss and Rayyan stand side by side.
A pyromaniac noon-sun blazes.
He, flamethrower of genocide
even shadows now erases
destroying with luminosity
burning with Nisan ferocity.
Two outlines have merged in one
melted in the furnace of the sun
left one form of shimmering light.
'Look out, look out' a cuckoo calls.
We seem to hear cascades, waterfalls
in this solar wilderness of white
cataracting with a double-splash.
(Just our two brers taking a slash.)

ii

(Rayyan.) 'You maybe think I'm green
bro, and yeah, I feel a twinge
ain't gonna lie, but I'd foreseen
the way this whole thing would hinge.
When I invited you to the club
I was foolin' with Beelzebub.
I knew Sajjid was cool with true Jews
it was a test, bredda. You had to choose:
play it safe and go back home
or risk your life for our friendship;
and fam', I didn't see you slip
or go in any yellow syndrome;
try to back-out or talk about risk.
Bro, you stood there like an obelisk.

iii

'You know me, I got loads of women
runnin' me down, I can't move for skirt.
My phone's jammed, my inbox's swimmin'
(I'm known in Nazareth as King Flirt)
with messages of textpectation.
It's not machismo, affectation:
I just love females, their company.
Imagine this world woman-free
dude, life would not be worth living.
But Jalilah's special, she's so chilled
she's no overspoilt, silver-spoon child
(like me). Allah and His lawgiving
brought you two together, bro, it's good.
Plus, you proved yourself: I knew you would.'

iv

Down the hill to Sajjid's black X5
they walk together, Rayyan's right arm
round Moshe's shoulders. The four-wheel drive
purrs in the shade of a Royal Palm
parked in a lookout-point's lay by
on Highway 899 (historically
the old freeway of the deep north
with east-west traffic back and forth:
the old road of the British Mandate).
'Listen, star, I'm goin with Sajjid
to try and source him some superweed
up at the border, the interstate
Blue Line, and we'll check you later
(leave you with Laurence as "curator").'

v

Moss nods. Rayyan slides in front
turning head to grin at Jalilah
as from jacket he drags a blunt:
Rayyan, the superhip hash-dealer.
(Yet he is so much more than this.
He is the true antithesis
the opposite of the clichéd stoner:
he is a poet and a loner.
The phrases he's just said to Moshe
are so elegantly expressed
in sentences truly the finest
Arabic (of poets) can essay
they bring tears to his friend's eyes.)
Which now Moss wipes away and dries.

Sliding in beside Jalilah
Moss feels totally together
sprawling back, dreadlocked heart-stealer
lounging on the smooth black leather
accepting the spliff from Rayyan
who, exhaling, says: 'Sajjid, drive, man.'
Under liftgate Shaza coughs
while Rayyan from front-seat scoffs.
(Aziz, with Shaz, also gives a bark;
sheep-like, he adds his own 'ahem':
but that's the last that's heard from them
for a while.) Sajjid slides from 'park'
guns the four-by-four up 899
Bimmer gliding like a black feline.

vii

Laurence, over by the right window
also beside Jalilah - sandwiched -
hands a disk to Rayyan saying: 'Throw
this in the player, cuz.' Outstretched
his arm is a bridge of ebony.
The zoot is streaming ribbony
blue smoke backward through the car.
'Jalilah, you're the rapstar
spit some lyrics, girl, we payin' heed.'
Laurence, his magnetic eyes
half-closed, seems to energize
Jalilah, as, from stick of weed
he drags a lungful of hot poison
strong enough to free soul from prison.

viii

Yet obstinately she stays silent
as her backing-track swirls through
toxic smoke; as gunship's violent
slashing again breaks into
soundfield, making it gyrate
the stereo-image moving eight
ways at once; as dark moody synth
waits for adolescent wordsmith
to drop her devastating flow
spit her poem in its atmosphere.
'Yo, Jalilah, man-dem wanna hear
words from you, rap-commando.'
The Zambian, marijuana-stoned
speaks as if gender were dethroned.

ix

'I'm not in the frame of mind, you know.
Still, though, I'd like to hear Moshe;
me, right now, I'm a little low.'
Jalilah has no more to say.
She gazes up the endless sun-drenched
expressway, delicate fists clenched.
Her big moment has come and gone.
Homeward-bound to Lebanon
she's going back to Shatila's hell
without a hope, empty-handed.
And now she's stupidly demanded
too much. Can a Hebrewman rebel
pass judgment on his own tribe
instantly slam down an heavy vibe?

x

A Jew, he may have nothing to say
oppressor today, no more victim.
'So how's about it then, Moshe?'
She sounds angry, out to convict him.
Her mood of the garden has vanished
the angel of that place is banished.
'Are you gonna break the speed limit
crash-on-thru at words-per-minute?'
Moss takes the spliff from Rayyan.
'Yeah, Jalilah, I'll give it a go
drop my little Hebrewman flow
ridin' the Sajjid caravan.'
Hand-stabbing, lips streaming blue smoke-trails
Moss raps, in longer breaks, inhales.

The Rambam's rap to Jalilah's backing-track.

It's the done thing, it's a true say
it's The Rambam comin' with a dark flow, yeah.
From Rambam to Rambam, hot damn
I am that which I am, yes ma'am.

The name's Moshe, I'm not Israeli
I'm the Jewish Prime-minister like Disraeli
representin' true Jews of the Middle East.
We're universal donors, bloodtype O
like you, from Beirut, from Cairo.
We say 'nowhere-to-go', 'airtime-zero'
for racists & haters like Iago
who, blow-by-blow, push the Palestine under.
Apartheid-ways must be put asunder
I know many-many wanna say 'yo-yo'.
I'm askin' Israel to give back the land
from Jordan right down to Netanya's sand
I'm sayin' to the Zionist rightwing and Co.
Israelis, so-called, listen up, understand
your landgrab is a no-no
you can't carry on with this gung-ho
leggo all stolen property, bro
drop the supremacist lingo:
'If I sneezed you'd fly out the window'.
Man, you need to have a sit-down with your ego.

Right now I'm gettin' off on my Slingshot sermon,
you can hear me from Eilat over to Mount Hermon.
C'mon, humanity, c'mon, c'mon

Hebrewman, Christianman, Mussulman
prayin' together and sayin 'Amen'
prayin' against the Armageddon.
It ain't harmless games like backgammon
we playin' here, it's atomic demon
we up against. This war we've begun
Solomon himself is confused on this one.
Long time ago we held things in common
the lemon trees and the glades of almond.
Now intercommunion has gone
we greyed out the harmony, the good fun
they will not load, they will not summon
like a system-failure in the new aeon.
Abandon all hope if you can't get it on:
we'll go from ethnic cleansing to annihilation
every mother's son, every last one
An' it's all down to Mammon, down to Mammon.

So let me hip ya to some history classes
let's get out some long-distance fieldglasses.
What passes for fact is a heap of excuses
for history on Babylon syllabuses.
When Britain redraws the old atlases
in twilight of 19th century
some jumped-up imperial jackasses
stick their long noses in Palestine
after the Ottoman decline
seekin' to selfishly redefine
the borderlines of the Arab world.
That's when the sufferin' Jewish masses
in Europe get told 'bout some freedom-passes;

but Theodore Herzl's no prophet like Moses
he opens up a Red Sea of bloodshed
sending all the wrong messages.
Hee-haw, hee-haw: it's Herzl the Mule.
The name of Herzl embarrasses
Jewish history, the man's a fool
because his supremacist doctrine dismisses
Arabians as ignoramuses.

So then begin the dark passages
from hostile Russia, Christian Spain.
that long black river of Jewish pain
flowin' east to the new domain
frightened peeps with nuttin' to lose
a so-called homeland at last to gain
in territories touted as empty terrain
in a cynical propaganda campaign.
Then down comes the Nazi night, inhumane.
And the river turns into a flood of insane
magnitude, so many refugees
fleein' the death-camps for overseas
no way in Ashkenaz to remain.

At first they bought the land legit
said: We too eat bread. Understan', please
we need to sustain in the shade of these trees
sit down, for so long we've lived on our knees.
At first it was fine between neighbour and neighbour
the women helped each other out in child-labour;
but now comes the Zionist land-grabber.
Check out the book by Karl Sabbagh

'Palestine': the man's a scholar.
And soon the dream begins to shatter.
"Only thus" the paramilitary settler
swears as he becomes sharpshooter
under darkness working to scatter
villager and hill-dweller.
And so commences the time of terror
as the Stern Gang begins to slaughter.
And the ethnic cleansing of Palestine
in '48 isn't far behind
when the whole Jewish people lose their mind
collectively become cruel and blind;
and machine-gun fire on moonless nights
stutters, and nuttin' else really matters
'cept the new Israeli flag which flutters
blue-white - and red - with blood-splatters.
And they drive a million people out
to make a homeland without a heart.

Now the mic's more powerful than the gun
but it's a hard fight, it's a hundred-to-one.
Even those who admit our Final Solution
say 'Well, you know, what's done is done
past is past, can't be re-run.'
But there's no future for any one
Israeli or Palestinian,
no security under the sun
with the truth 'bout the past in prison.
Once we were smashed under the Hun
we went down under the Zyklon;
now we seal off and we cordon

we bulldoze and we flatten
we say the Nakba did not happen
we beat up and we bludgeon.
But the whole world is lookin' on
from Al Jazeera to CNN.
Peeps see the truth and they reason:
'Why the second-class citizen
if Israel is such a beacon?
Why should the colour of someone's skin
mean they live under suspicion.'

And so we go on, and so we go on
drawin' closer to the Armageddon
circlin' the plughole in slo-mo.
Yeah, but mic-over-gun is more mojo
& Slingshot Hiphop is my weapon.
yeah, Slingshot Hiphop is our weapon.
From the Lion round to the Virgo
big-up peeps, a new time's begun.
You and me say the word 'Amigo'.

Moss & Rayyan say the word 'Amigo'.
Shalom, salaam, peace, big-up amigo
R Underground, big-up amigo
Tamar Nafar, more love bro
Liron Te'eni, big-up amigo
MWR, more love amigo
The Philistines, big-up amigo
We7, big-up amigo
Hadag Nachash, big-up amigo
E148, big-up amigo

Alon de Loco, more love amigo
Palestinian Rapperz, big-up amigo
Shalom, salaam, peace, big-up amigo
Shanaan Street, big-up amigo
Mahmoud Shalabi, big love bro
Arapayet, come on with your flow
Abeer Zinaty, big-up amigo
Jalilah, yeah, more love amigo
Shalom, salaam, peace, that's how it go
Benny the B, big-up amigo
Subliminal, even, wake-up amigo
stop with the showdown promo
more love and big-up your true self, bro.
Stormtrap, yeah, big-up amigo
Boikutt, yeah, big-up amigo
Aswatt, yo, respect amigo
Moss & Rayyan say the word 'Amigo'
Shalom, salaam, peace, that's how it go
Yehoshua Sofer, big-up amigo
Shadia Mansour, more love amigo
Mook E, more love, big-up amigo
Rayyan & Moss say the word 'Amigo'
Moss & Rayyan say the word 'Amigo…'
Yagga YO.

Rayan rides the fader to zero.
Sajjid's machine, gliding like a jet
whispers with highspeed airflow.
We study Jalilah's silhouette
as, on her contoured left cheek
her long fingers blindly seek
something resting on her silky skin.
Now she brushes toward her chin;
what's she looking for down there?
That tiny stain on her turquoise
bomber-jacket, is this what annoys;
is this the shadow of a tear
fallen from overclouded skies
the dark heaven of her eyes?

See Jalilah in profile
pulling down headscarf with fingertips.
Is that the faintest trace of a smile
playing with the curve of her lips
where her mouth-corner's outline
becomes too elusive to define?
Illegible, the secret written
there, yet her lower lip, just bitten
seems to give the unrevealed away.
The Rambam, beside, eyes closed
cool, detached, super-composed
feels her slender hand interplay
'accidentally' with his: all alone
her little-finger touching his own.

xiii

His little-finger, operating
autonomously, hooks over hers;
her baby-finger, vacillating
hesitantly half-withdraws
finds itself locked down and trapped
her whole hand suddenly wrapped
in his with no escape: she wriggles
for a moment, then she giggles;
looks at Moss and with free hand
strokes one fingertip below her eyes
cloudy and misty, like troubled skies
where storms brew above a troubled land.
Sajjid breaks the silence from the front:
'Moss, bro, you span the Hellespont.'

xiv

'Like that Sultan Mehmet Bridge
across the Bosphorus, east to west
you crossover with your knowledge:
your heart's deep, brer, you know you're blessed.
Man, your lyrics rule the scene
comin' like Buckminsterfullerene.
I want you on the bill, September
like I said earlier, remember?
It's you on stage with Jalilah
you two look so good together.
We'll do first in Transworld's nether
regions, then aim for Ramallah
Tel Aviv, Jerusalem, Al Kuds
you'll go down a storm with the kids.'

xv

'Can you drop Hebrew bombshells?'
(Moss had rapped in Arabic.)
'No probs, Sajjid, it's in the braincells.'
'K then, dude. Your flow is sick
man; different to Jalilah, for sure
but coming from the same heart-core.'
Now X5 glides onto grassy verge;
doors swing and passengers emerge.
As liftgate rises Shaz and Aziz
disentangle and emanate
blinking. 'Yo, you two, blind date?
Get a room.' Rayyan's interviewees
titter and blush, brush themselves off.
'All right' goes Sajjid, 'blast-off'.

xvi

'See you round sunset, like half-seven
enjoy the Rainbow, ketch ya soon.'
(The sun's still giving his fire-sermon
from the pulpit of the afternoon.)
'Remember landmines like I said
up near Lebanon they're widespread
keep on paths and trails, alright?
We'll be back before the fall of night.'
Rearwheel-drive of Sajjid's X5
excites the dust, raises a cloud.
Silence. Shaza to the ground is bowed
letting imprisoned toes come alive
tearing-off hot, adhesive trainers
where feet have lived in containers.

Jalilah does the same. In the dust
her foot makes a beautiful sphinx
half-angel, half animal-of-lust
(resembling a pan-pipe, a syrinx).
A green sign reads: 'Ma'arat Hakeshet
Rainbow Cave' - just that couplet
in Hebrew, English, no Arabic
a sign for the Islamophobic
traveller in the Western Galilee.
Now there's no one by the highwayside.
A trail leads where hardily reside
mountain-goats who climb the almond-tree
chewing brown diamonds of Nisan
earthy nipples of the Green Woman.

xviii

Now they're underneath a stone rainbow
hanging between sky and ground;
arc of rock against - spread out below -
vast panoramas: eastward, snowbound
Lebanon, southward Galilee
westward the Mediterranean Sea
with Nahariya, Akko, Haifa
even, possible to decipher
through blue haze forty miles away.
A rock-dove calls across the canyon
to his exquisite companion
hidden from the glare of the day
in a secret cleft out of the dazzle
waiting for him to solve her puzzle.

'Here am I; and where are you?'
Against her call, hear Laurence drumming
his hand-drum gentle as her love-coo.
Somewhere we can hear Aziz humming
some old Palestinian love-song.
(We can catch Shaza humming along.)
But what of Jalilah and Moshe
our bittersweet songbirds, where are they?
Flowering almonds make their shade:
a nut-orchard on the crag's verge.
From blue distances landmarks emerge.
'Look, tha's where, two nights back, I played
at my birthday on Lake Galilee.'
He points. In order to really see

Her head inclines against his arm
as ocean-vistas stretch out
neither so tranquil nor so calm
as the emotion brought about
by resting one sweet moment thus.
'Will we ever ride that bus
down to Sinai, do Sajjid's gig
in Transworld, make it real big
to spread the message of the One Love?'
She doesn't answer, seems miles away.
'Jah decides what's comin' anyway.'
'Are you a Jew or a Rasta, bruv?'
'Well, same thing to me actually
tho' airheads in the tribe disagree.'

xxi

'The first Christian church was Jewish
so who can say we rejected Christ?
Now straight Christians don't cherish
   Bob Marley, call him Antichrist
   but the man was the living Jah
   a supernatural prophet, yeah.
   So history repeats, you know.'
The Galilee, spread out below
appears to take these words to heart
   hallowed in the blue distance.
(Jalilah seems to drift in a trance.)
   'Now Rasta is gonna kickstart
the New Age with more-level vibes
   uniting all Abrahamic tribes.'

xxii

'"The first civilization was black"
so said the Prophet of the Winged Horse
"And the last one will also be black."
But you already knew that, of course.'
'You're like Majnoun, as mad as him
with drugs; you talk like the seraphim:
you're crazy and you're out of your mind.'
   Yet Jalilah's ear is inclined.
A jet of blue crosses Rainbow Bridge
exhaled by Moss. Jalilah breathes deep
   resting in his arms, lightly asleep.
Let's leave them like this on a ridge
   where pink almond petals rain
   high above the Galileean Plain.

CHAPTER

12

i

Dusk comes down an almond grove
precursor of potential night;
hear a lovesick wood-dove
harmonizing with twilight.
Airs sweep a hillside, a warm breeze
fans pink rain from perfumed trees
rainfall with the scent of marzipan
sweet, heavy, spiced as cinnamon.
Here's an up-to-date shepherdess
vaguely out of Grecian fable
asleep in the glade, desirable
in tight denim jeans, modern dress.
A sunbird hovers, electric-blue
drinking from a chalice of pink hue.

ii

A falcon's scream in mid-dive
at two-hundred miles-an-hour
targeting a dove (which won't survive
the airstrike of the superpower
lord of the wind searching out his prey)
wakes her boyfriend at close of day:
who turning on a bed of blossom
looks tenderly toward his handsome
girl sleeping through the raptor's cry.
On her back she lies, ankles crossed
slim feet bare, both lightly glossed
with colour fallen from on high
petals decked there like pink gems
(only as described in poems).

iii

Time passes in the beauty-spot.
Toes gently flutter and twitch
fan themselves as if too hot;
back-and-forth they sway and switch
positions, waving like small fronds
dancing like tiny magic wands.
Jalilah, dream-bathing her feet
in mountain-water fresh and sweet
warm fountains of a thermal spring
some sacred source of the hills
which gently on her instep spills
(experience refreshing)
surfaces from sleep, toes in spasm
skywalking still some dream-chasm

iv

Which separates her from her life's goal
feeling a divine sensation
as if barefoot her own soul
walked on dew's dawn-condensation.
Awake now (troubled by this world's fire
where we cannot have what we desire)
she suddenly knows her worst fears
realized: a rain of scalding tears
falls softly on her naked feet.
She sits bolt upright in alarm
(this is bad, this is so haraam)
stiffens her back, prepared to beat-
off a rapist to the last breath
resist a fate worse than death

v

Yet waits. Why Moshe's muted sobbing?
Did he molest her in her sleep?
Virgin fears set mind throbbing
but heart makes a sudden leap
in faith toward a certain fact:
she knows herself to be intact.
The kick intended for his face
to fend off maidenhead's disgrace
remains unlaunched, tense, potential.
'Wha' you doin', man, you lost the plot?
Get up, Moss, I'm scared. Thanks a lot.'
(Hysteria is exponential.)
'Hey, I'll kick you, Moss; 'scuse me
did you try to abuse me?'

vi

'Wha' you so sorry about?'
He drops his forehead on her instep
dreads in sandy chaos spreading-out
across her ankles in a yellow web
wildman dreadlocks fanning there
the tangled Nile-delta of his hair.
The sinking sun's over the world's rim;
at Rainbow Bridge day grows dim.
In the west one last luminous streak
shines as a broken, choked-back sound
(from a chain-leashed watchhound)
seems to say one who cannot speak
(guarding his mistress' domain)
tries to communicate his pain.

vii

Half-words, slurred and muttered
(like a drunkard's in a thunderstorm
against wind's screaming uttered)
are indistinct, speech devoid of form:
'Through Abyssinia a full circle . . .'
But there is no direct sequel
to these words, just another phrase:
'We made a promise to the last days
saying we would not return.'
'Moss, get up, I don't understand.
Wha' promise?' Jalilah's hand
reaches out to show concern
strokes tenderly Moshe's shoulder.
(What has made her instantly bolder?)

viii

A sunset out of science-fiction
metallic gold and electric-red
beautiful beyond description
transpires westward. The solar head
right at the frontiers of daylight
makes the stratosphere ignite:
gilt and scarlet clouds make staircases
for exits of gods and goddesses
leaving the arena of the human
world for other destinations
promising further visitations
when they will again illumine
earthly horizons and perspectives
extend their powerful correctives.

ix

At the apex of Rainbow Bridge
silhouetted against the west
Moss and Jalilah form one image
standing so close, two abreast
(unified in our symbology).
'My tears were an apology'
he whispers in her shrouded ear
through jet-black tresses entering there.
'Don't be angry or offended
I didn't mean anything bad.
Such an awesome time we've had.
Truly, man never intended . . .'
'So wha' were you sayin' sorry for?'
'Only the Hundred Year's War.'

A good moment to meditate
now, under this ravishing sky
as Moss' words in dusk vibrate.
Some might hear a rallying cry
as love brings these two together.
Others might question whether
it's demographically correct
for enemies thus to connect.
We have no answer, nothing to say.
Let these two, who have much in common
speak for themselves above the canyon.
Here they are, on Rainbow Bridge, halfway
from this side (from that side over there)
where a stone arc passes through the air.

They're at the highest point in this world
silhouetted against *their* glory
in each other's arms deeply furled.
Is there more to tell of their story
as the sun goes sinking in the west?
(These two belong among the blessed
in those enchanted isles which exist
beneath the sunset, fortunately kissed
by the flaring dreadlocks of The One
for whom there is no difference
who has no human preference
whose house crowns the city of the sun
who says: 'Good and bad in all races'
who looks into hearts, not faces.)

xii

One last kiss at the bridge of hope
one last word from insane Majnoun
trembling on the rainbow's slope:
'We'll hook up in Sinai real soon.'
Now shadows act as thieves of light
thickly conspire with oncoming night
to rob the world of colour and joy.
(There is no hope where they'd deploy
long grasping fingers of the dark
to hold in check, sometimes violently
those who through the twilight see
the devil's cloven trademark;
those changed by self-illumination:
they, themselves the transformation.)

xiii

O vertigo, you've a lot to learn.
Look, here at Ma'arat Hakeshet
as the four sky-quarters turn
these two swear they won't forget
though dusk-shadows fill the mind
(as the sun leaves the world behind).
An iPhone rings, a hand-drum ceases
pulsing with a tempo which decreases
which falters and dies out with a tattoo.
Shaza screams: 'They're at the highway.'
A frightened wood-dove flutters away
it's rendezvous-time, Eden, adieu.
One final look at Palestine
spread out in a ray of sunshine.

xiv

Black X5 is covered with dust.
(O, Khayam, do you harmonize
with one whose strings are red with rust
though unshattered? Yes, you sympathize:
it's hard to live where nothing seems
any more permanent than our dreams.)
Sajjid's right-foot is flat on the X
(when you gotta go, you gotta flex).
The Bimmer, with horsepower galore
flies up Highway 90, northbound.
No one talks, there's not a sound
apart from slipstream's phantom roar.
They hang a left at Kiryat Shmona
head for the hills on a fast-burner.

xv

The car is rammed with cannabis
(the good old Zahret el Kolch?)
literally every last crevice
secretly crammed with so much
resinous gear it's ludicrous.
If only it were less noxious:
the whole interior reeks of the drug.
And that's without the blue fog
streaming from a zoot in Rayyan's hand.
This is well-dangerous territory.
Everyone's real jittery
trusting venture to go as planned.
Aziz and Jalilah have to cross
a frontier famous for chaos:

xvi

The interstate borderline
between Lebanon and the land
which has always been Palestine
now called Israel; heavily manned
by the IDF and Hezbollah
facing-off, killer-to-killer
across a wooded limbo of barbed-wire
gun-emplacements, where crossfire
is frequent: a frontier, it is claimed
by far the most dangerous on earth.
Jalilah really proved her worth
crossing into Israel (so-named)
via this modern stretch of hell
so her dark rap could cast its spell.

xvii

They're in the Finger of Galilee
where Israel points at Lebanon.
From Manara the Hula Valley
sparkles below; with pure oxygen
the night-air of the mountain braces.
A stream plunges headlong, races
downhill, silver sound fragmenting;
gradient's one-in-three, unrelenting.
Another left, they're on a dirt-track.
The four-wheel soars here easily.
It's all a blur; heads spin queasily
drifting round a tight switchback.
Now they halt in a cypress-glade
lights off, pointing up road unmade.

xviii

They're on the Blue Line at 10 pm.
In the dark Moss holds Jalilah
whispers 'Till Sinai, yeah.' (For them
the promise of Shangri-La:
Sajjid's projected desert-fest
to put Slingshot Hiphop to the test
with the hope of another meeting
the chance of a romance less fleeting.)
'Respect, rapstar, Jah bless your homeward
crossing, think you're one crazy diamond.
Allah keep your soul in the highland.
May everything move straightforward
so we meet and link again down south.'
(See the tremor at Jalilah's mouth.)

xix

This is zero-hour for her heart.
Anticlimax begins now, it seems.
Shatila's a dead-end for her art;
no living soul there ever deems
Slingshot Hiphop worth attention.
She's only one voice of dissension
where the choirs of tradition sing
songs that have an antiquated ring.
Now she's met a dude she likes
not a child of Ishmael
(what's the difference, who can tell?)
a descendent of Isaac's
(through whose dreads she whispers low 'n' sweet)
'I loved it when you cried at my feet.'

xx

'But trees in winter give no shelter.
'Scuze me for earlier, my near-kick;
mind was goin' helter-skelter.
If I was cold it's 'coz I'm homesick
like all outcast Palestinians
exiled tonight - for what sins?'
In the darkness a flashlight winks
a prearranged signal blinks.
(Simultaneously chopper re-sounds.)
All get out, Sajjid says: 'Keep low.
Aziz, Jalilah, go, go,go!
But parallel tracer-rounds
blaze - no! - and from a horror-flick
comes a girl's stricken scream of panic.

xxi

Instantly Moss sprints into high-beam
racing in the night, madman
pounding the dirt-track, bloodstream
ice-cold, heart in overdrive. Rayyan
yells: 'Bredda. Fuck's-sake, keep down.'
Now as tracers burn the night a clown
head-over-heels suddenly tumbles
into the dim-lit backroad crumples;
as, further on, Aziz lifts the girl.
High-beam dies as chopper bellows.
Searchlights fall, fanning yellows:
pencils of illumination whirl.
Through criss-crossed hell, Laurence 'n' Rayyan
race out to Moss as searchlights scan.

xxii

Sajjid spins his four-drive in the dirt
one hand to blurred wheel, holding his phone:
'Seems she ain't too badly hurt.
Wha' about Moss?' (Rayyan's face alone
says everything.) 'Right thigh's bleeding
red cascades of blood.' Now speeding
down a mountain-road - no lights -
the gunship gets the car in its sights;
loses the target on hairpin-bends.
Shaza's headscarf is a tourniquet.
Hospital-on-wheels, a getaway
vehicle dizzily descends.
A moonless night in Galilee;
and on this road only faith can see.

UNHOLYLAND
BOOK TWO:
JALILAH

CHAPTER

1

i

A lightning-bolt's jagged scar
zig-zags on a mountainside:
road z-shaped and angular
through a descending countryside.
And we are riders in freefall:
down a mountain's granite wall
twisting in two-wheeled cliffhangers
we plunge, dumbstruck passengers.
Behind a predatory machine
whines and throbs, dives and follows
as darkness mercifully swallows
a speeding car only dimly seen.
Real or metaphorical?
Literal or allegorical?

ii

Fugitives on a road benighted
twisting through dizzy switchbacks
with fuel-gauge (of greed) red-lighted
motionsick, panicked to the max
we snake and turn in midnight's
obscurity without headlights
as bottomless cataclysmic gulfs
promise to annihilate self's
unity on pre-imagined rocks;
to precipitate to an abyss
to suffer a collective death-kiss;
to be shattered with aftershocks:
oneness of humanity
in absolute disunity.

iii

Bad luck: roof-rack's just come loose
torn-off an aerial, we're finished;
the end of satnav, no damn use
a hi-tech future's just vanished.
On the left we've a slow-puncture
socialism's at a low juncture;
on the right a rear-mirror's cracked
looking backward's no way to react.
The A-Z got used for roaches
maps disintegrated long ago;
black hood's steaming, coolant's low;
global-warming-time approaches.
The situation as we scream
round existential bends: extreme.

iv

The gastank's full of human blood.
We filled-up with a strange nozzle
resembling, with no unlikelihood
a submachine-gun's steel barrel.
We're headed for religious wars
having invented the unjust cause
which makes all other wars ethical.
(In His name it is heretical
to fight the jihad, the crusade.)
Are we doomed to planetary discord?
In the background is that Dark Lord
who rides the iron rotorblade
fallen angel of the dark side
driving us to race-suicide.

v

Down below is our deathbed.
(Driver's fighting with the wheel.)
A drop to hell is straight ahead
one tiny strip of alloyed steel
can never stop us crashing over.
No way now to outmanoeuvre.
Karaaang! A sense of timelessness
ecstasies of weightlessness.
(Hark, a void whistles strangely?)
And now someone is dreamboating
hypnagogically floating
another world, aerial and stately
far from precipices, gunships:
stretching out mysterious wingtips.

A young girl lies on her right side
left arm bandaged-over in white.
Faint pink rays on stone walls slide;
eyelids flicker in dawn sunlight.
A pinup Eminem looks down
upon the sleeper with a slight frown
implying he's profoundly aware
concerned for one lying here?
Pensively, from a great distance
the idol studies the crumpled bed.
A breezeblock-section behind his head
contributes an urban ambience
from darkened heavens of Detroit
(which ain't middleclass Irondequoit).

Bedroom's just makeshift cabin
grafted onto a stone roof, lifted
high over Beirut's dustbin
zone to which exiles have drifted
a million souls on their knees:
Shatila of the proud refugees.
A futile sun this morning winks
ascending through reds and pinks
offering cloudy assurances
blandishments, vague promises
displaying hypocrite purposes
tinkering with appearances.
(The sun is a politician
rising to fame, high position.)

viii

Yet here's a truly Great One
(an angel sent to intervene?)
falling out of the rising sun
heard before his form is seen.
Whispering rhythms beat the wind
as two black flights, tightly pinned
suddenly expand to brake
two jet-black parachutes, opaque
precision instruments creating
lift and drag. See: a streamlined
skydiver, every plume aligned
(the bird in midair hesitating)
comes in to land, double-checking
exactly who stands on roof-decking.

ix

It's Big Aziz, so familiar;
for sure we've met Aziz before.
Look, he leans by bougainvillea
framing small white rooftop door
gazing into the low sun squinting;
seeing black carrier-bird glinting
coming down the dawn-skyway:
firebird riding a sunray
angel breaking the new-day's seal.
Gazing up his eyelids narrow.
Falling downwind like an arrow
what will this messenger reveal
this genius of the sun, his black
racing-pigeon, his iyad: Mushtaq.

x

Homer's treading loft-trapboard
when thunderous shadow dimming
the skyline suddenly veers toward
Shatila: gunship skimming
housetops, bulbous silhouette
chopping brutally so-quiet
dawn-air, shuddering concrete
with rotor's throbbing crossbeat.
Mushtaq skids on plywood-square
sheering-off in panic-reaction
the steel monster of police-action
a vast hawk as far as he's aware.
Aziz rips out two white earbuds
starts to whistle as the chopper thuds.

xi

His calling for Mushtaq, scared;
the whirring of the bird's takeoff;
the Aerospace Super Puma's weird
pounding, juddering, quickfire-cough:
all these sounds sequentially
multiply exponentially
travel backward, work behind;
enter Jalilah's dreaming mind
in reverse, so she with a shiver
wakes to sounds which in her dream
sounded long before, far upstream.
(Strange how time's hypnagogic river
reverses and sends retrograde
sounds which register before they're made.

xii

When the hourglass of the ages
turns upside-down, the time-sifter;
and when time's fragile turning pages
move in the hands of the Age-shifter:
all's torn to pieces, forced apart.
Orders are reversed, empires depart.
Dreams are prescient, full of light
thrown into the world's dark night
as sleep's hazardous quicksands
suck dreamers down into themselves.
Each in the collective psyche delves
deeply penetrating quantum-lands
where time's non-linear as it streams
through the country-of-what-only-seems.)

xiii

Jalilah lies here half-awake
watching the shifting dawnlight.
It seems to her some earthquake
has shaken the world in the night.
She suffers a recurrent dream.
In its turbulent slipstream
she returns to the Blue Line
where fact-and-fiction intertwine
where angel, demon interchange
faces and personalities
where mysterious dualities
make certitudes rearrange.
She lies here with a shattered feeling
sense of self in chaos reeling.

xiv

Always it starts the same way:
she's riding in Sajjid's X5
with Shaz, Aziz, Rayyan, Moshe.
They're rapping together, spitting live
droppin' lyrics to her backing-track
dark, downbeat; till sudden switchback
makes the black car careen and tip.
At speed, traction gone, it starts to slip
toward the verge, metal screams
as they scrape along the guardrail:
Sajjid's hands in steering flail.
(This is how you navigate bad-dreams.)
Sometimes there's a gunship close behind.
(Useless to repeat: 'A state of mind'.)

xv

Tarmac's hidden, undefined
headlights are shot-out or shutoff;
they're on a death-road, cornering blind
a hairpin-bend's extreme dropoff.
Sparks fly up from the guardrail
grinding and crashing; it must fail.
As they plunge out into space
she turns to look at Moshe's face:
sometimes he's her arch-enemy
triumphing in her destruction
gloating over her seduction.
And sometimes there's such affinity
between them that she screams his name
as they fall like a star aflame.

xvi

Yet strangely, as they plunge to death
whether he's angelic and benign
whispering 'salaam' under his breath;
or whether demonic and malign
in his face 'haraam' writ large
there's always an erotic charge
to this end-phase of the dream
as over rushing airstream
she faintly hears Rayyan, Moshe
still dropping their two-bro-flow:
('You, me, say the word 'amigo')
as heart-stoppingly the runaway
black X5 plunges into hell.
(And with the car the whole world as well.)

xvii

Waking, Jalilah feels deluded
(like that tightrope-walker who outstretched -
while a phantom-crowd applauded -
cable on the floor, and nearly retched
as she crossed imaginary gulfs).
She'd rather be in hell in handcuffs
than lying in this stupid cot-bed
listening to Aziz (airhead)
whistling for his bird, Mushtaq;
his thoroughbred Egyptian
his long-distance champion.
She yawns under tedium's attack:
today she has to go to school
with injured arm, *so* uncool.

xviii

Like some maiden-in-distress
in a turret of breeze-blocks
she's a fairytale princess.
Far below among fountains peacocks
against rainbows preen and strut.
(Jalilah lies here, eyes tight-shut.)
In a dappled shade, at a chessboard
two princes, her jailers, like her bored-
out-of-their-minds, gape over moves
which hardly signify, don't amount
to much. Now even time's lost count
as on the sundial a shadow proves
showing in accordance with the facts
how the endless hour still protracts.

xix

Ah, the gardens of adolescence
where boredom's the only flower
where sickly drifts of black incense
drug neurotic cherubs, hour-by-hour
with that subtle narcotic, self-doubt.
One day, the secret is found out:
acceptance; till then the world's wrong.
Life's an out-of-tune pop-song
which pities itself in syrupy
language strung on basic chords
which the neonate applauds:
that adolescent symphony
which sees revolutions - coming soon -
based on lying-low, in bed, till noon.

xx

Jalilah's not as lax as these
naïve angels, she's wide-awake.
See her scribbling, pressing on her knees
latest rap-poem. It's her take
on smoking: nicotine-addiction
her brother's juvenile affliction.
(Yet she can be as bad as him
chain-smoking with no interim
when she feels so vacuous within.)
But here's more than teenage headshake
this is modern-world heartbreak
love's sorrow with a gritty spin.
Let's have a quick peep at her pages
where, in Arabic, she rages:

xxi

'Here are hearts like ashtrays, full
to overflowing with butt-ends
all dragged-on, each a hot pull
till stubbed-out chatting to friends.
Now someone for a gaslighter gropes;
here's the smoking debris of hopes:
failed affairs, extinguished loves
lipstick-stained 'to-be-disposed-ofs'.
(Sandcastles, with amputated limbs
protruding, safeguard us.) Lovesick
we plead for one last cancer-stick
to calm us down as good Muslims.
Pass me, like a joint, to someone else
when you feel the next burning impulse.'

xxii

We can see why Headmistress
has issues with Jalilah; who keeps
for bad times only, under mattress
a pack of Cedars (conscience weeps)
dirt-cheap Lebanese tobacco
(her favourites are Marlboro)
coconut-flavoured superkings.
The Nato occupation brings
cheaper Virginia to Beirut.
But still Jalilah can't afford
Marlboros for under-mattress hoard.
(Down there's also one small zoot.)
Jalilah thinks a Muslim girl
should move - breathe - in the modern swirl.

CHAPTER

2

i

We leave Jalilah in clouds of smoke.
(Who approaches? Hurrying upstairs
Mum coming to give her a poke?
She'll find her precious girl in tears.)
We turn back to where our narrative
became previously so negative
collapsing suddenly on the Blue Line
(most dangerous, most dracontine
frontier on our small blue planet)
where the Finger of Galilee
touches the Land of the Cedar Tree
where, with a hand of granite
Israel says to The Lebanon:
'Stop, don't cross the Rubicon.'

ii

Events ensued so torrentially
back then, seven long days ago
there was no space sequentially
(in sonnet's rapid onward flow)
to pause in that cypress-glade
loud with gunfire, cannonade
full of burning acrid haze
tracer-ammunition's blaze
(deadly tracks of phosphorous
which follow, muzzle-to-target
the speeding steel of each bullet
so marksmen can be murderous
in their aim; which is, of course, to kill
though most only speak of 'weapon-skill').

iii

Jalilah, winged in her left arm
felt a bullet graze her shoulder.
Seeing the girl had been brought to harm
Moss dashed out, acting much-older
than a brer just turned eighteen;
like some soldier in a battle scene
took a hit in his right thigh.
(Chopper overhead let fly.)
Two heroes, Laurence and Rayyan
through pyrotechnic tracers
(bruvvas with backbone, brave death-dicers)
out toward our lone madman ran
scooped him bloody from dirt-track
sprinted for Sajjid's X5: dashed back.

iv

Jalilah, dragged by Big Aziz
to safety, never saw the moment
MC Rambam crumpled to his knees.
To this morning she's ignorant
(like Aziz) of what transpired
the night everything backfired;
when they almost died on the Blue Line.
She's heard nothing on the grapevine
about events in the aftermath;
had zero news (since mobile-phones
are now Nato-hacked in all zones).
Not one word has found an airpath
between, say, Shaza and Jalilah
flying Nazareth to Shatila.

v

Radio-silence can be a blessing.
(Telecommunications suck
when, pinpointed to a coffee-ring
your phone makes you a sitting-duck
in some covert sting-operation.
Entrapment can be temptation;
peeps do get pressured into crime:
it happens in the States all the time.
A mobile rings in a honeypot
someone with a gangster-lifestyle
who's pushed you with a greasy smile
with greedy eyes like yours, bloodshot
watches while you take the call
which is your ultimate downfall.

vi

Soon it won't even be legal
to leave house with phone turned-off.
Surveyed by some orbiting eagle-
eyed satellite, you won't have burned-off
two inches from your own front door
before you're in the sights of the law.
No one's defending the gunslinging
coke-snorting, chaos-bringing
gangsters with religious streaks
fiends who make the sign of the cross
before they drop some crime-boss
using tried-and-tested techniques:
drive-by, urban ambush, hit-and-run
where the bystander's the 'hotcross-bun'.

vii

The system breeds the underdog.
His violence is only copycat
behaviour; he's in the red fog
just like the cop with his landsat
tearing crosstown; who won't stop
till he's gotten-off another pop.
He lives to recriminate:
he is the shadow of the state.
They're mirror-images of rage
cops and robbers, feds and crims
pigs and cons: fore-and-hind-limbs.
Twin-studies prove it on the page;
psychologies are just the same:
it takes two to play this puerile game.)

viii

That said, let's get back on track;
enough with the analysis.
(Philosophy must not hijack
momentum, bring paralysis.)
Free of civilization's wreckage
future-cities of the Golden Age
will rain their dancing-platforms
with coloured holographic ice-storms
streaming on a cosmic generation
who'll praise God with soles of their feet
singing, 'Fallen women of the street
are higher in their degradation
than the self-righteous man of law
who would brand his own mother whore.'

ix

Back to the 'story', let's have more
facts-and-figures from that point in time
when Sajjid gunned black four-by-four
out of cypress-glade at sixty. (I'm
assuming you've read *The Rambam*
Part One of the Unholyland slam-
poem peeps are talkin' 'bout;
or will be soon, it ain't even out
as She dictates the present sonnet
to one ambitiously musing;
one, as-it-were, presuming
'overheating under the bonnet'
so-to-speak. A metaphor
chiming with theme we're looking for.)

x

Sajjid's four-wheel-drive spins dirt.
(Zero-to-sixty never happened
so fast, never did gangsters splurt
so rapidly through darkened
backstreet urban territory
from gruesomeness, scary 'n' gory.)
Moss, behind, in pools of blood
whispers 'Jalilah', his face pallid;
as Shaza, with a laugh, rips in half
evergreen rayon hijab
(nothing lacklustre or drab)
destroying precious headscarf
binding it onto Moshe's upper thigh
through gritted teeth mumbling 'Tough guy'.

xi

As down dirt-track's cypress avenue
Sajjid pushes through at-the-double.
'I'm always doing this for you
can't you just stay out of trouble?'
'He's circling back' volunteers Rayyan.
(Tourniquet on the wounded man
stops red arterial spurting.
Moss, unconscious, not even hurting
now, lies back in Shaza's bloodstained arms.)
Sajjid hits tarmac, reardrive spinning
rubber on asphalt. 'From the beginning
I said you'd sound frontier-alarms
coming here for the Zahret el Kolch.
Now look, we under 'da big squelch.'

xii

Shaza hisses like a teased snake
breathing poison in her brother's face:
no blubbering in her bellyache.
Burning backwheel-scream fills space.
The gunship on the mountain wheels
searchlight scanning black visual fields.
Sajjid, right up on the windscreen
pierces the night with eyesight keen
probing mountain-road: subvisible.
'Shaz, sis, don't run your motormouth
we'll talk 'bout all 'dis shit down south.'
(Rayyan's guilt is audible
as frustration with his sister
makes *him* start to cuss and blister.)

xiii

Laurence joins the tense exchange.
'Saw worse in the Second Congo War.
Once we're off this mountain-range
we'll get help, he'll survive for sure.
I estimate it's non-fatal;
we'll get him into hospital.
Hold tight, Shaza, sweetness, don' blow it;
he'll come through, trust me, I know it.'
Sajjid, calculating bends
at high-speed in midnight darkness
sees the truth with great starkness
has no time to talk to his friends:
road is a twisting roller-coaster;
behind, the 'bird is getting closer.

xiv

Bright tracer on nearside shows
streaking, luminescent in flight.
'Hold on, peeps, off-road here-goes;
son-of-a-bitch has low-light
devices in his arsenal.
We'll *all* end up in hospital
unless I take chances, so sit
tight, I'm not takin' a hit.'
X5 leaves the ground on the next curve.
'Sajjid, drive, man.' (From Rayyan.)
Groaning like Leviathan
four-litre V8 in reserve
with four-thousand cc pushing
gently on raw granite crashing

xviii

Using sensors skilfully
running in max-traction mode
the beast-vehicle wilfully
(built for rigours of off-road)
rides 'intelligently' on the rocks.
Sajjid, handling eight-speed gearbox
takes a route roughly parallel
to the descending highway, well
back from the main-route snaking
down the mountain, in stone flank hewn.
Sinister gunship occludes the moon
hovering ten minutes, making
the dark night vibrate and rattle
till the sky-beast gives up the battle:

xvi

Sheers-off suddenly to the south
pulses away into the distance
crossing the moon once more in its path.
Rayyan: 'Excellent riddance
fuck-off back to where you came from.'
Nightbird still tickling his eardrum
Sajjid swiftly negotiates
some olive-woods, navigates
now with headlights, finds the road
hangs a right, slams down the x.
The black machine, free of all checks
seems, like a panther, to explode
with energy, to surge in freedom.
(As in some ad's make-believe kingdom.)

xvii

The lights of Kiryat Shimona
flicker from Manara heights:
hopeful proximate corona
shining amid dark indefinites.
'There's a 'Frontline Emergency Room'
down there somewhere; I assume
they'll be ready to do transfusion.
I saw a flash on television
two weeks ago, that's how I know.
Shine your iPhone, Shaza, please.'
Rayyan gave his sister's hand a squeeze
turning from the front. Aglow
the LCD shows Moss Rambam's face
drained white in ominous grimace.

xviii

'We ain't got that long, you know.'
Sotto voce, Laurence tells his fears.
'It's gonna be, like, touch-and-go
to save this bro.' Only Rayyan hears
the Zambian's extreme prognosis
whispered in his ear, diagnosis
based on bitter personal insight
where Coltan and Wolframite
are driving-forces of the vast war
tearing Africa apart
ripping out its conflicted heart.
Laurence knows about blood-loss for sure
he's seen the Congo bleed to death
where multinationals of the earth

xix

Drive kids of seven to the mines
at gunpoint, with plastic flashlights
so psychopaths in limousines
can chat on smartphones and lightweights
as they roll through Eurozone cities
the businessmen of proprieties.
Rayyan nudges urgently Sajjid:
'Bruv, we gotta make top-speed.'
(Speedo rightward from a hundred
climbs, starts clockwise to rotate;
now reads one-three-five on the straight-
section down which they thunder.
Until badass SUV's horsepower
takes them to one-fifty miles-per-hour.)

xx

Through outskirts of Shimona
slowing slightly - like the Shuttle
de-orbiting over Arizona
glowing with re-entry's subtle
fire - they burn to a standstill
beside a young dude on a downhill
freewheeling through night-suburb.
Sajjid slews-up onto the kerb
with glass rolled and sweat pouring:
'Need the Ziv Emergency Room.'
The dude sees demons through the gloom
as Sajjid screams over the roaring
dust-caked Bob Marley and the Wailers.
Terrorists, these wild night-sea-sailors?

xxi

But he stays cool; says, in Arabic
(though Sajjid's bellowed in Hebrew)
'Straight on six blocks, one K and a schtick
you'll see a roundabout, do
the third exit, leave at three-o'clock
you're there. Yo, guys, best of luck.'
The bro is smoking a little blunt;
he offers it (surreal moment)
just as handlebars eclipse in smoke
from spinning backwheels, as his face
vanishes without a trace
in burning Michelin's poison-toke.
(An exit from where rockets zoom
at the speed of sound, with sonic-boom).

xxii

'Please, Allah, it's not a hollowhead
the kind which blow up in the flesh.'
'Well, better hospitalized than dead;
we'll link soon, we'll synchromesh.
    Still 'n' all, I feel cold-as-ice;
not good leaving, but what choice?
Our bro Moss is one-in-a-million
but he's Jewish, we're Palestinian.
Sis', don't fret for our rhymeslinger
    you know that cat has x lives
you know the man of Allah survives.'
'It's such a shock, just such a zinger.'
    (Conversation in a getaway
    auto on a midnight highway.)

CHAPTER

3

i

The door flies wide, Tasneem is here
angry with her beautiful laggard
teenage daughter, who, with trailing hair
stands by window, bent and haggard.
   'What's that smell of coconut?'
'Just my new shampoo.' 'Well, shut
   that draughty vent immediately.'
      Jalilah does so obediently
(she daren't play rebel with Tasneem
      who confiscated Eminem
   last month on a maternal whim)
   mumbling: 'Another bad dream
   last night, I've slept so poorly.'
'Well, tonight you go to bed early.'

ii

'How's the shoulder?' 'Still painful.'
Tasneem believes what she's been told
re injured arm. Her brain's full
teeming with carefully-coiled
falsehoods and fantastic lies.
She would like to demythologise
her daughter's life, already taking
a direction groundbreaking
bending many a golden rule.
But she believes Jalilah's fibs
mostly accepts her wild ad-libs.
'Never mind, get ready for school;
and with your long hair wet in future
don't stand near windows, silly creature.'

iii

Tasneem's tired eyes have let her down
(sense of smell as well, in point of fact).
She too's had a bad night, and her frown
right now reveals sleeplessness' impact.
Twelve to three, semiwaking
she spent subconsciously matchmaking
mentally placing young men's faces
near her daughter's, reviewing cases
(background, prospects, looks, disposition)
one-by-one, a thankless task
since, in Shatila-town, a death-mask
is deemed the highest acquisition
for one without nationality
proof of his non-identity.

iv

At four a street fight broke out
feral shouts, intoxicated screams.
Husband Tareef slept throughout
(yet Jalilah heard them in her dreams).
Now Tasneem, standing at frontdoor
asks herself just what it's all for.
The dusty alley in early light
bears marks of the nocturnal fight.
On the road a bloodstained teeshirt
seems to say 'Clear me away
I don't belong in the light of day
my owner's gone down beneath the dirt.'
Jalilah quits the house in blue-jeans
as Tasneem snorts (there've been many scenes).

v

She's on the verge of saying something.
'Ma, no crack-of-dawn rows this morning
please, my brain's hotwired, I'm suffering.'
Tasneem accepts the early-warning
strokes her firebrand on the head.
'Hey, your hair's bone-dry. You said . . . '
'Ma, you promised, please give Dad a kiss.'
(Wow, a confrontational near-miss.)
Jalilah trudges off through garbage
trapped between traditions and fashions.
She must go to school or no rations
for her family in bondage.
Still, today she'll see Ishfaq, her friend:
and then confidences shall extend.

vi

The dark subterranean trench
she passes through is not a street
offering an intestinal stench
half-latrine, half-abattoir. Concrete
tenements, ramshackle towers
(where twenty-thousand neighbours
stack themselves into a crowded sky)
claw at each other with all-awry
aerials, dishes, drains, etcetera.
Over narrow, sunless lanes
power cables, in gigantic chains
hang like electronic viscera
the guts of some monstrous beast
swollen from a man-killing feast.

vii

This is Shatila at street-level.
On first-floor, passing the veranda
the body-mass of the Devil
in the form of an anaconda:
sixty-thousand volts of power-supply
wrapped in propylene snakes-by
cheap wooden shutters; sparking
in the rains of November, arcing
(barely-insulated) night-and-day
through Lebanese rainy-season
in Shatila's dismal prison
(December down to early May).
Jalilah walks schoolward, mood black;
then, for some reason, thinks of Mushtaq.

viii

Up on rooftop things are not so bad
sea-breezes blow through South Beirut.
Up there Aziz maintains launchpad
for racing-birds - angels - who execute
great circles and ellipses, flying
where the air is better (shying
away when Nato helicopters
make hallucinated raptors
larger than they have a right to be).
Jalilah loves the wheeling flocks
which turn around the towerblocks
swooping over grim Shatila, free.
Often at sunset she sits up there
sharing with Aziz his love-affair.

ix

He worships these beings of the sky
whose orbits seem to bless the houses
underneath; who seem, as round they fly
to rescind evil spells and curses
with circles made above the town.
Often, like Aziz, she'll sit down
to watch his racing-birds unconfined
whose swift magic-passes spellbind.
Following their movements she can lift
her broken spirits through the cloud
when low skies would enshroud
Shatila in the wet-season's shift.
His pastime of pigeoneering
she finds in him endearing.

x

Now through some nameless alleyway
she trudges east to Ramallah School.
Half-naked shoeless kids at play
under sagging snake-guts act the fool
shout-out a foul, obscene greeting:
'Slut, you'll get an arse-beating
today from the United Notions.'
These scatalogical commotions
leave our schoolgirl quite impassive.
She clumps along in cheap trainers
mumbles: 'Are you guys entertainers?'
For all her life she's had to live
emotions hidden, face blank.
She walks on through sunless alleys dank.

xi

She passes bakery, water-tower
crosses Abdul Nasser Boulevard.
Now she's made it, on the hour
and there's Ishfaq in schoolyard.
Now she can open-up and speak
without feeling some kind of freak.
But bell goes for 'Folk-orchestra'
first this morning, the sickener;
for the good of her Arabic soul
she must be tortured with instruments
whose very names are irritants
to Jalilah, who loves rock-n-roll.
(Well, she doesn't like Death Metal
for her Tupac is fundamental.)

xii

Ishfaq, who's a Maronite Christian
introduced Jalilah to rap.
(Her parents once lived in Britain.)
At one-o-clock the two friends clap
hands in a high-five, make for sunlight
near the lemon tree. 'So uptight
Jalilah, what's the matter?
C'mon, open-up, gimme blatter.'
'Honest, I don't know where to start.'
'All right then, how was Jezzine?
Your cousin Haniah?' 'I haven't been . . .
Ishfaq, I need a heart-to-heart
but not in noonlight. Tonight, your place?'
'Cool then, and afterwards, cyberspace?'

xiii

Beirut on its peninsula
Pearl of the Mediterranean
now shines through a crepuscular
atmosphere, almost subterranean.
Nightfall already? What's the deal
what's the rush? Has the sun's red wheel
rolled over the horizon so soon?
Can that be the big Nisan moon
over Lebanon Mountains there?
Is this pearl so deep in the sea
that it only shines invisibly
through a melancholic, dusky air?
(Here's the explanation, clear as day:
two girlfriends chatting on homeward-way.)

xiv

'Got some amazing new links
to show you, you are gonna die;
but what's hot on your plate, you minx?
You've been catching feelings, don't lie.
You've been up-close with some guy, true?'
Ishfaq keeps up this hullabaloo
all the way to her hillside home
high in Ashrafieh. So lonesome
is Jalilah (as eastward they walk
as they start to view, behind, downtown
Beirut sparkling in her evening-gown)
she finds it not dark enough to talk.
(She trusts her stuff's totally vaulted
with Ishfaq.) Now they've halted

xv

Look, in a little park. What next?
Ishfaq's bigging-up some earworm
some webcast that's: 'Kinda oversexed
Jah', you're gonna love this choon longterm.'
Does the phrase trigger confession?
Is it the place, with airs that freshen?
She fumbles for pack of Cedars.
(We really need to be lip-readers
to get the all words that follow.)
'I never went down to Jezzine
I lied to everyone, I've been
in Israel; and yeah, I met a fella
a DJ and a rapper who I like.
That's the problem.' A lightning-strike

xvi

Far out in the Mediterranean
makes the whole atmosphere
incandescent, almost alien.
(Of course the momentary flare
could be because of the blockade
some Nato-led naval fusillade.
Lebanon's writ of execution
was the Syrian revolution.
Her ports are full of fighting-ships
while Nato forces run a vast airbase
out in the B'qaa, face-to-face
with Damascus, massive landing-strips
Stratofortress-capable.
These days hell's inescapable.)

xvii

In the dark, Spring's first firefly
twinkles through the park. (Blinkbug
patrolling its airspace with fly-by?)
A pungent trace of the green drug
drifts from deeper shadows; while a flute
flutters on night-airs of old Beirut
caressingly, somewhere over there.
'Honeybabes, you *what*? You went *where*?
'Yeah, I know it sounds unreal;
Haniah's parents were away.
I had the long school-holiday...
I was smuggled into Israel.'
A motorbike putters through the glade
two brers onboard in stoned cavalcade.

xviii

Tomfool laughter spills through the night
two conspirators playing-the-arse
making their temporary flight
through brief heavens. On short grass
the pillion-rider falls in hysterics
clutching his belly in high antics.)
'And?' 'Well, Sweetness, where to start?
Got a Nato missile in my heart
direct hit on Jalilah-central.'
'Wha' you sayin?' 'Lemme finish.'
She plays with Ishfaq's Punkyfish
jacket - trendy - fingers soft lapel.
(Her friend's family are well-to-do;
Christians here, often, the chosen-few

xix

In Lebanon, some who've done okay
down the centuries, wielded power.
Ishfaq's people, in an earlier day
harvested the sweet orange-flower
on this very hill, within this glade
where, now, an urban park is made.
Ishfaq, herself, citing her 'worldview'
demanded she be put through
school with the hopeless refugees
from Shatila. Her Dad went mad -
there was nothing he could do - he had
to listen to her long complex pleas.
Full of the sweetness of Neroli
Ishfaq's golden heart: pure and holy.)

xx

'Explain, you cow, I'm in suspense.'
'Okay, hold tight, here we go.
You remember, from those rap-events
last summer, Shaza and her cool bro
Rayyan? Of course you do, "He's hot"
you said; got excited on the spot.
Well, Rayyan knows this club-owner
near Nazrat - loaded Sufi loner -
who's into Slingshot Hiphop bigtime.
He runs this literally underground
nightclub with everything: surround-sound
visuals, blah-blah. *He* asked me to rhyme.
Rayyan (who supplies him) said my act
was hot in Beirut: club was packed.

xxi

'I do my set, the stuff you know
the Zambian plays hand-drums for me.
Then it happens - when my flow
is done - after *Palestine*. I see
Laurence reach out both his hands
yank this good-looking guy (who stands
next to Rayyan, his twin) up on stage.
Now, in the middle of this space-age
club, he joins our hands together!
I try to disengage, the crowd
is screaming my name out loud;
I'm confused, like, really untogether.
We end up dancing, which breaks the ice;
get talking a bit, he seems real nice.'

xxii

(Ishfaq giggles.) 'We go on the roof
with the owner: science-fiction place.
My new friend seems strange, aloof;
    I see such sadness in his face.
We're all chattin' 'cept him, then Shaza
(you know that girl cuts like a razor)
cross-questions Sajjid, the owner.
(Rayyan's building pipes, that stoner.)
    Suddenly, taking a big risk
    (suspecting, already, perhaps)
I ask my mystery-guy if he raps?
Then at sunrise, with the sun's red disc
emerging, out comes something new:
Rayyan's best-friend's an Israeli Jew.

CHAPTER

i

With brake-screech an obscene expletive
with black skidmarks still smoking
glowing on the apron of the Ziv
the X5 stands here (still evoking
Unidentified Flying Objects
skyramps, spacecraft, shuttles, rockets).
One door's open: the front-right.
Now Rayyan (man of spaceflight)
comes running with whiteclad medic.
They slide Moss out with help from Shaza
(covered with blood, does nothing faze her?)
glide him into the pyramidic
building, ultramodern glass and steel.
Rayyan flies back: and that's the whole deal.

ii

Automobile takes off in the night
doing Space Velocity Seven
thundering under the starlight
transmission overdriven.
A CCTV camera blinks:
'Get those number-plates,' it thinks.
An intern with a big clipboard
inexplicably has been ignored:
she sucks her teeth, gets dramatic
choopsing and clucking over her form
(bureaucrats in Israel, the norm).
Her friend goes: 'That X5, fully sick.'
Through Prada eyewear intern glares;
at cloud of moonlit road-dust stares.

iii

If all this weren't so near-to-tragic
we'd collapse in hysteria
surrender to jocular magic
go over to the parking-area
build a spliff and say: 'O fuck it!
Pretty people kick the bucket
every day, disappear like smoke:
we crow awhile and then we croak.
We're the jibb from which Jah inhales
our burning bodies give Him bliss.
Life is just a hit-and-miss
affair which ends when Jah exhales.'
(All stoners know the mood descends;
yet for Jah the High never ends.)

iv

This is no time for getting wasted
though some say the bad trips are the best.
(When psychotropic drugs are tasted
you can put that theory to the test
ramp-up tension with a risk or two
float your boat out to that deep-blue
where Satan keeps his special storms
for those who like to push the norms;
then you can decide for yourself.)
Right now, here's one straight-out cynic.
Our mainman's in that spooky clinic
bleeding to death - near the ice-shelf -
helpless, isolated. Cue for action;
this is no moment for abstraction.

v

Plus, it seems from what Shaza blurted
when she lost her cool in the car
drugs were the reason Moss got squirted
on the borderline (How hip! Ha-ha.)
That quest for the Zahret el Kolch
backfired, nearly dropped in the gulch
one burning wreck with black catherine-wheels
spinning where the Devil does bad deals.
Drugs do represent a left-hand-path
toward enlightenment, that's a fact.
There is some kind of Faustian pact -
do the metaphysical math -
where drugs, as external agent
try to mimic the refulgent

vi

Light of the superconscious world.
Alchemy speaks of false elixirs
which force the doors of the otherworld
when we drink from those 'cement-mixers'
which turn up in Hieronymus Bosch.
Some will mutter: 'Load of tosh'.
Yet many die of nirvana
who get drunk on too much prana.
Overfasting can kill you as well.
Kundalini-recovery
is a new-age growth-industry
for peeps who've seen the dark angel;
in flower-gardens of damnation
the downside of illumination.

vii

Speaking of such cosmic topics:
consequence hangs in the stars.
Let's forget psychotropics
to such themes say our 'Au revoirs'.
Let's follow Moss through his ordeal
ride with him his fortune-wheel
steeply tipping now, it must be said
toward the lowlands of the dead.
Good God, he's lost a pint of blood
he's verging on desanguination.
(Let's hope that's an exaggeration;
but Shaza's sandals in some red flood
have stepped on the road to Nazareth:
sticky with the red stuff of death.)

viii

We're in the Ziv Emergency Room.
'Ballistic trauma.' 'Entry and exit
wounds.' 'Okay, bring up screen-zoom
I wanna see more.' 'Haemolytic
reaction?' 'No.' 'Okay, we proceed.'
'Transfusion trolley now?' 'Let it bleed.'
They've clocked our man's blood-type O
(in a full-blown medical scherzo)
it's probably on ID card.
This is fairly minor, basic stuff
classic practice, straightforward enough.
Here we don't see, frontline-scarred
some kid who needs a face-transplant:
tragedy is then omnipresent.

ix

(How does some young Romeo
conscripted into standing-army
face blown-off, deal with that cameo
role in which a strange taxidermy
makes someone else look still-alive
makes them superficially survive
though, in fact, playing a minor part?
Change of skin is not change of heart.
Most men would prefer to be
bitten by a canine with rabies
than deal with screaming newborn babies.
Women are the frontline soldiery
giving birth, torn asunder for love.
That's how girlfriends face the one above.)

Gliding through a strip-lit labyrinth
fluorescent maze of wards and clinics
see our hero, blue-eyed hyacinth
tripped-out under strong anaesthetics
mind gone, body in baggage-reclaim.
The phrase 'By any other name'
keeps repeating, without volition;
discorporated, his condition.
He dream-haunts that almond-wood
near Rainbow Bridge, against blue sky etched.
Jalilah lies there outstretched
in the pink shade. It feels so good
where the sweet-smelling trees are rooted
just to watch her sleep, barefooted.

xi

Her breath cycles lazily.
An almond-rain, rose-coloured, falls
a pink blizzard drifting hazily.
Far down below a wood-dove calls.
In altered states he enters her dream;
but her dream has a comfortless theme.
She listens to the voice of reason
against herself commits treason:
'Perhaps I'm just suppressing desires
but to love my arch-enemy?'
(Behind a cloud the sun looks gloomy.)
'To hell with all romantic fires,'
she whispers. Still, just the same
she adds: "By any other name."'

xii

Days sequence in a pink blur
(that almond-rain is falling still).
Fog fills a world of thought-transfer
(most would agree this man's very ill:
a blue line is his heartbeat on-screen.
A *blue line*? Repeating? That could mean…)
Sometimes he's in a little park
above a vast glittering city: it's dark.
someone's talking to her best friend:
they sweetly communicate.
She speaks his name; it's getting late
strange forms with half-shadows blend.
A flute, behind the conversation
augments a climate of frustration.

xiii

Fluttering back and forth, bittersweet
it sings and sobs, starts and stops.
There are mists of self-deceit;
there are high sunlit hilltops
which pierce the clouds with insight
where daring wheels in free-flight;
a multicoloured bird madly
describing freedom's melody.
But obscure skies close down again
dim with rain. Discordantly
the flute turns cold, mordantly
expresses only doubt and disdain.
Saliva froths from fevered lips
airy waveforms morph into whips.

xiv

Heart-rate increases; the blue line
turns red: the graph of its lash
becomes strangely serpentine
snaking on flesh. Hatred's gash
cuts furrows in a world-map.
Xenophobic visions mantrap
men behind walls of raised skin
congealed blood. (Fear is mortal sin;
borderlines are the world's whip-scars.)
The red turns black and gangrenous
the summer-heats are ominous.
On a desert-planet like Mars
oasis-waters are seething:
the atlas of this world is writhing.

xv

Steel-clad reptiles with poison-
fangs across dry wastelands wind.
God sends fevers of a hot season
hells of the hallucinated mind
to burn all lunatic-flagellants
with scourges made of arrogance
with horrifying hooked tails
with evil masochistic flails.
Snakes curl round the red planet
driving wars of separation
stirring nation against nation
smashing against cities of granite
making them crumble-down and crash
under a demolishing whiplash.

xvi

Stones feel these thrashings in their bones
these punishments of delirium.
Each wailing-wall of division groans
as falls the iron flagellum
which makes, with each cruel descent
one from another different.
The very mountains try to complain.
They feel a penetrating pain
as the whole planet is striated
with demarcations, borderlines.
Mineral flesh is full of landmines;
and mankind is lost in hatred.
Now comes a woman's voice, even worse
than the sound of God's final curse.

xvii

'Mr Rambam, wake up. No, don't laugh
you need to sign this document.
Plus you need to take a polygraph
lie-detector test. You're being sent
to another hospital underground:
down there they don't fool around.
You've been calling on "Dr Venus"
to mend you; but intravenous
heroin is what you need tonight.'
(It is the voice of the duty-nurse
which cuts like a flail, a whip, transverse.)
'That'll put you completely right
in time for your move tomorrow.
We'll see your back without sorrow.

'You've been fevered, very restless
bordering' - that word - 'on demented.
Mr Rambam, I'm relentless.
I'm going to talk till you're tormented
into waking-up, it's that simple.
We need this bed for other people;
there could be a war any minute.
On inspection - on a ward-visit -
I could have the Chief-of-Staff
walk in here right now and give me hell.
Mr Rambam, you hear me quite well.
You have to take a polygraph
because your friends are terrorists.
All their names are on our lists.

'You're going to military hospital.
We see from your Te'udat Zehut
you've just turned eighteen. Well
you know that's true, beyond dispute.
Eighteen means you're a big boy now
the personal can't overshadow
the national destiny of our land;
Israel comes first, you understand.
You might be back in here one day
you might need help with your face.
What if the final landing-place
the destination of a Stingray
(I'm not joking) lay between your eyes?
Then we'd need, surprise, surprise

'To look after you again.
Hizbollah are getting hotter
their Zelzal missiles fall like rain.
If that happened - what's the matter? -
you'd need more than Elastoplast.
Aha, I'm getting through at last.'
(The Hula Valley's the heart of hell.
It's full of that smell
which hovers near burning-grounds
when Saturn lights black fires
for male-children, funeral-pyres
which flare up on sacrificial mounds
burying their bones in quicklime
deep in his warlocked wintertime.)

xxi

He's wired to the truth-machine.
Twenty sensors and electrodes
a crown of thorns, are there to screen
in twenty different bleeping modes
perspiration, pulse, breathing-rate.
Rays look to see if eyes dilate.
Time now to administer
truth-drugs, narcotics sinister
nothing recreational.
A trembling electronic hand
(old Saturn of the Fatherland)
scribbles nothing inspirational.
Scopolamine is the alkaloid
which drives his soul toward the void.

xxii

Flashes of memory cyclone.
Israel Vibration: Rudeboy Shufflin';
a scene from The Guns of Navarone.
(In sunny cliff a dove is ruffling
feathers: preening, calling, cooing.)
Hour-after-hour: the interviewing.
'Hakim Faizan al-Filasteeni.
Ayyub Atif al-Filasteeni.'
The total unknowns make him glad;
they've nothing real, they're nowhere near.
Yet something else makes him fear
makes him feel he's going mad.
In this long-drawn-out sadistic game
he must never even *think* her name.

CHAPTER

5

i

'OMG, you are not serious?'
Phosphoric moonlight fills the glade:
Luna's large and imperious
Chrysler Liberty Renegade
her chromed and aerodynamic
cloud-cruiser glides the panoramic
heavens of her beloved Beirut.
She really digs her brand-new brute
in its V12 horsepower takes delight.
Now that the sun has gone to bed
(that somewhat ageing baldhead -
her husband - who likes an early night)
she's out kerb-crawling Jounieh
a far-from-salubrious area.

ii

Here are the super-nightclubs
where sexslaves dance in white hotpants
for older dudes (sometimes for wolf-cubs)
married-men with dental-implants
modern men of liberal Lebanon
lonely guys, who, off-and-on
come here with no real expectations
of anything but quick erections;
who flee hither from life's enfolding
claustrophobia and sadness
with no great romantic madness
driving them or beautifully gilding
dreams of a second, younger wife.
(Number One's been known to take a life.)

iii

Luna's not interested in these
of course; she's cruising for young studs.
She's had many lovers: Lebanese
Americans; Arabs and Yehuds.
Now that Nato soldiers are here
it's open-season for her next affair.
Her Powertech purrs like a big cat.
A well-hung Brit would knock her flat
could really give her a hard time;
he who'll give her a good scalding
absolutely won't be balding.
She's looking for manflesh in its prime
able to sweep her off her feet.
(She floats down a Jounieh backstreet.)

iv

Yet Luna has so many faces
from nymphomaniac to sublime
priestess of feline graces.
She's not just out for a good time
she's into relationship-building
too; which is why she's lip-reading
every last word Jalilah says
in the light of these silver rays.
(She's far above the circulating
harlotry of the vice-belt
the champagne-dinners where nothing's felt
amidst the pimpish calculating:
'How many clients-per-hour
in the marketplaces of amour?')

v

In cheap turquoise bomber-jacket
here's the true goddess of the night.
Away with that sordid flesh-racket
where 'virgins' stir a drunken fight
pole-dancing in a house with red doors.
(Still, of course, there are goodhearted whores.)
Yet here's the sinlessness of heaven
for which God's saints have striven
supercharged with a rebel-soul
who won't play the automaton
who won't be some female simpleton
who passively does just as she's told.
Let's listen, like the eavesdropping moon
as Jalilah and Ishfaq commune.

vi

'OMG. I don't believe it
how did you deal with the static?
Spill, tell all, how did you leave it?
Obviously too problematic
to pursue the dude.' 'Didn't say so.'
'Lilah, I don't… You kid me? No.'
Even her best friend is shocked.
A new bombardment has rocked
old Beirut on its foundation.
A vacuum-blast? A phosphor-bomb
for whose cold fire there is no balm
but only slow-burning damnation?
'So what the bleep happened next?'
(Interrogation bottlenecks.)

vii

'Exact sequence I misremember
it's all a sun-drenched, sleep-deprived blur.
In embarrassed silence September
came up. (Sajjid's a raconteur.)
He's gonna mount a "Burning Man"
in the Sinai Desert, that's the plan:
Slingshot Hiphop and Israeli rap
coming together to bootstrap
peace-and-love in the Middle East.
I've a slot, according to Sajjid
if he can get the papers I need
a passport for the border-police.
Then Moss - this Jew-dude - said something
which really got me, something scathing.

"Slingshot will dominate the battle
with dark substance, ocean-deep.
Israeli rap's lightweight material
forty-winks-lyrics, half-asleep.
The Nazi death-camps were yesterday
now we go the genocidal way
push the steel-grey in the West Bank.
(It ain't wordplay from a Sherman tank.)
Hip-hop's all about the downpressed."
Ishfaq, he hit the zone of my heart
my 'enemy' talkin 'bout my art
in such a cool way, fully-blessed
when my own flesh-and-blood can't see
the spirit of the times driving me.

ix

'I'm not quoting word-for-word
but his sense was crystalline.
It knocked me out, what I heard
was so on-point. Some borderline
transculturally-closed inside me
was destroyed, ceased to divide me.
Still I saw through. "Okay, true-say
but you maintain there's no way
a Jewish rapper could militate?
I don't buy that." He looked shocked
frightened almost, kinda tongue-locked.
And that's how we started to relate.
"Hebrew rappers chat a bag of breeze"
he repeated. "No real expertise."

x

'But I flipped back: "Uh-uh, I believe
flowin' on a high alpha-wave
a Jewish rapper could achieve.
He'd have to be seriously brave
love his people, but love the truth
even more. A bigmouth mighty-youth
a badass man, he wouldn't give a damn
he'd spit his wisdom: Blam, blam, blam."
I didn't speak with velvet tact.
Initially, at first, he looked
well-stressed, properly spooked.
(I'd called the dude in actual fact.)
Anyway, to cut to the chase
Moss took my challenge with good grace.

xi

'And that's how we started chatting.
Edgy stuff, substantial t'ings
conversational acrobating
flight above a gulf with rugged wings.
Rayyan and Sajjid were well-blocked
stoned out of their heads (we both clocked).
Shaza had wandered out with Aziz
down the hillside, through the lemon-trees.
My rash heart was knocking like a snare
beats-per-minute. (Ish', do you get me?)
It was like temptation set me
up with the thought: *"We could go there!"*
I should've found somewhere to sleep
but my rebel-soul took a leap.

xii

'I don't remember who suggested
a stroll in lucid morning-air.
All I recall is feeling tested
offering up a crazy prayer
as we snaked down through the garden.
In the sun's glare I asked for pardon
if I strayed from the straight path
if I asked for Allah's pure wrath.
Beneath His solar-angel's hot glance
we threaded by a sycamore
(feelin' myself like some Jounieh whore).
And so began a devil-dance
in the shade of that symbolic tree.
Ishfaq, you have to pity me.

xiii

It was all so innocent.
I heard Laurence's clay doholla
start to speak some slow, ancient
Zambian rhythm, irregular
now beating faster, like my heart
coming from the garden's upper part
somewhere hidden. That intricate pulse
helped our communicative impulse.
We'd been silent descending the hill;
I'd drawn my veil down, so the fringing
hid my eyes, not from sunlight cringing
but to stop them, against my will
wandering around the lovely place
coming to rest on his, Moshe's, face.

xiv

'We chatted in the shade more freely.
Talked 'bout the blues of old Missouri
Roots Rasta, Dub, Hiphop. We really
clicked: into Ali Farka Toure
Robert Johnson, I Vibrations.
(Talk impeded other temptations.)
He told me he'd seen I Vibes live:
"Modern black prophets in overdrive
angels on crutches" was his description.
"That was way-back, long ago" he said
"riding my Dad's shoulders, his bald-head
grasped in my hands." What a depiction:
a pre-teen beside Lake Galilee
beginning for the first time to see.

xv

'Two worlds met under that sycamore
fused in green rusticity.
We talked more openly than before;
there was deviant felicity
in my footsteps (the ground must have felt)
as we moved across a sunny belt.
The shadows said: "Go back, go back."
The sunshine said: "You're right on track."
Under a cypress, near a fountain
I peeped out at my dreadlocked friend.
he'd let his tresses, sun-gold, descend.
A dove came down the bright mountain
its wingbeats slow, like airy footsteps
saying: "Wonder's at your fingertips".

xvi

'She fluttered into a dark-green tower
as the fountain whispered my name.
The gardens held me in their power
inscape and outscape were the same.
I looked up into the cloud-stacks:
there, in perspective and parallax
wind-shifted castles of romance
moved foundations by happenchance
mirages of the air-country
where I found myself that morning
carried-off without warning
to the summerlands of fantasy.
The sky's topography, rearranged
mirrored confusion in me: changed.'

xvii

The full moon above a dark square
acts strangely, attempts to shine
deeper into the park; tries to hear
what's murmured in this saturnine
corner of the metropolis.
'So that was it? A morning of bliss
brief flirtation, some lightweight sinning?'
'O no, that was just the beginning.
My sweet catastrophe, heaven-sent
(at this stage I'm only half-hearted
I'm only now getting started)
was a mystery incipient.
Only at the fountain did I learn
how it felt for hot lips to yearn.

xviii

'To burn for something not-of-this-world.
A thirst came over me in the shade.
We moved to where cool water swirled;
our hands and our feet were sprayed.
I spun too, as spiral waters rolled;
my senses were not to be controlled.
Desire, as beautiful tormentor
told me what my lips were meant for.
I looked at Moss. Did he understand?
Did I ask him silently
my heart beating violently
to stretch in the fountainhead his hand?
Touching his wet skin I drank
then from that hand backward-shrank.

xix

'Trouble was in his turquoise eyes
bluer than those of Eminem.
(You laugh, Ishfaq; babe, I tell no lies
there are no contact-lenses in them.)
It was not timidity, but fear
he had offended, come too near.
Or, reluctantly, he looked at me
and thought, as I did: "The enemy."
We both recoiled; yet in my throat
thirst-quenching, cooler and sweeter
than this world's ordinary water
like Issa's water of which John wrote
I tasted some inebriant.
Thought: "Moss is no-way arrogant."

xx

'He backed-off. I made some smalltalk
hid myself in empty shadow-play;
we were the sun's puppets, made to walk
with rays for strings, a predestined way.
A pigeon-hawk hovered in the sky.
A dove, alarmed, fled his evil eye
from the path into her cypress-tower
it was about the noon hour.
"You really have to leave today?"
His intonation of that seven-word
sentence made my heart fly like that bird
up into her fortress straightaway.
But I didn't show my joy, Ishfaq,
I just chatted about "getting back".

xxi

'Sweety, listen, I know this is bad
but it's late, Dad will soon be angry.
I'm gonna do a Shahrazad
leave you suspended and hungry.
Let's meet tomorrow at Pigeon Rock
after school, say 'bout five o'clock?
By the sea, while the sun's setting
I'll tell the rest, without letting
one disastrous detail go astray.'
'Promise?' (Look, Luna is leaning
down into the small park, gleaning
every last word of this roundelay.)
'Yeah.' 'No webcrawl?' 'Not in the mood.'
'Me neither, your story's my soulfood.

xxii

'Still an' all, you're naughty. Just one hint?'
'Okay babes.' (Jalilah is so warm
with her friend.) In Luna's cool glint
look: something way beyond the norm.
'Casually, I asked what Moss was doin'.
For him, he said, there was trouble brewin'.
He said he had to shave dreadlocks clean
cut them down to serve the war-machine.
Trust me, babes, that came like a bullet
he seemed so sad and vulnerable.
The sun went behind clouds, unable
to shine any more, not a raylet.
Now look, Ishfaq. Here, behind my head
hidden, see, I grow a single dread.'

CHAPTER

i

Today a morbid sky shudders.
Something low under the horizon
murmurs distantly, rumbles, judders:
faint-sounding, jagged unison.
Other than this faraway drone
this undersong, this undertone
all is still, eerily so. For spring
there seems a check on everything
as if the vernal throne lay vacant.
Has the May Queen abdicated
is her green reign terminated?
Has her season-wheel in the Levant
turned backwards, spun retrograde?
Where is the sunburned flowermaid?

ii

Why this stagnation in Nisan?
Why this dustbowl-atmosphere
this sterile air? Since time began
Arcadia and Eden have been here.
This is Samchuna of long-ago
hunting-park where royal Pharoah
traced the leopard through papyrus-lands;
where panther-blood smoked on his hands
tracking-down the black cat to her lair:
Semechonitis of the Egyptians
garden of lyrical descriptions
paradise of legend; verdant sphere
wonderland sylvanian
in the old Mediterranean.

iii

Here were islands of the graceful crane
long-gliders of the cloud-world;
the painted-stork in summer-rain
clattered her bill, great wings furled
wading lakeshores through sweet-flag.
Here, her prey, the painted-frog
folded her tadpoles in dead leaves
learning from the spider (who weaves
in last-year's green her new cocoon).
Here the brown-bear fished cascades
surging down the alder-glades
snatching trout from streams at noon
raiding out of hollow oak-trees
yellow syrups of wild honeybees.

iv

(What is that subsonic drone
what's that low-frequency humming?)
Here, in the age of the flintstone
at the time of fire's coming
with the red spark born of friction
when the flame was science-fiction
man ranged through this paradise
flexing his hand: prehensile vice.
Here in the Dead Sea Rift Valley
secrets from the earth he wrested;
here he tried, honed and tested
prehistoric technology;
built his fires along the tranquil lake
watched his smoke across the water snake.

v

Here he became eco-poet
watching the changeful waterscape
charting his world, learning to know it
observing his Goddess shift her shape
naming her numberless visitant
bird-tribes with wondering-hesitant
liquid-echoic syllables
with joy in so many variables
catching the splash of aquatic birds
howl of the lunar wolf lovemaking
paw-step of the bear, earthshaking:
all his onomatopoeic words.
Here he saw the streamlined she-gazelle
fell beneath her mercurial spell

vi

Found the principle of likeness
the first time, in the first instance
comparing his woman's litheness
poised in moonlit firedance.
Here he made a reed-vessel of sedge
crescent-shaped, beside the curved lake-edge;
pushed outward in his first boating
to where the white lotus was floating:
the lily of the wetlands
sunlit wonder reflecting-back
snow-white on the waters black
to which she had stretched her hands
thing of greatest beauty in his world.
And from his hand the first gift unfurled.

vii

Here, through papyrus jungle
sailing waterlogged meadows
he saw the sun through green tangle
took notice of time-shadows
on the spangled surface of his lake
saw transmigrant clouds make
exit in the colder time of year:
their flightpaths meant winter was near.
And when they came back from the south
reappearing with the cyclic sun
his snowcapped mountain's tears would run
with glad rivers full of foam and froth.
The birds moved him to idolatry;
soon followed heliolatry.

viii

(What's that subsonic, man-made
sky-jarring, distant monotone?)
What's left of the moon makes him afraid.
Now he safeguards family alone
hoards rice and maize just for them.
Ice-age memories (that great wintertime)
make him stockpile, garner and reserve.
Now he needs many eunuchs to serve
his interests; he fears the unforeseen;
maintains ten-thousand dog-slaves;
as tyrannic overlord now craves
to lay hands on everything between
earth and sky, and let bondservants fall
sacrificed. (He builds a city wall.)

ix

Now he crushes-down at lake-edge
the green feathery-crested one;
now he smashes papyrus sedge
flattens it under a puzzled sun.
He needs to more accurately tally
all that is his in the big valley:
he's not interested in sundried clay
which took his reed-pen's mark yesterday.
Now facts and figures are mounting;
giant wheels of lore fade, forgotten.
(He sends a curse on the unwritten.)
Now he brings himself bad luck, counting
(since he knows exactly what is owed).
There are priest-scribes and a penal-code.

x

Now the Lord of Lower Egypt
marches for the City of Jasmine.
With the horn-bow he's equipped;
ripping the world apart to win
Shang fabrics, shining, silken, lacy
for his Foremost Noble Lady.
The oryx and gazelle go down.
(The sun wears an anxious frown
as he crosses over Samchuna.)
Reed-beds fall for the reed-arrow;
the angry sun seems to narrow
his eye in disgust. Lady Luna
cries a silver tear on the lake;
insomniac, walks the sky, awake.

xi

Old-world pigeon-flocks still wheel
the water-valley in summertime;
tribals still fill the wicker creel
dark-skinned men of the dreamtime.
But Indo-European Hittites
now war with southern Semites;
Indo-European Philistines
battle here with Proto-Byzantines.
From this point on there'll be no peace.
The Assyrian is coming-through
next year; in his worldview
Samaria's existence shall cease.
From Shalmeneser to Sargon
his bloodlines rule over Babylon.

xii

(What's that sound of low thunder
why does Spring seem so hesitant?
Has May been crushed to death under
a four-spoked sunwheel militant?)
It is the Lord of Akkad who rolls
southward his hurricane of souls
with cavalry and siege-tower
first military-industrial power;
with tactics never seen before
archery and charioteering
logistics and engineering:
now are the first days of total war
ethnic-cleansing and scorched-earth.
(Feel the winged-bull-angel's angry breath.)

xiii

The sadness of these victories
echoes by the Waters of Merom:
across the lake, sound-trajectories
shudder from an Israelite wardrum.
Waveforms break the ancient mirror;
the warriors of Dan draw nearer.
They burn the City of Leshem
(which is 'The City of the Gem')
and now it is the City of Dan
which shelters in the Iron Age
as time turns another page.
The war-crimes of Capricornian man
flare up for the idols of Micah
tin-gods who rape the Shekinah

xiv

Who steal the silver from her veins
who break her radiant flesh with mines
murder her in military campaigns
offer, to the superstitious, signs
indications that somehow declare
the Lord is in their dark warfare.
The milk-and-honey-land of Canaan
the green valley of 'Earth-Heaven'
Semechonitis, is no more.
Yet still to the land of three rivers
Mount Hermon from the east delivers
snow-cooled waters of the valley-floor.
(See, three sources of the Jordan:
the Hazbani, Banias and Dan.)

xv

And still within a setting alien
thrives a vital, verdant biosphere.
Still, here, five-hundred-million avian
winged travellers of the air
stopover year-by-year, transmigrant
nations of the wind, significant
visitors to the lacustrine world;
where, now, the lotus has unfurled
white stars of ivory perfection
on the black Waters of Merom.
Africa-to-Europe (to-and-from)
here is the locus of connection
on the long flight of attrition:
vital zone of intermission.

xvi

(What is that ominous, faltering
subsonic, super-low vibration?
What forces are altering
a green birdland-waystation
oasis on the endless flyway
from Mozambique to dim Norway?
Look, the horizon seems to tremble.)
Now the Israelites of the Bible
are scattered through the whole earth.
Only the proud, black-skinned Bedouin
lives on islands deep within
Hula's great swamplands henceforth.
He herds the wild water-buffalo
great-horned, splay-hooved, tortoise-slow

xvii

Captures some crusading knight
who strays into the hinterland.
(It is the end of his good fight
in Palestine; his skeleton and
armour become ritual
objects in a cult unusual.
As holy rider made of steel
he is a saint who cannot feel
the pain of this world in his shrine.
Through silver metallic skin
now well-rusted from within
his skull is regarded as divine.
He influences the summer-skies;
shining like them, he never dies.)

xviii

And now it is the Ottoman Turk
who rules Palestine from the north.
He fears the Bedouin who lurk
within the swamps, gives them wide berth
subduing in the nineteenth century
the whole Levant; his point-of-entry
through Samchuna naturally.
He'll drain the marsh eventually
wipe-out the pagan fishermen.
A hundred years he plans and plots;
the enterprise, waterlogged, rots.
He gives the project to the Frenchmen
(because the Franks are so damn-clever)
but the scheme drags on forever.

xix

And now it is the century
when new order rules over nature.
Now science plans to bury
superstition and conjecture.
Black-skinned phantoms fade away
their island-customs have had their day:
now is the dawn of understanding.
'Cannons! The white men are landing.'
From the Mountains of Naftali
the wolf can see, coming closer
a canary-yellow bulldozer
grazing in the Hula Valley.
He wonders: 'Does this beast have calves?'
(But Big Cats don't do things by halves.)

xx

A huge D9, with galvanized shed
(sunshield) over cabin for driver
with blade and ripper crawls ahead
widening the Jordan River.
It's summer, Nineteen Fifty-Six.
We're crossing now the River Styx
toward a ghost-countryside
where Mother Earth is crucified.
A whole ecosystem goes extinct
as this massive dissonant machine
cuts an ever-deeper mud-ravine.
(Yet still there is an indistinct
low subsonic humming monotone.
What other beast is coming to this zone?)

xxi

'Look, God built me for this job.
My children will be the killdozers
who, in spite of stone-throwing mob
(armoured crawler-tractor trailblazers)
will flatten the Palestinian towns.
With ultimatums and facedowns
how else to clear Unholyland?'
The voice is guttural, offhand
workaday, matter-of-fact
objective, scientific, cool.
(The speaker seems nobody's fool.)
Yet look at this dead soil, cracked
smoking like the mouth of hell's hound
as if fires were burning underground?

xxii

Once white clouds of egret whirled.
Now, topsoil gone, eroded, rain-thinned
here's a wasteland of the netherworld
crossed by the cold Sharkiyah-wind.
The light is dull under clouds of dust;
carbon-fires rage within the crust.
Productivity was brief.
Bad-tempered (with handkerchief
on bald head) a red-faced birdwatcher
dyspeptic eco-tourist, slaps a bug
in the reserve. With shoulder-shrug
(with small interest in blue flycatcher)
asks himself - does he philosophise? -
'What's that thundering in paradise?'

CHAPTER

7

i

A black moon rumbles in the west
throbbing spheroid, menacing shape
its monotone weirdly manifest
in the dead-still valleyscape
which acts as resonant enclosure
where soundwaves bounce-off picture-
postcard flanks of Mount Hermon
snowbound, hit the slopes of lemon-
groved Naphtali (as in a soundbox
where amplitude is reconfigured
by reflection and recaptured
as sonic energy unlocks).
A black sun crawls up the sky:
scarab beetle out of sci-fi.

ii

A Sikorsky 'Hurricane-Maker'
armoured gunship of conquest
climbs steadily, a sky-shaker
rising uncannily from the west.
Not difficult to identify
this massive pulsing dragonfly:
here is a titanium thunderbird
suddenly seen, previously heard
monstrous airborne revenant
strange three-engined, seven-bladed crane
coming back to Samchuna again
antithesis of all transmigrant
air-nations of yesterday.
Giant wind-lord, do you overstay?

iii

See the red-faced eco-tourist gasp
on wooden pontoon walkway stop.
Nikon, look, from sweaty clasp
he lets unceremoniously drop
to decking where it takes a snap
(captures sweaty foot in close-up).
Heavy-lift cargo helicopters
may resemble hovering raptors
mirror jet-black mutant nighthawks
from some futuristic videogame
yet no one thought such strange birds came
to Hula Valley Nature Park's
tidy little eco-sanctuary.
Seems we wrote Nature's obituary

iv

Too soon, a green world isn't lost.
The Hula Restoration Project
after the eco-holocaust
has indeed managed to resurrect
one-hundred and twenty species;
including the Anopheles
mosquito; which armour-plated
bloodsucker has anticipated
this beast-of-the-air-beyond-belief.
(One more thought before we get too smug:
no joke to be bitten by *this* bug.
Night-fevers would be very brief
malaria would seem the common-cold
once this monster got ahold.)

v

The seven-winged Sikorsky hovers
downwash raising thick black dust.
Our stout eco-tourist recovers
Nikon from decking. Zoom thrust
out toward the Hurricane-Maker
turbulence means the snap-taker
gets a grainy shot of the gunship
blurred (as rotorblades that whip
on General Electric turboshafts:
blades of titanium-fibreglass).
Floating bridge, wooden overpass
trembles in the black aircraft's
hover-mode air-displacement squall:
windstorm of the chopper's landfall.

vi

Sky is being torn asunder
air's being whipped into submission.
Our fat man, open-mouthed in wonder
watches Sikorsky take position
settle with power onto the ground.
Rotors spin down to zero-sound;
troubled waters cease to vibrate.
(Lake Agmon, toxic with nitrate
pesticides and fertilizers
milky agrochemical soup -
ghost of Hula Lake from the landscape
drained by the yellow bulldozers -
reverts to sluggish apathy:
main function to poison Galilee.)

vii

Now something eerie happens.
Distantly, through eucalyptus trees
it seems as if the earth opens.
(Our eco-tripper falls to his knees.)
Silently, without engine-furor
the chopper sinks through valley-floor.
In slow-motion, rotors spinning still
(like scarab-beetle into dunghill
like black sun going underground)
the Sikorsky starts to disappear
downward, like some bathysphere
plunging out of sight without a sound.
Nikon crashes out of sweaty hand
snaps again, this time, in Disneyland.

viii

With cold hissing servo-clunk
elevator-helipad deadlocks.
Compressed air and lubricant gunk
puff and bloop as gunship docks
hydraulically at base of liftshaft.
Arc-lamps train on the giant craft
set down on a rectangle of green
artificial meadowland, obscene
likeness of Samchuna's valley-floor.
Now a young dude with dark-blond dreads
blinking under bright overheads
limps on crutches through fuselage-door
flanked by a military nurse
deplaning from flying warhorse.

ix

Down the open backramp he swings
ashen passenger from iron skies.
(We've seen before these broken wings
which trail behind when freedom dies
when crippled men clutch at straws
when motive-power fastens claws
on stick and prop - and aspirin -
where desperate ones, from life's trash-bin
clamber up toward the light of day
try to climb a steep flight of stairs
get out-of-doors, far from cramped despairs
still defy old gravity's foul-play:
war-shattered men, polio-victims
all who've lost the use of limbs.

x

We've seen these dreadlocks, too, watched them fly
when godmen danced on walking-sticks
and walking-aids, I Vibes standing-by;
when, in a Hi-8 vid, Roots Radics
dropped *Greedy Dog* on Lake Galilee;
when vibrations became brotherly
as a young-boy rode his Daddy's neck
as Lascelle's dead limbs left the deck
as Skelly broke into a skank
'Two-Stepping' on crutches with a smile
evoking the prophetic lifestyle
as Apple G went 'Down di Flank'
making mystic moves on his handstaff
lifting up his broken lower-half.)

xi

Downward, haltingly, someone swings.
No coloured stage-lights, only arc-lamp's
harsh rays hideous brightenings
illuminate this loading-ramp's
indented steel. There's no applause
as, on steep rake, two crutches pause
between serrations, grip with rubber
grab every notch with non-slip fiber
to hold-up and prevent from sprawling.
Tall military nurse alongside
guides this invalid with swinging stride
pendulum-gait, stops from falling
one who must have taken some deathblow.
Look at his diffuse, strip-lit shadow.

xii

Ventilation-systems whirr
visceral ducting-pipes whisper.
The male-nurse mutters: 'This way, sir.'
(Somehow atmosphere seems crisper
here below than in the dead valley
up above, 'disabled' fatally.)
Through underground glades travelators
glide past cool fountains; elevators
made of glass fall to subterranean
levels deeper, still concealed
in this duodenal sub-world sealed.
A Phoenix palm flies downward, avian
whose biosphere's a transparent box.
See: a green helicopter docks.

xiii

A room lit by rectangular suns
perspex clouds of mercury vapour.
Here, in phosphor's cold fluorescence
coloured swirls on ice-white paper.
'The Ziv sent your dactylogram;
most unusual, Mr Rambam.
A great number of fingertip-whorls
means you're what our analyst calls
a "lone-wolf": focussed, independent
inflexible, no team-player.
(As scientist - no soothsayer -
I'm still aware of the transcendent.)
Here's a psychometric questionnaire;
fill it in when we're through here.'

'Let me come right to the point.'
(The speaker is one of two.
Good-cop, bad-cop, it's a joint
entity that mounts this interview.)
'Israel needs men of your kind.
Most in the Mossad could be defined
as teammates or 'synergic' agents;
they don't have that true ambivalence
which makes solo operators rare.
Most spooks work together: one unit
interdependent, closely-knit.
The men we're looking for never share
with anyone their identity
remain an unknown quantity.'

'We've watched you over time, Moshe.
Can I call you by your name?
Your type will always break away
from those who play the mutual game.
We know you have a 'friend' in Natzrat;
we know his name if it comes to that.
(The Ziv don't have our resources
for tracking down dark horses.)
We know you visited Transworld;
have been able, too, to establish
you hung-out with Sajjid Darwish
afterward. We need detailed
information about his plans
to send transcultural caravans

xvi

'Down into the Sinai Desert.
Darwish interests (and worries) us.
Good intelligence could alert
our hit-squads, which would be a plus.
You need to reconsider, Moshe.'
(On the wall a lily-pond Monet
somehow mirrors an earlier theme
seems, behind the speaker, from a dream;
symbolizing, half-familiar trope.)
'See the poet as undercover-
agent, most-secret-observer
ghost invisible on radarscope:
master-spy outside the cult of norms
taking mental-notes in thunderstorms.

xvii

'Think how the two professions
fuse, overlap by definition.
Spies, like poets, ask pointed questions
report from an oblique position
far out-of-sight, underground, unclear;
practice other voices, insincere;
invent faces, roles; assume, discard
trappings of some dangerous charade
involving simultaneous pretence
calculated schizophrenia.
Then, too, we find satyromania
a common bond; do you not sense
how spies and poets both deploy
the old subconscious playboy?

xviii

'Poets have a reputation
have they not, in this department
where opportunistic relation
explores, in some well-bugged apartment
ulterior sensuality;
where hidden eyes, for posterity
record what happens when desire
collides head-on with the thief-of-fire;
when both curiosity and fear
crash and penetrate right through
the ring-pass-not of stupid taboo
crossing some forbidden frontier?
That girl Jalilah's so attractive;
your romance could be lucrative.

xix

'Do you get my drift, Moshe?
State-secrets obviate the law
redefine the term "to betray".
Poets, too, in order to know more
must smash codes, isn't that so?
I'm paraphrasing Arthur Rimbaud
your rap-god, who saw fit to act
as if outside the human contract
as if he were some time-lord
committing the most idyllic crime:
drugging and raping his muse sublime
down in the dark sewers he explored.'
(Someone's thoughts are overground
in the sunlight, not down here, earthbound.)

xx

Listen: 'For I rather to be
where the grass is green always.'
Listen: 'Sittin' under a tree
where there's a running stream, yay.
Yet because of the situation
down here inna Babylon. . .'
From far above this hygienic air
this fake, greenhouse atmosphere
synthetic and insufferable;
far from white-suited technocrats
from beyond a world of thermostats
claustrophobic, inescapable:
sunsplash-music comes floating, gliding
folk-fables on Rasta-grooves riding.

xxi

(An antiseptic chamber of rage
where evil lures a freedom-fighter.)
'Think, Moss. Birds of freak plumage
recessives, impure, blacker, whiter
than average, differently-coloured
are rejected, badgered, tortured
ostracized and eliminated.
Think how the albino is hated
hunted in Africa as 'other'
white ghost-human of witchcraft
murdered in Tanzania, outcast
dismembered by his darker brother.'
(It is another voice, keen, suave, cold
more sinister a hundredfold.)

xxii

There's still a shade-tree full of singing
in the sunlight: a green opera-house
loud with songster-solos echoing
where a small bird serenades his spouse
where trills fill homes of chats and robins
where late-Nisan hangs coloured ribbons
here and there to celebrate the spring.
(Down here, still, an impulse to sing.)
'For as he was crossing the bridge
so then he looked down in the water...'
A song about a solemn matter
a song about deceptive knowledge;
a song about a black reflection
a shadow-dog: only projection.

CHAPTER

i

See, on this bench, sixty setting suns
in miniature reflect from shades
sloped in ranks; brown ones, blue ones
their coloured-lenses in cascades
mirroring the sundown many times.
Strangely an icecream-vendor's chimes
blend with glissando seagull-screams.
Caught in horizontal sunbeams
here's a street-sweeper of the corniche
his turquoise uniform and cap
slightly dusty as he works to trap
a just-discarded scrap of quiche
now suddenly snatched from trashsack
in a kamikazi gull-attack.

'These birds are laser-guided, no lie.'
Jalilah smiles, leaning on raked
balustrade of warm brushed-steel; sky
behind her to the west is streaked
laterally with oranges and pinks.
Dudes in dark hoods cruise past; one winks
at gorgeous Jalilah standing here
in turquoise herself, her long hair
hidden under black headshawl.
She blushes, as a virgin should
when flirty rudeboys, up to no-good
generate hot glances at nightfall
from eyes which say: 'The hour of the wolf
is when a young girl must guard herself.'

If only she'd grabbed those sunglasses
tried - too dear - five minutes earlier.
These wolves are gonna make more passes
they're turning back, looking deadlier.
'I would deflower you, little girl'
they seem to snarl; red tongues flick and curl.
Their eyes, beneath shadowy hoods
are those of wild beasts from dark woods.
(This is mental, where's Ishfaq?)
They glitter and they flash with lust
these eyes which say: 'Angel of dust
seize joy before time, masked in black
hijacks your beauty, turns to ashes
those lips, those cheeks, those curved eyelashes'.

iv

'Ishfaq, what took you so long?
We said five, it's now gone-six;
I've just been hit on by King Kong
in a tracksuit trawling for chicks:
get me outta here, I feel abused.'
The offender wants to be excused
but she also needs to tell her friend
burning news. As these two wend
from esplanade down to the sea
let's stalk them - kinda espionage -
as they wind down toward la plage:
walk behind them hiddenly.
'Lilah's nervous, still panic-attacked;
Ishfaq bubbles, slightly lacking tact.

v

'Babes, forget about psychic rape
I jus' got flamed in this chatroom.
Truly it's a tale of netscape
from the land of nom-de-zoom.
I was in Rapmonster (Mocospace
maybe) chattin' bout rap and race
talkin' bout Israeli hiphop
jus' sayin' no Jewish rappers drop
A-class lyrics, as you said yourself
when we were talking the other day.
Suddenly, like a Stingray
this guy comes up in my face by stealth
really starts to thunder and aggress
gettin' all obscene in his address.

vi

'Blatantly the guy was Israeli.
For screen-name he'd taken "ziontrain"
from that UK dub-section, early
90's. (Remember? It did your brain
when I played you their Terror Talk.)
Well, this d-head tried to walk-the-walk
but stumbled and got left behind.
I went: "Zion is a state of mind
not a state in the Middle East."
That went down like sixty slaps.
He started floodin', shoutin' in caps
comin' on like the rampant beast.
That's why I'm late, babes, 'scuze, my bad
but this intruder got me real mad.

vii

'I do remember Zion Train
mixed-ethnicity, white-rasta
UK Dub from a higher plane
a little bit like Zoroaster.
By the way, funny you should cite
Israel's rap-desert tonight.'
(Jalilah's expression's faraway
looking back to Sunday-
dawn on a hillside in Galilee.)
Now the girls are on sandy beach
far below trendy corniche;
where dirty-talking rudeboys set free
that dark elan-vital (that force
found everywhere in the world, of course).

viii

Twenty toes wriggle in warm foam:
a school of dolphins curvaceously
plunging through blue aquadrome
endless water-rides of the sea;
all of them marine acrobats
from birth, ocean's aristocrats.
In spacious free-state of the deep
they cartwheel, they pirouette, they leap
surfing through the coastal swells;
the Spinners and the Heavisides
the Snubfins, the Lords of the Tides
Pantropicals, Water-Gazelles.
See, babies play with bubble-rings;
they've never heard of water-wings.

ix

Ten pairs of amphibious toes
play sensual aquatic games
just like some school of Bottlenose
waterdancers with whistle-names.
Venus glides past in her white shell
handtrailing blue mirrors, truth-to-tell
straight from that beautiful mural
marvel of a Cretan palace-wall
where playful orcas smile from frescoes
painted many thousand years ago
our ancient friends of streamlined flow
as shapely as these sprayflecked toes.
(Good in foaming surge to liberate
feet entombed in sweaty leatherette.)

x

The muse today strides bare-breasted
through clouds which are superior waves.
Yesterday her poor nerves were tested
underground, where spirit craves
sky, sunlight, crystalline sea-air.
(Flux and variance condemn us here
where see-sawing change dips-and-dives
where assurance crashes and revives
following old sinewaves of fate
as we rollercoaster dolphin-style
through duality with forced smile
cresting, plunging through sinuate
existence like the rock-dove
whose flight ripples after making love.)

xi

'So tell me more, cut the suspense.'
(a monologue on the seashore).
'Take me back into the present tense
what happens next? You're falling for
him bigtime?' 'Well, no, as I recall
after the enchanted waterfall
on the highway north, we never spoke;
I felt low, and ganja-smoke
jus' intensified my downcast
mood, kinda like decompression
after a deep dive. Expression
must have reflected my outcast
feelings leaving Palestine;
land I could long ago call mine.

xii

'Laurence tried to boost the mood
told me spit to my backin'-track.
Babes, trust me, I got flat-out rude
bitching like some egomaniac
primadonna-diva seein' red.
I dared Moss to spit instead
prepared for this Jew-dude to flop-it.
This was the way, I thought, to stop it
kill our embryonic romance
abort feelings, rip out sentimental
attractions, likings accidental
conceived in random circumstance.
Ishfaq, I made a big mistake
motivation to myself opaque.'

xiii

The sun is kissing the skyline
lips of red caress ocean;
the sea murmurs in her sleep, sign
she feels some new and deep emotion.
'I remember how his flow started
lifting me up, heavy-hearted
afraid of going back to Beirut
scared of tasting forbidden fruit.
I know we've often said in the past
I even repeated yesterday:
"Jewish rappers have zero to say."
Well, Moss was about to bomb-blast
heart 'n' mind, penetrate 'n' destroy
this way-cool Marley-esque Jew-bwoy'.

xiv

'Ok, back in the present tense;
I'm in full-on panic-attack.
Car's dense with poison-clouds, intense
blue fumes. I'm high! My backing-track
pulses low through whirling toxic smoke
on playback. Now, between toke-and-toke
Moss starts movin' words like chess-pieces.
I'm like "Wha?'" as heart-rate increases.
This bro's takin' no prisoners
flowin' smooth as silk in Arabic
strategies of language fast 'n' slick:
he's up there with top practitioners
makin' mincemeat of Zionism
as I face: emotional schism.

xv

'Coz like the Mediterranean Sea
my mother cries Palestinian tears.
(Tonight's full-moon-to-be greedily
sucks salt tides of our despairs.)
'Sometimes, Ishfaq, my moon's a morgue
full of children's bodies, an iceberg
floating in a night-sky-ocean
white slab of a cold black heaven.
I say to myself "What's he to me?"
But, sweetness, struck by lightning
I'm split by fire; which is frightening
because sentimental amnesty
(something schmaltzy 'n' 'romantic')
ain't me either; seems inauthentic.

xvi

'In the space of five minutes
his rap-thunderbolts rip me apart.
Yet someone still self-incriminates
as raw senses jumpstart ice-cold heart
with the thrill of true connection;
as feelings take a new direction
so fate suddenly seems less bleak
(while a stupid tear sits on my cheek
and "rat, tat, tat" goes my heartbeat).
"Rayyan, restart that choon" goes Sajjid.
It plays real low as X5 at speed
eats the highway north in noon-heat.
Then, while I'm thinkin', Ishfaq, my hand
makes a move completely unplanned.

xvii

'Sajjid's talkin', not sure 'bout what;
mos' likely he's bigging-up Moshe
callin' him "rapstar", sayin' he's hot.
Like I say, this little giveaway
teardrop's parked under right eye:
not visible, hidden; but as I
go to brush it down, naughty left-hand
little-finger moves too - understand? -
contacting on cool black leather
skin touched earlier at fountain
in the sunny green mountain
when we two drank together.
Babes - shameless bitch! - I did the thing
with two fingers interlinkin'.

xviii

'Acting, like: "Wait a sec there, whoa!"
Moss shifted his hand away.
(Sajjid was talkin 'bout "tomorrow
in the peninsula", come-the-day
with The Serious Road Trip:
all his wicked plans to let rip
a wilderness megafestival
Burnin'-Man rap-carnival
for Arabs and Jews alike.)
But then Moshe slid back over mine
wrapped my fingers with a quick entwine
just as Sajjid went: "On-mic
you'd look amazin' side-by-side.
You two, ride or die? You gonna ride!"

xix

Now, Ishfaq, now, my *visible* eye
let down a dopey lil' droplet
on my blue jacket, too-late to wipe dry.
"This is Montague v. Capulet"
I thought. "Girl, you in-deep right now."
I still have this vivid flash of how
turning, I looked him in the eyes
thinkin': "Love sees no boundaries"
gazin' through conflicted tears.
Then it was time to say good-bye
at the Rainbow Bridge layby
to Rayyan, Sajjid, those racketeers.
(Who're doin' some mad drugs-deal
at the Blue Line: dangerous for real.)'

xx

The day is hardly colour-fast
the sky of light is dispossessed;
the sun is sending out his last
red beams of twilight from the west.
Our two friends huddle closer now
like lost sheep when the sun says 'Ciao!
I'll find you again, my little ones.'
For a moment a sunray brightens.
(Round Pigeon Rock a cloud orbits:
sweep of shadow in dark atmosphere.)
In semi-darkness the heart can share
more easily; murkiness permits
clarity sometimes. (Where extremes meet
boldly, in broad daylight, walks deceit.)

xxi

Solar god's down in blaze of red.
In a scene from modern tragedy
he'd seem to have laid his head
(like poor President Kennedy)
on a bloody execution-block;
here simulated by that Van Gogh
who paints with wind, shifts coloured clouds
action-painting pitch-black shrouds
across stormy evenings portending;
whose easel's this sad world without rest
where portrayed are worst and best.
'I'll tell you too of the dark ending
which turned our Galilee Sunday
into some well-fucked-up screenplay.

xxii

'But first, invite you to Rainbow Bridge.
Ishfaq, for the first time in my life
I felt like some girl from the village
meeting, maybe as his future-wife
her shepherd in the almond-wood.
I swear-down, we were both so good.
It's borin', there's nothin' to tell!
I'm still a virgin, not yet in hellfires officially burning;
though senses, as they say, at sunset
catch alight.' (See, our Juliet
mimes how Tamadur would sing
long ago: "Winged thoughts after dark
every word burning like a spark".)

CHAPTER

i

'You're barkin' for a greasy bone
dropped at midnight under a bridge;
barkin' for nothin' but fear of own
shadow: without self-knowledge.'
(MC Rambam impudently hums.)
Someone's finger on formica drums
tapping on veneer a wooden beat.
This is bureaucratic defeat
rout; someone's run-out of brainwash.
'Good-cop', more friendly, frank (much younger)
gazes, full of immigrant hunger
over strip-lit room at our man Moss.
He'll be Mizrahi or Maghrebi
newcomer to Israel, maybe

Eastern or north-African Jew
Babylonian or Carthaginian;
he's a Third World man of sunburned hue
but not Falasha (Abyssinian).
He's more relaxed than Ashkenazi
Iron John: expression crazy.
Here's a second-class citizen
apologetic denizen
of a state which gives scant respect.
(He's barely better than an Arab.)
After a lifetime of rehab
slow assimilation will perfect
his three kids, find them less false.
The other dude's something else:

iii

Russian blood perhaps, imperious
type, brute-force and hardline bombast
mixed with humourless, all-serious
materialism; out-to-do-his-worst;
extraction very likely Ukraine:
son of that difficult terrain.
A revolver bulks his black jacket
(that's no scrolled medical-packet
A4 notes on present patient
neatly rolled into a cylinder)
obviously holstered near left-shoulder.
Misgivings are incipient:
a William Burroughs lookalike
sinister, gentlemanlike.

iv

'We all need a friggin' fresh-air-break.'
(The Mizrahi; with permissive smile.)
'Central lake-garden? Let's take
this buttoned-up fool to Emerald Isle
for twenty minutes?' (Nessim Saatchi
speaks, accent still traced with Iraqi
dialect of childhood mother-tongue
the Arabic he spoke when still young
living in a tent-city near Lod.)
'Mr Rambam has simple options:
either he makes clear adaptations
or we cut down his Schwarze god
shave his dreadlocks off tonight;
tomorrow book him an army-flight.'

v

(Iron John of downturned, mordant smile
heavyweight, stone-expressioned;
tone of voice, attitude: hostile.)
'Week-in, week-out we've questioned.
Is the Egyptian government
backing the Transworld experiment?
One last chance, anything to say?
Or tomorrow you'll go the same way
you came into the Hula Valley
but you'll fly out another machine:
our Sikorski Aircrane Eighteen.
headed, incidentally
for a base in the Negev desert
south of Beersheba, so unpleasant.'

vi

'Still, let's try the overground.'
A room lit by rectangular suns
deep in the earth underground.
(We must not think of hidden guns.)
A strange trio moving in the night
through mazes of artificial light
on travelators, silver stairways
where fluorescent timeless days
cast a subterranean spell.
This is where hypervigilance
spins round in eternal war-dance;
where psychologically sick men dwell
in rubber rooms, scanning for danger
in war-haunted modes of behaviour.

vii

This is where they hide the one
who can't be seen in daylight, face
shorn-off like side of gammon
whose artificial cheekbones replace
human smile with imitation grin.
Here they keep hidden within
(wreckage of secret crusaders)
a war-machine's heroes; brave soldiers:
the undead, never seen in public
men who'd terrify everyone
if they tried to walk under the sun.
(Down here it's more pragmatic
not to speak of the world above.)
Yet in the depths you'll find love.

viii

She aids him of the blast-wound
hit by high-velocity shell;
serviceman lost underground
in hospitals of living hell:
missile-damaged, war-deformed
some survivor now un-uniformed;
crippled and quadriplegic
billionth victim of strategic
'mistakes'; with other brain-dead
sensory-and-motor zombies
remembering not armies
but operating-theatres instead:
battlefields of that death-struggle
where surgeons with slim chances juggle.

ix

Through labyrinth of glass and steel
tunnels of metallic twisting
passageways oesophageal
on-and-on, further persisting;
constantly auditioning
faint-songed air-conditioning:
low peristaltic whisper.
Sometimes fresher air, crisper
breezes-in from central void
bringing atmosphere's excitation
allowing light and ventilation.
(Sun, moon, elements: all employed
in the world of the earthscraper
still a dream for the developer.)

x

A shock to be out in starlight
on roofdecked surface of the lake.
(Subterranean's been overbright;
too-long forced staying-awake
has left no sense of day-night difference.)
MC-R feels a wave of reverence
under the nocturnal stars
decoding incredibly Jalilah's
stellar profile momentarily;
dark-headscarved, her luminous face
superimposed, star-flecked, on black space
etched in light extraordinarily
against night-sky's obsidian:
her silhouette in the meridian.

xi

A wooden pontoon with pine-decking.
There's Mount Hermon's white, moonlit ridge
in the distance eastward. (Just checking
where we stand from this dark bridge.)
Shadows move on shadowy water.
Probably some dog-otter
reintroduced to nature-reserve
making moonlit waters swerve
speeding in semi-playful dive
after carp or plump catfish
huge flat tail-appendage's swish
sharply perturbing with sideways-drive
smooth Lake Agmon's silvery surface.
(No reason to be nervous.)

xii

A bridge sways uncertainly.
Three figures on low pontoon hasten
(they 'float-walk' we'd say, mistakenly).
Our man leans, shadow misshapen
over water, reading black tablet
affixed to obelisk by islet.
(A disbelieving headshake.)
'The centrepoint of old Hula Lake'.
Now Nessim Saatchi leads the way
and the assassin brings up the rear
Moss inbetween (without fear
without a thought of foul-play?)
seeming to glide on silver Agmon.
(In the night-air, scent of lemon.)

xiii

Moonlit quicksilver's chromed brilliance
makes a mercurial dimension
like some off-world experience
(from wilder shores of invention).
Our man's relaxed, leaning backward
one elbow acting buttress on hard
timber-rail still studying night-sky.
'So, draft-dodger, you gonna comply
deal, bud, to clear the mess you're in?'
(Addressed by the Mizrahi
ignored by Ashkenazi.)
'Wha', like some Babylon-mannikin
puppet of the secret police
crap cheapo wooden chess-piece?

'Man, outta my face with that poor stuff.'
Moss hoists-up gun-metal-gray hood.
Mizrahi laughs at this rebuff:
'Bruuuv, got some puff here so-effin-good
never know, might make you change your mind.
Down below, fair enough, you declined
but up here?' Nonchalantly
darker-skinned Mizrahi instantly
unpockets what looks - yes - like a spliff.
(Pale Ashkenaz has turned his back;
see his stern silhouette of black.)
Mmmmm, pungent grass, get a whiff
someone's got proper drugs. Now Nessim
replies to something just said to him.

xv

'Only the best weed for the Mossad.
You'd wanna work with us 'n all
if I detailed weedkillers we've had
floating round here 'after nightfall
(not that spies are ever non-spies).
Check with our psychic-warfare guys
they rate this Afghan Trainwreck best.'
He offers red-tipped cone. 'Fully blessed.'
MC Rambam hoovers lethal haze
sucking on the mother-joint.
(Kefitzat ha Derach! Flashpoint!)
'Mmm.....' He shoulder-taps Ashkenaz
spins him, off-balance, surprised
(eyes blazing madness undisguised).

xvi

Long blue outbreath of Trainwreck
jetstreams to central forehead;
Glock falls nonviolently to deck.
Moss goes "S'okay, no one's dead.'
But Ashkenaz is out-of-action
shows no conscious reaction
when MC Rambam drawls these strange words;
doesn't startle when a night-bird's
strident call's imitated by him.
Eyes stare at infinity, glazed;
the 'bad cop' is seriously dazed:
exeunt for Ashkenazim.
A streak, forty minutes of arc
slices rapidly across the dark.

xvii

Anti-Lebanon flares a moment
Mount Hermon flashes, snowbound.
Spicy pine and patchouli-fragrant
cannabis resins drift around;
musky ethers race across the lake:
Hula breathes deep, comes awake.
Primal ventings, watery cavortings
combine with draconic snortings.
(Horned with two fantastic crescents
something's being born in thick brown mud.)
A shadow stirs with turbo-blood:
vastly-trumpeting angry presence.
Now whole shoreline heaves up in flux
with cries of startled lakeside geese, ducks.

xviii

Saatchi backs off, stumbling in reverse;
pontoon sways in quicksilvered night.
(Preparing to flee he bawls a curse
from supernatural scenes taking flight.)
Facing forward, he nonetheless
backtracks in worsening distress
as drastic forces seem to bulldoze
shoreline, as something bellows
(deep basso-profundo howling)
echoing on Agmon lake rudely.
Old 'Iraqi' mind confusedly
imagines marsh-monsters prowling;
madness in the boatman on the shore
which never had been found before

xix

Terrible Hufaidh within the swamps;
remembers such things as someone rides
straight for him on a brute which stomps
mud-shallows by island-watersides
churning yellow oozes in moonlight
(the ghost of a medieval knight
mounted in white skin of lunar steel?)
riding - and guiding with bare heel -
a mammoth looming bulk with horns
lumbering, cascading bright water.
It is the Swamp-Arab: marsh-dweller
believer in djinns and unicorns
who, wading too far in the wetlands
wandered many years bewitched islands;

xx

Who nonchalantly, insolently
rides now between black scimitars
in green swimming-trunks, innocently
as if joyriding under the stars;
who holds, inexplicably
impossibly (unmistakably)
a shoulder-launched ATM
(this freedom-fighter from Bethlehem).
With ski-goggles and keffiyeh
with massive spliff - more like a missile -
with dirty-bomb wi-fi'd to mobile
he looks hardcore Hezbollah.
(Alongside streak watersnakes
dog-otters leaving moonlit wakes.)

xxi

He babbles a pagan alphabet
waving, hands Ferris-wheeling.
(A pre-Islamic green cigarette
puffs toxic spirals unreeling.)
Saatchi panics completely
as the ghost-rider neatly
lassoes him with a reed-lariat
pulls him now behind his chariot;
makes him a skier on Hula Lake.
In moonlit freedom a moment
he treads the watery element
dog-otters, catfish in his wake.
(Saatchi hears his own mad laughter
mirroring across the water.)

xxii

A face from the firmament
smiles like Inanna, sky-crowned.
(Funny, we thought she was just figment
of someone long weeks underground.)
She watches closely as our hero
disappears, slowly fades to zero
riding his black ship of the morass
(still puffing stick of killer-grass).
Here is that man who jumped the road
not long ago; so no surprise
to see him dematerialise
as it were, proceed in quantum-mode
from a-to-b strangely-projected.
But *she* is most unexpected.

CHAPTER

10

i

The shepherd of planet-flocks
scans for a wandering one
sends searchlights, love-beams, flaring locks
flying from him, the shepherd-sun
a real-life herdsman with storm-lamp
(in rainswept mountains cold and damp)
directing flashlight's dying ray
to find some small animal astray
sweeping rugged crags and ledges
up in the high Carpathians
or in the blue Appalachians
searching along windy ridges
for some little stranded beast:
so the sun looks back toward the east.

ii

So he finds the faintest spark: our globe
silhouetted by the Milky Way.
The shepherd-sun sends out a probe
to where our world, gone astray
shivering in interstellar space
cold, distressed, in the darkest place
balanced on the edge of undoing
awaits last-minute rescuing.
(The Good Shepherd in the space-age
still understands our situation
arms-race of nation-against-nation
where future weapons-systems engage;
He has not forgotten our distress
where megadeath is part of progress.)

iii

This faint spark's actually a spleeff
not another planet, doomed, off-track.
Someone we know, in head-kerchief
Jalilah, as always, fringed in black
blue jacket purple in half-light
afterglow of reddish April night
(where Beirut sparkles on the coast)
drags on a zoot, getting the most
out of Ishfaq's juicy green reefer.
(Ishfaq is a druggy one
party-animal; more like a nun
Jalilah is no such raver.)
But right now, for real, she needs a draw:
she's a whole deal to confess for sure.

iv

'So Shaz' kicked shoes off and barefoot
vanished with Aziz cool 'n' blase.
(She's changed since she was in Beirut
a year ago, in every way
different from the girl I met then.)
Alone with Moss once again
I felt shy as the pre-fun-
loving Shaza. In noon sun
we stood there tongue-tied strangers.
In big dumb embarrassment
I knelt down on a dusty pavement
under a sign warning of dangers,
landmines. 'Keep to the path!' it read.
(That meant something else in my head.)

v

'Hard under my bare feet stones judged me
unforgiving; as Moshe's guiding
hand and arm gently nudged me
stopped me dazedly colliding
with rocks, trees, *goats* would you believe?
Divided, half-knowing, half-naïve
sleepier than Issa's disciples
I moved through shadow-dapples
in a trance-state, somnambulating.
In the car so totally depressed
I'd put this Jew-dude to the test.
Now, no longer negating
but with brain one-hundred percent blank
I climbed the mountain's sunburned flank.

vi

'In the heat we got near Rainbow Bridge;
Galilee lay stretched out below.
Then suddenly on sun-drenched ridge
we saw a scary bearded fellow
a billy-goat in an almond tree
among the blossoms clambered there, free-
of-the-earth and eating the green fruit.
My heart seemed to be following suit
ascending into perilous heights
to taste something young, pure, sweet.
Sharp stones ripped the bare soles of my feet
but deeper down I fantasized delights.
We stopped, laughed at the daring beast
busy with precarious feast.

vii

'I'd had no sleep for two nights.
Laughing still at our aerial goat
funambulist of green heights
we entered now a more remote
glade overlooking Rainbow Bridge.
Moss in fallen leaves made rummage
taking hurtful rocks away for me.
And I, Ishfaq, under a fruit-tree
fell to my knees, finally sat
under a pink almond canopy
depressed and at the same time happy
making of my jacket a blue mat.
"We'll cross that bridge later," Moss said.
I went: "Cool, 'coz right now I'm half-dead."

viii

'And sank cross-legged; Moss did the same:
I smiled at what he offered next.
"Thinkin' of changin' my stage name
to Ramjam you know, for me that checks
more boxes, still sounds Jewish
but gives the oldskool a newish
twist; plus it rhymes with that crazy goat
right out there on long thin limb afloat.
He must have a name like that
the way he pushes the envelope
like some cabledancer on a rope.
I've been, too, a drunken acrobat
all these last forty-eight hours."
His fingers twined with wildflowers

ix

Restlessly, gently as he spoke.
A little red ranunculus
the one called Adonis, never broke
as he turned, without being careless
its bright head, playing pensively
lightly, not doing harm, plaintively
speaking as the poets would say:
"Forty-eight hours from my birthday"
(I watched the dance of his left hand
stroking that red floret of the land)
"yo, I tell you blatantly
feels like I'm in quantum-mode.
Yeah, MC Ramjam's jumped the road.

x

"But my journey's nuttin' to yours."
White rains slanted through the grove
with light breezes. There came a pause
the low song of a rock-dove.
Gazing south through flowering trees
to where in blue haze Lake Galilee's
silvery plane glinted far away
I saw a waterside birthday-
party as Moss painted his big night;
told his so-mysterious story
explained how a celebratory
moment became nocturnal flight.
"Israel's birthday ends in tears
in '48, and mine now appears

xi

"To be goin' the same way
as I gun my wheels to Nazareth
hittin' that predetermined highway
to nearly die on my day of birth
caught in the riots, skull bashed
old black BM burned, my baby trashed.
But *destiny's* transportin' me here."
As the word hung in scent-laden air
my head to his shoulder lay inclined
headscarf trailing over his arm
as he pointed south. In great alarm
I straightened up, state of mind
confused in the sunny paradise
since to be up-close with him was nice.

xii

"I hit the road. But you, driven out
in the Catastrophe long ago
find the courage to come back without
papers, passport, like some commando
Lara Croft travelling by night
with twenty-twenty eyesight.
Me? I ain't goin' no IDF
I'm stayin' stone-free for def:
with friends I fight for the right to rap.
How come Israel's so screwed-up?
'Coz when man speak some go: 'Dude, shut up.'
Can't take that retro-racist crap
I hear from a minority.
An' *fuck* military authority.

xiii

"'Scuze the cuss" he snorted "I'm upset;
jus' like to take you to a movie.
You seen 2Pac in *Juice* yet?"
"No." "It's cold, forget lovey-dovey.
But stayin' on topic (blat, blat, blat)
come stay this summer in al-Nazrat."
"Not simple as all that, Moss."
"Rayyan's mum's cool, 'Ma' Shabash
she'd take care, hide you in Nazareth.
Then we could work on Sinai
plan with Transworld up the road nearby."
"Shatila is a living death
but I have all my fam there
overnight can't, like, disappear."

"Understood." I gave a silly yawn
the dreary thought of Shatila
got me weary and careworn.
Fate seemed even crueller
as pink flower-drifts scattered
through the glade. Then, nothing mattered
Ishfaq, babe, as I, half-reclining
watched almond-bloom softly declining
through the overheated noonday air.
"From al-Andaluz an old story
tells of a snowstorm illusory"
(I heard these words half-aware)
"a make-believe winter-show
blizzard winds made to fiercely blow

"For a princess, whose prince-magician
planted almonds in a grove
near her window, so their fruition
cast fantastic snowflakes for his love
clouding past her castle-balcony"
(his voice was low monotony)
"white on the wind, simulating snow
for a princess who wished to know
other lands, different ways.
She even dreamed an evergreen
something else she'd never seen.
Remember? Way back in those days
long ago in Andalucia
our ancestors held each other dear?"

xvi

'I murmured something as words droned;
conscious his hand brushed my feet.
(I must have been totally zoned
all that smoke inhaled on the backseat.)
Then, Ishfaq, I surrendered
and leaning back on him I slumbered
maybe an hour or more, I dunno.
I dreamed I walked in deep snow
where a tall sun-kissed pine-tree
arrowed up into pure blue.
Dream-within-dream, that pine-tree too
imagined in a distant country
a palm-tree, like him looking upward
tossing her rebel head heavenward.

xvii

'Then I was back in Palestine
tending my grandfather's sheepflocks.
Someone warned of a landmine
as I searched among barbed rocks
barefoot for a little one astray.
I climbed higher the whole day
into the mountains calling her name.
Always echoes came back the same
slapping in my face the name I cried
where a sun of punishment prevailed.
Naked feet felt they had been nailed
by stones of the mountainside.
Like Issa, crucified in my dream
I bled for love in a mountain-stream.

xviii

Waters lapped toes and ankles
playful, sensual, soothing.
I dipped in spinning blue sparkles
torn skin, cooling and smoothing
as a voice flowed silver: "No return"
The Rambam said. "Even if you yearn."
Soft words eased away my pain.
"There were Palestinians in Spain
long ago, perhaps our ancestors... "
I heard, very slowly waking
fragments, traces, dimly making
sense, as if giving answers
to questions hundreds of years old
ripping off some ancient blindfold

xix

Like Laurence when he tore headwrap
in Transworld, under the hill
when I'd dropped my *E Cleansin'* rap.'
Jalilah slowly inhales her fill
from Ishfaq's green zoot, tasty draw.
(Behind her, romantic on the shore
blinks insomniac unsleeping
Beirut, her nightwatches keeping.)
'I woke with arcane words in my head
to find Moss crying at my feet
experience bittersweet
sensation unexpected.
Embarrassed stupefaction
segued to a different reaction.

xx

With his hot tears on my skin
I sensed he was apologising
(each tear burning, too, with my sin)
for all the bitter, agonizing
struggle of my people to be free.
His act of contrition touched me.
Yes, Ishfaq, I knew virgin anger
in confusions of languor
truly still semi-sleeping;
but I felt too a romantic thrill
belonging to some idyll
with pure fury out-of-keeping.
My whorish heart was hammering
as Moss lay there murmuring.

xxi

"Kick him in the face" reason said.
"His tribe ethnically cleansed your bloodline
he coulda raped you here." But heart said:
"His kissing of your feet feels divine
nothing done from arrogance."
(A softer side took this stance.)
I made him stop, half-jokingly;
he was good as I provokingly
told him off. Then we sat side-by-side
holding hands in that God-hallowed place
till I couldn't see his handsome face
as shadows crossed the green hillside.
Then, through hours of sundown
till the daystar lost his solar crown

xxii

'We talked 'bout omnipotent music
proud beauty from worlds above
transmitter of the mystic
soundwave of One Big Love.
"More Slingshot in Palestine"
we chanted in-sync on steep incline
descending hand-in-hand, ledge-by-ledge
as the sun hung red on the world's edge.
"You hit me deep in the car!"
lips confessed on arc of stone
spun in an emotional cyclone
into his arms, like some falling-star.
Ishfaq, I could no longer resist;
and on Rainbow Bridge, at last, we kissed.'

CHAPTER

11

i

Over Beirut the moon tilts her head
cocks an eyebrow, lends an ear
(well, a crater) to what's being said
cranks the ignition of Chrysler
Renegade and rides out the night
heading for Jounieh's overbright
playground of pretend happiness.
(Her chromed 4X4's built to impress
sure on the floor, with V12 traction
to get her out of trouble
fast when some alcoholic rabble
runs riot, faction-to-faction
pimps-v-clients inevitably.
Loud brothels vent these equally.)

ii

The super-nightclubs are on fire
with 'virgins' winding in hotpants
backsides, magnetising desire
in gangsters, businessmen, heirophants
all sprawled in the Grand Lodge of false love:
lewd boozers, dog-priests, giving a shove
when sleazy half-pissed onanism
threatens to slosh some girl with jism
spray some tart from beneath a table.
The rites of these shadow-men
the issue of their lethal semen
mock the one whose long sable
hair trails down in ashtray's dust
doing in these nights the thing she must

iii

When she's enslaved at seventeen
younger too (no one's that fussy).
This lass does needles, easily seen
in the scrawny arse of the hussy
just another piece of pussy sold
where virginity's price is gold
got through arms or drugs or both.
This goddess has forsworn her troth
come to be unfaithful to herself.
(Hymen in a broken heart weeps.)
This prostitute no longer keeps
that photograph of her other self
her dear boy, in cheap little purse;
lives beneath oblivion's curse.

iv

White slaves, Abyssinian maids
minus passports, souls confiscated
the lost-and-found of vice-squad raids
with international, complicated
histories behind squalid lives:
here are teenage proxy-wives
bodies just game-zones to him
for whom the world's a sexual gym.
Outside Madame Luna cruises
through Jounieh, goes her usual route
purring down backstreets of Beirut
using her crescentic disguises
all her noms-de-guerre as femme-fatale
To track her silver moonboat: futile.

v

Luna's more interested
in our idyllic narrative
than in the just-attested
history of girls forced to live
by the sweat of their private parts
in prostitution's sordid marts.
That's why she's closely listening
(silver Chrysler glistening)
as Jalilah takes up her romance;
her slender ankles moonlit
where surf breaks on a golden spit
at Pigeon Rock, by night-sea's expanse.
(Of course, the moon's heard nothing yet:
prepare four quatrains and a couplet.)

'On the night-road to the Blue Line
we hardly spoke; to judge by Sajjid's
big smile drug-deal had gone jus' fine.
Tokin' a weed-loaded firecracker
jokin' 'n' smokin' at high speed
Moss still linked with my baby-finger
hidden down on cool black leather.
Secretly we stayed bound-together
interfused by sympathetic light
rays of harmonious energy
lending us an air of synergy.
Everyone sensed vibes were right.
(But everything's proper messed-up now:
I'll never get to Sinai no-how.)

'We did a left at Kiryat Shmona:
climbing to Lebanon stars glimmered.
(Bound for the hills on a fast-burner
between us big emotions shimmered.)
Flying toward the Blue Line
a ripped Rayyan, sky-high, mood fine
started talkin' up good times coming.
We all vibed with; simply succumbing.
"The Mafqat: sublime desert-venue
functioning as stargate and wormhole
for Slingshot Hiphop's cosmic role.
That whole gone-crazy Serious crew"
(Ray' was babblin' like a buffoon)
"hittin' Sinai from the UK soon."

'With the Bimmer's engine screamin'
suddenly I noticed the smell;
had the feelin' I was dreamin'
but knew that all noticed it as well.
Ishfaq, the bomblastic car stank.
Zahret el Kolch! Palpable and rank:
strong-strong odours of cannabis
which no one could possibly miss.
I sensed the perfume of that resin
(transhipped in bulk, concentrated
narcotic-of-choice often freighted
through Shatila by night-liaison).
The moon listens-up and leans closer
following our black landcruiser.

'Sajjid lowered his front right
letting into car interior
oxygen of the mountain, black night-
air, his purposes ulterior:
dispersing - all clear now -
by obvious means, anyhow
fumes of the turbocharger:
omnipresent stench of ganja.
Sweetness, I know that car was loaded.
Under floor-panels drugs were rammed
near the gas-tank kif was crammed
perhaps in special rims commoded:
the Zahret el Kolch was everywhere.'
(Israeli government's nightmare.

x

Arms are smuggled at the Blue Line.
Freedom-fighters, Hizbollah, Hamas
inward-bound to captive Palestine
nailed a hundred years upon her cross
often rendezvous, pass over here
at night, infiltrating where
security is super-tight
slipping through dangerous twilight.
Yet Israel fears one thing more
than Semtex, Zilzal and Katyusha
coming all the way from Russia:
the drug Israeli kids adore;
Zahret el Kolch, which frees the mind
for that reason hated and maligned.

xi

The moon is closely monitoring
(making certain she hears right)
both X5, northward motoring
and the lonely shoreline in the night.
She glides between two narrations
two nocturnal situations
one in the Finger of Galilee
one by Mediterranean Sea:
superslick, quick in her manoeuvres
physically fluid in her phases.
(The moon can be in two places
at once using smoke and mirrors
natural quicksilver magic.
Luna's her ancient, inner logic.)

xii

'Rayyan mentioned a double-act:
Moss 'n' yours-truly in contraflow.
I said: "Call us *'Suicide Pact'*."
Ray' went: "*Jalilah n Romeo*".
Er, hilarious? Yet as we laughed
a helicopter's rotorshaft
thundered across the Hula Valley
a big gunship hovering vastly
in the darkness. We went silent.
Familiar, not anomalous
the thing still sounded ominous:
iron whirlybird hell-sent.
Sajjid jumped in against the flyby:
"You two will blaze in Sinai."

xiii

'He spoke kinda uneasily
as the gunship ranged over Hula.
"We make that gig" drawled Moss breezily
as chopper, now perpendicular
buzzed the car, flying like a bullet.
Laurence, who'd been a long time quiet
went: "Jah bless the Serious crew."
These words dispelled bad voodoo
squashed a pessimistic atmosphere.
Then Moss said somethin' way-cool
as gunship, like vampire-ghoul
droned, intimidated from midair:
"Two nights back my burning need
was running in the dark for weed."

xiv

'"Addicted to the thought of hash
psychologically wallowing"
(slipstream's phantom-roar, backwash
sways the moon in night-flight following)
"I thought it was the Zahret el Kolch
I was lookin' for, needed so much
smoke which sets your soul aglow.
Rayyan, my bredda, my proper bro:
he's the reason I cut loose
lef' my so-called brothers, petty
walked-out my own birthday-party.
Pursuit of weed was jus' an excuse.
Peeps, for me this freakin' roadtrip
's'all about intense friendship."

xv

'The chopper died, banked-off in an arc.
We heard a silver stream fragmenting
saw Manara's spangle in the dark
climbing gradients unrelenting.
"I burned halfway-to-hell Friday-night;
there was nearly one-less-Israelite.
I was three-quarters barbecued
when Shaza (more love, Shaz') rescued.
But man survived to hear Jalilah
spit baddest, hardest lyrics ever
blatantly lay-down and deliver
superconscious Slingshot, rapstar."
(On backseat his hand and mine
made a deeper intertwine.)

xvi

'"See, Rastas are also Israelites.
Abrahamic revelation
today, right now, *tonight* unites
one planetary Rastanation
under Jah. I Vibes 'n' Bob Marley:
rock-prophets for our time, holy
messengers of Tetragrammaton.
The old secular automaton
zoned on booze 'n' chemical drugs
has no future, dead already.
Stateside? Rap's gettin' ready
to transcend the mindset of thugs.
Yo, peeps in Japan (makes so much sense)
are singin' with Jamaican accents.

xvii

'"Rasta's changed the world forever
a natural mystic's in the air.
Black, yellow, mixed-race, whatever
don't matter: Aquarian time's here.
Big, broad and massive on the frontline
stand up for your rights in Palestine!
(Dreadwave's comin' down from the sun.
That's wha' man been sayin' from day-one.)"
Rayyan went: "For real, my roots-bredda
I know where you're comin' from:
Slingshot Hiphop's droppin' a love-bomb.
Like Rimbaud said 'I is another'
and, you, bruv, show me daily
one love from a righteous Israeli."'

xviii

Luminescence of moonlight
on the night-sea seems now to unlock
secrets glittering just out of sight
in Jalilah's eyes at Pigeon Rock.
Yet she holds back in her account
hesitates (premeditated taunt?)
'It's late, Ishfaq, I must hurry
Tasneem 'n' Tareef will worry.
As you know my father's health is poor;
knife-grinding with a three-wheeled handcart
has nearly broken that dear man's heart.
Imagine trundling door-to-door
crying aloud "Scissors and knives."
Once upon a time we'd other lives

xix

'Nobles of the old homeland
many moons ago. And now this:
a proud landowner, horseman grand
traipsing through Shatila's shit 'n' piss
sharpening blades never sharp enough.
Tareef's memories play so rough.'
Jalilah fingers the single dread
fallling discreetly behind her head.
'Honeybabe, don't pause me *there*;
let me roll another zoot.'
(Ishfaq is in hot pursuit
of more mysteries, all's far from clear.)
'How the bleep did you come to harm?
Did a bullet do that to your arm?'

'Trust me, it'll keep for nex' time
let's leave things at a high point:
Sunday-night I saw a war-crime.
Don't bother with another joint
the two T's are waitin' up for me.
Will I never, ever be free?
Am I not to escape Shatila
Jalilah Zahlan, freewheeler
free as the racing birds of Aziz?
I suppose I'm asking for the sky
when it's impossible to fly:
young girls are so hard to please.
Godsent fate: I must not attack it.'
A tear drips on her blue bomber-jacket.

xxi

(Luna's often seen babes in tears
teenage Eurotrash abducted
the currency of flesh-racketeers
girls mysteriously conducted
far from their homes to the Middle East.
Women's rights are, to say the least
anaemic in Beirut, deathly-pale.
It's easy to trade behind the veil
smuggle white-goods all wrapped in black.
Cairo and LA are actually
in some ways, pornographically
for instance, close: nymphomaniac
cities given to prostitution,
old ambiguous institution.)

xxii

Love's tears are salt waves breaking
on an indifferent coastline.
Each one shatters, earthshaking
ocean-wall of aquamarine
the cyclic end of every surge
toward the land, cruel verge
where yearning for the other batters
on stone, in multicoloured spatters
fills the void with rainbows of heartbreak.
The forsaken sea cries one vast tear
longing for her lover insincere.
How much more pain can ocean take
as she smashes salty kisses
born from loneliest abysses?

CHAPTER
12

i

Tasneem is having a bad night.
Sleepless Tareef coughs, expectorates
airways exploding like gelignite
till a coughing-fit abates.
His is a bronchitic physique
rainy winters have made him weak;
working street-zones dawn-to-dusk
has left him a depleted husk.
Tasneem fears it could be TB
the doctors want to see x-rays.
Now disturbance from alleyways
below wakes him, he gropes to pee
staggering blindly through tiny flat
spluttering and frightening the cat.

ii

Insomnolence tonight
on Tasneem's part is mostly about
Jalilah - below, street-fight
escalates with curse and shout -
who got back late from Pigeon Rock
hot with fever, giving Mum a shock.
'Ma Zahlan put her straight to bed
vinegar compress to forehead
rubbed cold feet with sesame oil
placed in fresh socks onion slivers
to counteract the shivers.
Now Tasneem lies here in turmoil
worrying about boyfriends and drugs;
bothers Tareef, who just coughs and shrugs.

iii

Dawn enters, stage right, on tiptoes
trying not to wake anyone
a harlequin in blue-and-rose.
(Ironic, this rising of the sun
in pleasant and comedic outfit
when all below are so hard-hit
submitting to so much, each soul.)
But see, daystar on dawn-patrol
illuminates someone on housetop
who kneels - prays? - in black-and-white
combats, camouflage jacket
trainers (which didn't cost a packet
Nike clones) keffiyah in-flight
twin-coloured in the wind fluttering
all of a duplex patterning.

One name repeats in his prayer.
'Show me where my Mushtaq flies
I ask, implore. *Mushtaq!* Ah, there!'
A shake-of-the-head as hope dies;
hope soon followed by another
which a cloud manages to smother
after a second bird is spotted.
Here we find Big Aziz, squatted
beside pink bougainvillea, feeling
really fearful for his great black.
'Mushtaq, my hero, please come back.'
He rocks on fake trainers, kneeling
asking Allah to send home the bird
bringing from his Shaza her true word.

Two homers went to Nazareth
secretly, three days ago, smuggled
there by truck, hidden underneath
old tyres and tarpaulins muddled.
One, winner of the race from Gaza
carried his proposal to Shaza;
the white hen of Nahr el-Bared
wore a note asking her to wed.
Answer will return with Mushtaq
his brave storm-riding Egyptian
his marvellous racing-pigeon:
he will bring her message back.
What's that, his champion in the clouds
where, southward, morning-mist still shrouds?

vi

Another speck of false promise.
Every morning Aziz comes here
to scan the heavens, his premise:
Mushtaq will bring word through the air.
Is this another trick of dawn-light
simulating his bird in flight
his ebony pure-bred sky-king
in his element, on-the-wing?
'It's him circling, look, no?' Aziz squints
as an arrow falls from the zenith:
plummeting black windlord white with
telltale brightest underwing glints.
The prayers of Aziz have not been spurned:
'Mushtaq, royal one, you have returned.'

vii

The homer folds his flights descending
at one-hundred miles-per-hour
outspread tail half-extending
to aerodynamically empower
guide to the tiny trapboard
over which he's so often soared
towering above Shatila
watched by Aziz, Jalilah.
Skydive ends with black wings fanning
in the last few seconds of descent:
braking of precision equipment;
with Aziz rapturously scanning
every move and whistling low
as iyad comes rapidly below.

viii

Mushtaq spins, trumpeting one time
on landing-platform of his loft
swiftly telling his sublime
story in liquid tones so soft
boasting his great poem of the sky.
(The hens within look up at his cry.)
Now he traps through wire-gate;
now Aziz reads of his fate
removing from metal leg-ring
(trembling, holding his breath)
the message from Nazareth.
What word from Her does Mushtaq bring?
His cry of joy reaches Jalilah
sleeping (with help of an inhaler).

ix

In breezeblock rooftop bedroom
Eminem, the blue-eyed, the adored
studies our heroine through dawn-gloom:
during the night her temperature's soared.
Is he concerned for his teenage fan
acting the perfect gentleman?
Is she like Hailie Jade for him?
Or will he, by some twisted whim
pull a gun and shoot her down
side-splitting a nasty-arse laugh
(after signing an autograph)
Slim Shady from the bad side of town?
Jalilah's having a schizophrenic
nightmare: hallucinogenic.

Fever-driven is the dream
in which she crazily rehearses
subconscious feelings extreme;
where certainty reverses
suddenly without warning:
memories, desires churning.
By her feelings she's convicted
yet her emotions are conflicted.
Ultra-rebellious nature
turns against one she's fallen-for;
makes her name herself 'shameful whore'
hating this sentimental creature.
She fears a romantic phantom
dreadlocked and 'wasim' (handsome)

xi

Dreams of a sanatorium
where shadows of yesterday
amplify her delirium;
where many murdered haunt noonday
where stagnant memories recreate
the massacre of Forty-Eight;
where only lunatics can live
because of the past's abrasive
presence in the atmosphere.
Now in a narrative-twist
he's her gaoler-psychiatrist;
and strangely she wants this, feels no fear.
(The fever's vicissitudes
play with verisimilitudes.)

xii

Prone but restless in crumpled bed
with a temperature in the top-room
high in her concrete breezeblock shed
she burns-up in a functional tomb.
Eminem, modern seraph
angel with sardonic laugh
rap's inflammatory anarch
chats 'bout old times in trailer-park;
compares those with hers in Shatila
going: 'No real difference:
two shitheaps'. 'Kinda makes sense.'
(See the dry lips of Jalilah
moving as she tries to reply.
What's that wing-beating in the sky?)

xiii

Delirious in bed of rags
she suffocates as cinematic
dreams untwist, consciousness zigzags.
The air in her ramshackle attic
is stale, yesterday's sea-breeze
is nowhere; in chesty wheeze
she confesses to pinup idol
dark feelings suicidal
urges to cut her slim wrists
old compulsions to self-harm
at thighs, ankles and forearm.
See the clenching of her fists
as she sleeptalks out-of-her-head
rocking in her cheap cot-bed.

Night-terrors of childhood are back.
Here comes old sleep paralysis
creeping up in a dawn-attack
with spooky, eerie proneness
as if a corpse had come from below
someone buried many moons ago
onto the sleeper clambering
a foul ghost remembering
what it was like to be alive:
the nightmare smothering weight
seeming now to asphyxiate
Jalilah as, fighting to survive
she heaves-off phantom (with bedclothes)
achieves at last a peaceful doze.

Crisis is over. Fever's fire
still simmers-on in her bloodstream
but, tangled still in mental barbed-wire
wingbeats sound, cooling, in her dream.
(Is she now asleep or awake
as her bro cries out at daybreak
as Shatila's dawn-peace shatters?
She's in the present, all that matters
conscious only of subtle thunder
whirring of powerful wings
as some dream-messenger brings
an aerial mood of wonder
takes her to a high place of sunlight
calm after her delirious night.)

Look! Jalilah's sceptical headshake
at sense of having been here before
where, incredibly, a snowflake
tumbles through a pink arbour.
Is this old Samchuna perhaps
far away from everyday maps?
(In a worried mother's bad dream
she's with druggy Ishfaq: poor Tasneem.)
She hears a heavyhearted lovebird
crying in the shadows of her fate
calling through the sunlight for a mate
song forever unanswered.
In this high wooded timberland
is she transported to fairyland?

She recognizes Rainbow Bridge
and the pink glade, beautiful.
He's beside on the fragranced ridge:
powerful, powerless, pitiful.
(He has kissed her feet in repentance;
she has made her show of resistance.)
Now, on arch of coloured stone
flowing together, their words are blown
by a sudden supernatural wind
transmitted mysteriously
southwards over all Galilee.
Their two freestyling raps combined
fill a dream-sky from this bright hillside
thundering-out, strangely amplified.

xviii

From the zenith with colours ablaze
horizon-to-horizon aglow
overwhelmed she drops her gaze
from the meridian, glances below.
Lowering her eyes she looks beneath
as they freestyle on one wavelength
(while Moss stares endlessly above).
Suddenly she knows that she's in love.
(An impossible dream-vista
where bell-like African music tolls
for a hundred-thousand souls
gathered in one vast arena
stretching from Cairo to Baghdad.)
'OMG, this is so damn rad.'

xix

Hear Jalilah with fevered handsign
whispering - but not in Arabic -
Ishfaq's acronym-of-the-divine
faint in the stifling acoustic
soundstage of her tiny room;
where, in early-morning gloom
dread of God wakes in her heart.
Amazing, this sense of the Apart
bearing-down in holiness
changing this stale, sweaty air
into something aromatic, rare:
a new atmosphere, no less;
as if a mountain-dove had flown-by
coming down with freshness from on-high.

She studies him; he looks faraway.
(Aziz with Shaza's letter kneels
beside Jalilah in ecstasy.
'Sis, she said "Yes."') Wheels-within-wheels
turn suddenly till he's disappeared.
She stands all alone with a weird
weightless sensation in her spine
tingling, pleasurable, divine.
(As shout from brother Aziz
in time perpetually extends
as dreaming marvellously ends:
his cry somehow means 'Action-freeze.')
Jalilah wakes and scrutinizes
her brother's face, recognizes.

xxi

'Any improvement, sis?' he whispers
conscious he's been preoccupied;
now concerned for his sister's
health, she having very nearly died.
Mushtaq in his cupped hands sits quiet
recouping after heroic flight
happily triumphant in return.
'Sajjid has passports, Jah', so don' burn.
We meet at the Rafah Crossin'
in Aylul. In Aylul, Inshallah!
What else? That dreadlocked Jewman Musa
exploded a military coffin...'
Mushtaq's eyes are bigger than moons.
Jalilah drifts back into dreamzones.

xxii

Again the sky's strangely coloured
ordered with an interplay of clouds
whose metallized tints, hues altered
remind of those bright blues-and-reds
filming small pools, roadside puddles
when lubricant swirls and muddles
in fascinating complexes
labyrinthine vortexes:
green-and-purple-burnished spirals
kaleidoscopes of spilled engine-oil
helical, reflective as tinfoil;
kinetic windows of cathedrals
shrines found by the wayside sometimes
when dirty water swirls and transforms.

UNHOLYLAND
BOOK THREE:
THE SINAI

CHAPTER

1

i

In the star-temple of conception
another poem comes to birth
in fiery pangs of new perception
as sunlight strikes the dark side of earth
spinning out of widespread negation
doubt, denial, desolation.
Screams of painful genesis
alternate with ecstasis
as a third-born song surges
in paroxysms of agony
(through a night of ebony)
with bloody pushes, red urges
(out of absolute interdiction)
out of uterine constriction.

ii

In obscurity a poem's born
speechless, gasping, half-strangled
by its own birth-cord at dawn
star-covered and star-spangled;
as drugs are poured into the spine
as endorphins and dopamine
flood the heart of the birth-mother
(who is Muse, of course, to none other
than embattled Voice of Kings Cross
still striving for Her blessing
still to variance confessing)
with haemophilic blood-loss
the condition of delivery
for poems of brilliant livery.

iii

From Her great womb of what is true
come these sonnets into sunlight;
from tremendous skies of royal blue
from turquoise-lands of The Mafqat
(with sunsets of metallic pinks).
All here is written as She thinks
worth to be disseminated
where so many have awaited
problematic and dissident
truths from Our Lady of Sinai;
who makes these earthbound lines to fly
upward with transcendent argument
toward the zenith which She holds
in Her hand, full of blues and golds.

Gazing down, She sees (and shows)
over Innsbruck, in the Brenner Pass
cruising through supernatural snows
in slow-motion, with inertial-mass:
eight pantechnicons, big roadrangers
(posing to motorists real dangers)
vast roadtrains of the transit-route
gigantic flat-nosers, nothing cute:
Volvos and Mercs, Scanias and MANs
accelerating on saddlebacks
sliding round hairpins, switchbacks
like metal-skinned ophidians
dancing to a sinuous groove.
(Some serious convoy on the move.)

Check these monsters, well-laden.
Hear them grinding in low-gear
hot transmissions overdriven;
drivers scanning mirrors from nearside, double-clutching at each shift
as round icy switchbacks they drift;
with that technique known as 'floating'
(better driver-health promoting)
keeping crash-box disengaged
without the curse of pedal-crushing
(through the Brenner passes rushing
where wars of fire-and-ice are waged).
Ah, the Goddess has brought forth
giants of the European North

vi

Whose knees go wrong with RSI
as tendonitis fires their joints;
who stress their lower forearms, try
to crash through natural breaking-points
as four limbs take repetitive strains
multiplying rheumatism's pains.
Deep-vein thrombosis? Ever-pumping
a clunky pedal, clumping
foot-to-floor, hour-by-hour
(never slackening in the least)
can easily provoke *that* beast;
regulating engine-power
manually, mountain-driving;
human spirit just surviving

vii

Laden indeed. Such landtrains
through the Italian Alps snaking
with tailbacks in the granny-lanes
(thank God the scenery's breathtaking)
leave high Sarentino filthy
make Mezzaselva's air unhealthy
with diesel-stench, acrid, intense
the Tyrolean air thick and dense
with particulate. Sometimes
stoned drivers (in sedentary mode)
sleeping at the wheel lose the road
on twisting, turning mountain-climbs.
(Sit still in a cab-over a week:
bye-bye that truck-driving mystique.)

viii

A-million-miles-away at midday
high on methedrine and mind-escape
(skillet-face flying-down motorway
inflamed liver in bad shape)
dreaming back to sleazy sexcapade
in some Inzing lay-by gettin' laid
you fail to swerve around a 'gator
to this world say: 'See ya later.'
(Good riddance to joints like meat-grinders.)
A death-tunnel lies straight ahead;
an H-bomb flashes in your head.
(Watch out for the old blinders
ten-wheeling through the rainy Brenner
all the way here from old Vienna.)

ix

Let's stay in the land of the living
keep it real, avoid the disconnect
hold to a course unswerving
zoom-in on primary subject:
eight-truck convoy on the move.
(A promise: poem shall improve.)
Are septum-piercings, eyeball-tattoos
mohicans, seat-length dreadlocks, clues
to who's headed where, what's doing?
(Cab-soundsystem's cocoa-butter
not the rig of your average trucker.
Hey, if yours truly is reviewing:
'This rich, dark, velvety sound
absolutely does not fool around.')

We catch riffs of conversation:
'... so that's how I joined the world's most
rock'n'roll aid-organization.'
(Music's going like the Holy Ghost
truck's out in the hammer-lane
flying like a huge freight-train
following the ten-wheel in front.)
Driver gives a happy grunt;
she's about twenty-five maybe
possibly pushing thirty;
her passenger's modishly dirty
one enormous black military
combat-boot straddling the dash
as he knocks from red-hot spliff grey ash.

'Watch-out for snakes in the grass;
Italians love radar-traps.
Back there in the Brenner Pass
we got the better of speed-cops
but here? I'm gonna tell Law
up ahead in the front-door
we can relax, we doin' very
good to catch that Greek ferry.'
(Dreadlocked speaker dials smartphone.)
'Lorcan, bruv, slow down, the views.
Law, listen, bro, let's just cruise.
Man, you goin' like a cyclone;
it's on-the-spot-fines y'know
'n' cops here're more corrupt than 'ho.'

xii

Hey, check that logo on the cab-crest
up there on streamlined fairing.
What does that symbol suggest
what's that hieroglyph declaring?
A red London double-decker
('Woah, das ist sehr lecker.')
trails a cloud of red, green and gold
all around our lonely blue world.
Drivers on the E45
blow horns and wave like crazy
as they clock this Rasta daisy
meaningful, quaint, so-attractive
high up on the crown of each truck.
One dude even screams: 'Viel gluck.'

xiii

Gazing down from (Her) blue zenith
all carry supercool logo;
every one of these mammoth
roadtrains (count 'em: eight-in-a-row)
descending mountain autostrada
at high speed, driven with ardor
sports this livery, this brilliant
so-original, so-different
mindblowing wonderful motif.
We heard this bunch were gonna let rip:
this has to be the Serious Road Trip.
'Hey, dude, beyond all belief.
Blow your horn, give this crew their propers.
These peeps are total showstoppers.'

'Didn't they go out to Kosovo
sometime in the late nineties
not really all that long ago?
Didn't they throw full-on parties
in Bosnia, then bus kiddies out?
War-children, that's what they're about.'
'Correct, they bought an old Routemaster
in London (nothing mightier)
paid for out of unemployment-dole;
drove it into the Balkan States
ignoring suicidal death-rates
not a bulletproof-vest in the whole
vehicle, clowns not guns on board.
Rainbow Warriors: does that strike a chord?

xv

Our driver is very thoughtful
poised behind big steering-wheel:
bewitching, regal, very youthful
driving her MAN. (You would kneel
in the highway before this queen
this nonviolent mujahideen
in charge of huge ten-wheeler.)
She's a total showstealer:
turquoise teeshirt, tight blue jeans;
headwrap some dayglo stocking;
trendy pink Raybans blocking
glare from gigantic windscreen's
prismatic flashing wraparound.
Hey, this woman's so bleepin' sound.

xvi

She'd say 'Who me? I'm just a clown
forget the queen, a weird scene
all that toadying goin' down
High Grovel 'n' all that's inbetween:
I'm just here to make peeps laugh.
If you want my autograph
no-way, I'm not a star, I'm a moon
spinnin' round my life, a goon, a loon.'
Well, sometimes she shines like the sun.
And now, on the highway to Trieste
she's on the up-curve of her life-quest
heading southward on the long run
down to Palestine and Sinai.
(Hey, when you're making moves don't time fly?)

xvii

'So, Skidz, say how things kickstarted
for you, man? How came the message
to head for territory uncharted
when you booked the first bus-passage
over the English Channel to France?'
Tika checks her passenger askance;
'Tika' (from Connaught) her convoy-name.
"See, I played a waiting-game
through the Eighties, then I saw the light.
Winter evening; Camden High Street:
a random cinema's tempting heat
sucked me out of the aimless night.
See, I had a presentiment.
Flick was no disappointment.

xviii

'First thing I noticed was the smell
through the foyer: totally rank.
Racing up a tatty stairwell
breathing very deep, mind blank:
African headcharge everywhere
(you just had to suck it from the air)
I entered an abyss of laughter:
whole flea-pit was full of Rasta.
Film was Cecil B. DeMille:
"Ten Commandments". (Better believe it
not a whiteskin there to receive it.)
That night for true I travelled uphill
by coincidence bizarre
met the brothers who trust in Jah.

xix

'Then everything fell into place.
Squatting a bus-depot in Kings Cross
in Battle Bridge, we called it 'Airbase'.
Dub and One Big Love: the ethos.
(House was comin' up, the new wave.)
Right there we did the world's first rave
with Wildchild 'n' Mutoid Waste
Sequenzi 'n' Tech-Tribe: barefaced
madness, lightshows from Go Green
acrobats, fire-eaters, clowns
totem-poles, therapeutic splashdowns.
We launched "The London Love Scene."'
Tika glances left with slight
flicker (driving to Skidz' right).

xx

'An old red London bus in there
a 73 (remembered well)
engine gone, bodywork fair
became my pad: in red shell
my bedroom was on the top-deck
my office in the lower wreck.
That's where I dreamed up SRT:
one stormy night it just came to me.
We'd buy a Routemaster 'n' drive it
worldwide in the name of one love.
(I was sleeping on the deck above.)
No way did I contrive it:
the Road Trip started with this dream
by the River Fleet's sacred stream.'

xxi

'For real? The Fleet, I heard 'bout that...'
(Tika accepts spleef from Skid.)
'Didn't someone go mad in a squat
'n' write an epic poem?' 'He did
I've met the bloke. Heard him spit live
for four-thousand peeps in Ninety-five
when they launched his *Vale Royal*
at - if you please - the Albert Hall.
"Voice of Kings Cross" they call him now.
Spesh has read, says it's way-cool
futuristic but same time old-skool;
psychogeographical, no-brow
literature like Rimbaud:
Deep London, if you need to know.'

xxii

With Euro-plates and GB stickers
eight pantechnicons fly south.
Marijuana-smoke in blue whiskers
trails from Tika's half-open mouth.
What's the payload of these roadtrains
(now safely back in granny-lanes)
full of superhip Londoners
clowns, DJs, dancers, weirdos, stoners?
We'll have to see, time will tell.
Coasting down past Lago di Garda
saving gas with the 'road-glider'
God bless this strange caravel
sailing swiftly into the unknown.
Life itself is a combat-zone.

CHAPTER

2

i

The sense of an urban graveyard:
debris of collapsed concrete
skyscrapers fallen earthward;
from time-to-time the bittersweet
scent of death on evening-air
blending enigmatically here
with frankincense and camphor
floating on the breath of the seashore
as blue smoke coils from a silver tray
carried aloft, funneling behind
as shadows through dark ruins wind.
What procession of obscure feast-day
under way in this twilight
threads a rubble-littered bombsite?

Fragrance spirals, uplifting
medicinal, faintly vanillic:
sweet clouds of benzoin drifting.
Suddenly flares a candlestick.
Now bright-sounding handclapping
palms in time together slapping
comes echoing: a pilgrimage
(through reek of raw sewage)
appears to navigate these ruins
as, mingling with styrax and myrrh
odours to fragrances defer
(as poisons to antitoxins).
The besieged must be marrying
among themselves, merrymaking.

iii

Hand-drums sound in shades of gloom
upbeat nuptial cadence.
That man in white must be the groom
so young, lit by incandescence
as flambeau sways. He's just a boy.
(It would seem nothing can destroy
the dream of two hearts to unite
when lovers keep that flame alight
though thousands lie buried alive
by blitzkrieg and bombardment
in blockade and besiegement.
Somehow the brave still contrive
to honour love when life's in eclipse
when the sky's about to collapse.)

iv

Here's a fortress behind the world's back
hidden in the land of suffering
where the sun at noon turns black
with sacrificial offering.
Here's a city ramped on a hot coast
where souls burn in the lowermost
furnaces of genocide.
Here rage Baal-fires of infanticide
in the killing-fields of Samaria;
here a husband dances in madness
wife's corpse on shoulders, his sadness
mounting into dark hysteria.
Here the meaning of a siren:
the dismemberment of children.

v

Welcome to the country of shadows
hidden deep in the world's core.
Orphan-gangs teem here; war-widows
with raw memories endure
where firestorms of sorrow
rage continuously below
blazing-up with a black sun's light
(fiercer than some airstrike tonight).
Down here with incendiary anger
fury erupts in red explosions
detonating doomsday emotions.
And blood explodes as human magma
born in the volcano of that heart
which has seen its own flesh torn apart.

vi

This is Gaza, metropolis
sloping away from a sunken sea
(poisoned cesspit) populace
pent in limbo indefinitely
under seige by land and ocean.
In a city hot-as-an-oven
beside eerily empty beaches
where a repetitive sun bleaches
everything into sameness
in that sickness called 'occupation'
under humiliation
a people completely tameless
call on prophet Muhammad: 'Save us.'
call upon Allah, upon Jesus.

vii

Benzoin and myrrh, bittersweet
swirl and gyre in the sky of mind.
Somewhere far-off a drumbeat
very softly seems to unbind
the hypnotising spell of fear
falling as a faintly-chanted prayer.
Yet rhythms, with exhilaration
bring a new air of frustration:
hand-bells, handclaps - diminishing -
remind us of a wedding-party
(we weren't invited, what a pity)
through the darkness vanishing.
The besieged are marrying
among themselves, merrying.

viii

Despite an affirmative role
Gazans still fool about marriage;
say 'A life-sentence of the soul
traps a man in a beautiful cage'
poke fun at one who wears a yoke
becomes a beast, no more 'a bloke'
wearing round his shoulders proudly
harness, while fat lady-wife loudly
orders him, overloaded: 'Left, right'
goads him ahead through pouring rain.
And yet the custom must remain
since we've seen, this terrible night
touching proof that love survives
even as the demon warhead dives.

ix

Our fatalistic eyes lift in hope
(trusting in God-given evidence
over a rubble-strewn slope
following trails of frankincense)
to see where the holy smoke is going.
A glimpse of the bride in flowing
finery, in her womanly pride
weeping father by her side
(we might even hear a few jokes)
would lighten mood, fairly sombre.
This night's been harsh. Shocked and sober
ceremonial rites of these folks
sacramental celebrations
matrimonial situations

x

Might restore our faith in love
shaken with these towers to the ground.
Isn't that a white fantail dove
released with wing-whirring sound
from the depths of this battered town
between tall buildings overthrown
fluttering up into night-sky?
(Where, in stellar glory, we espy
eastward the Summer Triangle.)
From heart-shaped basket see her climb
flying as symbol of peacetime
like an all-forgiving angel
upward to the Northern Cross.
And here indeed is pathos:

xi

A man in white, a prince of light
questions, asks, as children lie
in dusty vaults of a bombsite
sealed away from the night-sky:
'Why must these go down this way
crushed under towers which splay
their limbs (as if still jumping-out
to ambush Mum and Dad without
realising no-one's surprised)?
The raptures of innocence
brought to this for no offence;
our babes in rubble-graves, sacrificed
smashed into the ground like refuse:
military-industrial child-abuse.'

xii

On edge (but unafraid of death)
we've caught-up and we overhear.
By many roads (out-of-breath)
we're going all the way to Beit Lahiya
beyond Jibaliya camp, north on
the old coast-road to Ashkelon;
where the whole world stood disgraced
when two Cast Lead tank-shells laid waste
the UNWRA school at al-Fakhura:
white phosphorous to eat the flesh
of children, six and seven, fresh
victims for Baal the child-devourer.
'Weddings?' Disoriented, shattered
some ask: 'Has love ever mattered?'

xiii

'Can life go on as normal
when they return our infant-dead
from realms of the infernal
with shrapnel lesions to the head?'
(Questions posed by those who walk
past Jibaliya camp, wretched talk
among the wedding-guests. And yet
while most break-out in cold sweat
there's too, a mood of excitement
as, slightly lemony, balsamic
spicy fragrance - Islamic
Christian, Judaic - sends enticement
saying 'Come away from sorrow;
still be strong enough to follow.')

Impossible to see the groom's face
as he leads his caravan along
gliding through a night of null space;
as a dull, distant, ominous song
hums and murmurs from the zenith
like the mantra of some Goliath
brooding over Gaza: hubristic
(something in the sound sadistic)
making a Dajjalic counterpoint
to chanting of wedding-singers
jingling of bell-ringers
dancing on without constraint
to doumbek: bright rimshot beats
echoing through unlighted streets.

Some guests look up, briefly mumble
'To hell with that mother-in-law
who forever has to grumble
person peeping round the door
with flat-as-a-pancake phrases
sticking her long nose into places
where she has no right to be;
bad-mouthing; perpetually
belittling when she should shut-up.'
'Nah, that's the Zenana' someone drawls
'nag who suspiciously eyeballs
husband's every move, big dustup
imminent if he steps out of line:
wife whose main function is to whine.'

xvi

Listen, an explosion of laughter
mingles with finger-bells and zills;
hilarity rings from our zaffa
winding through Gaza in the sand-hills.
'Confusion to the zenana.'
(Detect a whiff of marijuana?)
Other smoke bathes the city faintly
tonight (aroma less saintly):
ammoniac stench of Qassam-fire:
rockets which give the oppressor
the chance to scream 'Transgressor'
when all who require truth entire
understand exactly the reverse
throw that barefaced lie out on its arse.

xvii

(An apology for Forty Eight
even at this late point in time
would go some way to stem the hate
building with crime upon war-crime.
Study Einstein's letter, harangue
launched against the Stern Gang
April tenth, following Deir Yassin
the day after that obscene
bloodbath, sadistic, sickening;
in which he names as criminal
Zionism: with subliminal
propaganda, slickened spin
electing itself 'peace-activist'
when Is-nah-real is the 'Terrorist'.)

xviii

'Here's a joke. At three in the morning
suddenly the lawn wants cutting.
Hubby Shazad's smoking, yawning;
Zenny the Scold: "Iffing and butting?"
(No public parks or even children's
playspaces here, let alone gardens.)
"In pitch-darkness trim the grass
woman? Your PMT will pass."
"Hot damn, husband, cut that lawn tonight.
You'll never get it done by day
(when no one can sleep anyway)
so mow from dusk till first-light."'
(High above a consort's moaning
midnight lawnmowers are droning.)

xix

One more: 'Bumblebee excitation
behind our breezeblock ceiling
last night brought irritation
triggered once again that feeling:
buzzing which circles endlessly
coming-and-going incessantly
blend of model-plane 'n' moped.'
Then an explanation registered.
With fishing-rights disputed
in the rainclouds looking for food
(with outboard-motor from Evinrude)
a poor fisherman, persecuted
goes trawling overcast skies
in the folktale 'fishing-skiff-which-flies.'

xx

In the mother of fortress-cities
siege-castle of shaky towers
(Hasankeyf of stacked cavities)
a population cowers
in apartments so packed and cramped
no sound between two homes is damped
until a wedding-feast's declared
until a wedding-song is aired.
(What's that mantra humming from on-high
whine of some old nag's cussing?
What's that dull, distant buzzing:
'Who shall live and who shall die?'
A machine with power to decide
means humanity's race-suicide.)

xxi

Long ago across painted ceilings
Yohanna cherubs dragged banners
telling of wonderful proceedings
(wedding-feasts, breakfasts and dinners)
held in honour of true love.
Now the only angel above
Gaza's breezeblock tenements
trains science-fiction instruments
on our little winding cavalcade
threading through the ruination:
angel of assassination.
But still our guests seem undismayed:
listen to their surrealistic jokes.
What is it with these crazy folks?

xxii

Wheeling through the Milky Way
the Arabian phoenix known as Rukh
gliding across Gaza, far away
at the siege-town takes a closer look.
Wingspanned Gienah-to-Delta-Cygni
passing over Gaza City
she wonders if a miracle
something metaphysical
has taken place by any chance?
Has the star called Sadr flashed
the luminescent river splashed
to somehow make these earthlings dance
at a marriage in a warzone?
Answers to such questions are unknown.

CHAPTER

i

We're still in the Pentapolis
in penitentiary Gaza
to the north of the necropolis
passing through an unlit plaza
in that vast concentration-camp
where two million souls cramp
into less than one-forty square-miles:
population of 'hostiles'.
Here an elongated corridor
the bandage of the Middle East
adheres to a narrow strip of coast
ten-mile-long dressing for a shore
blood-soaked, gangrenous underneath:
to tie-the-knot the worst place on earth?

ii

In Gaza, tattered band of gauze
tightly stretched across burning wounds
tonight 'fighting for the cause'
means getting married as a drone sounds
demonic epithalamia.
(We're far from Mesopotamia
songs of the bull-horned lyre
turquoise eyes flashing soul-fire
as someone sings of dense black stars
governing the galaxies with love;
marriage, lowered from above
gift of Annunaki avatars
from heaven to the fertile crescent
when gods on earth were everpresent.)

iii

Gaza is a giant flesh-wound
in the side of humanity.
To wash clean such a blast-wound
would take the Mediterranean Sea
and more, the Atlantic too.
(Heavy-hearted, we continue;
is that a smoke-spiral through the dark?
We search with a question-mark
also over ourselves, strangers here.)
Those who are soon to become one
carry an immense torch like the sun;
whose light shines everywhere
not just for this nation or that
(according to cosmic fiat).

iv

Getting married in the drone-wars
promising the vows of union
seemingly (and surely) ignores
end-time mayhem and confusion;
saying 'We'll build a pleasure-dome
(though you'll see only a humble home)
right in the mouth of your hell.
And if the demon would expel
evict by demolition
(grey, armoured-plated killdozer
pushing over homes in Gaza
steel death-machine of attrition)
in twenty seconds of destruction
he brings about love's reconstruction.

v

'Because of course, endlessly
Golden Ages forever return
spiralling forward celestially;
since high ideals will always burn
more brightly than overcast hatred
born of darkness in the Age of Lead.
Just as no winter can kill the spring
(of ambiguous blossoming)
the Platonic Year's starwheel spinning
makes the spirit in us expand
brings back the old Summerland
as it was in the beginning.
Music lubricates that machine
giving to an age its golden sheen.'

Such microtonal cantillations
from this African woman-singer.
So haunting her ullulations
(she is the frankincense-bringer).
She might be from The Mahgreb
sweet-voiced Moroccan folk-celeb;
or maybe from Mauritania
she brings this old song of Arcadia;
solemnly, underneath balcony
where stand proud groom and bride
smiling in white, side-by-side
soaring upward in sweet agony.
(An African hand-drummer
adds more pzazz to the drama.)

vii

We follow up some breezeblock stairs
clearly bomb-damaged yet swept clean.
Apparently the elevators
here for seven years have been
out-of-action, inoperable.
But wedding-guests are unstoppable.
Climbing like the red gazelle
they scamper up black stairwell
three-flights-in-no-time, while we race
grannies, geriatric grandads
mothers carrying half-grown kids;
really struggling to keep pace
with everyone. What a people
the Gazans, what a people!

viii

They say this tower is haunted
by the ghost of Sozomen.
Well, none seem at all daunted
as they scramble another broken
pitch-black flight, without a light
pounding through what seems a building-site;
with gaping holes in outer-fabric
(which leave one feeling acrophobic)
reeling around some precipice
still - in theory - unafraid
with neither railing nor balustrade
in case a foot or hand should miss
purchase in dust, come unstuck;
if you, climber, should run out of luck.

ix

Mountain-sick (it's only the third floor)
we've made it to the love-feast
heart in upheaval (and footsore).
Now for marriage in the Middle East.
Doors festooned with palm-leaves
archways made of green sheaves
we push through with hyper crowd.
There's the bride, tiara-browed
throned beside husband, their chairs
raised on a dais. But wait a schtick
this is just *too* fantastic.
(Excuse disbelieving stares.)
That's Aziz sitting beside... Shaza.
O what? Our lovebirds wed in Gaza?

x

How did they even get here;
the intent was to meet at Rafah.
('Nother story. Through the atmosphere
Mushtaq the Mighty carried afar
love-letters sent by pigeon-post.
Hey, straight-up, this is the most.)
Aziz, raven-bearded, wears a look
different when clean-shaven; we mistook
him in unlighted streets outside.
Check that cool 'SS' on his hand
penned in henna, love's hot brand:
initials of his gorgeous bride
Shaza Shabash (hers alone)
interwoven with his own.

xi

Shaza and her man sit enthroned
in a cloud of soothing frankincense
while Katb el-Kitab is intoned;
as open windows admit intense
music, as dancers intertwine
whirl in the circle, walk the line.
Down in torchlit square below
that must be Lawrence in full flow
driving forward the Shamaliyya.
(Who down there can be head-man
if not charismatic Rayyan
leading where one needs - heh - stamina?)
Beginning to make sense now
it's all still a fantasy somehow.

Woah! That's about what's left to say.
Lost for words and dumbstruck
a glad day indeed. (What cliche.)
But joy is precursor of good luck!
And laughter, like music, is a tongue
a language full of meaning, sung
in a sense, a universal code
unlocking when worries unload.
(Contractions of the diaphragm
not those arising when nervous
or if just appearing courteous
ease some emotional traffic-jam;
allow to wordlessly extol
that often-inarticulate soul

Who finds the party a nightmare;
where, chattering, the circulator
in every corner vents hot air;
where the common-denominator
is small-talk, gossip 'n' hearsay.)
This night says, in a personal way:
'Palestine's here to stay, full stop.'
(See these unbeaten Gazans bop.)
Shaza's face! A mirror of bliss
sipping old-style rose-petal sherbet
raising her wildflower bouquet
as she recieves from her man a kiss.
(Big Aziz moved faster than Mushtaq
to get his wedding-night on-track.)

xiv

All the flowers of Palestine
are in these slender hands tonight:
Star of Bethlehem and eglantine
the briar-rose, pink and white
sweet-smelling, apple-fragrant;
cyclamen, shy but vibrant
gentle, delicate, ever-hiding
herself from midday's blinding
sunlight of The Galilee;
and, naturally, the 'Awb Innoom
remembering in scarlet bloom
the fallen (as in Normandy)
flashing torch of memory:
signifying, declaratory.

xv

For even while the living marry
they too must somehow sleep at night.
(When love-feast's epic story
is finished the overwrought
young couple still has reflection.)
And flowers speak of imperfection
beautiful, transitory spring
the ephemeral in everything
save love's glowing central core
which outlasts briefer petals;
whose sad loss still unsettles
within ourselves so unsure.
(Underneath an iron flail
at the tests of love many fail.)

xvi

'God has made me a poet of joy'
sang Jallalaudin Rumi.
Those who claim we are just the toy
of evolution end-up gloomy
selfish and suicidal;
if life is all about survival
certainly these are not the fittest.
In fact they view God as the fascist
who runs the concentration-camp
called life; and these are impoverished
by such a world-view, almost punished.
From that low point let's take a jump.
(Because we can still autolocate;
we write our own kismet, our fate.)

xvii

'The arc of the moral universe
is long, but bends toward justice.'
Meditate these words before you curse
atheists (so-called) think twice.
Only he who serves can walk free.
'Esclaves, ne maudissons pas la vie.'
Holding her wildflowers, Shaza
sorrows for the state of Gaza
even as she sees her dream come true.
Married now to handsome Aziz
(he's the only man she sees)
she's still committed to that breakthrough
in consciousness: Slingshot Hiphop
truly aiming for God's mountaintop

xviii

Where all is holy, holy, holy.
(Though no reconciliation there
the truth revealed unwholly.)
Tonight as we celebrate here
the brutal desert is not so harsh
as daily life down in war-torn Wahsh
when black plumes of fragmentation-bombs
bear away the souls of their victims.
(If we're talking about hubris
the inability to climb down
take-off a monstrous brazen crown
then we're talking about Iblis.)
For the children they scatter poppies
when the diggers come for their bodies.

xix

A drum is pounding in the night.
(Not for the march of the janazah:
slow left-right of funeral-rite
when baillif-death, ever-eager
passes in the dark with ravens
bound for the nether-regions
having taken possession of goods
long owed him, against the odds.
Who amongst us dreams they die?)
Big rugged beats accelerate!
It's Lawrence leaping-in with great
bassdrum hooked on broad waist-tie
pumping-up the volume as he comes.
This is how a masterdrummer drums.

xx

Bless them both on their path ahead.
Look, a second, velvet-sleek dove
shyly peeps from heart-shaped red
basket; now, see, flutters above
beautiful (as all, delighted, gasp)
'dovecote' parting at the hasp
(the way a loft's unlocked at dawn
just when the sun is being born
so first-and-fastest birds explode
pouring in pale trains to untrap
through the door's wide-open gap:
thunderous racing-birds in cloud-mode).
Release of this divine creature
makes a highlight: charming feature.

xxi

'Get it on, play the coffee-grinder.'
'Highly, highly, highly, high.'
'Go down and hire me a childminder.'
Party has suddenly started to fly.
Hey, postpone your departure
prepare yourself for the rapture.
A mystery-man's gonna spin the decks
later, they say, he's bound to flex;
for-def rapstars will drop something
real Slingshot on the mic tonight.
(Whole situation's taken flight.)
That dangerous bass-drum pumping
night-air means only one thing: destroy.
(With x-amount of guests jump for joy.)

xxii

Shaz' wears a corsage on her wrist
made with medallions of rockrose
badge of pink already kissed
fifty times by Aziz, whose nose
explores the floral bracelet's charm.
Kisses (his) would travel up her arm
if Shaz' allowed in front of guests
her beau any closer to her breasts
alluringly discreet in white lace.
He wears a double-edged expression
docility mixed with aggression
as his bride pretends to slap his face.
So they rule, King and Queen of Gaza:
Big Aziz and his delicious Shaza.

CHAPTER

i

Has the world transformed tonight?
Or has the union of opposites
been powerless to bring respite
even as the enemy commits
more crimes against humanity?
Kings and Queens? All is vanity.
Look, in trains petitioners extend
hoping for some dividend
from the hierogamic alliance.
Where is the Shekinah of Godhead?
Are the power and the glory dead?
Where now is sacred dalliance?
Superficial is attraction
in the age of distraction.

One day these lines will seem old-fashioned
far away in some dim tomorrow
when, just as now, impassioned
singing of some house-sparrow
(where the house is the universe)
will call in verses pungent, terse
for the extirpation of wrong
in some plaint (possibly overlong).
Until then make do with these
which you mistakenly call mine
where an angel aquiline
or serpentine (just to tease)
dictates in the tongue of my time;
reinforced, of course, by rhyme.

iii

Our gathering is bittersweet;
it bears the mark of our condition.
Near midnight, above Mansheiya Street
where Shaza's uncle, a physician
Masoud Shabash, has lent his house
to his niece and to her proud spouse
there comes a lull in celebration.
(Backlash of desperation?)
Two interruptions of the feast
have dealt peeps a nocturnal jolt
one a supernatural thunderbolt
unexpected to say the least.
It seems there has been penetration
through the doors of perception:

iv

Old Saint Sozomen's been seen.
Someone, chilling on the third landing
reportedly, in a 'widescreen
moment', saw a tall man extending
two spectral hands as if to bless;
odd in modality of dress:
ectoplasmic revenant
some spirit-world visitant
eerily attending the wedding:
a supernatural presence
putting in an appearance
mysterious lights shedding
with an otherworldly air
on our (already sparkling) affair.

v

Then a wife - all-too-real - with speeches
very loud (as drone overhead
buzzed east of Gaza Beaches)
scarier than the eidolic dead
vented on truant husband hot air;
almost drowning-out in dark square
still-peppy guests, with jubilant yelp
all doing the 'We've come here to help';
with highly-disciplined jumping
(al-Shamaliyya leaping-madness)
happily exorcising sadness
(to someone's cool bassdrum pumping)
with hard-to-execute manoevres
complicated dance-procedures.

Midnight: catch the whirr of an oud
sinuous lines of a player
sliding on his fretless lute
gliding idea-to-idea
with fast liquid fingerings
ever-changing colourings.
It is a magical technique
that renders this melody antique
(a love-rhapsody of old Persia)
in which the ear imagines
the song of endless fountains
in some paradise of inertia
where indolence is discipline
and doing actuates mortal sin.

vii

As Shihaad plays for our young couple
honeyed offerings of song
Aziz pulls on hubble-bubble;
while regal Shaza sweeps sidelong
flashing looks and proud glances.
Now through royal court advances
none other than Sajjid (ill-at-ease
as usual, greeting her and Aziz)
lurching unsteadily through the room
where guests chillax on long cushions
deep in murmuring discussions.
As he sways past, some peeps assume
sitting-postures or just turn their heads
half-elevating on sofa beds.

viii

Everyone's heard of Sajjid:
heretic, demon, angel, cherub;
legendary soul. 'Difficult to read.'
'Murky, his underground club.'
'Yeah, but he's so down with the rap-scene.'
(Where 'to rap' means to intervene
in a hellish spiral of hatred
driven by protocols outdated).
'He thinks a transforming sonic-wave
from underground Slingshot Hiphop
could surreally flip-flop
status-quo in Israel.' 'Naïve!'
'Childlike, mystical, ingenuous.'
'Hopes impossibly tenuous.'

ix

Sajjid offers congratulations
takes long pull on shisha-pipe
(apple-and-mint cooling-filtrations
managing subtly to enwrap
tobacco in delicious vapours).
'Aziz, bro, I give you propers
you've married the Nazarene princess.
Cuz, for your marriage with Shaza, bless.
Sorry to miss the ceremony
heard the speeches were for-real.
Marriage in a warzone ain't ideal
but, yo, blissful matrimony
wins every time, innit bro?'
(Big Aziz.) 'Ah, Sajjid, you know.'

x

'Btw, any public-speakin'
from yourself would be a plus.
Got x-amount of peeps beseechin'
every minute, makin' bare fuss.
Brers want the hottest update
verified, you get me, the facts straight
from the man with the peace-plan.
(News never hits this bantustan.)
What's good wid' Project Sinai?
Right now most are on tenterhook;
man has heard rumours on Facebook.
Peeps are down, Sajjid, I won't lie.
All wanna know things can shift;
in Gaza, bro, they need uplift.

xi

'Gimme fifteen, have you seen Rayyan?'
Sajjid's thinking: 'Zahret el Kolch.'
Eyes twinkle in a face deadpan:
he'll walk (and talk) with a crutch.
Right now, worn-out, exhausted
after dealing with five-hundred
emails in the space of one week
if he absolutely has to speak
(Sajjid's idea of hell-on-earth)
he really needs 'rebirth via weed'
something to get him up to speed
before attempting a 'Wordsworth'.
(That's one way for the taciturn
to verbally - and herbally - burn.)

xii

Following our man Sajjid downstairs
we find Rayyan (ever-the-player)
in smokey flicker of torch flares
still dancing the al-Shamaliyya.
High-jumping, see the demon rise.
In zero-gravity he flies
frisking alongside nubile ladies;
where some veiled formation eddies
in lines and semicircles skipping;
paired now with wildest Rahiq
her beautiful hair, lustrous and sleek
swaying - black - with motion of her tripping.
Sajjid holds two glasses of mint tea;
clearly he should have made it three.

xiii

Ten minutes later Sajjid, airborne
himself (no dancer, reserved Sajjid)
re-climbs the stairs, less withdrawn
in his hand one phat half-stick of weed.
Are you wise, Sajjid Sharif
stopping here to finish off that spliff?
This is the infamous third landing
where Sozomen (mind-expanding)
gave two guests a nasty fright
looming out of nowhere in the dark
(as in some cheap amusement-park)
appearing at the stroke of midnight
(whose grandfather saw Alaphrion
exorcised by Hilarion).

xiv

Now, dripping with perspiration
we're entering the shrine of union
staggering into main-reception
where newlyweds, still in communion
only with each other sit enthroned
side-by-side, seemingly zoned
on purest matrimonial bliss.
(The strongest drug is Shaza's kiss.)
We sense this space is sacrosanct.
(Somehow the clock of life rewinds
fastening the tie that binds;
we seem with the ancient world hand-linked
witnessing love's induction:
timeless rites of conjunction.)

xv

'Ahem...' A speaker on the mic.
Time to meet: Dr Masoud Shabash.
(Guests experience attention-spike.)
Likewise his sister: Noor 'Ma' Shabash
who has come here from Nazareth
(slightly flustered and out-of-breath;
all those flights for someone her age?)
who radiates so much courage
standing at her brother's side
dressed in long calico, elegant
nothing flashy or extravagant
genial with motherly pride.
Masoud famously treated a man
surely not a Hamas partisan;

xvi

Someone with heartbeat flatlining;
brought him back from the dead
a fighting-man, no longer winning
his endless war, full of lead
(thanks to nocturnal outgunning)
someone taken down while running
through the zigzag concrete casbah
which is ever-besieged Gaza:
conscript-soldier of the IDF
stopped in his tracks, defeated
(from book of life almost deleted)
on operating-table left
for a hunk of defunct flesh:
till Masoud began his midnight sesh.

xvii

Here and now, the man in question
a wedding-guest raised from the dead:
Motel Cohen, still slightly ashen
but alive-and-well and breaking-bread
with the people he once hunted
through the maze of Gaza, confronted
by the simple fact of commonwealth:
'I am in truth another yourself.'
(In time the heartless god of war
will alter his malign expression
from behind a mask of aggression
let flow iron tears to answer for
shadows projected everywhere:
dark acts done from primal fear.)

xviii

Look at Mr Cohen right now
(as Dr Shabash begins his speech
presenting Sajjid; taking a bow
smiling round the room at each
person individually).
Do we observe, residually
resentment in him, anxiety
here and now in this society?
Not at all, we see a young man
with emotions running high
fighting down an urge to cry
trying his best to stay deadpan
during Masoud's introduction.
What's the most obvious deduction?

xix

'Well, my friends, on love's holy day
someone who's gonna say words now
does things his own visionary way.
Undoubtedly you've all heard how
he built his club in The Galilee
underground, experimentally:
Transworld, a legend already
with its futuristic, heady
mix of traditional Arabic
culture and Slingshot Hiphop
which has been called "Bedouin-Pop"
redefining tribal aesthetic.
Now I've rolled my drumstick, here's the chief:
please will you welcome: Sajjid Sharif.'

'Ladies and G's: "Love's to be."
The marriage of Shaza and Aziz
means "Love's reinvented" to me;
seems symbolic for the Middle East.
Here's a princess of Palestine
descended from a Nazareth-line
stretchin' back into the distant past
and a prince who's been outcast
exiled to the death-camp, Shatila.
These two've joined hands, Allah bless them.
I know with me you wanna say "Amen."
Listen, I'm no fortune-teller
but when I see this beautiful twosome
"I know a change is gonna come."

'That's a songline from Sam Cooke
my number-one black vocalist.
Sam took from the Christian's Holy Book
not obedience to the racist
doctrines of the southern slave-states
but that freedom which annihilates
prejudice and apartheid.
We ourselves now have to decide
how to overthrow injustice.
The ways we've tried in my belief
have given no lasting relief.
One way I myself dismiss:
the argument for insurrection
(as pointing in the wrong direction).

xxii

'All brave talk of crushing Israel
ignores the Samson Option;
as revealed by Vanunu's bombshell
Dimona's in full operation.
Someone, pushed to the limit
might possibly wield the ultimate
thermonuclear holocaust.
No second-strike or counterblast
will ever win back one green spring
our planet stone-dead and damned
into a radioactive wasteland.
My dear friends, I'm so sorry to bring
gloom to Shaza's wedding-feast.
But there's one way to lockdown the Beast.

CHAPTER

5

i

'Imagine a voice out of hell
penetrating armoured steel
speaking to the heart of Israel
from our century-long ordeal
dispossessed of motherland
driven out by despotic hand.
Imagine, from beyond the grave
a transformative soundwave
eerie with sadness, rage and hope
transmitting truthfully, without hate
the secret word that changes our fate.
Peeps would shout from the housetop
if they knew of such a voice;
like me, they'd exceedingly rejoice.

ii

'I know that prophetic voice is here
among us now in this room;
yet it's often buried, lost somewhere
in a subterranean catacomb
under old rubble of the past.
We've always known that poets are last
to be noticed, first to be suppressed;
truth's always an unwelcome guest
at the strident banquet of idiots.
But now we have a new twist
on what's accepted or dismissed.
The whole issue neatly pivots
on the clash of civilization
versus glocalization.

iii

'Some of our wisest elders
have a spiritual blindspot
make stupid, obvious blunders
analysin' Slingshot Hiphop;
sayin' the voice of Arabian rap
screams from the cultural mantrap
which is mainstream America;
work themselves into hysteria
on the subject of heresy.
Hey, old man, are you not aware
hiphop is counterculture's prayer?
Don't be overly hasty
to confuse Western pop-sedation
with PR speaking for our nation.

iv

'Peeps, I'm wired 'n' over-tired.
Very possibly I've blurted
a bag-o'-breeze, now it's backfired
- heh-heh - preachin' to the converted.'
(Crowded smoky room's spellbound
nobody making slightest sound;
there's no lack of concentration
lapse of anyone's attention.)
'Alright, the latest on The Sinai
comin-up, but first, check the detail
the drift of a just-received email
from someone many deify...
Nah, hold tight, I'll deal with that
later in this little chat...'

v

In Sajjid's veering discourse
do we possibly detect
exponential rising-force
snowballing mental effect:
psychotropic shift, mindquake
from Rayyan's reinforced spacecake
eaten half-an-hour ago
in Mansheiya Square below?
Most likely. Yet sarcasm
eccentricity and charm
most effectively disarm
listeners, whose enthusiasm
excuses sequential shifting
off-topic lateral drifting.

vi

'In fifteen minutes a Greek ferry
docks in the Sinai port of Arish.
From this point forward in theory
we nonviolently unleash
the dream-weapon of One Holyland.
Zero-hour, for which we've planned
is here; now our huge endeavour
moves, though sceptics have said "Never"
and many sensible have doubted.
No problem; our colossus walks tall
making headshakers look small;
as we stride across flouted
limits and demarcations.
Yo, peeps, it's action-stations.'

vii

The smoke-blue room, odoriferous
with mint-and-apple waterpipe-fumes
explodes suddenly with thunderous
plaudits; shouts from other rooms
adjoining now compound acclaim.
Lawrence, muscular hands aflame
fires a long rolling tattoo
bigging-up One Holyland's breakthrough;
blasting from between his thighs
a flourish of commendation;
the rush adding to anticipation
as his vibrant doumbek cries
like some sunchild from outside time
uttering at birth a magic rhyme.

'Check me, I ain't sayin we're there yet;
we face a dicey operation.
Two weeks ago my first death-threat
caused some self-examination
generated a few night-thoughts.
There've even been dark reports
saying the Mossad are watchin' us.
But nothin' is bewitchin us;
man ain't even spooked or bothered.
We've got a so-solid connection
promising overtime protection
a partnership in which we're honoured.
Peeps, into the Wilderness of Sin
we go with the Bedouin.

ix

'With three-hundred warriors to guard
we're heading into the deep south.
The pastoral Qedar will guide
as we thread that labyrinth
of dry-rivers and ravines
with our heavy road-machines.
Some are true nomads of Sinai;
others are men of the nearby
Negev: Tarabin and Azazma
peoples, al-Tayaha tribesmen too.
Having such aid is a breakthrough
since we face a big dilemma
the peninsula being dangerous;
beyond-belief treacherous.

x

'Peeps, the Egyptian government
offered a military escort;
I refused such accompaniment
wanting nothing of the sort.
Armoured personnel-carriers
versus camel-mounted warriors
no contest, right? Now lemme explain
the eight-pantechnicon roadtrain
disembarking from Brindisi
'bout now.' (Sajjid checks wristwatch).
'Here's the new face of outreach:
The Serious Road Trip: most jazzy
aid organization on the planet
more than rock-solid: made of granite.

xi

'These guys and gals with no money
drove a double-decker London bus
straight into the death-agony
of Bosnia, that disastrous
overboiling of ethnic war;
then in the lethal downpour
rain of genocidal bombs
gathered kids (with Dads and Moms)
held a party in the mouth of death
(with the missiles screaming down
on trampolines and painted clowns).
So was born a true and lucid faith
flowering as all else falls apart:
touching efflorescence of the heart.'

xii

A droning from the night-sky
as Sajjid continues talking.
(Maybe in midnight flyby
some fallen-angel stalking
humanity, eye wide-open
paranoid, of stealthy motion?
Otherwise just neighbours mowing
the grass; or the odd cloud-going
fishing-trawler looking for a catch
up there in the atmosphere of dreams:
nothing here is what it seems.
As long as it's not Lady Mismatch
frostier than the tramontana;
some formidable zenana.)

xiii

(A young woman interrupts.) 'Sajjid
you never said 'bout the email?'
'Sorry, sis, nearly there. I need
to more fully - lemme first - unveil
exactly what we're planning.
This dream of our caravanning
began when The McCool Foundation
looking long at our situation
pointed to the Parker James Peace Trust.
(The famous war-painter, as you know
died insane but wanting to bestow
his millions on a charity robust
enough to work in Palestine
real enough to cross the danger-line.)

xiv

'I told Parker James 'bout my dream
to do a Burning Man in Sinai;
they loved the whole outrageous scheme
and SRT went on standby
apparently well up for it:
everything seemed a perfect fit.
(Our venture was always ordained.)
Only one problem remained:
how to get both sides onboard?
Where would we find the Jewish bods
prepared to risk unfavourable odds
(repping for an enemy abhorred)
soldiering into a wilderness
outnumbered? (Too much stress.)

xv

'At this point I grew my beard
with a punishing online regime.
(Of course several here volunteered:
big love, Shaz', for your precious time
given when your thoughts were on marriage.)'
Sajjid, balding, with stooping carriage
fingers luxuriant chin-growth;
and suddenly, seeming less loath
to speak, pulls himself up straighter.
'Every last peace-group everywhere
on the planet got our crystal-clear
circular e-flyer, our bold letter
inviting all to adopt our stand
in proclaiming One Holyland.

'We spoke of a "peace-caravan"
"a rehearsal for unity"
"a non-violent bi-partisan
experiment in community."
We guaranteed everyone
absolute protection from day-one
joining us on our mission:
our visionary expedition.
We talked of the power of sand
(semiconducting silicon
fired-up by the ancient sun)
to change our minds, make us understand.
We spoke about an exodus
from all normal consensus.

'The response was overwhelming!
From One Voice of Peaceworks Foundation
came the first green light, affirming
our "stellar manifestation".
(Who could remain the pessimist?
With eighty-one peeps on our guest-list
we all felt much less like amateurs.)
Then we skyped, met on monitors
with Combatants for Peace;
who said very much the same thing;
offering for def to bring
numbers that would only increase.
(Arab and Israeli ex-soldiers
more-than-used to many dangers.)

xviii

'Next we heard from The Abraham Fund
giving an establishment thumbs-up;
saying "Even the most hardened
squares could not resist"; which sums up
the truth that mainstreams can change
that some there are within hearing-range.
TAF covenanted fourteen jeeps;
linked us to a raft of young peeps
burning to ride our peace-convoy.
Then came Sanea al-Salaam
(aka Oseh Shalom)
who sent just one word: "Attaboy"
but backed it up in reality
with grass-roots solidarity.

xix

Hand in Hand, Children of Peace
Act Beyond Borders, Ta'Ayush
Meet, Stand Up and Comedy for Peace
all answered in one big rush.
(That was our most full-on week.)
Not a single negative critique
just wave-on-wave of constant support;
way more than I would have thought
possible; with big props and praise
from Olives of Peace and Green Action
Roots project. Work-satisfaction
hit mega-levels, O my days!
The Institute of Circlework
vowed three women's groups at a stroke.

'Just Vision and Hamidrasha
Aix, al-Tariq and Peace Oasis
all said it would be their pleasure
to take the road with our peace-circus:
adventure in loving-forgiveness
pilgrimage toward cohesiveness
journey toward justice, path to light.
Peeps, I could stand here all night
naming those who've pledged from the heart:
RHR, Valley of Peace, Mejdi;
NeuroBridges and Peace Already;
everybody wantin' to support;
bringin' skills, expectin' troubles, thrills
ready for slips 'n' blips (and sand-hills).

'More champions of our cause
could (till dawn) be added to my list
realistic people seekin' the stars:
Friends of the Earth Middle East;
Neve Shalom; Tolerance Monument;
The West-Eastern Divan: excellent.
My own Sufi master suggested
an eight-spoked logo, requested
octagonality as binding
motif of our balanced vision
mark of our superbonded mission:
Islamic, on every mosque winding
with geometric inner meaning;
the signature of Christ, Christening;

xxii

'The eightfold wheel of Ezekiel:
octagonal universal seal.'
(Our main-man pauses.) 'O well
I've chatted 'n' blatted a deal
but everything remains to be done
we're only too aware.' (Someone.)
'Wait, dude, the xyz email
you never gave one detail;
Sajjid, bro, listen we need t' know...'
But see our man has vanished from sight;
like The Rambam he's taken flight
leaving afterburn and afterglow.
Does Sajjid also 'jump the road'?
(Sure, when his head's in overload.)

CHAPTER

i

Three a.m. on Gaza's skyline.
The constellation of The Swan
describes a cruciform sky-sign;
showing the night is nearly gone
since her flight into the west
almost-over, so-far-progressed
means, soon now, in slow-motion
she'll land on the Pacific ocean.
She wonders, crossing Palestine
if there is rest for any soul
caught in Gaza's stricken castle
concrete fortress of the coastline?
Questioning, she glides over
so-compassionate observer.

ii

Do they still revel in the ruins
(who have nothing to celebrate)
birthdays, marriages, reunions?
Are these, with a people prostrate
in devastation, still observed
among a population unnerved
whose orphan-children barely speak
utter only monosyllabic
fragments of speech, because no word
can communicate the pain;
whose language cannot contain
such emotional darkness, inward
fearfulness: shellshocked four-year-olds
sons and daughters of war-torn households.

iii

(Thoughts of Cygnus passing above
Palestine at three in the morning.)
Something else hard to believe:
look, in spite of air-raid warning
wailing-out from Gaza City
two lovers in obscurity
half-hidden on a Mansheiya roof
seem to offer living proof
romance remains alive-and-well
even as the screaming warplanes spew
even as superdrones continue
to scan and probe the citadel.
(Cygnus also sings when dying
like these lovers death-defying.)

To look more closely at the couple
(not to run some security-check)
The Swan bends down her neck so supple
three light-years in length (one parsec)
intending to caress these two
fold them from the inshore dew
keep in her wings from coastal fog;
which in pre-dawn is prologue
to warmth of more-friendly morning.
These lovebirds: some just-married pair
entwining in the shadows here?
Cygnus attaches great meaning
to the dalliance of two doves
in breezeblock rooftop alcoves.

Leaning a streamlined neck below
she drops her head, still gliding-on.
The double-star, Albireo
(representing both eyes of The Swan:
one large and bright-orange-hued
the other bluish-green when viewed
through stellar dust-clouds faraway)
narrows down to distantly survey.
The Swan's a romantic at heart
sentimental too, for sure;
no monstrous drone-voyeur
Peeping-Tom of devious resort.
Innocently she wants to eavesdrop
overhear these two on rooftop.

Even so our white supergiant
swishing through cosmic infinity
bending her slender neck so pliant
also wishes to observe, surely
the faces of this couple hidden
deep down in the forbidden
worlds where Hamsas and Garudas
seldom venture (as intruders);
where Rocs and Firebirds don't go
since they are of the excarnation
not in the flesh of condemnation
where mortality prevails below.
(Indeed, patrolling the altitudes
she sometimes tires of star-clouds.)

The Eagle of the Arabs flies lower
curious to learn how love sustains
where little is clear to man 'the knower'
except that pleasure has its pains;
where time is the worm in the clay
which mines a little more each day
which fast-consumes the human core
till all again is dust as before.
(Can these two be Shaza and Aziz
seeming quite familiar in half-light;
or is this just a trick of eyesight
where daybreak gradually rallies?)
He wears shoulderlength dreadlocks
while a black-fringed headscarf blocks

viii

All starlight from her shrouded face.
Cygnus, with bird's-eye-view unclear
approximating now from deep space
brushes the upper atmosphere
with her wings, nearer reaching.
(Orbit of Jupiter approaching
she understands she's got it all wrong.)
Yet how wonderful after so long
to see Jalilah in her blue
bomber-jacket, huddled by white wall
out of the night-wind with her 'downfall':
bad-boy draft-dodger Moss, cool Jew.
What's new? These two reunited?
Their brave love-affair reignited?

ix

Did it ever really fizzle out?
Who ever said the thing was dead?
Times were difficult without a doubt;
what matters is the road ahead.
All humanity wants to believe
in paradigms of perfect love;
dreaming still of some dimension
without exhausting mundane tension.
But that's the sovereign-state of Cygnus
great domain of boundlessness
special place of flawlessness
which cannot here apply to us.
We shall not in this sphere liaise
as in a more exalted phase.

x

Yet see how these lovers huddle
out-of-the-wind in each other's arms;
they seem in affectionate cuddle
one (four-armed) being which performs
some sacred dance of intimacy
(far away from race-supremacy).
Cygnus herself is affected
to see the contraries connected
as in her world, perfected zone
far away from our asymmetry
her realms of light-geometry
nearer to the non-existent Throne.
(Hear the wind jet over each pinion
as she swoops in homage to union.)

xi

Jalilah whispers in Moshe's ear
something fierce, something tender
too faint for Cygnus to hear.
Entranced by mysteries of gender
The Swan descends further, further
burning herself now, used to ether
not to the gross atoms of our skies.
(Dangerously close Cygnus flies.)
All at once driving wind lulls
words become distinguishable.
In-between gusts The Swan is able
to decode, in certain intervals
conversation on the skyline
where two amorous entwine.

xii

'For me, when we hit the road
(with outriding Bedouin)
it'll be anxiety-overload!'
'K, but in the Wilderness of Sin
with the Serious Roadtrip tribes
we'll be soakin'-up nomad-vibes...'
'Moss, as a Jew ain't you shit-scared?'
'Yeah, but Jah kills fear, rest assured.
And down there, under the Milky Way
sleeping side-by-side - sheesh! - who cares?
(Angels will be guarding unawares.)
Yo, let's jus' do it day-by-day.
Plus, for you, it's just as edgy;
ain't 'bout genealogy.

xiii

'"Don't know much about history"
(Moss croons in Jalilah's hair.)
"Don't know much biology."'
'O, that's by Sam Cooke, I swear.
Sajjid was mentioning him.'
'You're my click, my synonym.
How come you know that old-school choon?'
Now a love-song's words are strewn
syllables missing on the wind
cold from the Mediterranean.
(Jalilah hums a Palestinian
folksong; her phrases, misaligned
into the frigid night are tossed;
fierce words about a love long-lost.)

xiv

The Roc of the Arabs swoops lower;
sky flashes electricity.
The lovers sense a higher power
some otherworld entity's
auroral light across Gaza:
energetic extravaganza
emanating from the zenith
as if sensory bandwidth
had suddenly been maximised.
(Jalilah.) 'I'm only guessin'
but a supernatural blessin'
which can no-way be analysed
is comin down on One Holyland.'
(How much does Jalilah understand?)

xv

Night-sky faintly undulates
multicoloured, shining like satin
as if somehow Northern Lights
played an atmospheric pattern
powered by a million megaherz.
A dancer, swaying rainbow skirts
seems to move to music unheard
glimmering, flickering skyward.
Hems and fringes in slow-motion
resemble ethereal driftnets
as she, ballerina, pirouettes
tiptoeing across a sky-ocean
where continuously seraphim
in spectral shoals many-splendoured swim.

xvi

By chromatic wonders captured
impossible transparencies
Moss 'n' Jalilah, enraptured
view the shifting frequencies'
prismatic wavings of chiffon:
inexplicable phenomenon.
Watching the magnetic weather
Moss thinks to holler his brother
Rayyan (snuggled with Rahiq
further down the housetop sheltering
fog-nestled). His words, faltering
prove him too wonderstruck to speak.
(Listen, he articulates a sigh
staring spellbound at a tinted sky.)

xvii

His way has been transcircular
roundabout, tangential, strange
since the Blue Line; since Hula
(when he really jumped out-of-range).
It's been a loop and an ellipse
equivalent to a few earth-trips
round the sun, eerie revolutions.
Does Jalilah want explanations?
No, she's just so glad he's here
having made it into Gaza
for the rites of Aziz and Shaza.
They stand, hand-in-hand, stare
study the celestial display:
sky's electrical ghost-ballet.

xviii

'"But I do know that I love you"
(Moss lilts softly at Jalilah's ear.)
"And I know that if you love me too . . ."'
Jalilah tilts her head to hear
(nearer, nearer, doing nothing wrong)
simple words of Sam Cooke's hit-song.
'BTW, do you think Sam Smith
fit to be mentioned in the same breath
as the mastersinger himself?'
Jalilah's question is a direct
attempt to cautiously deflect
attentions of the big-bad-wolf
now pretending, acting babyish
while sharpening his fangs for her flesh.

xix

The house of one column and nine doors
has never been safe against attacks
by lycanthropic carnivores
who know how to arrange comebacks
where a window of perception
left open means: self-deception.
(There shall be other sweet onslaughts.)
Now, the night of contaminant thoughts
with auroras enigmatic
wonderfully intense colours
gives way before first-light-pallors:
eastern sunrise, how dramatic.
(Cygnus has withdrawn to the west
but it's not the end of her quest.

xx

She will be watching, with the moon
our caravan of dreams descending
through the deserts of Majnoun.)
Jalilah, as always quite unbending
where her boyfriend is concerned
has, it seems, very-recently learned
more tricks to keep his wolf at bay
maintain a safe level of love-play.
(Moss, comprehending, simmers down.)
'Yeah, he's not Slingshot Hiphop
but Sam Smith is intelligent pop
with a voice truly from Motown:
best UK act since The Beatles;
maybe one of the immortals.'

xxi

'Btw, that email mentioned.
(Sajjid Sharif is such a tease;
everyone wanted to get straightened
with some authentic certainties:
nothing like officialdom.)
You know the facts? Who was it from?'
(Now Jalilah has the upper hand
in that oldest war of the heartland
where adolescent lovers won't
be friends, with superior smile
one saying: 'U have to wait a while
'coz I know something U don't.'
In truth she's longing to reveal
though lips refuse to unseal.)

xxii

This morning's sun's a diplomat.
He'll find an elegant solution
(great solar aristocrat)
a way forward from retribution.
'I'll tell you, though you're a criminal;
that email was from Subliminal
who says he's buryin' the past;
but still preparin' rugged bombast
for the battle in the sand.
He's bringin' many rappers too
(some bad-boy called Impromptu).
It's rock 'n' roll, it's One Holyland.'
A little spat is over; the sun smiles.
He's happy when the world reconciles.

CHAPTER

7

i

Shadowmouth is bitching, complaining
constantly because nothing's right;
dusk-till-dawn scorning, disdaining
she brings a thousand sins to light.
From daybreak to sunset she grumbles
thunders, nags, niggles, rumbles
rattles on and reverberates.
(Her sister always corroborates
everything she says, all of the time.)
At nightfall she's under the weather.
(Nothing worse than a spot of bother
on the horizon at bedtime.)
Rhyme nor reason shall excuse you:
Shadowmouth will abuse you.

She visits your house without warning
pokes her nose in, misconstruing
innocent fun-and-games, frowning
arguing, brewing trouble, spewing
advice in her superior tone:
that whining automatic moan.
She gives your spouse a nasty fright
turning up in the dead of night
ever-hovering in the background
on the lookout for problems.
Everywhere in your breezeblock slums
Old Zenana's always around;
jibber-jabbering through phoney smiles
she needles, she vexes and she riles.

iii

'It's for your own good' she mutters
taking over your own house;
every stale cliche she utters
is cleverly-disguised abuse.
Here comes (with throaty monotone
as musical as Dad's grindstone)
Mum-in-law as counterterrorist
ticking-off her to-do checklist:
from rooftop hear her growling.
(A sheet hung out to dry the old bag
misinterpreted as a white flag;
which caused her a lot of scowling:
'A surrender of the enemy.'
No you crackpot, you dummy.)

iv

This morning, much radio-chatter.
Monitoring the Rafah Crossing
she reports as 'No laughing matter'
the convoy she sees amassing
just to the Egyptian side.
Information's classified
but we've got our own connections
know well Shadowmouth's inflections;
quickly find her frequencies
recognize at once her call-sign
(cold, harsh, jagged digital whine)
complaining of delinquencies.
(Finding reasons to be annoyed:
Shadowmouth's way of being deployed.)

v

'Vast numbers of horseback Bedouins
are meeting Gazan SUV's
rammed with peeps (doing wheel-spins
in the sand with sudden flurries)
driven by young dudes noisily.'
Now Shadowmouth uneasily
reports movements of the Red Crescent
shipping a marquee hospital-tent;
also notes numerous motors
fast-outbound from the West Bank
(monitored by an Egyptian tank)
full of weird Jordanian characters.
Everything's going just as planned:
apartheid versus One Holyland.

vi

A three-day mass-visa-clearance
means the besieged can exit
Gaza with Egyptian concurrence
thanks to Sufic Sajjid's closet
dealings at diplomatic levels.
(He sometimes has to talk to devils
political somnambulists
disembodied sleep-walkers, 'realists'
as they name themselves proudly:
ministers, lawyers, chiefs-of-police
men whose palms he needs to grease
amply while they lecture loudly
on probity, dignity and law.
Sometimes too he oils an office-door.)

vii

Wheels are rolling in from the Negev
all-terrain landcruisers and estates
(listen to that badass Nissan rev)
quite a number with Israeli plates.
Looks like the caravan of peace
is not some ludicrous caprice
after all: backing that consensus
witness the media-circus
building on the highway to Arish:
Voice of Palestine, BBC
Al Jazeera, Fox and Nile TV
El Chourouk and Channel 10 (sheesh)
CNN, Rusiya Al-Yaum
France 24 and Al Alam.

viii

Behind: the fortress of sorrows
siege-castle of ruined towers
city without tomorrows
where desolation overpowers
two million cramped and packed
into the microscopic tract
the world knows as the Gaza Strip.
Ahead: the unknown of the roadtrip
into the landscape of nothingness
the negative terrain of Sinai:
monotonous, windswept, dry
zone of unvarying sameness
vast and undifferentiated
empty and unregulated.

ix

Everything behind seems unreal:
the birthday beside Galilee;
that flight in a black automobile
to Nazareth; the wrecked car weirdly
burning in a midnight of near-death;
that vertical moment of rebirth
when Moss fell under Jah's spell
in the darkened club, an infidel
converted by truth and beauty;
even the idyllic dawn-garden
hillside with the view to Jordan:
all seem faraway in honesty.
(Hidden in the past, lost to sight:
a girl weeping on a beach at night.)

x

They say we wake from this life
into light infinitely stronger;
they say we enter afterlife
scanning backward no longer
leaving all ambition behind:
dreams to oblivion consigned
buried under time's shifting sands
with Ozymandias in shadowlands:
forgotten as yesterday's shards
in dust, until that summary
cleansing of our memory
as unconditional love discards
from consciousness fragments, ghosts:
old phantoms of sublunar coasts.

xi

We know sea-change and transition
away from materiality;
in a flash, in juxtaposition
see our souls against totality
each a fragment of that anti-sun
we call the monobloc, only One.
All we leave behind is nothing
in the light of such awakening.
No more caring for what only seems
we leap into God's firestorms
burning-up anthropomorphic forms;
and so our existence becomes
fused with that supreme fire
which carries every soul-spark higher.

xii

We don't know what's in Sajjid's mind
(Shadowmouth would understand it all)
as down the road to Arish we wind
in that (famous) jet-black cannonball
trusty, dusty four-wheel drive
so powerful it seems half-alive:
aforementioned high-speed Bimmer.
(Nothing on the road looks trimmer.)
Perhaps it's all about changing gear?
The Sufis are millennial, true.
(We've an automatic option too;
important to make that crystal-clear.)
Maybe it's essentialism?
Or even quintessentialism?

xiii

Who knows? It's Biblical, Koranic
in the sense that solitudes
attract the messianic
individual in episodes
celebrated in desert-myth;
where a man like a monolith
legendary one of departure
embarks on lone adventure.
There are madmen like Majnoun
who sojourn in the wilderness
long out of too much tenderness;
hiding from the gibbous moon
which wears Her silver headband:
La Belle Dame Sans Merci of the sand.

The Prophet's ships crossed many deserts:
spice-caravans in starlight
driving through the void which converts
everything to the Infinite;
flotillas of a hundred or more
crossing nothingness from shore-to-shore
alone in the night, navigating
camel-bells tintinnabulating.
Jesus conquered the wilderness
where vipers sleep beneath the stone
where cities shimmer in a dream-zone
full of rage and bitterness.
Musa led his people to the fire
which burns away all false desire.

xv

Rimbaud had a hunger for the waste
gun-running to Menelik.
His own past had been erased:
the opiated, alcoholic
London-days in old Kings Cross
when he worshipped decadence, chaos
but sang in the oasis of dawn
against the modern Babylon.
Artorius, sunchild! Show your face
as it shone when you went out alone
through the desert, Rasta, to atone
in Abyssinia's furnace.
You, genius, were so pure
all seasons you could endure.

xvi

And Dostoyevsky, your mirror
stands opposite your legend
condemned to outer Siberia
in early manhood's whirlwind
long before predestination
gave the poet incarnation
Holy Russia's laureate;
prophesying the idiot
atheist Soviet Union.
Only a near-death firing-squad
made him hear the whisper of God;
and ten years of lonely communion
on the steppes before he could return
with his new word to torch and burn.

xvii

Shadowmouth is tracking westward
along the coast-road to Arish.
Does she detect and duly record
aromatic plumes of hashish
trailing backward from our motorcade
most noticeable clouds of high-grade
Zahret el Kolch, delicious resin?
(Are those lefty, liberal vermin
puffing their never-ending reefers
as they caravan to rendezvous
with that gone-crazy London crew?
Let's hope no drivers get brain-fevers
behind the wheel: signage is confusing
up al-Kantara Arish cruising.)

Anyone snoozing's a murderer:
eight-hundred-plus jeeps; the road's rammed.
Check this horseback desert-wanderer
who, alongside-riding (monogrammed
headscarf flying in the wind
criss-crossed, black-and-white intertwined;
his chest diagonally-decked with belts)
protects One Holyland from assaults:
warrior-nomad of the lands
lost to drifting dunes long ago.
You don't wanna cross this amigo;
check out the kit in his waistbands.
He makes Clint Eastwood look a peacenik;
yet something here of the beatnik.

xix

It is Budayl of the Boqom tribes
(whose bloodlines are ramified
who traces back to Taraba-times
in the lost valley, deified
hair-raising dude) leaning to X5
out-of-saddle, doing forty-five
on mindblowing black stallion
(mph of course) riding pillion
his ten-year-old son, Baligh
up behind poppa on the horse
(the little fella, too, looking fierce
showing neither fear nor fatigue).
Budayl, descendant of Joktan:
here to safeguard the caravan

xx

A poet who lives for poetry:
fire in the blood of the Bedouins.
(The river of modern floetry
traced to its origin begins
somewhere in Arabia
probably, though suburbia
births in a synchronous cradle
the modern song of the turntable:
Sincere, UK-garage two-step
'Just look... what is done for me';
Klashnikov, and that man Lowkey.
Humbledown if you wanna rep
for higher ends; to justify
call only upon I-and-I.')

xxi

That is why Budayl is onboard.
He's been to Transworld plenty times
was there when Jalilah overawed
with her poignant, burning rhymes.
(Those lines about the Stern Gang
brought hot tears; eye-water sprang.)
As well as dowser and rainmaker
Budayl is also the best tracker
by far in the Sinai Peninsula.
On camel-back (with roots-god
Bob Marley on his ipod)
he 'eats the tarantula'
sniffs the ways unerringly
finds oases reassuringly.

xxii

What are he and Sajjid discussing
laughing through rolled window at speed?
What Godsend is Sajjid promising?
'Kay, this is all 'bout that pressing need
with every car under scrutiny
to facilitate a green journey;
simple principle and popular.
Each vehicle must be fuller-
than-full: environment comes first.'
(This one's pretty damn-overcrowded;
yet behind tints all is shrouded.)
The desert-air after a cloudburst
is what they dream about in heaven.
(Yet how these dunes ask to be driven.)

CHAPTER

i

Shadowmouth's delivering intel
circling the old port of Arish
watching our eight-truck caravel
crawling centipede of yellowish
sand-hued, supersized pantechnicons
Volvos, Mercs, Scanias and MANs
filing out of the customs sector;
where an Egyptian inspector
has almost had a mental collapse
due to strangeness of what he's seen
the sheer scale: something inbetween
a carnival of peace-shocktroops
and the roadcrew of The Rolling Stones
with spiritual overtones.

His call to Cairo (intercepted)
resounding with perplexity
(bounced-back to the Mossad, decrypted)
betrayed total incredulity
when, from within the Administrate
the Office of the Governorate
someone simply said: 'If weapons-free
see them through, emphatically
no argument: let my people go.'
(That was the actual phrase used.)
The port-bureaucrat, deeply confused
by this dictat from 'The Pharoah'
(great man in charge of all Sinai)
complied with the word from on high.

iii

Another drone-intercept
to lead-cab from local SUV.
(Shadowmouth is so adept
in eavesdropping, so gossipy;
the old crone makes it her business
to snoop, apply guesswork, assess
often wrongly, all she sees;
yet can't tell the forest for the trees.)
Up in the front-door, of course, it's Law:
Lorcan from Donegal, Celtic
anarchic-stroke-aristocratic
Irish royalty of yore:
the Celtic order of legend
in his blood, its light undarkened.

iv

'Law, One Holyland, it's Rayyan
bless, man; in less than five hang a right
for Hazna, 'n' don't miss, Lorcan
or you wind up in Gaza tonight.
Two miles down the road you'll see our dust.
T'ings tense out here, bruv, vibes are robust.
We're waitin on the verge. As planned
the Red Crescent will go out beforehand;
then your first four artics'll roll-through.
following al-Hillal al-Ahmar;
then (definitely, Law, yes, star)
we come off the sand behind you;
and after your last trucks the Red Cross
form the trusty "tail of the horse".

v

'Tarabin and Aquila flank us
tribal outriders to either side;
Sawarka, too. (Who all outrank us;
who would have been the first to guide
but they gave position, pride-of-place
to al-Hillal al-Ahmar.) They'll pace
us at, like, twenty-five, thirty-five.
Trust me, bredda, we'll survive
only with the Bedouin, simple.
As you know, Somalian gangster
rules Sinai, many jus' youngster:
over here, that's how it crumble.
Blood, soon-soon check you in view.
Star, we lookin out for you.'

vi

Crackly Lorcan, on speakerphone
comes back with wonderful accent;
break-up not affecting liquid tone
warm, faraway, super-present
all at the same time. (What a voice;
straight out of the pages of Joyce.)
Shadowmouth listens attentively.
There's no way, substantively
she can block these communications.
Monitor is all she can do
the hyper-diligent shrew.
'Cool, Ray, for the clarifications;
more love, bredda, 'n' I jus' wanna say:
One Holyland all the way.'

vii

Zoom out to big panorama.
Many caravans have left this port
for the land of the Chimera:
burning zone of no resort
inferno of the bond-slave
scratching his God-name in a cave;
escaped from the coppermines until
he becomes the desert-cobra's kill
coiled in some cool, dusty canyon;
where excavators of turquoise sweat
singing under drivers heavyset
songs of the chaingangs who carry on
bitter service of the master:
the animals of Cleopatra

Pack-donkeys of Solomon;
chanting toilers for blue stones
eternally-shackled bondsmen
slaving through desert-cyclones
dust-storms: miners of old Sinai
men and women, sentenced to die
where acid waters make azurite
drip through copper to green malachite;
where the dream of blue sky underground
sacred turquoise, magical
mineral treasure, mythical
stone of lustrous wonder is found:
connected with heaven always
image of the halcyon days.

ix

Turquoise-stacks lie to the south:
The Mafqat of prehistoric mines
where the Nephilim of sky-birth
found the blue gem which outshines
all others, prizing it, vivid-blue
(not with more subtle sapphire's hue)
first symbol of heaven-on-earth
patently, often set in worth
near gold, thought in value beside.
And what can be better than heaven
where all our sins are forgiven
and none from justice can hide?
(Tell that to Anunnaki slaves
in the mountains digging their own graves.)

x

Traded by Turks in Frankish lands
Sinai's aquamarine sky-stone
became 'turquoise'. (Language hands
riddles spoken in an undertone
associative blunders of tongue
down the centuries, among
all peoples, coded and obscure.)
From mountain-cities, as Nishapur
transported, refined and polished
the Persian fluorescent for the blind
victory-stone from a sky-vault mined
shines, cerulean and untarnished
promising to set spirits free:
the stone of bright-blue eternity.

xi

Imagine celestial Yerevan
constructed from turquoise blocks of light
(only the blue of Rimbaud's eyes can
compare) composed of filtered sunlight
ultramarine material
dazzling and ethereal
floating down into this world
so all souls may be world-healed:
a city founded for everyone
built from topaz, lapis lazuli.
It's the New Jerusalem we see.
(A city one would wish to call Zion
but for associations recent
which make the poet reticent).

xii

'Good and bad in all races':
(The Emperor Haile Selassie.)
We shall find faith's interspaces;
forward to Zion with urgency.
'Get up, stand up, stand up for your rights.
Get up, stand up, don't give up the fight.'
'Sometimes like water they seem to flow:
these architectures of indigo
desert-cities formed in a crescent.'
'A blue-shifted underground star
always, even when seen from afar
the ultimate antidepressant.'
(From 'The Mythology of Turquoise.'
text of insight, charm and poise.)

xiii

Returning focus to today
consulting once again the expert
what has Shadowmouth to say?
From her vantage-point covert
has she noticed anything amiss?
From heights of superior hubris
has she zoomed to proximity
complacent with anonymity
where a conspiracy of silence
condones automated execution
a false sky-god's final-solution:
obscene distancing of violence
all done in the name of safe-keeping.
(While man's conscience is sleeping.)

xiv

Here two operators scan Playboy
while console pilots to perfection
computing the sweet-spot to deploy;
who murder nursing an erection
kill coming, then flick back to mag:
bimbo-time again, the mental shag.
Such inhuman procedures
such transhuman mergers
with the machine-carnivore
mean demonic embodying.
Such imaginary journeying
to the pits of porn-enhanced war
shudders poor souls conducted
into something so corrupted.

xv

Who needs Shadowmouth's evil eye
to see the whirlwind Rayyan mentioned?
Hard through dust-screen to quantify;
there must be a thousand cars stationed
down there, very possibly;
more than a thousand probably.
(Someone's predicting hatred
has to explode, hot and red.)
Yet Sajjid, cosmic organizer
man of moves and stratagems
already has deep mechanisms
in place, in case: his tranquilizer.
(The Institute of Circlework
people have done their homework.)

xvi

Roadcamp One on the noon-verge
is surrounded by drummer-women
some young, some seemingly of great age;
all their hand-drumming solemn:
a slow, calm heartbeat of power
(not beats-per-minute but per-hour)
pulsing into the dustcloud
apparently extremely loud
though in reality very soft;
just coming so much from the center;
music seeming somehow to enter
not through orifices, right-and-left
ear-canals' spirallic chasms
but from internal abysms.

xvii

Big censers spiked in sand smoke with blue
ribbons of frankincense trailing.
(Which soothing fragrance takes us back to
Gaza, senses sweetly assailing.)
Here comes The Serious Road Trip!
Tension suddenly seems to flip:
a thousand horns blast suddenly.
A shout goes up, blatantly
ecstatic sound of unanimity.
On lead-cab, London-bus-logo
high over cab-fairing, halo
tricoloured, means nonconformity.
(Sign of red-and-green-and-gold
something ultra-modern, so old.)

xviii

The circle of hand-drummers
escalates tempo a tiny bit;
across the dunes latecomers
hear rhythms the djembes transmit
accelerate; and they know
One Holyland is good-to-go.
The Serious Road Trip's front-door
driven dead-slow by mohicaned Law
follows through behind the Red Crescent;
the first of four trucks rolling southward
very slowly, coming afterward
(paying homage to risk, everpresent)
giving the ambulances room.
(A scene from Mad Max II: vroom, vroom.)

xix

Drummers have melted into a coach;
landcruisers, SUVs, are making
agreed main-highway approach
tightly-wedged behind truck-four, taking
places on the road in triple-file.
Sajjid's X5 (machine of style)
showing the way (just for today
going first) leads on the driveway:
two-lane blacktop heading due-south
in almost ritualistic silence.
Up-front a Red Crescent ambulance
flashes, but no siren-mouth
screams; the whole atmosphere just hums
in semi-silence (eerie with no drums).

xx

Late-afternoon on the Hazna road
advancing into Ard al-Fairuz;
by Israeli drones shadowed
through the Land of Turquoise:
country of blue-green crystals.
Struggles other than rap-battles
lie ahead, more probably than not.
What was that? Another gunshot
from Tarabin and Aquila
outriders on ardent stallions?
A warning to alien battalions?
(Some feared Somalian arms-dealer
snaking his transhipments through the sand
cargoes of death, deadly contraband?)

xxi

Twilight asks that prayers be said
deep bows be made, meditations:
Roadcamp Two is a few miles ahead.
Big Toyotas have taken stations
four, parked in prearranged stasis
around the rim of the oasis
preconfigured for optimal sound.
PsychoacoustiX Sensurround
one of London's most roots DJs
just at moment of early sunset
will be launching his Cosmic Dub set
(in the day's slowly-dying phase)
when caravan rolls to a stop
when its tight-sealed windows drop.

xxii

Playlists have been discussed for months;
Roadcamp Two is a crucial juncture.
Aesthetic weaknesses and strengths;
sensitivity to culture;
all picks must be really dope.
(Music's been under the microscope.)
Raps from anywhere on the planet
are excluded as too passionate:
no Tupac, no Lowkey, no Dam
no Subliminal. For voices
there are more irie choices
to keep the family Abraham
from going into versus-mode.
This is one decisive crossroad.

i

Listen, the hushed voice of Jalilah
(in dark, fringed headscarf clouded)
anxious-yet-defiant, low whisper
in black X5: way-overcrowded
(as gunshots sound from nomad outriders
shrouded wilderness-ambassadors).
'In the face of death I can say
what I like' is the simple way
Jalilah justifies to herself
an astonishing outburst:
the top-secret thing she's just
confided to the dreadlocked wolf
sprawled beside her on the back seat.
(Giving thanks for aircon in this heat.)

ii

We don't hear a distinct response
more than a free-and-easy grunt
from Moss: super-breezy nonchalance.
See: he clenches a streaming blunt
(now releasing blue narcotic wreath)
seemingly affixed between his teeth
(not anchored in place by lips).
But there's touching of tense fingertips
near smooth, black, sloping leather-seat;
predicament has clearly impacted
with gunfire crazily protracted.
And someone's said something indiscreet
because Jalilah blushes crimson
at whispered comeback brazen.

iii

Those are real cannonades, God knows;
parallel salvos chattering, intense.
Through landcruiser's tinted-out windows
(as light becomes at sundown more dense)
there's not really much to be scanned:
just dust-clouded amber wasteland.
But these are the trade-routes of death.
Somalian arms-shipments by stealth
cross this landbridge in quick succession
ferrying Qassams to the Strip;
to be tunnelled-in and let-rip
from parking-lots, zones of 'aggression'
launched, of course, in self-defence
from the Gazan side-of-the-fence.

iv

Dropping past saffron-coloured dune
southbound convoy decelerates.
(Wait, in loud tints some 'late-afternoon'
chocolate-box cliche perpetuates
painted Arabian sunsets
- stop! - in garish ultraviolets.
Here is something different
pastel image more ambivalent.
Through a sterile - future? - wilderness
a long metallic roadtrain
navigates desertified terrain
hot plain of indistinctiveness.
Has global-warming intensified?
Is a world committing suicide?)

v

As motorcade slows in grove of palms
plantation shaded and tranquil
(whose psychogeography welcomes:
this island-oasis, sensual)
Imperial Zion's soundsystem
broadcasts a legendary riddim:
(while frankincense streams soothingly)
greatest modern love-song, movingly
making the sand-islet holy-ground.
Setting sun looks on in wonderment
forgets tired disgruntlement
tunes-in to the spiritual's sound
as Marley chants *No Woman, No Cry*
in the wastelands of Sinai.

vi

Dreads beside artics, black-and-white
march in sandals through the dune;
trod through a luminous twilight
kicking-up clouds in late-afternoon:
baddest Rainbow Warriors around.
PsychoacoustiX Sensurround
has dropped the groove of love 'n' peace:
Prophet Bob's timeless masterpiece.
(A long centipede of sand-hued trucks
now parked, unloads clowns on cycles;
and jagged cultural icicles
seem to melt a little, stomachs
tensed for fight-or-flight relax.)
But Marley steals the climax.

vii

Music's apparently reached
Somalian ears: Small Axe
has biggaliciously preached.
(Bob has stopped the arms-dealer's attacks.)
The Bedouin remain en-face
fiercely circling watering-place
showing the antagonist no chink
coming only one-by-one to drink;
approaching small waterways
(vigilantly entering)
on foaming horses cantering
travelling sometimes sideways
(with eyes in the backs of their heads)
smoothly controlling thoroughbreds.

viii

A possible armistice agreed
makes safer this hazardous place;
providing what Sinai-nomads need:
a semi-pastoral breathing-space;
in conducive air a setting-free
in God's negative eternity.
Some who've crossed an empty tract
(mere nothingness to be exact)
seem to have found a zone of prayer.
Those who've endured a brutal sun
(though the journey's only just begun)
now meditate Palestine's despair
imaged in huge red solar disk
sinking bloodily in dusk.

ix

'Yes, I remember when we used to sit
in the government-yard in Trenchtown
observing the hypocrite...'
(No slackness can pull this irie down.)
Circlework women-drummers throb
in-sync with Trenchtown-prophet Bob
as dusty jeeps discharge passengers
Palestinians, Israelis: strangers
face-to-face, certainly, with fears
distrust just beneath the surface;
with differences of 'race-and-race'
not confronted for a hundred years.
(There's only mixed ethnicity
within one race of humanity.

x

Of course Diasporan Jews
largely invented the spiritual
supermarket, so profuse
with offerings multicultural:
aisle-upon-aisle of lateral choice
to make the customer rejoice:
a sutra of Buddhism here
echoing a Zen koan there;
with inner practices exotic
disciplines of ancient India
alongside some new zeitgeist-idea
all designed to calm the neurotic
dweller in modernity
still longing for eternity.

xii

Yet overstanding has revealed
that he whom this seeker really seeks
is close at hand, not far afield.
In truth, with time-and-tear-furrowed cheeks
if he look again he'll find him where
he's always been since yesteryear;
even since the time of the garden:
still keeping the fasts of Ramadan
still seeding orchards of salvation;
tending olive-groves, rearing horses;
speaking with atavistic voices
his 'Welcome home': revelation
one day uttered near the skyline
by a hill-farmer of Palestine.)

xiii

Check that choon: Dimi Mint Abba.
We heard it under a previous moon
when the queen of desert-cantata
sang in Transworld; as wheels-of-fortune
span on dancefloor: Moss 'n' Jalilah:
Dimi, great Arabian vocal-star
voice of the Twentieth Century
(O Casablanca of treachery).
Dimi, Mauritanian warrior
non-violently with Art's Plume
fighting only low-caste stigma, shame
of the Iggawin: vast class-barrier.
Who, against all comers in Tunis
won The Umm Kulthum. O pure bliss.

xiv

Through half-light two sweethearts loom:
(as Cygnus hovers just underneath
eastern skyline; as bass-drum boom
heartbeats in the music's depth)
Jalilah, sweet-sixteen-and-a-half
hiphop genius in a headscarf;
Jewman Musa (with his Gaza flag)
Rasta Jew-kid MC Scallywag.
Listen to that microtonal chant:
O Lord, bring apartheid crashing down.
(Dimi serenades at sundown
our twin-souls with deep, vibrant
slow-pulsing rhythmic mastery;
asymmetric mystery.)

xv

Walking side-by-side real close
in occidental sunset-glow
boldly holding hands (shyness adios)
checking now Sajjid's on-mic flow
(grandmaster of ceremonies)
somatic testimonies
tell us these two are in love;
hint and suggest more thereof
halfway to Hazna at Roadcamp Two.
Yet with so much else going on
who pays any heed except The Swan?
(Some, indeed - it's true - might take issue
if they heard the truth from 'Jahlilah'
as she signs herself now: way-cooler.)

xvi

Doors fly open up-and-down
shepherded middle-section;
at the periphery of the unknown:
venture against circumspection.
Flags, red-and-white, black-and-green unfurl
glowing, in semi-darkness whirl.
Here come King and Queen of Gaza
Aziz and his delicious Shaza:
outspoken Nazarene princess;
see, with her one-week-stubbled man.
(Looking way more 'built-to-plan'
much happier, not the usual mess.
Married-life certainly seems to suit;
he's less cyborgian, way-more cute.)

xvii

Aziz, terrible-looking bruvva
big, broad 'n' massive like a door
now acts more the classic lover
no longer stone-faced sorceror-
cum-bouncer-from-outer-space
big amigo with so-scary face
cyborg-of-yore. (Seeming a zombie
nerve-racked, harassed and flabby
hubby-from-hell, jealous 'n' hating
we'd have to dismiss the married-state
pity his hard-pressed, harried fate;
speak of cages, sweet traps of mating.)
Yet as now revealed (who's always been)
the gentle giant we've just seen.

xviii

Who still scans, droid-like, after Moshe
(certainly in Wahat al-Salaam)
tracing his outline with laser-ray
as Jahlilah rests on his left-arm.
Moss, sauntering-on unabashed
seems in wishful-thinking wished
dead with this dark look from Aziz.
(Are there dormant jealousies
in this poisoned dart askance.)
Cygnus, rising over Calcutta
distantly overhears a mutter
grunt of rage, detects the evil glance
Moshe's way, watching it align
with our Rastaman: cast malign.

xix

Either his wife's been telling Aziz
Moss is a bad influence on Rayyan
leading him down a road of sleaze
(blood-brothers of the morphine-clan)
to sordid ghettoes of addiction;
or else she's spun no-such fiction
told instead the innocent story
(eternal and transitory)
young girls tell of perfect first-love.
(Such secrets never should be aired
or virginal heart-feelings bared.)
Did she once love her bro's main-bruv
(save a life felt to be worthless)
his Nazarene dove of loveliness?

xx

Budayl flies past on jet stallion
Jarir, 'Puller-Onward', speeding
who thunders his rider along
on four rapid winds, conceding
nothing to the desert-sandstorm
lord of onward-momentum
in impetus and driving-force
resembling some poetic horse
best-compared to a dream-charger
black, muscled, flexible, majestic
in forward-motion: fantastic
Jarir, legendary steed, larger-
than-life, of God-like demeanour:
phantom flying-horse of literature.

xxi

Marley's black-madonna Mary
wails beside Gaza's war-widows:
ghostly on truckside-screens, eerie
faces looming from twilight shadows.
Past lamenting daughters of Adam
frankincense and myrrh windstream
from fairing of a MAN cab-over
(serving as tower for projector:
solar-powered nickolodeon
eco-cinema, with optional
pedal-function, exceptional
dreamchild of its custodian
dreadlocked Skidz; Rayban'd assistant:
Tika from green Connaught, radiant).

xxii

The sun loves every rainbow-logo
red-green-'n'-gold on each cab-fairing;
loves, too, that pumping dub-tempo
skanking slow with so much heart-caring
syncing with the eight brilliant signs.
He's tickled in his solar turbines
by the old London bus
in orbit with so little fuss;
feels like returning to the zenith.
(But luckily he thinks again
keeps his cool and counts to ten
forbears to burn and sunbathe
when what's needed is twilight
to give these travellers respite.)

10

i

'My dreams last night weren't smothered
by the horrendous weight of a house.'
Orange sandstone bluffs, time-weathered
in lucid distances slowly pass
in crystalline tones of light
painted supernaturally bright.
Over the central Tih Plateau
in searing noon, convoy-on-the-go
through white-hot nullity winds-down
one strip of tarmac in nothingness
crossing desolate Sinai, treeless
(of Biblical, Koranic renown).
'My dreams were so wide-awake
I was lost in wonder at daybreak.'

ii

Jahlilah's Arabic: sublime.
(Silence in X5, like a tomb.)
Now, after morning-long climb
out of Hazna, mountains loom
shining-out distantly, far onward
over tableland (searching southward)
the blue-stacks of Gebel El Igma;
where thrustings of granite and magma
design a titanic landscape
a tremendous lunar world
spectacular expanse, fold-on-fold
peak-upon-peak down to Sinai's cape
(where twin gulfs unite in the Red Sea)
panorama of infinity.

iii

All night watching the caravan
from the zenith vigilant, wary
protective with her wingspan
(where circumstances vary)
Cygnus looked-out for Jahlilah;
made her dreams spectacular
circumnavigating galaxies
flexing giant white wings with ease
(far from oases in the sand)
where grains of light numberless
lie scattered in a star-wilderness
astronomically grand.
Backward-looking, whisper-tentative
hear Jahlilah's silver narrative.

iv

No one else says a single word
as convoy snakes waveringly south.
'I dreamed about a firebird
who spoke a paradoxical truth:
"Palestine will rise from ashes
when non-violence vanquishes."
Nothing spins in CD tray;
blue smoke spirals from an ashtray
(helix which means 'someone getting high').
Bedouin, now on camelback
alongside our roadtrain track
over sand, reflexes in standby
outriders against cliffs of limestone.
See, their camels smile at the unknown.

v

Who were waiting in acacia-woods
at Hazna, place of water-supply
behind, below; who now upwards
slow, sandy gradients ply;
these far-celebrated animals
(famously-humped desert-mammals)
who thirstlessly, ship-like, triumph
sailing across the yellow gulf
between Aqaba and Suez:
absolute endurance-in-motion
crossing sand-equivalents of ocean
creatures of patience and noblesse;
who, nevertheless, can and do snap
(in a cameleer's mishap).

vi

The camel's eye and foaming smile
must sound alarms in cameleers
because, behind expressions docile
easygoing, lurks a beast which flares
suddenly: shadow-dromedary
the opposite of exemplary
who bites, sometimes fatally
bad-tempered brute who eats testily
who slashes with preternatural teeth
with ferocious capability:
dumb and helpless animality
condemned endurantly beneath
man, the tyrannical rider
high on his yellow desert-strider.

vii

Past Gebel Ras Gineina
east of Gebel Reqaba
under Gebel Gunna
over the Gulf of Aqaba
the Canyon of the Green Eye:
whose white-powdered sand-floors lie
outstretched under date-palm orchards.
Towards this wadi, always onwards
eight pantechnicons, big roadrangers
on punishing gradients exert
horsepower in the high-desert;
where arms-dealers still present dangers.
Yet sometimes exactly the reverse
thanks to music's power to coerce.

viii

(Somalians actually guided
through a sandstorm at one point.
It seems some gunrunners decided
to trade Kalashnikovs for a joint).
But there've been better surprises
(where noon-heat terrorizes).
Bound for the Wadi of the Green Eye
at Roadcamp Three a black rabbi
sang a lullaby in Amharic
through which mystically shone
the Magisterium of Prester John
(while Souljahs' calming, therapeutic
soundsystem purred in background
with tranquil dubs of ultrasound).

ix

The Ethiopian preached a sermon
near the Forest of Pillars
truly worthy of Solomon
(some of his lines were total killers).
He said One Holyland was blessed
both in concept and put-to-the-test
in the burning terrain of fact.
He spoke of a new kind of peace-pact
saying Palestinian and Hebrew
should not be divided any more
than the child Solomon swore
long-ago to slash in two.
He prayed that love would soon overcome;
chanting to a doumbek's low drum.

x

Through dusk, behind Blue Mountains
Mercs, Volvos, MANs now thread a defile
(guided-in by Tuwara chieftains)
negotiating, mile-by-slow-mile
a maze of canyons, coloured, seamed
top-to-bottom with layers formed
in porphyry and greenstone
shadowed basalt, lighter sandstone:
smooth-veined corridors of tinted walls
river-planed millennia ago
by watercourses in downflow;
where now, as night in Sinai falls
there seems no limit to hearing-range
in a silence absolutely strange.

xi

This is Roadcamp Four, the last
before the Wadi of the Green Eye.
Silence is interrupted by a blast
from a V12 mammoth nearby
revving on sand-mats. (Another surge:
clouds spinning at the amber verge.)
If more wheels stick in the wadi-bed
One Holyland will be dead
only half-started, so planned tactics
involve off-loading to the camels
soundsystems, lights and portables.
Such terrain's too tricky for artics:
the work of the pantechnicons is done.
(The poor camels' tasks have just begun.)

xii

The Canyon of the Green Eye
lies five miles into fantasyland.
No two-lane blacktop leads there, just dry
white-powdered, pristine virgin-sand.
(Now we break the tie with tarmac
rip-off its thin black lie, throw it back
in civilization's bloated face.)
From this point on we slow the pace
to a camel-walk, replace the wheel
with the dromedary's tassled rein.
Rayyan, Moss, Laurence, Aziz explain
tactics to car-drivers, who kneel
lowering tyres PSI
deflating partially.

xiii

Not one squalid incident
has coloured the venture thus far
as if some force had cleared all strident
angry thoughts from pure desert-air.
Sajjid's 'rehearsal for unity'
'experiment in community'
his 'non-violent, bi-partisan
Arab-Israeli peace-caravan'
has rolled triumphantly to this point.
The calm presence of Rasta elders
greybeards with dreadlocks over shoulders
solemnly passing chalice and joint
radiating equanimity
has helped bring unanimity.

And yet there is the battle to come.
Courtesy as order-of-the-day
will bow before the war-drum
when the dread time arrives to say
live-to-the-world what must be said.
(Only two networks imbed
with One Holyland consensually:
just al-Jazeera and BBC.)
The rap-war will feed to Youtube
in real-time (thanks to Trailblazer John
and his bad app 'Phenomenon').
From there every web-suburb
including Facebook's just a link
down the chain to everyone-dot-inc.

xv

Nightfall in Sinai: drumming-circles
form among sworn enemies.
A peace-pipe and a chillum cycles
between the 'generals' of 'armies':
Tamar Nafar and his rap-allies
Subliminal, with his Israelis.
Roadcamp Four is blessed as I Vibes
(crippled-angels of Rasta tribes)
chant-out: 'Yes, I'd rather to be
where the grass is green always'
as Apple Gabriel on crutches sways
down the plane of a Scania's proxy-
screen in the break of 'Greedy Dog.'
(O my days, his cosmic leapfrog.)

xvi

Pink twilight settles on the land
an atmosphere romantic.
Cygnus rising, mightily-wingspanned
overhears (Rayyan to Rahiq)
the usual bunkum lovers-in-bliss
burble as prelude-to-a-kiss:
'You're life's oasis, flower-maiden;
the sun shines 'coz you are a garden.'
Still, old cliches King Flirt's just uttered
(oversweet, his vocabulary)
whispered in pea-green temporary
home (among many, all-coloured)
are the testament of a city
built upon affinity.

xvii

'Tasneem wants me married soon!'
(Cygnus wonders who says this
trying from the orient to attune.)
'Same thing sucked-down my older sis'
Salimah in a whirlpool last year.'
Cygnus sees the twin-gulfs, very near:
deep Aqaba (thirty-miles or-less)
the shallow Straits of Suez.
'The guy's so vanilla-envelope
runs a little computer-shop
downtown Beirut; Tasneem can't stop
singing praises while I sit and mope.
Talkin 'bout grandchildren and money.
Security bringing harmony.'

Cygnus wonders: Whose tent is this?
Who speaks from the triangular
black, wedge-shaped wilderness
which is the Sinai peninsula?
Tone is silvery, familiar
melancholic with sense of failure
the voice of one like Sylvia
(who, suicided, sent a shiver
long-ago, never-to-be-forgotten
through London's archetypal skies;
she who tried to rhapsodize
single-motherhood and rotten
luck, abandoned to her lonely craft
while literary critics laughed).

xix

It's Jahlilah, nearly sobbing
fingering her single dread
(while painful hearts is throbbing)
asking herself 'Where has all this led?
Must I go back to Shatila
tear out by the roots my freewheeler
settle down and die of boredom
live the life of genteel whoredom
married to a computer-genius?'
(Cygnus watches a burning tear
fall down her blue top and disappear.)
'Housewives are heterogeneous.
Some new heart-stealer might give a knock
who knows, one day, with better luck.'

xx

Is this the brave girl who faked a grin
fibbing to Tasneem when cheap Cedars'
stench became - another sin -
scent of coconut-shampoo? Old scars
on left wrist (so visible)
seem to Cygnus plausible.
She's seen young girls, child-martyrs
ones whom teenage angst batters
destroy themselves sometimes to resist
characterization not-to-taste;
sighing-and-crying for the waste
when life's dullest chapters insist
you play the game by always trying
never, ever to be caught lying.

xxi

'Hey, in this southern wonderland
it's way-safer; I'm not gonna worry;
plus, I knew the odds beforehand.
Still-'n'-all, it's bare-jittery.'
Dishonestly, she talks herself down
from panic-attack, with strong frown
holds back idiotic second tear
afraid he'll see it hanging there.
(Cygnus understands her dilemma:
'Falling-in-love-with-the-enemy
versus return-to-nonentity.'
She weighs trauma-against-trauma
whispers some advice to the poor girl
secret word which makes her eyes whirl.)

xxii

Blue-streaming blunt seemingly affixed
to mouth, clenched, not held with lips
Mossman looks hundred-percent relaxed
as carelessly from him slips
(with modern inverse-gallantry)
'Would you then, like... marry me?'
He waits, with action indiscreet
brushing Jahlilah's naked feet.
(In canyon's silence uncanny.)
Complete peace reigns in southern Sinai.
Where, as Cygnus glides across the sky
a lizard, sliding from a cranny
in moonlight, snaps transparent eyelid.
(And suddenly our nightscene is hid.)

CHAPTER

11

i

Entering the ancient wadi
Canyon of the Green Eye
(Ain Hudra, frond-filtered, shady
where light seems to liquefy)
we cruise on sands levelled so flat
they look hand-planed (as even as that)
pure snow-white sands now tinted pink
with dawn-rays from the sun's red wink;
who, rising over the riverbed
(where our caravan's espied)
lifts his head, though preoccupied
deep in 'Guidebook to the Day-ahead'
knowing this a significant one.
(Believe when you hear it from the sun.)

ii

Who glances at Green Eye; who blushes
pinker and prettier as she smiles
fluttering now serrate eyelashes
in dawn-breeze, lifting palm-veils.
Twelve hours to the moon's full;
everyone's feeling a tight schedule.
A lot depends on whether
SRT get their act together.
Carbon-60 mainmasts should soon
stand palm-high in the oasis
killer-sound's crucial basis.
Wave field synthesis must, by noon
be tested for spatialization.
In the heat: vast mobilization.

iii

Unladen camels kneel in shade
ruminating thoughtfully
as glazed carbon stage-plinth (conveyed
in three cross-sections successfully)
locks together down on powdered sand
assembling as rapidly as planned.
The rising sun and Lady Green Eye
trade looks across a turquoise sky
exchange glances of astonishment
as deck-cabins are suspended
(pragmatic energy expended)
as rope-ladders invite ascent
into the DJ's wonderful nests
high between crystalline masts:

iv

Slender, superbonded towers
blend diaphanously with palms;
seem glass stems of giant flowers
springing upward with see-through plumes
(as some new flora of palm-orchards
or nesting-place of firebirds?)
Array is scanned, checked for sweetspots.
Running digital 'earshots'
monitors are raked to maximise
sound for mainmixer and stage-sector
fine-tuning each acoustic vector
where rap-acts will vocalize
where rappers will spit and flow live
from where One Holyland will arrive.)

v

Seated in a multicoloured ring
Circlework women-drummers
keep all afternoon outpouring
hypnotic rhythmic shimmers
(Palestinians and Druze
Bedouins and Israeli Jews).
From the shade their drum-figures entrance
with subtle hand-struck cadence;
learning from Laurence of Zambia
(Bantu master-drummer) to create
the lilting metres of six-eight
(African musical insignia)
the iron timelines of Caja
the phrasing-patterns of Kata.

vi

Ain Hudra: named for its green well.
(Where water is always to revere
in the brutal emptiness of hell
where heedlessness is no small affair
where men say 'water' under their breath
where wastage can be punished with death
insult of temerity
crime met with severity.)
Here, a verdant, lenient zone
atmosphere of lush date-orchards
desert-analogue of everglades
(high over which now hovers a drone)
opens unconditionally
welcomes nonjudgmentally.

vii

Well-water's now aquaducted
in featherweight transparent siphons
raised on pylons (also constructed
from carbon-60) glass-like sections
winding through the palm-orchards
to 'the-place-of-exploding-upwards'
where translucent cycling-basins
(designed by flowform-masons
beautiful concavities
reminiscent of sea-shells)
lure waters to meander-channels
where they play with gravity's
pull, cascading liquid quantities:
spiralling lucid vortices.

viii

The Fountains of Euphoria
symbolize One Holyland's
commitment to an idea:
dream which airily transcends
torpid earthbound politics
(non-reasoning of lunatics)
envisioning a single-state
where 'antagonists' reintegrate
trust again, where 'enemies' respect
redraw stiff-necked maps to recombine
as Palareal or Isratine
(whatever) the name to reflect
interconnect; all-the-way
saying: 'One Holyland, one day.'

ix

Over the Gulf of Aqaba
full moon rises like a lantern
to the chime of Laurence' marimba:
yellow orb transiting eastern
heavens, golden lunar lamp
illuminating the peace-camp
about to turn into battleground.
(Luna looks down in wonder, westbound
shining horizontally
amazed that all can unify
in the Canyon of the Green Eye
look at each other honestly.)
Now a battle for world-consensus:
millennial catharsis.

From the labyrinth of the Blue Stacks
where smooth-eroded orange sandstone
corridors twist in crazy switchbacks
Youtube sees a black rabbi intone
a prayer blessing One Holyland's
venture in possible quicksand;
listens to a Sufi imam pray
for the opening-up of love's way
across the wastelands of earth;
hears a Christian Rastaman
chanting for the One Love masterplan.
As Luna says to herself: 'Have birth
O Child-Tetragrammaton
only one, long-forgotten.'

xi

Burning Spear hits the soundsystem:
"Do you remember the days of slavery?
O, slavery days.' (Supercharged riddim
intensifies, revelatory:
slow, encumbered chant of pain
in which angrily red lashes rain
from the whip of an imperialist
white Jamaican colonialist.)
Circlework women drum along
jingling many an amulet:
'Usually pull-it, we pull it.'
Bassline of the legendary song
bubbles slow, big dub-prayer:
roots-testament of Burning Spear.

xii

For ignition of the lasers
ambient and downtempo
pads from quiescent synthesizers
drone with enormous afterglow.
Reverb-tails hang in sonic space
underneath cool doumbek, keeping pace
with loops of electronic soundwash:
beating pulse to tranquil backwash.
Now the Fountains of Euphoria
fly up with lucent carelessness
illuminate in weightlessness
lifting toward Utopia
the spirits of five thousand
seated on still-hot, snow-white sand.

xiii

Aquafer-waters exploding
(shot-through with iridescence
predetermined by optical coding)
generate intricate, intense
rainbows, defining spectra;
make the fountain a tiara
multicoloured: red, green, gold.
Easily five-thousand (all told)
congregated on warm sand
sitting, standing, kneeling, lying
with tricoloured waters highflying
seem crowned: a symbolic headband
ceremoniously given to each.
(See, then, some paradise-beach.)

Budayl takes the stage, in left-hand
beacon flaring vividly brighter;
black Mushtak in his right-hand
(Bedouin poet, freedom-fighter
torch of the lyre, singer in his prime).
'Peeps, One Holyland's here on time.'
(Budayl's master of ceremonies
because Sajjid on bended-knees
implored 'n' begged him please to MC.)
Oasis of the Green Eye
shimmers under a twilight sky;
handclapping ripples joyfully
across white ocean-even sand.
Five-thousand echo: 'One Holyland.'

Mushtaq's eyes are bigger than moons:
brave storm-riding Egyptian.
(Budayl's right hand gently cocoons
the legendary racing-pigeon.)
'Black Mushtaq, like my Lord Jarir
fly the peninsula's atmosphere
race with the news we're up 'n' runnin'.'
(Two orange eyes are glistening.)
'Tell them in Shatila it's all good;
tell the exiles "All-systems-go."
In the death-camp they should know
they need a lift down in the 'hood.'
With this last emphatic word
Budayl tosses high racing-bird.

Mushtaq, spinning into the zenith
in spirals (tracked by thousands of eyes)
now arrows free, uncircling, north-
eastward flying where Lebanon lies
behind the horizon a hundred miles.
'Okay, performer-profiles.'
(Mushtaq's vanished, magnetic-compass
guiding over vast landmass.)
'Later, peeps, you'll hear Jahlilah
her mind-bending phenomenal
flow: intellectual, emotional.
As Mushtaq reaches Shatila
(where our poet's from) she'll be onstage:
our al-Khansaa for the modern age.'

xvii

'Right now: MC's for tonight.
First-up, from Tel Aviv, TAF
The Abrahamic Family: tight
unit with attitude for def.
Then from occupied Ramallah
rap-messengers Inshallah:
name says it all. Then, next up
the explosive Turboprop
straight outta oppressed Jenin.
Then you get Noiz, antizionist
Israeli thrillers; then Coexist
sensational Jewbro from Lod, seen?'
Projections of Banksy's *Watchtower*
blitz a widescreen with play-power:

xviii

War-kids, gliding in bucket-seats
air-ride round an obelisk of hell
laughing as the watchtower rotates
(street-art's fairground anti-carousel)
their cries of joy carrying wonder
drowning-out rumble of war-thunder;
screaming as they orbit the snipers
(staring down with sceptical whispers).
'Then, blood, time for Dam!' (Crowd explodes
under deep-blue evening-sky star-flecked
with dazzling constellations decked.)
'Next, you-know-who.' 'Boo!' (Vibe implodes.)
'Right now: TAF. Give it up fo'
The Abrahamic Family, yo.'

Rap of The Abrahamic Family

'We rep for the whole A Family, yeah
one Moslem, one Christian, one Jew, yeah;
One love in the fam of Abraham, yeah
one big love in One Holyland, yeah.'

Differences do exist, that's true, yeah
but x-'mount of sim'larities shine thru 2, yeah
so from texts don't argue but from love
follow-through, yeah;
whining minor details just sucks man into
endlessly different fine-tunings of sects
construing doctrines (and histories related)
finding angles, insights, studying contexts
intellects dry-as-dust, well-inflated
sham-philosopher dogma-specialists
far from the superconscious catalysts:
the meditations of breaking-through, yeah
to the standpoint of the overview, yeah.

One love in the fam of Abraham, yeah
one big love in One Holyland, yeah.'

Rap of Inshallah

Under occupation, Allah akbah
my occupation: rapper.

Silver on my neck since Ramallah's
under a hail of lead. And when it flashes
watch out, my lil' brothers and sisters:
with steel impunity the bullet lashes
one-and two-year-old's as inhumanity invades.
Come holler-me, bro, in the air-raids:
check my headphone-mixes with jet-planes
(not fx but F16's in the cans)
in the sky for real above my studio
downgrading audio-quality
psychoacoustic sonority:
that's a typical scenario.

Under occupation, Allah akbah
my occupation: rapper.

Friends ram-raid businesses of settlers
tech-shops, jewelers, I know it ain't right;
I go along with a lot of heavy social pressures
try to say no and keep out the fight
with satanic weapons, stick to microphones.
(Don' wanna blast war-trumpet thighbones;
it's pagan when you blow peeps away;
last cries haunt man to dying day.)
'One Holyland' sounds meaningful
in vernacular-stroke-classical Arabic
Hebrew and English: and that's fully sick
a new definition of wonderful.
Under occupation, Allah akbah
my occupation: Arabian rapper.

Rap of Turboprops

Soundz of an Arabian tambourine
ringin' in the Slingshot Hiphop scene
swingin' in my birthplace, beloved Jenin.
With the dirty facts I'm comin' clean.

Dirty facts 'bout the true nature of Jihad.
Mos' piss-a-bed boys wanna be real bad
run up in your face with some attitude
(testosterone's in the young dude
firin'-up his adolescent spree).
The real Jihad is the war inside
yeah, the only war that can set you free
the war to make Satan commit suicide.
Yo, Israel's a fuckin headache, true
how much more genocide can we take?
But violent reaction's a fundamental mistake;
tha's exactly wha' the Shaitan expects of you.

The ring of an Arabian tambourine
soundin' in the Slingshot Hiphop scene
in beatz 4 my city of birth, Jenin.
With the basic facts I'm comin' clean.

Rap of Noiz

I'm a straight-talkin whigga by de name of Noiz;
I'll spell that backwards (for the schoolboys)
decipherin' the opposite of what I am:
encoded, encrypted anagram.

...
...
...
...
...
...
...
...
...
...
...
...

Rap of Coexist

Wanna show you the city-sights:
sinners and sodomites
hangin' from street-lights
dangling from building-sites.

'Backwardness out there is not 'pretend'.
Think of that medieval kingdom
made of sand. How to comprehend
a world where per-capita income
is sky-high but women can't drive cars;
or that land of the mad mullahs
where teens hang from tower-cranes
because they melt mental chains
binding them to yesterday
slaves of creeds and holy codes;
who'd skip down interesting side-roads
but end their lives on public display:

Lemme show you the city-sights:
sinners and sodomites
dangling from building-sites
hangin' from street-lights.

...
...
...
...
...
...
...
...
...

Rap of Da Arabian MC's

Every ghost-poet has another half
so lemme hip ya to my twin biograph.

I'm the carrier of Arabia
surrounded by xenophobia
urban schizophrenia.
I'm the righteous seer
from Mesopotamia
suffering insomnia
sadness of nostalgia.
Rap-animal exterior
deep poet of my area
I'm the carrier of Arabia:
I'm the carrier of Arabia.

Every ghost-poet has another half
so lemme hip ya to my twin biograph.

I live for euphoria
(one love's utopia)
sacred marijuana
in the new millennia.
I'm the carrier of Arabia
a forbidden encyclopaedia.
What's my contraband idea?
As far as I'm aware
(rap-animal exterior
deep poet of my area)
I'm the carrier of Arabia
I'm the carrier of Arabia.

Every ghost-poet has another half
so lemme hip ya to my twin biograph.

Rap of Subliminal

You know what, Tamar, I repent
if you take back callin' me a Nazi
on camera, that night we spent
filming *Channels of Rage*, nasty
name for your number-one cody
who acted sometimes like your humble roadie
makin' sure you weren't too stoned
for the gig in Lod (so it wasn't postponed).
Everything got so much harder

xix

Properly Sub gets a massive hand
echoing around the oasis;
retractions of this firebrand
rapper in the wilderness
show the force of One Holyland.
Eleven pm on floodlit sand.
(Shadowmouth, invisible drone
hovers, scanning from sky-zone:
'Confirm, target one to the stage'.)
Budayl announces: 'From Shatila
people, give it up for Jahlilah
now rapocalypse gonna rage.'
(Aziz, with stagehand armband
presses forward, SS on his hand.)

Rap of Jahlilah:

The Grindstone

In bad dreams of fevered sleep
a burning wheel of centuries
indefinitely, forever turns:
this is exile dragging on.

And how did we trangress, tell me?
As I toss, turn and chafe restlessly
on a rooftop in Shatila's dump
dozing lightly in the returnee-camp
in my breezeblock tomb tightly sealed
(in my little refugee-bedroom)
I dream my dad Tareef's healed
wake and hear in grey dawn-gloom
(damp nights of November, December)
his dry cough, making me remember
our broken sleep of displacement
insomnia of resettlement.

In bad dreams of fevered sleep
on a burning wheel of centuries
vast timespans turn and turn:
exiled aeons dragging on.

In Forty-Eight came hatred with exile
following hungrily on her heels;
near the old village in the green hills
the alien harrowing of our fields.
You, noble landholder of yesterday
saw them defile the mother-country

the 'sabre-tooth tiger' infantry
angrily hunting on the sabbath-day
even, with automatic rifles, modern
weapons in the service of catastrophe, then:
at the real beginning of the troubles
when we became dust, disposables.

In exile's sleep recurrent dreams
turn and twist with nightmare-scenes
enduring thousands of centuries:
timelessly, endlessly.

Defiance was always your strong suit
nothing ever glittered on principle for you;
now everything's rusted except hate.
A dirty trade for small revenue
knife-grinding with a three-wheeled handcart
has nearly broken your lionheart.
Embittered, I can't end up like you.
On my knees I cannot continue
living, I have to stand up and try
to be me somehow. And if I die trying
then dying's my way of saying
'fuck you' to the Zionist lie.

In bad dreams of fevered sleep
a burning wheel of centuries
indefinitely, forever turns:
our infinite exile dragging on.

In the concrete guts of Shatila
trundling your carborundum-stone
door-to-door and home-to-home

pushing your little handcart, three-wheeler
peeps give you scraps of this and that
an apron, a bike-pump, perhaps an old hat
as you go your rounds grinding knives and scissors
through Beirut's temperamental winters.
But I don't wanna be humiliated like *you*
when they call you 'one-step-from-a-hawker', 'tinker'
and your lionheart fills up with rancour
and you curse the homecoming of the Jew.

In fevered sleep a bad dream
burns for endless centuries
exile through indefinite aeons
in our dark penitentiaries.

Grinding afternoons with hacking cough
through overstacked tenement-block shadows
(wits sharp-as-ever when super-tough
gangster-clients lean from dirty windows
to hear the late-night prince of talkers
now become the prince of hawkers)
kids throw stones by the roadside
'hard as the thought of one's graveside'.
Your broken-down system no more immune;
in your hot bedroom you lie speechless
conscious of your own weakness
filling to the brim that night-spittoon.

Exile seems to feed well
on our wasted flesh and bones
as feverish, restless sleep burns
thousands of centuries.

So much friction across history
grinding uselessly, aimlessly.
(Sometimes you say you prefer to be
a knifegrinder than a terrorist Israeli.)
Three-sides-of-a-square meant exile
in the delirium of our uprooting;
and now when some pockmarked juvenile
teases in Shatila's alleyways, saluting
you, proud heart, as 'The Scavenger'
you would be our dignity's avenger
though you believe from Holy Koran
man must live in peace with fellow-man.

Exile's dream is a sick and bitter
nightmare lasting centuries
while slow aeons of cold rain
spiral down time's gutter.

So how do Israelis want us to act
with their 'Don't ask, don't tell' adolescent mankillers
roaming our streets, matter-of-fact
teenage mass-murderers slaughtering toddlers
in our hostage-cities: Bethlehem, Jenin.
These days you can't even buy an aspirin
when they gun you to the ground in Ramallah
in occupied Nablus, downtown Qalqilyah.
How react to arrest-operations
robotic soldiers at nightfall
blasting through a party-wall;
armoured killdozer's devastations?

This sleep is the death of our soul
in the dark night of banishment.

But we can't forget Palestine
through centuries of stone.

Favoured races, say Darwinians
survive, but not Palestinians.
But Dad, I ain't gonna be like you
I'm gonna rap-out, gonna rap-through
sayin: 'Puttin down the gun, pickin up the mic'
sayin: 'Words are the way to be warlike'
sayin: 'No peace without justice'
sayin: 'One big love in this oasis'

Bad dreams of fevered sleep;
a burning wheel of centuries
indefinitely, forever turning:
our long exile dragging on.

My grindstone is rap and sparks will fly
as in the rough trade of my dad, Tareef.
(Discordantly I testify
in the darkness declare my belief.)
Dull blades, my sharpening emery-wheel
will brighten, intensify the way you feel
save with verbal electricity.
Regardless of ethnicity
in One Holyland's theocratic state
we'd all once again venerate
one another unconditionally
once more love 'unrealistically'.

In aeons of midnight exile
long sleep is the death of the soul.
But I don't forget Palestine
through centuries of stone.

So if you wanna be a perfectionist
affirm your parallel religionist.
Fallin' in love with your enemy
is not necessarily blasphemy.
And, Daddy, like Issa I'm gonna do
the crazy thing no one would expect
do the one thing no one would do.
And right now I demand your respect
coz, Daddy Tareef, I'm gonna marry a Jew;
Mamma Tasneem, I'm marryin' a Jew.
And 'bout now I'm gonna introduce him to you:
his name, The Rambam (Go on, say 'Boo! Boo!')

xx

Green Eye blazes, thunders applause
for *Grindstone*, Jahlilah's rap
(where rugged hipster vocab explores
High Arabic in smooth overlap).
None mock as our dreadlocked outsider
MC Rambam, Rasta low-rider
slouches onstage, reticent
not exactly the spouse heaven-sent
Tasneem's been imagining.
(Budayl.) 'Peeps, it's MC Rambam.
Watch, he's gonna loose a Slingshot slam
for Palestine's un-imprisoning.
The time of freedom on the planet
is the dream of every street-prophet.'

Moss and Jalilah's Rap

Some call us Romeo 'n' Jahlilah
whatever, anyways we're the showstealer;
nex' one called us Suicide Pact
look, we're still here, message intact.
Gonna show you crossings-over of ethnicity
rainbow-bridges of unity;
gonna sharpen cutting-edges of perception
free those trapped in shadows of deception.
Sparks are gonna fly, lies are gonna die
burn-up in the friction of our double-diction;
with spiritual-political truth's non-fiction:
our double-act blazin' in The Sinai.

(Jahlilah, solo)

I was raised with usual stereotypes
born out of tense relationships
over the last one-hundred years:
'All Jews are bloodsucking profiteers.'
(Aggressive Zionist landgrab in overdrive
reinforced that whisper back in '45.)
Caged in the camp I didn't know any Jews;
I raged, thought it crazy to change my views;
then in a split-second The Rambam's
'Salaam, Shalom, Peace' hit me with wordflow
on the highway: lightning-strikes, thunderstorms.
Now that man'll tell ya wha' ya need to know.

(Moss, solo)

The night of my eighteenth birthday
my luck was sparkling like the Milky Way

like some supernova or cosmic ray;
but man felt in the dark like a sad castaway.
So to link for real with my soul-brother
over the hills from The Galilee to Nazareth
I flew, the night of the Gaza bloodbath
(with Rimbaud sayin' 'I is another').
On escape-routes from normality
from boredoms of conformity
I took-off like a gypsy in my old black car
following my boho lodestar.

(together)

We sharpen the cutting-edges of perception
free, trapped in webbed orbits of deception.
Gonna show you crossings-over of ethnicity
rainbow-bridges of unity.
I thought I was dealin' with narcotic need
runnin' in the crazy night for weed.
(At fourteen when Solomon quit smokin'
it was tough as his only son, I ain't jokin'.
He was a much cooler, more-expansive Dada
a li'l stoned, halfway-up Jacob's Ladder.
Funny, he still detects spliff a mile-off
with nasal radar. The old green cough?
You cannot get one past Solomon.
But to this day, like, clockwork-regular
once-a-year at Purim he does a Thai bong
though for Hasids that's irregular.)

Some call us Romeo 'n' Jahlilah
whatever, we're the showstealer;
someone else called us Suicide Pact
look, we're still here, message intact.

Anyways, makin' my midnight-dash
to score some resinous Zahret el Kolch
(down to my last Algerian roach)
my night-drive seemed all about superhash:
a quest for the definitive high.
I didn't know I was sayin' goodbye
putting old Galilee good-life behind
my so-called friends, jus' travellin' blind
to a voodoo appointment underground
with love-at-first-sight: a knockdown blow.
Deep in Transworld of the ultrasound
I looked through a spiritual window.

Some call us Romeo 'n' Jahlilah
whatever, we're the showstealer;
someone else called us Suicide Pact
look, we're still here, message intact.
In black headwrap a slim girl on-mic
delivered the histories malign:
her *Ethnic Cleansing of Palestine*.
These dreads of mine stood-on-end, like
as I heard her poem of damnation:
full-on flashback, hi-definition
scan of what happened in Forty-Eight
all related with no trace of hate:
just this young woman with eyes closed
motionless, as if sleeping
telling about the agonized
time of no safekeeping.

We sharpen the cutting-edges of perception
free, trapped in histories of deception.
Gonna show you transcultural ethnicity
rainbow-bridges of unity.

As she rapped, my ancestor's words
came flooding back, warning of hazards
from centuries ago, saying: 'No return
even if through long exile you yearn.'
In the blacked-out subterranean club
I seemed to hear (mind aswirl)
The Rambam, prophet of my tribe
speaking through this Palestinian girl
dark truths, lyrical, articulate.
His voice echoed in every sad verse
warning of the end-time-curse
after the genocide of Forty-Eight.

Sparks are gonna fly, lies are gonna die
burn-up in the friction of our double-diction;
with spiritual-political truth's non-fiction:
our double-act blazin' in The Sinai.
Peeps were shattered, deeply-affected
as she chanted the lost-village names.
From time-and-space I disconnected;
split-seconds existed other lifetimes.
Then, with hot tears in my eyes
('scuze me, I don't romanticize)
all blurred-up, looking through mist
(hey, man's no sentimentalist)
with consciousness on a new axis
with butterflies in my solar-plexus
I'm lookin' at the light of my heart
thinkin' the words: 'Till death us do part.'

Some call us Romeo 'n' Jahlilah
whatever, anyways we're a showstealer;
nex' one called us Suicide Pact

look, we're still here, message intact.
Gonna show you crossings-over of ethnicity
rainbow-bridges of unity;
gonna sharpen cutting-edges of perception
free those trapped in shadows of deception.
Sparks are gonna fly, lies are gonna die
burn-up in the friction of our double-diction;
with spiritual-political truth's non-fiction:
our double-act blazin...

xx

A sudden stroboscopic freeze
as cold light arrows, slashing the stage!
Moss collapses - mid-rap - to his knees
neck fountaining from red cleavage
bright arterial blood - frightening
deluge - pumping-out, glistening
spurting from a jugular shredded.
(Already half the deck is flooded.)
Jahlilah intercepts his fall
plunging downward to catch him
as he tumbles, trying to snatch him
red spattering black headshawl
blood staining blue bomber-jacket.
(Where is the ram caught in the thicket?)

Mossman's final syllables spit
faintly, meant for Jahlilah alone;
yet all distinctly hear and audit
as a blood-soaked microphone
still amplifies last words, whispered
swallowed, choked, sucked and slurred:
'Get off this stage, rapstar... jet!
Leave me, Jahlilah... just don't forget
babes, the bridge of hope,...' In despair
bending over blood-flecked lips
clutching with crimson fingertips
see our girl at black headscarf tear
making a bandage for a wound
to no avail to wrap around.

xxii

Against her scream all goes dark.
(Now a second enigmatic flash
lights stage-area, sudden and stark
across nothingness: cold hell-slash.)
Heart-rending, her cry intensifies
as Rayyan (dancer-every-time) flies
sideways in an acrobatic leap
swiftly manouevering to grab, keep
from strange lightning-bolts: too late!
Two red pools lie blending on the deck:
Moss bleeding from torn-open neck
Jahlilah, too, haemorrhaging, prostrate
how badly injured who can say
in this chaos? (Let us pray.)

CHAPTER

12

i

Overshadowing melodies
once more the sombre tone sustain.
Again sound pensive harmonies;
listen now for light-music in vain.
(Listener, if you are not inclined
to angular movements, if you find
too much pain in my dissonant theme
I also would awake from that dream
where bittersweet, unresolving chords
echo some troubled polyphony
haunting this life's symphony
trace of existential discords:
grating and unpleasant note
never from our human world remote.)

One who wrote this savage score
oldest Sacre du Printemps
we may reflect, is probably more
responsible than anyone
for a lingering sense of disquiet
in the core of the human heart.
O Lord, how are we to explain
the mystery of Your terrain
dark with hazard, plagued by horrors
country-of-the-hard-pains-of-birth
the worldly estate of the whole earth
poisoned with duality's flowers
where, for reasons which remain unknown
evil slashes down to the bone.

iii

When whole galaxies are bloodied
by the violence of necessity
no choice for us but to concede
we travellers in adversity.
(Is there small commiseration
in the thought that all creation
suffers inexplicable shockwaves
catastrophic negatives?
'This flesh is injured with all the rest';
comfort - some? - in the fact of boredom
generated by that arcade-game
which puts no player to the test?)
The mystery of our suffering
needs careful deciphering.

iv

We return - numb - to that wilderness
where Musa burned to make One Love
suffice: one decree of tenderness.
(His Decalogue was more adaptive
a second-best fallback approach
designed less straightforwardly to teach;
more to guide the perplexed
step-by-step with impressive text;
soon to be expanded by Levites
spiritual bureaucrats
multiplying caveats
for the bewildered Israelites
just celebrating delivery
from corporeal slavery.)

v

We are still in the Land of Turquoise
where a wolf with blueish torso prowls
stony wastes of Ard al-Fairuz
genocide dripping from its jowls;
where a bird with x-ray eyes
over the barren Mafqat flies
marking-out victims in the sand.
(Yet see how God's angels stand
in massed ranks luminescent
mobilizing to support
with rainbow-armoured escort
a disembodied soul's ascent
sounding a magnificent retreat
from what to us seems only defeat.)

vi

When the stealth-beam that killed The Rambam
left Jahlilah fighting for life
an ambulance flashing blue alarm
(frenziedly screaming from its roof)
thundered up the highway to Nekhel
with Red Crescent personnel
doing all in their power
in this catastrophic hour
to keep our heroine alive.
Some claim - probably delusion -
on the road a transfusion
helped Jahlilah to survive.
Was Moss Rambam's blood taken:
morbid yet romantic notion?

vii

Who knows? Some hip bloggers claim both
rappers were one rare blood-type.
(In cybernetic undergrowth
smoke 'n' rumours fuse with hype
generating urban myths
conspiratorial 'truths'.)
What is undeniable
factual and reliable:
long before the ambulance
reached the airstrip at Nekhel
unprecedented groundswell
not surprising in the circumstance
(a tsunami, to be accurate)
hit and rocked the internet.

viii

Trailblazer's feed to Youtube 'live'
had logged ninety-five million views
even before the laser's death-dive;
so when the planet clocked the bad news
saw assassinated in real-time
The Rambam (rapping mid-rhyme)
saw Jahlilah cut-down by stealth-drone
the datastream from Phenomenon
crashed several servers Stateside.
Many-more-million views then mustered;
meaning highest figures registered
ever; implying that, electrified
transculturally - almost at first-hand -
the world encountered One Holyland.

ix

After the strike by Shadowmouth
massive shock: even more defiance.
In immediate aftermath
in unstoppable alliance
one solid block of Jews and Arabs
(while Souljahs dropped dark, slow dubs)
crushed the stage chanting 'One Holyland'
'Jahlilah,' 'The Rambam.' On demand
red-green-and-gold laser-fountain
restarted, re-illuminated.
And, Rasta DJ's reinstated
Garvey's Ghost came haunting:
calming and elegiac
solemn, melancholy soundtrack.

x

Then Coltrane's *A Love Supreme*
resounded with sadness at Green Eye
faith in all great faiths the theme
(a requiem for what cannot die
from the jazz-divinity's
saxophone-of-infinity).
Moss was mourned by a wailing 'Trane;
Jahlilah was keened in each refrain.
Then Sajjid, at three a.m.
got up and moved everyone to tears
offering on-mic Sufic prayers
another sort of requiem;
but starting with the pungent phrase:
'We ain't hidin' from no death-rays.'

xi

'One Holyland has said with one voice.
The planet is contemplatin' now
our vision of non-violence:
One Big Love, one day, somehow.
Impossible to understand
Moss never made the promised land;
he'll never, ever be forgot
the man's a saint in Slingshot.
We light the candles for Jahlilah
in hospital at Sharm el Sheikh;
in the Land of Turquoise, we're awake
prayin' for her, the truth-teller
stayin' up all night askin' God
to spare the life of that sweet bod.'

xii

What of Big Aziz? Initially
of course he faced accusations.
All knew, as-it-were 'officially'
his sister's 'subversive flirtations'
left him restless, made him grumble.
At one point peeps saw him crumble.
The words: 'Mama, I'm marryin' a Jew'
hit him hard, forced his mind askew
made him raise a fist at the stage.
Then, nearby, some nondescript
(who later vanished) as Moss got dropped
pinpointed Aziz in outrage
making our bro blatantly to blame;
until, of course, truth's counterclaim.

xiii

At dawn news came from Sharm el Sheikh:
Jahlilah Zahlan was alive;
so many had prayed for her sake
peeps jumped for joy, in overdrive.
Good tidings gladdened five-thousand;
raised the spirits of One Holyland.
Simultaneously, by slow degrees
playing on still-shadowed palm-trees
golden daylight threaded pale air
as the sun took a morning-stroll
(a king beneath his cloud-parasol).
After this night, haunted with fear
it seemed an omen of rebirth:
the sun snatched from the jaws of death.

xiv

With Jahlilah out of danger
everyone turned to The Rambam.
His friend, Rayyan, in anger
(in greater sorrow) chose to declaim
a new rap by the dead man
written lying on the warm sand
under the subtropical stars
less than thirty-six hours
earlier (saved on Macbook Air);
from which extremely-battered machine
Rayyan, grave, in early sunshine
not smiling much (still debonair)
rapped the whole of *Moshe's Dream*
(in the wake of *A Love Supreme*).

Moshe's Dream

I spit my wisdom: blam, blam, blam
(know what I mean, don't give a damn).

Jah! Last night on warm sand awake
gazin' up at our local galaxy
drifting to sleep with frequency
suddenly I'm seein' Sharm el Sheikh
that gamblin' den of Eurotrash
where millions get gone, vanished in a flash
where there's no moral caveat.
'N' I'm thinkin': 'We different, we ain't like that:
sleazy, low-life blackjack junkies
smart-enough skin-deep dummies
playin' the star-crossed tables of fate
rolling the dice of "Never-too-late".'

I spit this wisdom: blam, blam, blam
(elliptical, don't give a damn).

Friends, when you see three sixes in a row
that could mean, like, revolution;
but that word don't impress much, no;
what dazzles me is transformation;
'coz Jah in His fiery chalice shakes
all destinies, all human affairs.
And Rastaman plays for higher stakes
on the roulette-wheel of the stars:
workin' with strong, raw energy
then bringin' cool feminine strategy:
Unholyland into One Holyland
transforming on Jah's command.

I spit this wisdom: blam, blam, blam
bringin my little slingshot slam.

Sharm el Sheikh is the mouth of hell
run by that mafioso iron-will cartel
who sell souls reduced as Shaitan's trash
marked-down, on-offer, for ready cash.
(I'm talkin 'bout those skin-deep winnings
by-products of unscrupulous spinnings.)
The Angel of the Great Rift Valley
with God's permission one day violently
will spill the tables of Sharm el Sheikh
shake them peeps till they're all awake;
coz right now, bredda, for real they're sleepin'
in small-hours dark fiends worshippin'.

I spit my wisdom: blam, blam, blam
(know what I mean, don't give a damn).

The Bedouin say: 'Sleep in a house
'n' soul goes creeping, small as a mouse
in dusty rafters, under floorboards
trapped in forgotten graveyards.
But sleep-out on Sinai desert-sands:
your dreamform night-body expands
into the cosmos, through the stars
climbing vastly-ascending stairs
through courtyards of an astral mansion
through gardens of green boulevards
to the city of the great palmyards:
and that is the way of ascension.

I spit this wisdom (blam, blam, blam)
I am that which I am, yes ma'am.

Suns and moons on a tree of light
you glimpse in visionary sleep, agleam.
And you leave your home in the middle of the night
consciously, because of this dream;
not resting in dust and shadows
driven-on by destiny's tornadoes
to be liberated from your past;
psychologically outcast
but closer to that possibility:
(balanced by nobility
tempered by humility)
enlightenment's divinity.

I spit this wisdom (blam, blam, blam)
I am that which I am, yes ma'am.

Rayyan went an hour-and-a-half
freestyling at sunrise. That man
grieved and moved, couldn't say enough
in rhyme for his friend; Rayyan
(king-of-the-underground-side-of-town)
rapped an obit which *really* got-down;
blew everyone at Green Eye apart:
accurate but coming from the heart.
He touched many; some were changed.
(Rayyan caught his friend so right
even the diehard anti-Semite
found some viewpoints rearranged.)
'He coulda played it safe, gone back home
but that wasn't the way with him.'

As Rayyan revisited the legend
(recorded in three movements here)
captured his longtime best-friend
('That sunlit bridge we crossed up there...')
something wonderful happened
impossible, unimagined
miracle of connectivity
digital interactivity.
Grief-stricken Solomon uploaded
to Trailblazer's capacious server
(so that his son could live forever)
the home-movies. Green Eye applauded
as screens positioned between palm-trees
carried footage: the video-diaries.

xvii

Skidz 'n' Tika were able to show
grainy clips from happy Goa years
(while Rayyan freestyled on his bro
sometimes coming close to tears).
In one, parked by lean-to of rattan
a split-screen VeeWee campervan
(vintage rat-look model, no hubcaps
roofrack fitted with surfboard-straps
the alternative road-machine
not exactly Hitler's dream-
vehicle, gaudy colour-scheme
psychedelic orange, army-green)
screamed aloud: 'Indian paradise!'
(Did not have to tell you twice.)

xviii

Then, on riverside white-sanded
on spacious sunny curvature
extended (palm-overslanted
straight out of travel-brochure)
seven-years-of-age in Lotus Land
at play on uneven ivory sand
somewheres in old Candolim:
Moss. And coming straight for him
on lumbering beast, dreadlocks flying
a god-form in sunlight aglow:
a boy on a swamp-buffalo
black twin, red-eyed, terrifying
apparition at the riverbend!
(Childhood's mythologic end.)

xix

In a second clip, aged eleven
you saw Solomon's son shouldered
piggybacking on his Dad, given
uplift (as *Greedy Dog* thundered
down Galilee) raised-high to see
three dreadlocks on crutches stone-free
unbroken, three bodies balancing
on sunlit lakewaters, dancing.
That great Israel Vibration gig!
life-changing for Moss Rambam
imprinted like a hologram
making an impression so big
he could never forget that day
shot shakily by Mum. (Giveaway.)

xx

One Holyland rolled on twelve weeks
longer than intended by Sajjid.
There had to be a few quick tweaks;
at one point Green Eye ran out of weed.
Flying-in from Addis Ababa
a chopper droned across Aqaba
with a gift from Shashamannaland
'da holy grail of contraband:
highland strain of Pineapple Kush
the Royal Queen mind-enhancer
Ethiopian answer
to the famous Zahret el Kolch.
'Or should that be "infamous"?' you say;
but that's the old view of yesterday.

xxi

Why argue the last breaths of my song
waste words when all remains unsaid?
(Much must be excused in works so long:
the night can't be all stars overhead.)
Speaking of stars: Jahlilah Zahlan
(Jah-Zah to fans) got bigger than
anyone else in Slingshot Hiphop
riding the global wave that put stop
to apartheid in the Middle East;
helping peeps slowly to their senses
making all see through different lenses.
When her debut album was released,
Rainbow Bridge, all heard her looking back
to her doomed romance on every track.

xxii

'A Jewish hero on the Arab street'
one reviewer commented.
'Genius speaks bittersweet
language, ecstatic and tormented.'
In these lyrics Moss is Majnoun.
His and his 'Layla's' misfortune:
'To love across battle-lines
to dance among the landmines.'
Lamentations of al-Khansaa
for a loved and long-lost brother
(who cast the shadow of the other)
live again in anthems of Jah-Zah:
legends of her brokenhearted ones
who love as ever-burning suns.

NOTES

BOOK ONE

Chapter 1

ii

'Two-armed beings': The Vedic literature of India carries references to both four-armed and two-armed beings.

vi

'Conceived in Goa': A massive ex-patriate Jewish community in Goa is comprised of many thousands of young Israelis who, unable to participate in the state-terrorism of their home country by reason of conscience, find themselves living a Californian-style beach-life on the western coast of India, where sunny seasons, cheap hotels, good food and plentiful drugs contribute to the atmosphere of a promised land away from The Promised Land.

'Dreadlocks in Moonlight' contains the wonderful phrase: '...valid at sunrise,' which probably suggested the allusion here.

'Lee Scratch Perry': The relatively unknown mad genius of reggae, mentor to Bob Marley, experimental maestro behind Black Ark studios in Kingston, Jamaica. Now married and living in Switzerland, Perry has renounced the Rastafarian sacrament of ganja, controversially stating that he needed to discover whether the music was coming from 'the herb' or from inside himself.

'Likewise mater': Controversially, women are conscripted into the Israeli army.

'Koan': A koan is the sometimes almost surreal riddle communicated by Zen masters to novice monks, who have to 'solve' their particular brain-twister by commenting on it in a way which accords with the spirit of Zen Buddhism. The same koan will be repeated day after day until there is some kind of breakthrough to enlightenment. Perhaps the most famous of these formulae is the question: 'What is the sound of one hand clapping?'

The object of a koan is probably to short-circuit merely functional finite faculties which would (as in the case of Richard Dawkins) idiotically pronounce on the non-existence of God while being unable to predict with any degree of certainty local events of the near future or even 'accidents' waiting to happen in the next five minutes. Yet even as professors of atheism agitate their jawbones and worry their brain cells to pronounce denial it is the Superconscious Lord of the Multiverse who has given them the ability to do so.

vii

'Burning Spear... Bunny Wailer, Ijahman': These are some of the greatest artists in the spiritual field of Roots Reggae. Bunny Wailer worked alongside Bob Marley for many years but has released many revered recordings in his own right. Winston Rodney, also known as Burning Spear, is regarded, like Marley, as a prophet of Rastafarianism (which is essentially Ethiopian Christianity filtered through the experience of diaspora and slavery). Ijahman Levi is celebrated internationally as one who preaches non-violent mystical Rastafarianism through his music.

'Israel Vibration': Israel Vibration, legendary living prophets of Rastafarian culture, are three singers who have performed for four decades with different groups of musicians, though most often backed by Roots Radics. Lascelle 'Wiss' Bulgin, Albert 'Apple Gabriel' Craig, and Cecil 'Skeleton' Spence met in a rehabilitation home for polio victims in Jamaica in the early 60s. They went separate ways, individually adopted the Rastafarian way, and formed Israel Vibration in 1969. The trio toured Israel some time in the 1990s and a rare film of that tour exists, titled 'Israel Vibration in Holy Land'. For the purposes of Unholyland a gig they performed on the coast of Israel is transferred to the shores of Lake Galilee.

'Isaiah 9.1.': 'Nevertheless, that time of darkness and despair will not go on forever. The land of Zebulun and Naphtali will be humbled, but there will be time in the future when Galilee of the Gentiles which lies along the road that runs between the Jordan and the sea, will be full of glory.' (New Living Translation)

Biblical traditions say that King Solomon gifted an upland plain among the mountains of Galilee to Hiram, architect of his temple, to which Hiram gave the name 'the Land of Cabul' which in turn evokes the name of the Cabbala. The Galilee in Hebrew is Glil haGoyim, which translates as the 'District of the Nations' and elsewhere in his prophetic book Isaiah refers to the region by this name.

There exist serious problems for millennialist and dispensationalist Christians who imagine that the creation of modern Israel in 1948 represents Isaiah's land 'full of glory' (a view popular in the United States and Canada). An immediate difficulty is that Israel is one of the countries of the world most hostile to the Christian message. Another problem concerns the interpretation of prophecies in Isaiah 10 which speak of the gathering of 'the remnant' and the restoring of the people of Israel to the land. The fact is that when Isaiah envisions this restoration he specifies that the Messiah – in charge of this great earthly transformation – restores and regathers all nations to himself, Gentile and Jew alike. To put it more clearly, the Messiah does not create an apartheid state.

Some Christians have deduced that simply because of the political existence of modern Israel the return of Christ is imminent; and many naive fundamentalists flocked to Jerusalem around the year 2000 to see the skies open. Important truths are ignored to sustain such illusions. Firstly, many eminent rabbis still believe today that Israel lost the land in ancient times because of disobedience to God. Secondly, the nature of the restoration predicted in the Old Testament by the prophet Isaiah is quintessentially peaceful, a state in which wild animals – interpreted usually as meaning hostile nations – no longer attack each other. Yet there is no peace in modern Israel, no security, no lying down of the lion and the lamb, no beating of swords into ploughshares, only the opposite, where the international military- industrial complex seems to use Eretz Israel as a laboratory for aggressive 'bleeding-edge' technology. Thirdly, any Christian with a conscience must condemn the record of human-rights abuse visited upon the Palestinian people by the war-machine and secret-police of Israel. (It is worth mentioning that such is the view of numerous 'True-Torah' Rabbis worldwide.)

In Unholyland the interpretation of Isaiah's end-time prophecies takes a different direction. Here the contemporary preachings of Rastas beside Lake Galilee and the emergence of non-violent truth-based Slingshot Hiphop appealing to both Arab and Jewish youth alike are seen as auguries of a new time, a new heaven and a new earth.

x

'Jounieh whore': By Middle-Eastern standards Beirut and its surroundings are considered an area of lax morality. Prostitution is well-organised and fairly pervasive, especially in the Jounieh district with its barely-disguised brothels known as 'super-nightclubs.'

xvii

'Greedy Dog': The lyrics of this piece, one of Israel Vibration's most powerful tunes, tell the fable of a dog trying to get home with a bone in his mouth but stopping on a bridge to look at his reflection in the water below. He opens his mouth to bark at the 'other' dog and, of course, the bone falls from his jaws, an interesting parable about illusory enemies and projected shadows, apposite in the context of Palestine.

xxi

'Orbit-scratch': A technique used by DJs. It is a type of 'flare-scratch' which starts with crossfader open. Then, while the fader is closed quickly, the record is moved and the process is repeated, with the sound cut out each time. The orbit-scratch is sometimes also known in the language of turntabling as a '2-click flare'.

xxii

'Bob Marley and the Wailers': When Marley became the first international reggae star, there was initial jealousy on the part of some Jamaican artists who never – at least in those days of the early seventies – gained the world-stage. According to one account, Marley was criticised in particular for driving a BMW. 'So. Now dat yuh reach de top yuh rollin' thru like big-shot, top man in de town, drivin roun in nice car, white-man-wheels, yeah?' (Marley, as everyone knows, was mixed-race, so this particular sting must have hit home.) Eyeing his detractor lazily through blue puffs of collyweed Bob drawls: 'Man, hold strain, relax yourself, yuh don even know wha' BMW mean, do you? Yuhjus' ignorant, man.'(His would-be judge looks puzzled.) 'Yuhsee 'dem t'ree letters right 'dere? Dem t'ree letters stan' for 'Bob Marley and the Wailers', yuh overstan? Don' forget dat. Learn yuh lessons, man.'

Two decades later a popular London derivation will explain that the three letters BMW stand for 'Black-Man-Wagon.'

Chapter 2

ii

'Nepheton': The Nepheton is a clone of the famous Roland TR 808, one of the first programmable drum-machines, originally created in early 1980s by the Roland Corporation of Japan. Original 808s are much prized; Moshe is mentally playing the Nepheton emulation made by DR16, 'remixing' the Israel Vibration tune Greedy Dog in his head. In Unholyland this is meant to symbolise a contribution to the transformation of Israel into a non-racist, non-apartheid state.

iii

'Slingshot tunes': Slingshot Hiphop is a powerful instance of glocalization, where a local trend becomes dispersed across the planet relatively quickly. The American genre, born in the Bronx in 1970s, had been reinvented and reinterpreted by Palestinian rappers by the mid-to-late 1990s. Seeking a name for their new school of angry – yet poignant and poetic – rap, artists like Tamer Nafer and others saw newsreel pictures of themselves challenging Israeli tanks with stones and brilliantly inverted the Biblical story of David (fighting Goliath with a sling) to reflect their national predicament. In spite of the vehemence of the name, the fundamental philosophy of Slingshot Hiphop is non-violent, proposing that the way forward for Palestinian freedom-fighters is to 'put down the gun and pick up the mic.'

iv

'Zahret el Kolch': This is a legendary variety of Lebanese hashish, hand-pressed as in Afghanistan, black outside and greeny-brown inside, very rare, quite potent and seldom exported. A Manali-strain (and so originally a Himalayan introduction) the Zahret el Kolch is produced, like most Lebanese hashish, in the cannabis-fields of the beautiful B'qaa Valley, near Baalbek in the east of the country, where cannabis-plantations have flourished for many thousands of years.

'Gold Leb': Three types of Lebanese hash are common: red, yellow (or gold) and black (the super-rare Zahret el Kolch described in the note above). The red variety is weakest, the gold can be quite strong when fresh, and all varieties have a spicy flavour which can sometimes be a little harsh.

xi

'a people expelled': After the destruction of the Second Temple and during the Hadrian persecutions (115–138 AD) the Jewish Diaspora – which started on a smaller scale in the sixth century BC with the conquest of the Kingdom of Judah by the Babylonian Nebuchadnezzar – began in earnest. The Romans outlawed many Hebrew religious practices and insisted that a statue of Caesar should be worshipped in the Temple at Jerusalem. This was fiercely opposed (as detailed in sonnet xi). In consequence, around AD 123 the Jews began organising guerrilla attacks, and – as always with violent forms of resistance – their Roman oppressors used these revolts and uprisings as the pretext for savage repressions. From this point onwards annexation was inevitable and total exile imminent.

'guidance secular': Zionism: which though it sounds religious, has nothing whatever to do with Judaism, being a purely political movement, founded by Theodore Herzl in the nineteenth century. (cf. note to Chap 11, x.) In actuality Zionism is a fundamental betrayal of Judaism, condemned by many Rabbis worldwide. Influenced by Darwinist ideas and imperialist race-supremacism, Herzl exploited the agony of the European diaspora to produce the political momentum which eventually gave birth to Israel, a secular state which has no right either to the sacred name of Israel or to the land of Palestine. (cf. note to Chap 11, x: Theodore Herzl.)

xiii

'Kibbutzim': Workers on a 'kibbutz'. There are still about 300 of these collective farms left in Israel, though, with the collapse of the communist-bloc and the loss of international confidence in socialism, the movement has nowadays largely adopted capitalist structures. In the nineteenth century Russian Jews escaping pogroms and blood-libels fled Europe, primarily migrating to the United States, though a minority went east to Ottoman Palestine where they purchased land and settled, forming prototypical kibbutzes, dressing Palestinian-style and living in harmony with the local population. Later, against the internecine convulsions of the twentieth century, mass immigration introduced a ruthless and invasive settler (mostly from the Soviet Union) who, fusing communism with Zionism, conducted an experiment in utopian living which paradoxically necessitated the constant presence of heavily armed guards. The collective farms of this era were extremely productive.

xiv

'The Bimmer's rearwheel': BMWs uniquely are powered by a rear-wheel drive-system which makes the traction of these vehicles very lively.

xxi

'Kefitzat ha-Derach': Cabbalistically speaking the ability to magically translocate. 'Jumping the Road' is not an out-of-body shamanic journey but a physical leap through a quantum portal which cuts out fractions of actual space.

Chapter 3

vi

'As Rastaman The Rambam truly': Rastafari is an evolution of Judaism, like Christianity and Islam, yet it is properly an ideology and a spiritual movement more than a modern religion. Its liturgy is based on roots-reggae music, its sacrament is cannabis (though not all Rastas partake) and its one God is Jah.

The Rastafari movement began in Jamaica in the 1930s yet traces its origins to legendary eras of Ethiopian history. According to Rastafari traditions Prince (Ras) Menelik I, the son born to King Solomon of Israel (c. 980 BC) and Sheba, Queen of Ethiopia, travelled back from ancient Jerusalem to the land of his royal mother, taking with him the Ark of Covenant. (It is generally believed today that the Ark has been hidden in Ethiopia for many centuries, from well before the time of Christ. Vide: Graham Hancock, The Sign and the Seal; the Quest for the Lost Ark of the Covenant, 1992.) In Ethiopia Prince Menelik set up a branch-dynasty of the House of Israel and at this point Ethiopia as a whole is converted to monotheistic Judaism. Throughout the Christian era the famous Emperors of Ethiopia (descendants of Menelik) are universally accorded the title 'Conquering Lion of the Tribe of Judah'.

Fast-forward to the eighteenth and nineteenth centuries and we find West-African slaves from Jamaica down to Trinidad reconnecting with these holy traditions through exposure to the Old and New Testaments of the Bible. Until the point in the late twentieth century when Bob Marley, as Rastafari prophet, makes of Western secular rock-music a vehicle for spiritual values in a way which sends a powerful cultural signal round the entire planet. (Not even Bob Dylan has the respect shown today internationally to this mixed-race messenger, 'born in a stable' so-to-speak, the most-loved and most-imitated rock-messenger of all time.)

The portrait of Moss Rambam in Unholyland was in some way influenced by the interesting cultural background of the New York-based Hasidic hiphop reggae phenomenon, Matisyahu. Matisyahu was raised in a secular Jewish-American home where he heard a lot of reggae; then, as a teenager, after experimenting with drugs and going on the road for five months, he had an epiphanic experience in which he discovered his religious roots in Hasidism; and finally, with rabbinical blessings, he returned to reggae and hiphop, beatboxing and MC-ing as a way of expressing his new-found spirituality.

Moss Rambam makes a different journey, moving away from the Hasidism of his father Solomon towards deeper Rastafari beliefs and projections, but there are parallels between his route and that of Matisyahu (who is known for collaborating with Muslim-American beatboxer Te'eni Mohammed.)

'The Rambam': Rabbi Moses Ben Maimon (Rambam is an acronym) is known in European culture as Maimonides and in Arabic civilisation as Musa ibn Maymun. He is regarded by many as the greatest Jewish philosopher. He was rabbi, physician, astronomer, astrologer, and one of the greatest Torah scholars of all time. Born in Cordoba in 1135 he died in Egypt in 1204. His Guide for the Perplexed (written in Arabic as Delalatul Ha'yreen) exerted a profound influence on Albertus Magnus, Thomas Aquinas and Duns Scotus. Maimonides' primary sources were the writings of Aristotle, Muslim philosophy and the science of the Middle Ages.

After fleeing Andalusia for the city of Fez in Morocco, The Rambam eventually found his way to Cairo where he became physician to Sultan Saladin. In 2010 his historic synagogue in that city was restored at the expense of the Egyptian government, an unusual gesture certainly.

The Rambam is surrounded with many legends. One story tells of his ability to 'jump the road' and this translocational power has been borrowed in Unholyland by his descendant, Moshe. (cf. note to Chapter 2, xxi)

Maimonides opposed the creation of a state of Israel in his celebrated 'Letter to Yemen' in which he warns that dire results will follow the breaking of one of the sacred 'Three Oaths' of Judaism, the first of these fundamental principles being that the Jews should not succumb to the desire to found a home-state. (Secondly, the Jews of the diaspora should not rebel against their host-nations. And thirdly, the host-nations should treat the dispersed Jews with mildness and tolerance.)

viii

'The Machsom Watch': 'Machsom watch is a movement of Israeli women, peace activists from all sectors of Israeli society, who oppose the Israeli occupation and the denial of Palestinians' rights to move freely in their land. Since 2001, we have conducted daily observations of IDF checkpoints in the West Bank, along the separation fence and in the seam line zone, on the main roads and on out-of-the-way dirt roads, as well as in the offices of the Civil Administration (DCOs) and in military courts. We regularly document what we see and hear. The reports of these observations are published on the Machsom watch site, and sent to public officials and elected representatives. Through the documentation which discloses the nature of everyday reality, we are attempting to influence public opinion in the country and in the world, and thus to bring to an end the destructive occupation, which causes damage to Israeli society as well as to Palestinian society.' (From the Machsom Watch website, www.machsomwatch.org.)

xi

'Paulus Hashishi': The main street of Nazareth.

xiii

'Tefillin': In orthodox Judaism a tiny case, made usually of leather, containing sacred scriptural formulae and worn in the centre of the forehead strapped over the zone of the third eye. A tefillin worn in this way is believed to aid prayer and meditation, to assist in the attainment of mystical states of being.

Chapter 4

'Yohanna ceiling': Salib Yohanna's painted murals and ceilings are now highly controversial in modern Israel, not because these derivative Italianate artworks have any particularly great aesthetic value but because they stand witness to a demographic Palestinian cultural background denied by many Israeli historians (with some notable exceptions, see the note to 'K'far Saf Saf' below). In the late nineteenth and early twentieth centuries these works were often commissioned by wealthy mercantile Palestinian householders, frequently in Nazareth. Many survive (as in the Habash mansion, Rayyan's family home in Unholyland) but many have been destroyed in suspicious circumstances. Those that do survive demonstrate clearly that a viable, sophisticated, articulate Palestinian culture did exist prior to the creation of Israel. They show that the Zionist myth of 'an empty land' waiting for settlement was a complete falsehood.

iv

'Widowmaker': The dangerous ballooning foresail known as the spinnaker so greatly accelerated sailing-ships that the bowsprit (to which the spinnaker was attached) became known in sea-jargon as 'the widowmaker' because vessels often wrecked themselves while speeding with this particular canvas spread to a following wind.

v

'Natzrat Illit': Natzrat Illit, a exclusively Jewish urban sector, dominates 'the Arab capital' of Israel in a threatening manner. On the heights of Illit (which name suggests 'elite') one can find western-type shopping-malls and cinemas, in fact all the luxuries of a modern consumer-playground. Yet nowhere else in Nazareth can such facilities be discovered, simply because they are impermissible under Israeli town-planning provisions. More sinister than the malls and cinemas of Illit is the quite infamous building of the Israeli Courts of Justice which frowns down on Nazareth at night, vast concrete facades uplit to emphasise its sombre presence.

'from the Mishteret a nasty kiss.': The heavily armed quasi-military Israeli police force.

ix

'A Sufi': The Sufi's love of hashish is legendary. This medieval mystical arm of Islam developed its taste for sacred narcosis at the time of the saint Haydar, an introverted and reclusive master who one day astonished his followers with uncharacteristic flights of religious eloquence verging on poetry. It was then revealed, by his own confession, that the master had wandered into a cannabis plantation where he had been instructed by Allah to consume the sticky psychoactive leaves in great quantities. The disciples themselves began to follow the saint's example and so the Sufi sect began its controversial progress through Islamic history.

The name 'Sufi' derives from the word in Arabic for wool, and denotes one who wears woollen robes. This is interesting in itself because woollen robes are associated in Islamic traditions with Christ, while cotton garments are linked with the Prophet Mohammed. (Peace be upon them both.)

x

'Green Men': A synonym for those who follow the Sufic school of Islamic theology.

xxi

'Bahamadia': Antonia Reed, the New York-based woman-rapper of outstanding range and sensibility, her super-laconic style involving complex wordplay and references to mainstream poets. She speaks, for instance, on her acclaimed 1996 album 'Kollage' of 'modern-day prophet, Rimbaud'.

Chapter 5

iii

'Abrahamic family': Meaning Jew, Christian and Muslim.

xiv

'Abdul the Merman': A character from 'The Thousand And One Nights', a poor fisherman miraculously translated to a subaquatic existence.

xv

'Azrael': The Archangel of Death in both Islamic and Judaic theologies.

xvi

'Byzantine scales': The Byzantine scale (aka the Double Harmonic scale) is probably the western diatonic structure closest to the microtonal scales of

Arabic music. Where H is a half-step, W a whole step and W+ a step of three semitones, the Byzantine scale is as follows: H, W+, H, W, H, W+, H. The scale is widely used in jazz and fusion.

The fourth mode of the Byzantine is the Hungarian minor, exploited by Bartok.

Chapter 6

'Looks for God in a hole in the ground': The world's largest and most ambitious machine, the Large Hadron Collider (or LHC) has recently been constructed under the Swiss-French border, a twenty-six kilometre tunnel designed for the purpose of discovering the 'God- particle', the famous Higgs Boson. Some physicists have expressed alarm that this atom- smasher (or Satanic Mill in Blakean terminology) is capable of producing 'small' black holes which could theoretically consume the entire earth; or generate 'strangelets' which could transform the planet into a lump of subatomic materia prima.

v

'Cafour': The green plant which grows in the garden of Cafour replaces in our hearts the effects of old and noble wine.

Give me this green plant from the garden of Cafour, this plant which surpasses wine itself in the number of people it enslaves.

For hashish-eaters and devotees of marijuana, for Sufis, poets and musicians, the Gardens of Cafour played a role in thirteenth-century Cairo similar (though on a much larger scale and for much longer periods of time) to The Golden Gate Park in San Francisco and Holland Park in London, when, in the late 1960s, the flower-children and the hippies made these green spaces their gathering-points for love-ins and happenings. Tragically, the Gardens of Cafour were ruthlessly destroyed by the authorities, and known eaters of hashish had their teeth wrenched out in public, presumably to stop them expressing the wisdom of the sacred herb. (It should perhaps be added here that most chemical marijuana or 'skunk' being hydroponically produced today in urban agglomerations is a dangerous travesty of the organic drug grown in natural surroundings. Lab analysis of skunk has shown that in this artificial version of the drug, while psychoactive chemicals which induce mental euphoria have been maximised, the whole complex range of subtle chemicals which stabilise the high, which make the experience mellow, are missing. This factor, by itself, can explain much of the undeniable psychosis associated with the use of chemical cannabis; though of course, times have changed and society itself is sicker, edgier and even more psychotic than it was back in the day of flower-power and non-violent love-ins, a point made in 6, iv.)

xii

'Oud': The eleven-stringed Arabian lute (al-'ud.) The pear-shaped instrument is fretless, allowing for expressive vibrato, slides and the microtonal string-stopping required in Arabic music. As in Greece, where the lyre was the instrument associated with poets, the 'oud has a long history of being used as supporting instrument for the spoken word. (Thus: 'that friend of ancient pastorals'.)

When opera emerged as the dominant musical art form of the renaissance period, it was widely believed that Italian composers had reinvented the Greek art of speaking poetry to music. Yet even the 'recitative' of opera (where the narrative action of the storyline is hurried along to the 'continuo' of simple harpsichord figures) probably bears little resemblance to the Greek and Arabic recitational conventions of long ago. In fact, opera has been spectacularly unsuccessful in presenting declamatory verse fused with music; it is difficult to find a single opera whose libretto is also first-class poetry. (Wagner's Parsifal for instance is a travesty of the great epic poem, Parzifal, by the minnesinger, Wolfram von Eschenbach.) Choral works and massed choirs do a superior job of presenting visceral poetry fused with music; one need only think of Orff's 'Carmina Burana' and Stravinsky's 'Symphony of Psalms'. But the pretensions of opera in this respect have led directly to the situation in which (to quote Yeats from memory) 'music, too proud to wear the garment of words' struts about, upstaging, in effect, the softly spoken, lyrical poet.

Hiphop and rap are far more effective than opera in presenting raw and poignant words in a hypnotic context; which should be the aim of this conjunction.

xiii

'Cheb Khaled': Cheb Khaled's work represents the high-point of modern Arabic music prior to the emergence of Slingshot Hiphop in the mid-to-late nineties. Khaled (based in Paris because of death threats from the religious right in his native Algeria) fused – in the form known as 'rai' – poetic lyrics with modern electronic western instrumentation, and his biggest hit Chebba became the internationally known anthem of contemporary Arabic culture.

xv

'Kfar Saf-Saf': These are names of some of the villages destroyed in the 1948 Nakba ('Catastrophe') in which 750,000 Palestinians were displaced in order to create the state of Israel. Many thousands of civilians were massacred in cold blood during this atrocious, shameful episode. The objective truth about the Nakba has been detailed more recently by the outspoken Israeli historian, Dr Ilan Pappé, in his ground-breaking The Ethnic Cleansing of Palestine. Pappe's study is unique because it represents the first attempt by a major Israeli academic to examine unflinchingly the truth about the events of 1948.

xvi

'The dead hamlets': This evocative phrase is borrowed from Iain Sinclair's psychogeographical masterpiece Lud Heat (Albion Village Press, 1973) which examines the East End of London through a lens of poetic esotericism.

Decoding sacred but desanctified terrain, Sinclair analyses the Nicholas Hawksmoor churches which, both by construction and alignment, overshadow this historically impoverished region of Britain's capital city. Sinclair speculates that the Hawksmoor grid of 'pseudo-churches' are connected with negative upsurgings from the collective unconscious, and act as focuses for morbid telluric currents, possibly generating, among other lurid manifestations, the Ripper murders.

Sinclair's play on 'hamlet' as both village and Shakespearian dispossessed rebel attaches itself easily to the motif in Unholyland of the ruined innocence of Palestine and the usurpation of that state.

xviii

'The whole Levant': An older name for the entire region lying along the coast of the eastern Mediterranean.

Jalilah's Rap

'I and I': There is a very ancient tribal greeting which says: 'I am in truth another yourself' and in this profound salutation is the essence of the Rastafarian 'I and I', which references a non- dual state of being where is no separation into 'you and me' but only the sacred unity of one love.

'The Red House': The infamous Red House plays a central role in the story of the birth of modern Israel. It was in this building, situated on the waterfront of Tel Aviv, that, on the 10th March 1948, eleven men, headed by David Ben Gurion, met to finalise the plan to expel Palestinians from their homeland. From that point onwards the Red House became the home of the feared paramilitary Haganah and their offshoot terror-organisation, the Stern Gang, named after its founder Avraham Stern.

Originally the Red House was the headquarters of the Socialist party, hence the name. Nowadays a Sheraton hotel occupies the site.

Chapter 7

ix

'Dun, dun, dun': This vaguely self-referential formula has an excusable basis in the nomenclature of a whole family of West African bass-drums (larger cousins of the djembe) which are known collectively, onomatopoeically – and conveniently – as 'Dun-dun' (also Dundunba, Doundoun and Dunun.)

xii

'If the eye were not a sun': 'If the eye were not sun-like, the sun's light it would not see.' Goethe (from the Preface to his Scientific Studies). A very old concept in the esoteric physiognomy of alchemy. The phrase may be borrowed from

Jacob Boehme, Paracelsus or Traherne (some of Blake's sources). The reader will kindly indulge this vague attribution.

xvii

'Dimi Mint Abba': Considered by connoisseurs the equal of Umm Kulthum, the greatest woman-singer of the modern Arab world, Dimi Mint Abba was born in 1958 in Mauretania and died in Casablanca in 2011 under suspicious circumstances while touring Morocco. Called 'the Diva of the Desert', Abba was a member of a hereditary caste of nomadic troubadours known in Mauretania as Iggawin. Like the sub-Saharan griot Salif Keita of Mali, Dimi suffered many indignities in her life (like many musicians worldwide she was considered 'low-caste') and made only very few recordings. Yet her 'O Lord, bring Apartheid crashing down' is one of the most searingly beautiful vocal performances in any repertoire, in any genre. Here, the singer's control of ullulation in the midst of complex melodic passages simply defies belief.

Many have contended that 'O Lord, bring Apartheid crashing down' did play an important part in the collapse of South African apartheid. Certainly Dimi's magnificent 'Sawt Elfan' (Art's Plume) proposes music as a spiritual weapon in the same way that Blake spoke of 'mental fight'. 'Art's Plume is a balsam, a weapon and a guide enlightening the spirit of men.'

xix

'Heine': Heinrich Heine (1797–1856) was born into a Jewish family in Dusseldorf but converted to Christianity in his late twenties, famously calling his conversion 'the ticket of admission into European culture'. (The Prussian government of 1822 denied Jews the right to academic positions and Heine desired a university career.) His early works embody some of the most romantic lyrics in German literature; his great love of Rhineland folklore infused his poetry with quaint supernatural themes. As time passed Heine's work became increasingly polemical and eventually the poet was forced into exile, spending the last twenty-five years of his life in Paris, where he married an illiterate shop girl with whom he apparently found great happiness; until the 'mattress-grave' claimed him. (Heine may have been suffering from syphilis; for eight years he lay slowly dying on a mountain of mattresses in a humble Paris bedsit, afflicted with excruciating pains in his spine.)

'Ein Fichtenbaum steht einsam' Ein Fichtenbaum steht einsam Im Nordenauf kahler Höh.

Ihn schläfert; mit weißer Decke Umhüllen ihn Eis und Schnee. Er träumt von einer Palme, Die, fern im Morgenland, Einsam und schweigend trauert

Chapter 8

v

'Auf brennender Felsenwand': This lovely poem, necessarily compressed in the Unholyland translation from eight lines into four, could be interpreted as expressing the longing of the diasporan Jew for the warmer zone of the Biblical homeland, but a simple romantic construction of the lyric connects it – gratefully – with the present text.

'Musa': The Arabic and Koranic version of Moses, Moshe, an important prophet in Islam.

viii

'Paradise Now': A film made in 2005 by Hany Abu-Assad which recounts the story of two young Palestinian suicide-bombers preparing for a mission into Israel. The movie is profoundly anti-violent and relates the narrative in a human, not a political way. Still, the Israeli government made strenuous efforts to have the film internationally banned; in spite of this Paradise Now won a Golden Globe award for best foreign-language film.

xi

'Carbon 60': Carbon 60, the third form of carbon (diamond and graphite being the other two) was unexpectedly discovered in 1985. Also called Buckminsterfullerene in honour of the visionary American architect, the Carbon 60 molecule (or Buckyball) may well prove the single most important technological discovery of the twentieth century. Currently the international military-industrial complex is researching Buckminsterfullerene's vast potential as a superconductor, designing futuristic machines of war based on the extraordinary strength of a molecule in which each of sixty faces is bonded with surrounding molecules, so that an Airbus 380 made of Carbon 60 could be picked up in one hand like a toy. Very little is heard of these developments for obvious reasons, ironic when one considers that Buckminster Fuller himself was a passionate believer in the philosophy of non-violence.

xviii

'Farmland in the Galilee': The Israeli Knesset has indeed passed such a reform legislation on behalf of the Israeli Land Authority, theoretically allowing someone like Sajjid, a non-Israeli, to buy large quantities of privately owned agricultural land in the Galilee region. One hundred and fifty square miles has so far been allocated for sale to the highest bidder, even if that buyer is not Israeli, and a further 150 square miles have been allocated for sale after 2014.

'Love must intervene': Unconditional love is the guiding principle of Sufism.

'say Darwinians': Alternatively, Zionists. Theodore Herzl and other figures in the early Zionist movement were deeply influenced by the racist and supremacist implications of Darwinism as it was understood and interpreted in the late nineteenth century (cf. note to Chapter 11, x).

Chapter 9

iv

'Satanic trip': Certainly the cruel and sadistic treatment meted out to the Palestinians merits this description. Yet the actions of many governments around the world could also be described in this manner, for instance the farming-on-demand of prisoner's internal organs in modern China; or the wide-ranging and clearly documented genocidal actions of multinational oil companies. It must also remain crystalline in this context that the historic demonisation of Jewish peoples in Europe for 'religious' reasons has been (and continues to be) of this order of evil, the famous blood-libel against the Jews being the worst example of this kind of prejudice and 'fear of the other'. Right down until the nineteenth century the accusation was made that the Passover Matzoh could not be prepared unless the blood of a Christian child was admixed with the flour. Posters warning parents that the date of Passover was approaching appeared on the streets of Warsaw until the very early twentieth century. Such manipulations of the popular psyche, such programmings of the collective unconscious – usually as the precursor to a fierce pogrom – also belong under the heading of acts which can only be described as satanic. (It should also be added here that repetition of the blood- libel echoes on today in the propaganda of certain more theocratic and fundamentalist Islamic states.)

One most painful psychological aspect of the situation in Palestine is that a people traumatised by two thousand years of persecution leading up to the Holocaust have almost no conscious understanding of the fact that they are blindly replicating patterns of terror, with the difference that they are now the perpetrators and the Palestinians are the victims. Recent social studies indicate that abused children will grow up to abuse others and this is the psychological mechanism driving Israeli intransigence in the Middle East.

x

'The Serious Road Trip': Between 1991 and 1997 the Serious Road Trip, who have been described as 'the world's most rock'n'roll aid organisation' 'brought humanitarian aid and its own unique brand of therapeutic entertainment to people in Eastern Europe, from the war-torn former Yugoslavia to Romania, Chechnya and beyond. Today, groups started by Road Trip members carry on the work and the goals of the Road Trip – to help people in difficulty of any kind, here, there and everywhere, particularly through the use of circus and street art.'

At the close of McCool (Goldmark, 2009) the Serious Road Trip are discovered engaged in a fictional mission to Palestine in which they take Palestinian and Israeli kids into the Sinai Peninsula desert for a hand-drumming festival of unity, and here in Unholyland is a reference to the same (notional) mission.

xiv

'Subliminal/Tamer Nafar': Subliminal is a talented (but now quite nationalist) Jewish rapper; Tamer Nafar fronts Dam, the brilliant Arab-Israeli rap-group from Lod in Israel. (cf. note to 11, x, Moshe's Rap.)

Chapter 10

'The unities': The basic building-blocks of classical Greek dramatic structure, the three unities of space, time and symbol. Among more modern European playwrights the French tragedian Jean Racine (1639-99) adhered quite strictly to these ancient requirements of Greek theatre; where the unity of time, for instance, stipulated that plot action should elapse inside a period of 24 hours; and the unity of space required the action to happen only in one location.

The downside of this venerable and demanding literary convention is that works constructed according to its standard sometimes appear formulaic and stylised. Unlike Racine, Shakespeare fundamentally dismissed the unities and gave free reign to his characters to exist outside such constraints.

vi

'Saladin/Lionheart': The point here is that the legendary friendship between Richard Coeur de Lion and Saladin very nearly resulted in an unusual and imaginative peace deal for the Middle East. According to many accounts, after the disaster of Hattin (when the relics of the True Cross were lost) and subsequent to the Battle of Arsuf (when the Christians prevailed and Saladin's invincibility was called into question) Richard offered his sister, ex-Queen Joan of Sicily, in marriage to Saladin's brother, al-Adil, a diplomatist whom Richard and many other crusaders admired greatly. Al-Adil was to retain all of Palestine under Muslim control and Joan would bring as her dowry to the marriage all the territories and cities conquered by the Lionheart. And as King and Queen of Jerusalem the couple would be guarantors and patrons of lasting peace in the Holy Land. Richard gave a magnificent banquet for al-Adil at Lydda to launch his bold plan. But Joan, Richard's favourite sister, quite used to being treated as a royal bargaining-chip, apparently expressed horror at the idea of marrying a Muslim. (Some say that Al-Adil, also known as Sephadin, also revolted at the prospect of marrying a Christian.) Whatever the truth, matchmakers and peacemakers were comprehensively defeated.

The legend does seem believable when one considers Richard's enlightened disposition, and his attitude towards both Muslims and Jews. (At his coronation in London in 1189 there was an outbreak of anti-semitic violence which resulted in many deaths, including that of the noted scholar Jacob of Orleans. Richard punished the racist rioters severely, causing Baldwin, Archbishop of Canterbury, to remark sourly: 'If the King is not God's man, he had better be the devil's.')

vii

'Arcadia': Arcadia (or Arcady) is a region of Greece supposed in classical mythology to have been the home of the god Pan. Situated in the southern Peloponnese, Arcadia became symbolic in the Renaissance period of an Edenic wilderness, a simple pastoral land of happiness; though an additional strand of secret melancholy can be found associated with Arcadia, best summarised by the famous 'Et in Arcadia ego' ('Even in Arcadia I exist') the 'I', of course, being mortality personified.

In 1503 the Italian poet Sannazaro, drawing on Virgil, published his astonishing prose-and-verse poem Arcadia and initiated the Arcadian genre in European literature, continued by Sidney. Here is Sir Philip Sidney (from his Arcadia) describing his utopian pastoral world complete with 'young shepherdesses knitting' in time with their singing:

There were hilles which garnished their proud heights with stately trees: hu[m] ble valleis, whose base estate semed co[m]forted with refreshing of siluer riuers: medows, enameld with al sorts of ey-pleasing floures: thickets, which being lined with most pleasa[n]t shade, were witnessed so to by the chereful depositio[n] of many wel-tuned birds: each pasture stored with sheep feeding with sober security, while the prety la[m]bs with bleting oratory craued the dame co[m]fort: here a shepheards boy piping, as though he should neuer be old: there a yong shepherdesse knitting, and withall singing, & it seemed that her voice co[n]sorted her hands to work, & her ha[n]ds kept time to her voices musick. (Renascence Editions, copyright © 2003 The University of Oregon.)

In Unholyland the poetic idyl of Arcadia thematically supports the Platonic concept of a golden age mediated through music and transcultural art forms. In recent years in Northern Ireland, The Pushkin Trust, a visionary project enjoying the patronage of Seamus Heaney and the Duchess of Abercorn (herself a lineal descendant of Pushkin), has brought children from both sides of the Protestant/ Catholic divide together to write poetry in pastoral surroundings, so helping young people transcend sectarian conditioning.

viii

'Pulsa diNura': The Pulsa diNura or Pulsa Denoura is an Aramaic term which translates as 'lashes of fire'. It is the name of a Cabbalistic ritual which is believed to obstruct or intercept the mercy of God so that a sinner is immediately confronted with his or her full spiritual liabilities. (The Torah however expressly forbids prayers which aim negative spiritual energy at another.)

In modern urban myth the Angel of Destruction of the Pulsa diNura has been invoked against both Yitzhak Rabin and Ariel Sharon. Rabin was assassinated by a right-wing Israeli fanatic a month after his cursing, apparently launched because he had signed the Oslo Accords; and Ariel Sharon, much criticised for withdrawing from the Gaza Strip, collapsed (he remains in a coma to this day) six months after his widely reported malediction.

xiv

'Hamza el Din': Hamza el Din (1929–2006) was a composer from Nubia, his main instruments tar and 'oud. In the 1960s, during the construction of the Aswan dam, his home village of Toshka was flooded along with most of Egyptian Nubia. El Din's music wonderfully evokes the vanished rural world of his birthplace. In particular, Escalay: The Waterwheel is widely regarded as a genre-classic, perhaps the first recording to become (around 1971 when it was issued on the Vanguard label) a successful world-music release in the west.

From the 70s el Din based himself in the States; he performed with The Grateful Dead on their Egyptian tour in 1978.

'vaporizer': The vaporizer is a modern digital equivalent of the traditional waterpipe, hubble-bubble or nargile. With this device, the cannabis is warmed to a precisely controlled temperature at which the precious material does not actually ignite but releases relatively cool and non-carcinogenic vapors. Vaporizers are widely used in more advanced American and Russian hospitals today; patients inhale the mists of various curative herbs and reap their benefits with none of the risks associated with smoking.

xxi

'Shahaadat work': The Shahaadat al-Bakaalouriya is a secondary education certificate in the Lebanese academic system.

xxii

'The tree of Ferdowsi': For the great Iranian poet Ferdowsi (940–1020) the cypress tree has many associations, some romantic, some funereal. Cypresses often form the focal points of Persian classical gardens.

Chapter 11

iv

'Blue Line': The Nato-demarcated border between Israel and Lebanon, considered the most dangerous frontier in the world.

x

'Theodore Herzl': Herzl was born in Pest, Hungary, on 2nd May 1860, the father of political Zionism and the Israeli state. He grew up in a humanist secular

Jewish home pouring scorn on Judaism and religion in general. He developed into a third-rate playwright and when it became clear even to him that he had no poetic talent whatsoever he became a journalist. In 1896 he published Der Judenstaat (The Jewish State). Right from the outset, his ideas were detestable to religious Jews who sought acceptance and integration into their various resident countries; who believed then, and still believe today – many of them – that dispersion is God's will for the Jewish people. ('Thou shalt be a diaspora in all kingdoms of the earth.' Deuteronomy 28:25.) Herzl's views were therefore regarded in rabbinical circles as proof of his rebellion against God. Indeed, very much a European of his times – racist, Darwinist and imperialist – Herzl's attitudes would fuel his ill-omened project, ensuring the convenient dismissal of an 'inferior' Arab culture.

In 1898 Herzl had an audience with the German Kaiser which proved most significant, legitimising his campaign in the view of the world. In 1901, he met the Sultan of Turkey and offered to consolidate Turkey's debt in return for access to Palestine, but this proposal was rejected. Nevertheless from this point onwards till his death in 1905 Herzl, with the backing of the Order of Ancient Maccabeans, a proto-Zionist British affiliation, began to promote ever- more-successfully the idea of 'a land without a people for a people without a land'.

In spite of the Zionist claim that the land of Palestine was 'lying empty' (cf. note to chap 4, i) Herzl, envisioning his future Jewish state, did not deny that Arabs would play a part in that state. However he foresaw no friction between Arabs and Jews, a remarkably myopic prophet. Herzl imagined that grateful Arabs would participate in a hybrid capitalist-socialist secular state, developing modern humanist/atheist principles while acquiring the skills of engineers and scientists alongside superior Jewish citizens: a pipe dream.

'Karl Sabbagh': Palestine: A History (2006) movingly documents the changes in Palestinian society as the Zionist state of Israel evolved in the early twentieth century. The author's father was Isa Khalil Sabbagh, the celebrated BBC Arabic Service broadcaster who became a culture-hero in Palestine because his voice – alone at that time – told the story of a people without a voice, representing the Palestinian narrative to the world. The Sabbagh family (who were Christian) were based in the northern Galilee in the town of Safad, famous for centuries as a centre of Cabbalism.

'R Underground... Mook E': These are names of some of the most celebrated rappers and hiphop artists in the Middle Eastern scene, many of them Arabic though a good a few of them are Jewish. Tamer Nafar of Dam and the Israeli rapper Subliminal were close friends at one time. (Subliminal discovered Nafer.) But the friendship acrimoniously imploded during the Intifada, as documented in the film 'Channels of Rage'.

xiv

'Sultan Mehmet Bridge': Spans the Bosphorus linking Europe and Asia.

'Buckminsterfullerene': Carbon 60 (cf. note to 8, xi).

xvi

'Tetragrammaton': The ancient Hebrew name of Jehovah (of which Jah is a contraction) is mystically composed of four letters (Jod, He, Vau,He) which correspond cabbalistically to the four elements.

xvii

'pan-pipe: syrinx': 'Syrinx' is the name given to the group of pipes bound together in the 'pan pipe'. The origins of the name in Greek mythology are fascinating. The goat-footed god Pan was pursuing a nymph through the Arcadian forests. This was Syrinx, chaste and virginal. As Pan gained on her she rushed towards a river and plunged out of reach, drowning, but also metamorphosing into a river-reed. Pan on the riverbank listened to the wind blowing through the flags until, inspired by unfulfilled desire, and to console himself, he cut reeds of differing widths, trimmed them to different lengths and bound them together to make the first pan pipe. From that time onwards he wandered through the mountains of Arcady playing an instrument which imitated both the sighing of a frustrated lover and the sad tone of the wind. Often Pan would play all night so that at dawn he would appear with mouth bloody, his lips wounded by his passion.

xxii

'Majnoun': Layla and Majnoun are the doomed lovers of Arab culture; their legend may be reflected in the story of Romeo and Juliet. Majnoun is one whose impossible love drives him mad; in which state, according to some variants of the narrative, he disappears into the desert to endure romantic disappointments alone. Of course Majnoun's lovesickness appears as madness to others, but the Arabic poets have been at pains to point out that the one who loves hopelessly is actually in a state of 'divine' insanity, very different to other conditions of mental breakdown. The type of love which cannot be realised in a physical sense is called in Arabic poetry 'virgin-love'; our closest term in the West is 'platonic love'. See Majnun: The Madman in Medieval Islamic Society by Michael Dols. (Oxford: The Clarendon Press. 1992.)

Chapter 12

xvi

'Blue Line': The Nato-demarcated border between Israel and Lebanon, considered the most dangerous frontier in the world.

BOOK TWO

Chapter 1

iii

'socialism's at a low juncture': Written before the arrival of Jeremy Corbyn in the politics of Albion.

'The A-Z got used for roaches': The thin cardboard covers of 'London A-Z' streetmaps were once-upon-a-time the mobile spliff-builder's material-of-choice for making the 'roach', hollow filter of a joint.

vi

'(which ain't middleclass Irondequoit)': Here, Eminem's semi-abandoned post-industrial hometown is contrasted with an upstate New York lakeside agglomeration that may culturally represent American complacency at-or-near its zenith. Irondequoit's northern border is the shoreline of Lake Ontario; its name, of Native Indian origin, was lent, no doubt unwillingly, by the Iroquois tribe. 'Gracious living' here finds a societal epicentre.

ix

'racing-pigeon, his iyad: Mushtaq': Iyad: a 'racing-pigeon'.

xvi

'in his face 'haraam' writ large': Meaning forbidden.

xxii

'The Nato occupation brings': Unholyland assumes that a Nato-led occupation of Lebanon has taken place in response to Syria's disintegration.

Chapter 2

xviii

'where Coltan and Wolframite': Sought-after minerals, often used in mobile phone technology but also resourced for military purposes, extensively mined in Central Africa with disastrous consequences for the people of the region.

xx

'Need the Ziv Emergency Room.' Israel maintains a huge number of medical facilities along its borders with Lebanon and Syria, there to cope with casualties of any future invasion from the north.

Chapter 3

x

'today from the United Nations': Palestinian refugees are obliged to send their children to schools run by the UN; if children do not attend such schools their parents receive no aid from the UN.

Chapter 4

xxi

'Scopolamine is the alkaloid': A 'truth-drug' derived from a plant of the Deadly Nightshade family widely believed to have been used by the Nazis, certainly today an ingredient of South American criminal subculture, used for 'zombifying' potential victims.

Chapter 5

xxi

'I'm gonna do a Shahrazad': Referencing the princess-storyteller in The Arabian Nights who prolongs her own life by never concluding a story at dawn (which would cost her her life).

Chapter 6

i

'Today a morbid sky shudders': Chapter 6 is intended as an Edenic/dystopian interlude, marking the halfway point of Unholyland and consciously departing from the tone and mood of the poem thus far to address one of the world's most serious ecological catastrophes: the draining of the Hula Valley by the Israeli government in the 1950's.

xi

'The Assyrian is coming-through': Tiglath Pileser, king of Assyria in the 8th cent BC, a military genius who subjugated most of the ancient Near East, inventing forced deportation of whole populations as a means of enlarging his dominions.

xiii

'echoes by the Waters of Merom': The Old Testament name for the great lake of the Hula Valley

xix

'Cannons! The white men are landing.' A Season in Hell, Arthur Rimbaud 'crossed by the cold Sharkiyah-wind': Name of a stormy east-wind in the Galilee regions.

Chapter 7

x

'as Skelly broke into a skank': 'Skankin' is Jamaican for dancing to reggae-music; 'Two-stepping' and 'Down di flank' are variant dance-forms.

Chapter 8

viii

'See, babies play with bubble-rings': Bubble-rings (or toroidal rings) are underwater air-bubbles which spin in vortices, rather like smoke-rings. Most cetaceans create these vortex rings, and in the case of dolphins they seem to be generated for pleasure, to be played with, as described here.

Chapter 9

i

'He'll be Mizrahi or Maghrebi': Mizrahi: a Jew from Iran or Iraq; Maghrebi, a Jew from Morocco.

ii

'maybe Falasha': Abyssinian.

The Falasha (or Beta Israel) are Ethiopian Jews whose legendary genealogy goes back to the celebrated son of Sheba and Solomon, Prince Menelik the First, who fled Israel with his father's hieratic treasure, the Ark of the Covenant; and went into hiding in mountainous regions of the Abyssinian homeland of his mother. This is the narrative with which Rastafari begins a dialogue with Christianity, Islam and Judaism, pointing out that a primogenital branch of the house of David set up at this point in history implies a continuity of revelation from Solomon to Christ in Ethiopia. This unbroken line culminated in the exemplary life of the Emperor Haile Selassie, the inspiration of Robert Nesta Marley (a child-of-two-cultures like Prince Menelik) whose father, Robert Norval Marley, belonged to a family of Syrian Jewish extraction, emigrants to Jamaica via Sussex.

There have been at least five waves of Falasha emigration to Israel beginning in 1936 and climaxing in 1991 when 15,000 Ethiopian Jews were flown out of politically-crumbling Abyssinia. The much-publicised airlift by the Israeli Air Force made world-headlines; but reportedly the Beta Israel have not been well-treated in the land of Solomon. A monstrous clandestine sterilisation program is only one of the indignities the Falasha have had to suffer in their adopted country.

ii

'He's more relaxed than Ashkenazi': Ashkenaz is actually the Yiddish name for Germany but the description 'Ashkenazi' has come to mean any European Jew.

Chapter 10

xiii

'You seen 2Pac in Juice yet?': The American rapper Tupak Shakur made his brilliant acting debut in Juice in which he plays an anti-hero drug-dealer who betrays his brothers as he rises to power on the streets.

xiv

'From al-Andaluz an old story': In the eleventh century Al-Andaluz was that part of Moslem-occupied southern Spain (corresponding to modern Andalucia) where Christianity, Judaism and Islam flourished side-by-side under an enlightened and tolerant dispensation, a far cry from the paranoid atmosphere created, a few centuries later, under the Inquisition.

Chapter 11

xvii

'Rasta's changed the world forever': If Bob Dylan is the lyric poet of rock then Bob Marley is its prophet. Roots reggae is regarded as a sacramental art-form by its originators and its liturgy carries a message of world-transformation.

Chapter 12

viii

'on landing-platform of his loft': Every professional racing-loft employs a similar methodology for 'trapping' birds. In a timed situation the homer descends rapidly to a large flat landing-table and (ideally) goes straight to the trapgates which brush his folded wings as he enters to have his ring removed and placed in the race-clock. Mushtaq is not racing on this occasion and he is permitted to twirl a few times boastfully on the landing-board.

ix

'Is she like Hailie Jade for him?': Eminem's daughter about whom he has written often and movingly.

ix

'Slim Shady from the bad side of town': Eminem's dark alter-ego, fearing and hating the fans who would devour him, rip him to shreds as 'the raving ones', the Maenads, ripped Orpheus apart.

'Dreams of a sanatorium': Objectively this sonnet refers to the Deir Yassin massacre in 1948. On the night of 9th April, the Israeli terrorist organization LEHI (also known as The Stern Gang after its founder Avraham Stern) attacked the village of Deir Yassin situated on the supply-road to Jerusalem (blockaded by the ALA, Arab League forces). There followed the massacre of as many as 245 people, including 30 babies. There was mass rape and lurid mutilation. Deir Yassin was the bloodbath that baptised the state of Israel at its birth. Stern Gang leader Israel Eldad wrote in his memoirs that "without Deir Yassin the State of Israel could never have been established."

In immediate response to the massacre, on the 10th of April, Albert Einstein wrote his unequivocal condemnation of the criminality and folly of what he defined as Israeli 'Terrorism.'

The village of Deir Yassin was never rebuilt and has become, in a macabre twist, the location of the largest mental hospital in Israel: thus, sonnet xi in this chapter of Unholyland.

BOOK THREE

Chapter 1

ii

'than embattled Voice of Kings Cross': Work on Unholyland commenced in 2009 in London and the poem was completed in 2015 in Dorset under duress.

iii

'from turquoise-lands of The Mafqat': An ancient name for the Sinai peninsula meaning 'land of blue-green minerals'.

iii

'truths from Our Lady of Sinai': 'Sinai' derives from the name of the Mesopotamian moon-goddess Sin.

viii

'you fail to swerve around a 'gator': Truckdriving parlance for a shredded tyre lying dangerously in the roadway.

xiv

'Correct, they bought an old Routemaster': The actual name of the classic red double-decker, the iconic London bus.

'High Grovel 'n' all that's inbetween': For Highgrove House, the residence of Prince Charles.

'when they launched his Vale Royal': In 1995 the present author had the good fortune to recite the prologue and a part of the first cycle of his epic poem Vale Royal before four-and-a-half thousand people at the Royal Albert Hall. This work, in 800 triads, had taken twenty-three years to research and write; many of those years were spent living rough in London derelicts and squats. The poem sets out a psychogeographical theory of the zone which William Blake made the centre of his Jerusalem; where Rimbaud wrote his Illuminations and dreamed his Season in Hell; where Thomas Chatterton plunged into an open grave three days before his tragic 'suicide'; where Shelley underwent the most extreme supernatural experiences of his life (as chronicled by Richard Holmes in 'The Pursuit'); and where Yeats lived for nearly three decades (the period of 'A Vision').

Vale Royal is concerned with the psychogeography of inner London, in particular the mysteries of Saint Pancras Old Church in Kings Cross, believed by many scholars to be the oldest Christian foundation in the western hemisphere, the first messianic (as opposed to apostolic) church, which in Vale Royal becomes the Church of the Pan Cross, built by Christ in Britain ('And did those feet' etc.)

Chapter 2

iv

'Here rage Baal-fires of infanticide': At certain points in the timeline of of the Old Testament the Jews absconded from the monotheistic worship of Yahweh (Jehovah) and were accused by their own prophets of placating the deity Baal with child-sacrifice, most notably in the Vale of Hinnom (Gehenna).

vi

'call upon Allah, upon Jesus': At least one percent of Gazans are Christians.

x

'eastward the Summer Triangle': The brightest stars (Altair, Deneb and Aquila) in three constellations (Aquila, Cygnus and Lyra).

xii

'the UNWRA school at al-Fakhura': During Operation Cast Lead, on the 6th of January, 2009, the Israeli military struck this school in the Jabaliya Camp in Gaza killing more than forty civilians, many of them children. The Israeli military lied about the incident, claiming that Hamas militants were firing on them from the yard of the school but UN (and other) investigations found this claim to be false.

'making a Dajjalic counterpoint': In Islamic theology the Dajjal corresponds most closely to the Christian concept of Lucifer. Satan is a materialist-reductionist, denying all possibility of Spirit, chaining man to the earth, imprisoning him in the tiny spectrum of his five senses. Dajjal or Lucifer, on the other hand, is concerned with offering man the chance to work out his own salvation through the 'miracle' of technology. The quest for Artificial Intelligence could be designated Dajjalic.

'Nah, that's the Zenana': 'Zenana' or 'nagging-wife' is the jocular nickname long-suffering Gazans have given to the drones which more or less constantly patrol their skies.

'hilarity rings from our zaffa': wedding-procession.

'Study Einstein's letter, harangue': Dated April 10,1948 and addressed to Mr. Shepard Rifkin (Exec. Director) American Friends of the Fighters for the Freedom of Israel, 149 Second Ave, New York 3, N.Y. Einstein's prescient and passionate letter reads:

Dear Sir:

When a real and final catastrophe should befall us in Palestine the first responsible for it would be the British and the second responsible for it the Terrorist organizations build up from our own ranks. I am not willing to see anybody associated with those misled and criminal people.

Sincerely yours, Albert Einstein.

Note the capitalisation of 'T' in terrorist; how prophetically looms that hanging-tree of a capital-letter now as the War on Terror launches its one-sided agendas across our world.

On the subject of Britain's responsibility for the establishment of Israel, two very well-defined incidents two-thousand years apart characterise British relations with Palestine. The first is the messianic visitation by Christ (in His early-to-mid twenties) to Britain as ramified and resumed in the Matter of Britain, a vast corpus of Dark Age and Medieval histories relating to precisely this subject; the second is the British 'Mandate in Palestine' which in 1948 mysteriously transforms into modern Israel. The first connection is a historical-mystical actuality of infinitely benign significance, the second (where Israel is racially, not culturally defined) at very least a grave error of diplomatic judgment, at worst an absolute cataclysm for the Palestinian people.

'the Arabian phoenix known as Rukh': The symbolism and mythology of the Arabian Rukh is very extensive. This is the immortal bird which carries off Sinbad the Sailor, a creature reportedly powerful enough to lift baby-elephants over mountain-ranges with ease, a bird which nests only on Mount Qaf; to be identified with the Persian Simurgh, the Jewish Ziz, the Hindu Garuda, the Native American Thunderbird.

Some of the oldest star-temples in the world have been found to be aligned on the constellation of Cygnus, also known as the Northern Cross. Some have speculated that Cygnus may be identified with the dove of the Holy Spirit in Christianity.

Chapter 3

viii

'by the ghost of Sozomen': Salminius Hermias Sozomenus, an important historian of the early church, lived (400-450 AD) in Bethelia (modern Beit Lahiya) in Gaza. He is interesting to modern scholars partly because he relies on oral traditions.

xi

'while Katb el-Kitab is intoned': The Moslem service of matrimony.

xi

'driving forward the Shamaliyya': A traditional dance form (or dabke) of Palestine often performed at weddings. The name al-shamaliyya translates 'We came here to stamp the ground (dance).' Ancient Middle Eastern marriage-rites ensured that a new home was both blessed and 'built', in the sense that its uneven earthen floors would be left flat and even after all the ceremonial dancing of the night before.

xvii

'Esclaves, ne maudissons pas la vie': 'Slaves, don't curse life.' (A Season in Hell, Arthur Rimbaud.)

Chapter 4

i

'Where is the Shekinah of Godhead?': The Shekinah is the feminine principle of Godhead in Cabbala, where female 'glory' is balanced with male 'power' in a manner directly parallel to concepts of androgyny in Shivite Hinduism (where the Shakti takes the role of the Shekinah). In Solomonic times sexuality - as evidenced by the Song of Songs - was sacred; and according to some Jewish traditions in the days of the Temple there existed on the rooftop of the temple-structure special kiosks where, on the Sabbath, the Rabbis would seclude themselves with their wives to bless the congregation below, since it is the Shekinah who presides over the welcoming of the Sabbath day, dedicated to her.

xvi

'till Masoud began his midnight sesh': The skill and dedication of Palestinian doctors is famed throughout the world.

xxii

'ignores the Samson Option': Israel is not a signatory to any nuclear treaties and has never even officially admitted possessing WMD's. However thanks to the revelations of Mordecai Vanunu, heroic Israeli peace-activist, the world is only too aware that this in fact the case. Vanunu, a former Israeli nuclear technician, was captured by the Mossad in Italy and clandestinely transported in a cargo vessel, drugged, to Israel where he served many years in solitary confinement and now remains under house-arrest. His crime: to reveal to the world via the Sunday Times (in 1985) that deep beneath the Dimona facility in the Negev desert was a subterranean nuclear bomb-factory.

The so-called Samson Option is the apocalyptic 'last-resort' strategy of Israel in which potentially overwhelming conventional attack from united Arab armies is met with a nuclear response which results finally in the destruction of Israel.

Chapter 5

viii

'Peeps, into the Wilderness of Sin': The Biblical name for Sinai in the time of Moses, referencing the ancient dedication of the peninsula to the moon-goddess Sin.

xiii

'began when The McCool Foundation': I ask my reader's indulgence for the back-story to this sequence of allusions. My verse-novel McCool (Goldmark, 2007) in many ways a prequel to Unholyland, is set partly in Lebanon, partly in London. At the conclusion of McCool the eponymous war-painter leaves his millions to a trust set-up in the name of the just-deceased soldier-husband of the beautiful woman he has seduced. Thus the Parker James Peace Trust comes into being.

There were already hints in the climactic chapters of McCool that The Serious Road Trip would be mounting a peace-convoy to Sinai for purposes contextualised in Unholyland.

xvii

'From One Voice of Peaceworks Foundation': Most of the peace-organisations mentioned in the following sonnets are real-world players in the Middle East and my hope in name-checking them in Unholyland is that in some small way the acknowledgement will assist their magnificent efforts, that they may all be increasingly proactive and that their visions of peaceful co-existence will be exponentially recognised.

xxi

'an eight-spoked logo, requested': Sajjid's spiritual-master's request for an octagonal logo is a reference to the geometrical image of androgyny. I expand on this symbolism at length in my first-published epic poem Vale Royal (Goldmark, 1995) where I designate the glyph of eightness 'the Pan Cross', the all-embracing cross. Vale Royal engages with the psychogeography of inner London, especially the mysteries of Saint Pancras Old Church in Kings Cross, believed by many scholars to be the oldest Christian foundation in the western hemisphere, the seed-foundation of the Celtic Church, the first messianic (as opposed to apostolic) church, which in Vale Royal becomes the Church of the Pan Cross, built by Christ during His mission to Britain ('And did those feet' etc. Will. Blake.)

Octagonality expresses the equilibrium of male and female cosmic forces. The 'Signature of Christ', the famous Chi-Rho Monogram of the Labarum, is octagonal. Octagonality lies at the very heart of Islam as evidenced by exquisite base-eight mosaics on all of the world's most beautiful mosques. In Old Testament holy scriptures the infinite eight decodes the Wheel of Ezekiel which spins through visionary elemental dimensions always seeking equipoise. Octagonality, too, underlies the most profound book of Chinese wisdom, the universally-revered I Ching where the arrangement of the trigrams on the 'Map from the River Lo' is eightfold and equilibrated.

Octagonality leads to transculturality, which is not the same as multiculturalism. In multiculturalism different cultures mingle but do not interact, while in the transcultural model bridges of theology, art and science actively create interchange and reciprocation between ethnic groups.

xxii

"Does Sajjid also 'jump the road'?": He does.

Chapter 8

vii

'for the land of the Chimera': Traditionally the land of the Chimera, Lycia, barren, despoiled by the monster's fiery breath, is supposed to have been in Asia Minor, but some have speculated that ancient Lycia was in fact the Sinai Peninsula.

Chapter 10

viii

'the Magisterium of Prester John': In medieval belief-systems Prester John (Latin: Presbyter Johannes) was believed to rule over a 'Nestorian' church somewhere in the orient. He was said to be a descendant of the Three Magi and was believed to govern a kingdom of wonders where unicorns roamed and the grail was manifest. At first the Nestorian church was thought to be in India (perhaps because of the mission of the disciple Thomas to Goa recounted in the apocryphal 'Acts of Thomas') but medieval notions about geography allowed for the existence of three 'Indias' and Ethiopia was definitely one of these. Prester John as an exotic 'Black Pope' symbolised to medieval Europeans the high priest of a universalised church; and in Unholyland he represents a modern equivalent, a reconciling influence in the Abrahamic family.

Chapter 12

'with a gift from Shashamannaland': Emperor Haile Selassie donated 500 acres of his own land to the Rastafari brethren in 1948. When the communist mass-murderer Mengistu came to power in 1974 (deposing Haile Selassie) he confiscated most of the land. At one point, after Mengistu fled the country in 1991 there were as many as 2000 (mostly Jamaican) Rastas living in Shashamane (to give the region its correct name) and there has been talk of reburying Bob Marley here.